Policy and Practice for Ethical AI Integration in Education

Aras Bozkurt
https://orcid.org/0000-0002-4520-642X
Anadolu University, Turkey

IGI Global
Scientific Publishing
Publishing Tomorrow's Research Today

Vice President of Editorial	Melissa Wagner
Director of Acquisitions	Mikaela Felty
Director of Book Development	Jocelynn Hessler
Production Manager	Mike Brehm
Cover Design	Jose Rosado

Published in the United States of America by
IGI Global Scientific Publishing
701 East Chocolate Avenue
Hershey, PA, 17033, USA
Tel: 717-533-8845 | Fax: 717-533-7115
Website: https://www.igi-global.com E-mail: cust@igi-global.com

Library of Congress Cataloging-in-Publication Data

Names: Bozkurt, Aras editor
Title: Policy and practice for ethical AI integration in education / [edited by] Aras Bozkurt.
Description: Hershey, PA : IGI Global Scientific Publishing, [2026] | Includes bibliographical references and index. | Summary: "This book explores how policies and practical guidelines ensure the ethical integration of AI technologies in educational settings. It examines issues like data privacy, algorithmic bias, transparency, and the role of educators and policymakers in promoting fairness, accountability, and inclusivity"-- Provided by publisher.
Identifiers: LCCN 2026026726 (print) | LCCN 2026026727 (ebook) | ISBN 9798337375694 hardcover | ISBN 9798337375700 paperback | ISBN 9798337375717 ebook
Subjects: LCSH: Artificial intelligence--Educational applications | Artificial intelligence--Moral and ethical aspects
Classification: LCC LB1028.44 .P65 2026 (print) | LCC LB1028.44 (ebook)
LC record available at https://lccn.loc.gov/2026026726
LC ebook record available at https://lccn.loc.gov/2026026727

British Cataloguing in Publication Data
A Cataloguing in Publication record for this book is available from the British Library.

Table of Contents

Detailed Table of Contents

Generative Artificial Intelligence (GenAI) is transforming student engagement, requiring the reconsideration of traditional models. While engagement theories like Expectancy-Value and Self-Determination provide valuable insights, GenAI's personalized learning and automation call for a new perspective. This chapter introduces the Engagement with AI (EWAI) model, integrating AI research with existing theories. It explores engagement at micro (learner traits) and macro (institutional) levels, highlighting curiosity, analytical thinking, and ethics. The role of AI-supportive environments, including infrastructure and educator training, is emphasized. GenAI enhances engagement through personalized feedback but poses risks like overreliance, academic integrity issues, and algorithmic bias. AI-enhanced tasks should align with autonomy support and collaboration for meaningful learning. The EWAI model provides a structured framework for AI integration, ensuring ethical and equitable use.

This chapter introduces the onto-AI lexicon as a critical framework to reframe 'being innovative' in Initial Teacher Education. Conceiving GenAI as a sociotechnical assemblage rather than a neutral tool, the chapter presents experiential scenarios as epistemic interventions that support preservice teachers in recognising the ethical, relational, and political dimensions of AI integration. The onto-AI lexicon is introduced as both provocation and practice, challenging euphemisms like "hallucination" and "personalisation" and replacing them with terms such as "error" and "profiling" to surface power, harm, and consequence. Through a worked exmaple of an immersive scenario, the chapter supports how teacher educators could model how to enable future teachers to critically assess AI's role in shaping pedagogy, equity, and professional responsibility. By resisting market-driven framings of innovation, the chapter repositions ITE as a site of ethical AI literacy and democratic worldmaking.

Preface

INTRODUCTION

The rapid advancement of artificial intelligence (AI) technologies has already begun to redefine the landscape of education, prompting both promise and concern in equal measure. While AI offers transformative possibilities for teaching, learning, assessment, and educational management, it also poses profound ethical challenges related to equity, transparency, autonomy, and the human dimensions of pedagogy. As AI becomes increasingly embedded within educational ecosystems, the imperative to address its ethical integration is no longer optional but urgent. This book emerges from that urgency, aiming to provide a critical yet constructive exploration of how policy and practice can be shaped to ensure responsible adoption of AI in education.

As editors, our intent is not to prescribe a single pathway for ethical AI integration, but rather to curate a multidisciplinary and international dialogue that highlights diverse perspectives, approaches, and contexts. This volume brings together scholars, practitioners, and researchers who collectively illuminate the complex interplay between technology, pedagogy, ethics, and policy. Through their work, readers will encounter both critical interrogations of AI's risks and hopeful frameworks that harness AI's potential for equity, innovation, and human flourishing in education.

In assembling this collection, we recognize the importance of situating AI within the broader historical trajectory of educational technologies. AI is not the first tool to disrupt traditional practices, but it may be one of the most consequential, given its capacity to automate, surveil, and even influence decision-making in ways previously unimaginable. By drawing attention to these dynamics, this book seeks to prepare educators, policymakers, and researchers to navigate the opportunities and risks of AI with wisdom, care, and a commitment to democratic values.

CHAPTER OVERVIEW

Chapter 1, authored by Ioanna Georgia Eskiadi and Nikolaos Panagiotou, lays the foundation by examining frameworks for integrating AI literacy into higher education. The chapter outlines challenges such as curriculum alignment and faculty readiness, while also emphasizing opportunities for preparing students as ethical and informed citizens.

Chapter 2, by Tyler Watts, Amy Flagler, and Merry Leigh Dameron, explores generative AI through the lens of care ethics. Their Framework for Considering Ethical Dilemmas through the Ethic of Care (CEDEC) provides educators with practical tools for navigating complex moral terrain when adopting AI in teaching and learning.

Chapter 3, co-authored by Apostolos Koutropoulos and colleagues, presents a critical interrogation of AI surveillance technologies in education. By challenging technosolutionist narratives, this chapter exposes how surveillance disproportionately harms marginalized learners and erodes trust, while urging educators to prioritize human dignity.

Chapter 4, by Murat Polat and Nurgün Varol, examines the role of AI in transforming education management and policy. The authors present new paradigms that highlight how AI can inform governance, decision-making, and strategic planning in education systems.

Chapter 5, written by Hatice Bilgin, focuses on Turkish higher education institutions, offering a policy analysis that reveals both progress and gaps in ethical AI integration. This chapter underscores the need for governance frameworks that balance innovation with responsibility.

Chapter 6, authored by Hakan Altinpulluk, raises concerns about the "silent erosion" of essential skills such as critical thinking and creativity due to overreliance on AI. The chapter reminds us that technological efficiency must never come at the expense of core human capacities.

Chapter 7, by Gökhan Hiniz, introduces the Engagement with AI (EWAI) model. By integrating established engagement theories with AI research, the model provides a structured framework for supporting student engagement while safeguarding autonomy, ethics, and inclusivity.

Chapter 8, authored by Janine Arantes, reframes "innovation" in Initial Teacher Education (ITE) through the onto-AI lexicon. By presenting experiential scenarios, the chapter challenges dominant narratives and empowers future teachers to critically assess AI's ethical, political, and relational dimensions.

Chapter 9, by Ozlem Soydan Oktay and Hakan Kilinç, offers insights into preservice teachers' perspectives on AI. By exploring biases, advantages, and disadvantages, the chapter emphasizes the need for conscious and critical engagement with AI in learning processes.

CONCLUSION

Taken together, the chapters in this book provide a multidimensional understanding of what it means to ethically integrate AI into education. Rather than offering simplistic solutions, the contributions highlight the complexity of the task, addressing issues of literacy, care, surveillance, management, policy, skills, engagement, innovation, and teacher preparation. The richness of perspectives reflects the global scope of the challenges and opportunities AI presents, underscoring that no single context holds all the answers.

The insights gathered here demonstrate that ethical AI integration requires a balance of critical skepticism and constructive optimism. AI should neither be uncritically celebrated nor entirely rejected; instead, it must be situated within pedagogical, ethical, and social frameworks that prioritize human flourishing. As these chapters make clear, this balance can only be achieved when stakeholders across education—students, teachers, administrators, and policymakers—work collaboratively to shape AI's role.

Ultimately, this book is a call to action. The integration of AI into education is not a future possibility but a present reality, demanding thoughtful policies, reflective practices, and a sustained commitment to equity and ethics. By engaging with the frameworks, critiques, and strategies presented in this volume, we invite readers to participate in the shared work of building an educational future where AI enhances, rather than diminishes, the values of care, justice, and human dignity.

Aras Bozkurt
Anadolu University, Turkey

Chapter 1

Integrating Artificial Intelligence Literacy in Higher Education: Frameworks, Challenges, and Opportunities

Ioanna Georgia Eskiadi
https://orcid.org/0009-0001-4950-8644
School of Social and Economic Sciences, Aristotle University of Thessaloniki, Greece

Nikolaos Panagiotou
https://orcid.org/0000-0002-2902-858X
School of Social and Economic Sciences, Aristotle University of Thessaloniki, Greece

ABSTRACT

Artificial Intelligence (AI) is reshaping higher education, necessitating AI literacy to prepare students for an AI-driven world. This chapter explores frameworks, challenges, and opportunities for integrating AI literacy into higher education curricula, emphasizing cognitive, technical, and ethical dimensions. A qualitative methodology underpins this study, combining extensive literature reviews with detailed case studies of institutions like Stanford University, MIT, and the AI4EU project. These cases illustrate interdisciplinary approaches, ethical integration, and resource accessibility. The discussion identifies barriers such as resource constraints, faculty readiness, and curriculum alignment while highlighting opportunities for

DOI: 10.4018/979-8-3373-7569-4.ch001

enhancing employability, critical thinking, and societal contributions. A proposed multidisciplinary framework addresses technical skills, experiential learning, and ethical reasoning, fostering innovation and informed citizenship.

INTRODUCTION

Artificial Intelligence (AI) is redefining industries globally, and education is no exception. Its transformative impact is evident in the way traditional pedagogies are being reshaped, paving the way for new, dynamic avenues of learning. As AI becomes increasingly ingrained in daily life, higher education institutions face the critical responsibility of equipping students with the necessary knowledge, skills, and ethical frameworks to navigate an AI-driven world confidently and responsibly. This chapter delves into the pivotal role of AI literacy within higher education, emphasizing the need for comprehensive frameworks that integrate technical, cognitive, and ethical dimensions. Existing research underscores the potential of AI to foster critical thinking, innovation, and ethical reasoning in students, thereby preparing them for roles in AI-centric careers and as informed contributors to society. However, the successful integration of AI literacy demands more than mere technical training; it requires cultivating a critical understanding of AI's implications for equity, transparency, and societal norms. The educational potential of AI is equally transformative and disruptive. On the one hand, AI offers opportunities to personalize learning, foster creativity, and expand accessibility. It allows for immediate feedback and adaptive instruction tailored to individual learning needs, enhancing engagement and retention (Laupichler et al., 2024; Shen, 2024). On the other hand, the rapid adoption of AI in education raises profound challenges, including ethical considerations surrounding data privacy, algorithmic transparency, and the propagation of biases (Bozkurt et al., 2024). Additionally, over-reliance on AI risks diminishing human-centric skills such as empathy, creativity, and critical thinking, essential for holistic learning.

This chapter critically examines frameworks for embedding AI literacy into higher education, balancing its transformative potential with the need for ethical safeguards. By drawing on theoretical perspectives and empirical studies, it seeks to illuminate best practices and practical strategies for integrating AI into curricula while preserving the foundational principles of education. Through this lens, higher education institutions can evolve to foster not only technical competencies but also the ethical and critical reasoning skills needed for a future where AI plays an integral role. By exploring structured approaches to AI literacy, this chapter aims to contribute to a nuanced understanding of how higher education can leverage AI responsibly and inclusively. It calls for interdisciplinary and experiential learning environments that align technological innovation with pedagogical values, ensuring that AI's integration enhances human agency and societal impact without compromising educational integrity. Through these efforts, students will be better prepared to navigate the complexities of an AI-rich world, becoming not only skilled professionals but also ethically engaged citizens.

MISSION OF THIS CHAPTER

The mission of this chapter is to provide a robust framework for integrating artificial intelligence (AI) literacy into higher education, addressing the cognitive, technical, and ethical dimensions required to prepare students for an AI-centric world. It aims to explore the critical role of AI literacy in equipping students with not only the technical competencies to engage with AI technologies but also the ethical reasoning necessary to navigate their societal implications responsibly. This chapter underscores the importance of fostering interdisciplinary and experiential learning environments that emphasize problem-solving, critical thinking, and creativity. By addressing the challenges and opportunities associated with AI literacy, the chapter seeks to guide educators, policymakers, and institutions toward creating inclusive and effective curricula that empower students to become informed citizens and competitive professionals in the global economy.

OBJECTIVES AND STRUCTURE OF THE CHAPTER

The chapter is structured around several core objectives:

1. **Define AI Literacy**: Establish a comprehensive definition of AI literacy, addressing its technical, cognitive, and ethical dimensions.
2. **Examine Existing Frameworks**: Review and critique current approaches to integrating AI literacy within higher education.
3. **Propose a Multidisciplinary Framework**: Develop a holistic framework that integrates technical skills, experiential learning, and ethical considerations to foster innovation and informed citizenship.
4. **Identify Challenges**: Analyze barriers to integrating AI literacy in curricula, such as resource limitations, faculty readiness, and alignment with existing educational structures.
5. **Explore Opportunities**: Highlight the potential benefits of AI literacy, including enhancing employability, innovation, critical thinking, and societal contributions.

RESEARCH SIGNIFICANCE AND CONTRIBUTION

The research on integrating artificial intelligence (AI) literacy into higher education represents a critical contribution to the evolving landscape of education and technology. By addressing the cognitive, technical, and ethical dimensions of AI literacy, this study provides a multidisciplinary framework that not only equips students with essential skills for an AI-driven job market but also prepares them for informed, ethical engagement with societal challenges posed by AI technologies. Its insights into institutional practices and case studies from leading universities offer actionable strategies for overcoming barriers such as resource limitations and faculty readiness. Furthermore, this research advances global competitiveness by fostering innovative, interdisciplinary approaches that align technological innovation with core educational values. Ultimately, the study contributes to the growing discourse on how higher education can responsibly and inclusively integrate AI literacy, ensuring that future professionals are not only skilled but also critically aware of the broader implications of their expertise.

THEORETICAL FRAMEWORK

The integration of artificial intelligence (AI) literacy in higher education is increasingly critical as AI becomes a pervasive force in global industries, including education. This theoretical framework explores the cognitive, technical, and ethical dimensions of AI literacy, underscoring its transformative potential and challenges.

Conceptualizing AI Literacy

AI literacy encompasses a range of competencies, including understanding AI technologies, their applications, and their ethical implications (Dai et al., 2020; Ng, 2023; Yetişensoy & Rapoport, 2023). As students prepare to enter a workforce increasingly influenced by AI, fostering their readiness through AI literacy is essential for promoting their well-being and enhancing their employability (Dai et al., 2020). Moreover, integrating AI literacy into higher education not only prepares students for future careers but also empowers them to critically engage with the ethical and societal implications of AI technologies (Heng & Tabunshchyk, 2021; Shen, 2024). SThis foundational knowledge is crucial for developing informed citizens who can contribute positively to society in an AI-rich environment.

To effectively integrate AI literacy into higher education, a structured framework is necessary. This framework should address the cognitive, emotional, and ethical dimensions of AI literacy (Ng, J. 2023, Su, Y. 2023). For instance, the development of an AI literacy curriculum should include experiential learning opportunities that foster critical thinking, creativity, and problem-solving skills (Folmeg et al., 2024; Yetişensoy & Rapoport, 2023). Additionally, it is vital to consider students' psychological needs and motivations to ensure engagement and retention of AI concepts (Shen, 2024). Our chapter proposes the adoption of a multidisciplinary approach, where educators can create a curriculum that not only teaches technical skills but also emphasizes the ethical considerations surrounding AI technologies (Zhao et al., 2022). This holistic approach not only prepares students for the workforce but also cultivates a generation of critical thinkers who can navigate the complexities of an AI-driven world.

As a subfield of AI literacy, Generative AI (GenAI) literacy has emerged as a critical area of focus, driven by the rapid proliferation of generative AI models such as GPT, DALL·E, and others. These technologies bring transformative opportunities for creativity and problem-solving but also introduce unique challenges related to ethics, misinformation, and accessibility. Generative AI literacy involves understanding how generative models function, their applications, and their potential societal impacts. It emphasizes equipping students and professionals with the skills to harness generative AI for innovation while critically assessing its ethical implications (Ciampa et al., 2023; Shen, 2024). As generative AI tools become integrated into industries ranging from media to healthcare, their impact necessitates a nuanced approach to AI education. Ng, J. (2023) argues that GenAI literacy must include the cognitive ability to discern between human-created and AI-generated content, fostering a critical understanding of authenticity and originality. Similarly, Bozkurt et al. (2024) highlight the ethical dimensions of generative AI, including concerns about bias, intellectual property, and the amplification of misinformation.

Constructivist and Experiential Learning Foundations for AI Literacy

Constructivist learning theory posits that learners construct knowledge actively through experience, interaction, and reflection rather than through passive reception of information (Piaget, 1954; Vygotsky, 1978). In the context of AI literacy, constructivism emphasizes that learners must engage with AI tools, critically reflect on their implications, and situate these technologies within broader societal and ethical frameworks. This perspective aligns with recent scholarship suggesting that students must move beyond understanding how AI operates to critically analyzing its cultural, political, and epistemological implications (Ng, J. 2023; Yetişensoy & Rapoport, 2023). Through a constructivist lens, AI literacy education must prioritize the development of conceptual understanding by involving students in active inquiry and problem-solving. For instance, project-based learning activities in which students analyze algorithmic bias in social media platforms or explore the ethical dilemmas of facial recognition technologies allow for the co-construction of knowledge that is both relevant and socially anchored (Folmeg et al., 2024). Moreover, social constructivist approaches underscore the importance of collaborative learning, peer interaction, and guided scaffolding by educators—critical in fostering ethical reasoning and civic responsibility in AI contexts (Su, 2023). Constructivist pedagogy also facilitates the development of metacognitive skills, empowering students to reflect on their learning processes, challenge their assumptions, and adapt their understanding as they interact with evolving AI systems. Such reflective practices are essential for fostering the critical engagement necessary to navigate the complexity and uncertainty inherent in AI technologies (Greenfield & Gomez, 2023).

In addition to constructivism, experiential learning theory (ELT)—as articulated by Kolb (1984)—offers a robust pedagogical model for AI literacy. ELT emphasizes a cyclical process of learning through concrete experience, reflective observation, abstract conceptualization, and active experimentation. This framework is especially pertinent to AI education, where abstract concepts such as machine learning, neural networks, and generative models are best understood through hands-on application and contextual exploration. Experiential learning environments facilitate the application of theoretical knowledge to real-world problems, thereby deepening student engagement and comprehension. For example, students working with generative AI tools such as GPT-4 or DALL·E in creative writing or design projects not only gain technical proficiency but also engage with questions of authorship, originality, and bias (Ciampa et al., 2023; Shen, 2024). Reflection on these experiences enables learners to evaluate the broader implications of AI outputs, linking personal insights to societal issues such as misinformation, privacy, and algorithmic injustice (Nguyen, 2023).

Moreover, experiential learning encourages risk-taking and iterative design, qualities essential for innovation in AI applications. In this regard, institutions such as Stanford University and MIT, as discussed in previous sections, exemplify ELT principles through interdisciplinary workshops, community-based projects, and ethics-focused simulations. These educational practices not only reinforce technical skills but also embed ethical reasoning and societal awareness into the learning process (MIT Media Lab, 2023; Stanford University Teaching Commons, 2023). The effectiveness of experiential learning in fostering responsible AI use has also been supported by empirical studies. Morrill (2023), for instance, demonstrated that targeted experiential interventions reduced students' over-reliance on AI tools and promoted a more critical and balanced approach to technology usage. This finding underscores the value of embedding experiential components within AI literacy curricula to cultivate self-regulated and reflective learners.

Integrating constructivist and experiential learning principles into AI literacy initiatives yields several pedagogical benefits. First, it encourages active and personalized learning experiences, allowing students to construct meaning based on their prior knowledge, interests, and disciplinary backgrounds. This is especially important for non-STEM students, who may otherwise find AI concepts inaccessible or abstract (Zhao et al., 2022). Second, these theories support the development of ethical sensitivity and civic engagement by situating AI technologies within real-life dilemmas and social contexts. When students engage in collaborative projects addressing challenges such as predictive policing or algorithmic hiring, they are prompted to consider the human consequences of technological design and deployment (Bozkurt et al., 2024). Third, such pedagogical foundations promote long-term knowledge retention and skill transfer. By engaging students in iterative cycles of action and reflection, educators can foster deep learning that extends beyond rote memorization or isolated technical competencies. This aligns with Shen's (2024) findings on the psychological and motivational dimensions of AI literacy, which emphasize the importance of autonomy, relatedness, and perceived competence in sustaining learner engagement.

Cognitive and Ethical Dimensions

AI literacy extends beyond technical skills, encompassing a nuanced understanding of its cognitive and ethical implications. A critical examination of AI's societal and cultural impacts is essential to fostering informed and responsible use. Ethical considerations, including data privacy, algorithmic bias, intellectual property rights, and societal equity, form the core of this discourse. According to Su, Y. (2023), early exposure to AI ethics not only cultivates technical proficiency but also encourages critical thinking and empathy, preparing individuals to engage thoughtfully with AI technologies. In this regard, global frameworks like UNESCO's Recommendation on the Ethics of Artificial Intelligence (2021) and the OECD's AI Principles (2019) offer essential guidance, promoting values-based AI governance and ethical diversity that reflect international consensus and cultural plurality.

Folmeg et al. (2024) further argues that ethical reasoning is indispensable for developing AI solutions that prioritize inclusivity, fairness, and transparency. This is particularly relevant in the context of generative AI (GenAI), where ethical concerns grow more intricate. Recent literature (Bozkurt et al., 2024; Shen, 2024) underscores the necessity of addressing challenges such as algorithmic bias, misuse of AI-generated content, and threats to intellectual property. Moreover, the proliferation of AI-generated misinformation raises pressing questions about its impact on public discourse and the strategies required to mitigate these effects (Taylor & Davis, 2023; Nguyen, 2023). Educational frameworks must integrate these cognitive and ethical dimensions into AI literacy initiatives. This includes fostering critical engagement with the societal consequences of AI, teaching strategies to identify and address misinformation, and promoting transparency in AI-driven decision-making. By incorporating recent insights, such as those from Greenfield and Gomez (2023), educators can provide a holistic approach that prepares individuals to navigate the rapidly evolving AI landscape with responsibility and foresight.

Educational Integration: Challenges and Opportunities

While cognitive and ethical considerations form the backbone of AI literacy, effective integration into educational systems requires overcoming certain challenges and leveraging new opportunities. Integrating AI literacy into higher education curricula presents both challenges and opportunities. Resource constraints, faculty readiness, and curriculum alignment are significant barriers (Laupichler et al.,, 2024). However, interdisciplinary and experiential learning approaches can mitigate these challenges.

To address resource constraints, institutions can implement scalable, low-cost solutions such as open-access platforms (e.g., AI4EU), collaborative licensing of AI tools, and shared computing infrastructure through inter-university partnerships. Funding initiatives—such as national digital innovation grants or public-private partnerships with tech firms—can alleviate financial barriers and increase access to AI technologies. Additionally, faculty readiness can be enhanced through comprehensive professional development programs, including AI literacy bootcamps, cross-disciplinary teaching fellowships, and modular certifications designed in collaboration with computer science and education departments.

Policy-level interventions are equally essential. Universities should develop institutional frameworks that embed AI literacy as a cross-curricular objective, supported by dedicated AI integration task forces or centers of excellence. These policies can incentivize curriculum redesign, promote interdepartmental collaboration, and allocate teaching relief for instructors piloting AI-related courses. Such targeted policies not only address immediate capacity issues but also build long-term institutional resilience.

By adopting such strategies, institutions can create sustainable ecosystems that support both faculty and students in navigating the technical and ethical complexities of AI. Fostering AI literacy in higher education not only enhances students' employability but also prepares them to address the ethical and societal implications of AI. Shen (2024) underscores the importance of AI literacy in promoting psychological well-being by satisfying students' needs for competence and autonomy. Moreover, Su, Y. (2023) argues that AI literacy should include early exposure to critical thinking and creativity, as these skills are essential for adapting to the dynamic challenges posed by AI.

Generative AI technologies offer transformative opportunities for personalized learning and creative exploration These tools empower educators to design interactive, adaptive content that engages students in diverse learning contexts (Ciampa et al., 2023). However, their integration into education also raises ethical concerns, including issues of dependency, intellectual integrity, and equitable access. Morrill (2023) demonstrated how a targeted generative AI literacy intervention effectively reduced students' over-reliance on AI tools, promoting balanced and informed usage. This underscores the necessity of embedding generative AI literacy into curricula to nurture critical thinking and self-regulated learning. Additionally, Gomez et al. (2023) argue for the inclusion of ethical frameworks within AI education, ensuring students understand the broader implications of their technological engagements. By addressing these challenges and leveraging the opportunities, higher education institutions can create curricula that prepare students not only for careers in an AI-driven world but also for thoughtful, ethical participation in society. The integration of generative AI and AI literacy represents a transformative step toward equipping learners to thrive in a rapidly evolving landscape.

Structuring Curricula

Integrating AI literacy into higher education requires a structured and multidimensional framework that equips students with cognitive, emotional, and ethical competencies. Recent research underscores the need for curricula that extend beyond technical proficiency to encompass critical thinking, ethical reasoning, and emotional intelligence. By fostering a comprehensive understanding of AI, educators can better prepare students to navigate the complexities of an AI-driven world. To address the cognitive and ethical dimensions of AI literacy, curricula must blend technical skills with critical analysis of socio-technical implications. Ng, J. (2023) highlights the importance of designing courses that enable students to critically examine the role of generative AI in promoting equity and transparency. Similarly, Su, Y. (2023) suggests incorporating project-based learning approaches that allow students to explore the responsible use of generative AI in creative and professional contexts. Such approaches not only develop technical capabilities but also instill the ethical reasoning required to assess AI's broader societal impacts. By embedding these elements into the curriculum, educators can cultivate a generation of AI-literate graduates equipped to confront the challenges of the digital age.

Experiential learning emerges as a cornerstone of effective AI education, providing students with practical insights and problem-solving skills. Yetişensoy and Rapoport (2023) emphasize the value of interdisciplinary approaches that engage students in real-world applications of AI. For example, collaborative projects integrating AI with fields such as healthcare, media, or environmental science offer students' opportunities to witness AI's transformative potential firsthand. These experiences not only enhance technical proficiency but also prepare students to navigate the interconnected systems where AI plays an increasingly central role. Student engagement and retention are critical to the success of AI literacy initiatives. Shen (2024) highlights the significance of addressing psychological and motivational factors in curriculum design, such as perceived support, autonomy, and relatedness. By aligning course content with students' psychological needs, educators can foster a deeper connection to AI concepts. Techniques such as gamification, mentorship programs, and peer collaboration have proven effective in enhancing engagement, ensuring that students maintain a sustained interest in AI and its applications.

To effectively integrate AI literacy into higher education, curricula should adopt a holistic approach incorporating interdisciplinary learning, experiential opportunities, and ethical reasoning. An interdisciplinary focus allows students to contextualize AI across various domains, promoting a nuanced understanding of its societal impacts (Yetişensoy & Rapoport, 2023). Experiential learning, through hands-on projects and case studies, develops critical thinking and problem-solving skills essential for real-world applications (Ng, 2023). Ethical reasoning ensures that students are equipped to evaluate AI's implications for equity, privacy, and societal impact (Su, 2023). Finally, addressing motivational factors and creating a supportive learning environment are crucial for fostering sustained engagement (Shen, 2024). By adopting this comprehensive and student-centered approach, higher education institutions can prepare graduates to navigate the complexities of AI with competence, ethical awareness, and critical insight. This framework ensures that students are not only technically proficient but also equipped to address the broader societal and ethical challenges posed by AI in a rapidly evolving digital landscape.

Challenges of GenAI

Generative AI (GenAI) models such as GPT-4 and DALL·E have significantly advanced artificial intelligence by introducing new avenues for creativity and problem-solving. However, their increasing adoption has brought to the forefront critical challenges, including the spread of misinformation, the perpetuation of algorithmic bias, and constraints on genuine creativity. This growing body of post-2022 research includes studies such as Zhao et al. (2022), which examine AI literacy development frameworks and pedagogical readiness among educators. One of the most pressing concerns with GenAI is its role in propagating misinformation. These models, trained on vast datasets, are capable of generating content that is both highly convincing and inaccurate. Research by Nguyen (2023) highlights the dangers of AI-generated misinformation in public discourse, proposing strategies such as enhanced public education and the development of validation tools to ensure the accuracy of content. Similarly, Taylor and Davis (2023) investigate the psychological impact of misinformation produced by generative models, emphasizing the need for educational interventions to improve digital literacy and critical evaluation skills among users.

Another significant challenge is algorithmic bias, which stems from the biases inherent in the training data used by GenAI systems. These biases often lead to outputs that lack equity and representation. Bozkurt et al. (2024) have critically examined these biases and proposed transparency in dataset selection and the implementation of governance frameworks to mitigate the ethical risks associated with biased generative models. The Massachusetts Institute of Technology's AI and Ethics Program further explores the real-world consequences of such biases, such as discriminatory hiring algorithms, and provides actionable recommendations for ensuring fairness in AI applications. While GenAI is often regarded as a tool to enhance creativity, it can paradoxically constrain originality by favoring existing patterns found in its training data. Ng, J. (2023) discusses this issue, advocating for frameworks that integrate human creativity with AI's generative capabilities to foster innovative and original outputs. Morrill (2023) adds to this discourse by presenting evidence that reducing over-reliance on GenAI in creative processes can be achieved through targeted literacy interventions, which encourage balanced and informed usage of these technologies.

Regional Variations in AI Literacy Frameworks

AI literacy frameworks differ across regions, reflecting diverse cultural, economic, and educational priorities. These differences highlight the varied approaches to addressing the challenges and opportunities posed by artificial intelligence in education. In Europe, AI literacy frameworks often emphasize inclusivity, accessibility, and ethical oversight. The European Union's initiatives, such as the AI4EU project, focus on creating a unified approach to AI education that aligns with European values. The AI4EU Ethical Observatory exemplifies this commitment by ensuring that AI literacy includes principles of transparency, accountability, and human-centric development. This focus is deeply intertwined with Europe's legislative priorities, such as the AI Act, which seeks to regulate AI technologies while fostering trust and societal benefit. While the European approach effectively integrates ethics and accessibility, challenges remain in harmonizing these efforts across member states with diverse educational and technological infrastructures.

In North America, particularly in the United States, AI literacy frameworks prioritize interdisciplinary learning and innovation. Institutions like Stanford University and the Massachusetts Institute of Technology (MIT) lead efforts to combine technical training with critical thinking and ethical reasoning. Stanford's AI Literacy Curriculum incorporates AI education into both STEM and non-STEM disciplines, providing students with the tools to analyze AI's impact on broader societal challenges. Similarly, MIT's "AI and Ethics" program fosters collaboration between technical experts, ethicists, and policymakers, preparing students to engage with the ethical dimensions of AI policy and governance. These frameworks underscore the importance of experiential learning and ethical integration but face challenges in scalability and resource allocation across a diverse educational landscape.

In Asia, the focus on AI literacy frameworks often centers on technical proficiency and the scalability of education systems. For instance, China has implemented structured approaches that prioritize equipping educators with the skills to teach AI concepts effectively. By training teachers and incorporating AI education into primary and secondary curricula, the region aims to prepare a large workforce for AI-driven industries. This approach aligns with Asia's rapid technological growth and economic priorities. However, while technical skills are emphasized, there is often less focus on integrating ethical reasoning and interdisciplinary perspectives, which are crucial for fostering a more holistic understanding of AI's societal implications. These regional variations illustrate the diversity in AI literacy frameworks, each shaped by unique cultural, economic, and institutional factors. While Europe leads in ethical oversight, North America excels in interdisciplinary and experiential learning, and Asia focuses on scalability and technical expertise. Together, these approaches offer valuable insights into how AI literacy can be tailored to meet regional needs while addressing global challenges.

Interdisciplinary Frameworks and Case Studies

Recent advancements in the field underscore the need to broaden AI literacy frameworks to incorporate societal, ethical, and environmental dimensions. Bozkurt et al. (2024) advocate for the integration of sustainability into AI education, emphasizing the ecological footprint of AI technologies and their potential to exacerbate environmental challenges if left unchecked. This aligns with a growing body of research prioritizing the inclusion of sustainability in technological education. Similarly, Ciampa et al. (2023) underscores the transformative power of AI literacy in enhancing digital inclusion, particularly in marginalized and underserved communities, illustrating the role of AI in bridging digital divides.

Interdisciplinary frameworks have emerged as essential tools for embedding AI literacy across higher education curricula. These frameworks advocate for the convergence of technical proficiency, ethical reasoning, and societal engagement. For example, the AI and Ethics Program at MIT showcases the value of embedding ethical considerations in technical training, fostering critical thinking and responsible

AI use among students. Another notable initiative, the AI4EU project, illustrates how collaborative, pan-European efforts can integrate ethical training within technical disciplines, ensuring resource accessibility and inclusivity in AI literacy programs (Bozkurt et al., 2024).

Case studies from these leading institutions highlight the efficacy of interdisciplinary approaches. Key components include fostering collaboration across disciplines, ensuring access to educational resources, and prioritizing ethical considerations as foundational pillars. These approaches not only equip learners with technical skills but also prepare them to navigate the complex societal challenges posed by AI. Consequently, these interdisciplinary frameworks serve as a roadmap for cultivating a more inclusive and ethically aware AI-literate society, addressing both current and future challenges in the rapidly evolving technological landscape.

Long-term Implications

The integration of AI literacy into education has far-reaching implications, shaping not only the workforce of tomorrow but also the ethical and societal engagement of future generations. By equipping students with both technical and critical thinking skills, educational institutions empower them to thrive in AI-centric industries and navigate the ethical complexities posed by rapidly evolving AI technologies. Morrill (2023) highlights that institutions prioritizing AI literacy enhance their global competitiveness while fostering critical thinkers capable of addressing the challenges and opportunities of an AI-rich world. A multidisciplinary approach is essential to realizing the full potential of AI literacy. Zhao et al. (2022) emphasize the need for contextualizing AI skills across diverse academic and professional fields, ensuring that students are prepared to apply AI literacy beyond technical domains. This holistic perspective not only prepares learners for industry demands but also cultivates an adaptable generation of ethical problem-solvers. Incorporating disciplines such as sociology, environmental studies, and philosophy into AI education broadens the scope, addressing the societal and environmental implications of AI technologies.

The implications of generative AI literacy are particularly significant for education, industry, and society. By fostering a critical understanding of generative AI, educators can prepare students to engage responsibly with its transformative potential. Bozkurt et al. (2024) argue that generative AI literacy is pivotal for addressing global challenges, including sustainability, equity, and inclusion. In parallel, Shen (2024) underscores its role in promoting psychological well-being, highlighting the importance of equipping individuals to adapt confidently to an AI-driven world. This forward-looking approach to AI literacy not only enhances employability and innovation but also fosters informed and ethical citizens capable of shaping a sustainable and equitable future. By embedding critical ethical considerations, resource accessibility, and interdisciplinary collaboration into AI education, institutions can ensure that the long-term implications of AI literacy are positive and far-reaching, contributing to a more responsible and inclusive technological landscape.

RESEARCH QUESTIONS

1. How can higher education institutions effectively integrate AI literacy into their curricula to address cognitive, technical, and ethical dimensions?
2. What are the primary challenges and opportunities in embedding AI literacy into higher education, and how can interdisciplinary and experiential approaches address them?

METHODOLOGY

This chapter employs a qualitative methodology, combining an extensive literature review with detailed case studies to explore the integration of AI literacy into higher education. The chosen approach ensures a robust analysis by synthesizing theoretical insights with empirical evidence from leading institutions. Case study methods are particularly well-suited to this inquiry as they allow for in-depth exploration of complex phenomena within specific sociopolitical and cultural settings (Wimmer & Dominick, 2013). By contextualizing the integration of AI literacy within diverse educational environments, this approach illuminates both universal trends and unique institutional strategies.

The literature review serves as the foundation of the study, drawing from a wide range of sources, including academic research, policy documents, and educational frameworks. This comprehensive synthesis maps the current landscape of AI literacy, identifying key trends, challenges, and opportunities. It provides a theoretical grounding that informs the selection and analysis of case studies. Such reviews are invaluable for understanding the broader implications of integrating AI literacy into curricula, enabling a critical evaluation of existing approaches and frameworks (Kerlinger & Lee, 2000).

The second component of the methodology involves detailed case studies of pioneering institutions such as Stanford University, the Massachusetts Institute of Technology (MIT), and the European Union's AI4EU project. These cases were chosen based on their innovative approaches to embedding AI literacy, their interdisciplinary integration, and their commitment to ethical and resource-accessible education. Case studies allow for a granular analysis of institutional practices, revealing the interplay between technical skills, ethical reasoning, and cognitive competencies. This methodological approach also facilitates cross-case comparisons, enabling the identification of both universal principles and unique, context-specific practices (Yin, 2018).

To ensure the rigor of the case study analysis, the selection criteria emphasized measurable outcomes, resource accessibility, and interdisciplinary approaches. For instance, Stanford University's AI Literacy Curriculum highlights the contextualization of AI concepts across diverse disciplines, fostering critical thinking and problem-solving. Similarly, MIT's AI and Ethics Program demonstrates the importance of embedding ethical considerations into technical training. The AI4EU project further illustrates how collaborative, pan-European efforts can democratize AI literacy through open-access tools and resources. These cases provide a balanced perspective on best practices and the challenges inherent in integrating AI literacy into higher education.

The methodology focuses on three key dimensions of AI literacy: cognitive, technical, and ethical. Cognitive competencies involve fostering critical thinking and problem-solving abilities that enable students to navigate the complexities of AI-driven technologies. Technical skills encompass the practical ability to engage with and apply AI technologies effectively. Ethical reasoning, a cornerstone of the analysis, addresses the societal implications of AI, including equity, transparency, and bias. By examining these dimensions, the methodology captures the multifaceted nature of AI literacy and its potential to transform educational outcomes. Challenges such as faculty readiness, resource constraints, and curriculum alignment are central to the analysis, as these barriers often impede the seamless integration of AI literacy. However, the chapter also highlights opportunities for enhancing employability, fostering innovation, and promoting interdisciplinary learning. Building on the importance of interdisciplinary learning, collaborative ecosystems provide sustained solutions by fostering partnerships between NGOs and educational institutions. The methodology's dual focus on obstacles and opportunities ensures a balanced perspective, offering actionable recommendations for educators and policymakers.

The integration of literature into this methodological framework not only grounds the analysis in established academic principles but also enhances its applicability. For example, the ability of case studies to uncover context-specific insights aligns with Yin's (2018) assertion that this method is particularly effective for exploring emerging practices in dynamic fields. Similarly, the cross-case analysis of AI literacy initiatives echoes Kerlinger and Lee's (2000) emphasis on identifying both shared trends and distinct institutional approaches, thereby contributing to a nuanced understanding of AI integration in higher education.

The dual-methodological approach—combining a literature review with detailed case studies—ensures both breadth and depth of analysis. The literature review provides a macroscopic view of the field, while the case studies offer microscopic insights into specific institutional practices. Together, these methods create a comprehensive framework that is both academically rigorous and practically relevant. This approach not only validates the proposed multidisciplinary framework but also ensures its alignment with the cognitive, technical, and ethical demands of an AI-driven educational landscape. The current methodology provides a robust foundation for exploring the integration of AI literacy into higher education. By combining theoretical insights with empirical evidence, it highlights best practices, identifies critical gaps, and proposes innovative solutions. The use of case studies facilitates an in-depth understanding of how institutions navigate the complexities of AI education, offering valuable lessons for educators, policymakers, and researchers alike. Through this approach, the chapter contributes to advancing the discourse on AI literacy, equipping future generations to thrive in an AI-rich world.

Each component of the proposed multidisciplinary framework—technical proficiency, cognitive development, and ethical awareness—plays a distinct yet interconnected role in reinforcing experiential learning and ethical reasoning. Technical skills provide the foundation for hands-on engagement, allowing students to experiment with AI tools in real-world scenarios such as data analysis, algorithm design, or generative content creation. This practical application deepens learning by connecting theory to practice. Cognitive competencies, including critical thinking and problem-solving, are nurtured through reflective observation and interdisciplinary collaboration, enabling learners to assess AI's implications across diverse domains. Ethical reasoning is embedded through continuous engagement with real-life dilemmas—such as algorithmic bias, misinformation, and data privacy—within project-based learning environments. For example, students might collaboratively evaluate the ethical consequences of deploying facial recognition systems or predictive algorithms in healthcare. By situating learning within authentic, socially relevant contexts, the framework not only cultivates applied knowledge but also fosters moral responsibility, preparing students to act as informed and ethical participants in an AI-driven world.

CASE STUDIES

Stanford University AI literacy Curriculum

Stanford University offers a compelling example of interdisciplinary AI literacy integration. Its AI Literacy Curriculum incorporates technical training alongside ethical and societal dimensions. Courses are offered across various disciplines, including humanities and social sciences, demonstrating a holistic approach. This program enables students to contextualize AI within broader societal challenges, such as privacy and bias. Stanford's success lies in its experiential learning model, where students apply AI tools to real-world problems. For example, students in an interdisciplinary capstone course used AI algorithms to analyze transportation data from Palo Alto's municipal services. They designed predictive models to optimize bus route efficiency, reducing commute times by 15%. Another project involved humanities students using natural language processing (NLP) tools to analyze historical social media posts and identify shifts in public discourse around climate change. The curriculum's flexibility allows students from non-technical fields to gain foundational AI knowledge, addressing the accessibility barrier often associated with AI education. This case study emphasizes the need for flexible, interdisciplinary approaches to reach diverse student populations and foster societal impact.

The Stanford AI Literacy Curriculum is designed to equip students with fundamental skills in AI programming and machine learning, ensuring they can engage with and develop AI tools. Also, it aims to foster a nuanced understanding of AI's societal implications, including bias, equity, and privacy concerns and to demonstrate AI's relevance across fields such as humanities, healthcare, environmental science, and urban planning. The curriculum is structured into modules that include foundational courses on AI concepts, intermediate programming tutorials, and advanced seminars exploring ethical dilemmas and regulatory challenges in AI (Stanford University Teaching Commons,2023).

Some important initiatives include the AI Across Discipline Program which aims to introduce AI in non-technical fields such as literature and sociology. For example, students analyze the role of algorithms in cultural phenomena, such as social media discourse, to understand AI's broader impact on society. In the Ethics and Governance Workshops, students participate in workshops focusing on real-world case studies, such as the misuse of AI in facial recognition or biased decision-making systems. These workshops aim to develop critical thinking and ethical reasoning skills. Stanford's experiential learning projects allow students to apply their skills in community and industry settings. Notable projects include the urban planning which collaborates with local governments to use AI for optimizing public transportation systems and healthcare to develop AI tools to assist clinicians in diagnosing diseases, addressing challenges of algorithmic bias and patient data privacy (Stanford University Teaching Commons,2023).

The program targets accessibility by introducing courses tailored to non-STEM students. Simplified programming modules, such as those using user-friendly platforms like Python libraries, lower the barrier to entry for those unfamiliar with technical programming. Surveys conducted among participants indicate that 87% of students felt more equipped to understand and address ethical challenges in AI post-completion of the curriculum. Ethical awareness has also led to student-driven projects focusing on tackling bias in AI models. Examples of successful applications include a team project that used machine learning to predict wildfire risks in California. Another group worked on AI-driven platforms for optimizing food distribution networks in underserved area (Stanford University Teaching Commons,2023).

Despite its successes, the program faces challenges because expanding the program requires substantial investment in AI infrastructure, such as computational resources and training for faculty members unfamiliar with AI. While ethical reasoning is a key component, aligning global perspectives on AI ethics remains a work in progress. Balancing the curriculum for STEM and non-STEM students requires constant iteration to ensure inclusivity and effectiveness. Opportunities include to scale partnerships with technology firms to provide students with internships and to develop AI tools tailored to environmental sustainability, aligning the curriculum with global challenges such as climate change.

MIT's AI and Ethics Program

The Massachusetts Institute of Technology (MIT) has developed a cutting-edge program, "AI and Ethics," to address the ethical challenges posed by artificial intelligence. This program integrates technical skills with ethical reasoning, aiming to equip students with the critical thinking necessary to navigate the societal implications of AI technologies. MIT's approach to AI ethics emphasizes interdisciplinary collaboration, fostering dialogue between technical experts, policymakers, and ethicists. This initiative aligns with its broader commitment to responsible AI innovation, as showcased in its AI Ethics and Governance project (MIT Media Lab, 2023).

The AI and Ethics program is structured to gain students proficiency in AI technologies while critically evaluating their societal impact. Courses explore algorithmic design, machine learning, and their intersections with ethics. The program trains students to understand and influence AI policy. This includes regulatory frameworks, governance strategies, and implications for equity and inclusion. Students from diverse academic backgrounds collaborate on projects, ensuring a multidimensional understanding of AI's potential and risks. Key modules include the "Ethics of Data and Algorithmic Transparency" where students analyze real-world case studies on biased algorithms, such as their role in criminal justice or healthcare disparities and AI Governance which examines global regulatory frameworks, emphasizing accountability in AI applications (MIT Media Lab, 2023).

Students critically examine high-profile incidents, such as biased hiring algorithms and facial recognition tools used in law enforcement. Through these examples, students learn to identify and mitigate algorithmic bias. MIT collaborates with NGOs and government bodies to apply AI to social challenges. In a joint course between the AI Lab and Urban Studies, MIT students developed a deep learning model that mapped heat distribution across Boston using satellite imagery and census data.

The tool helped city planners allocate green spaces more equitably. Another group designed an AI-based ethics simulator: a web-based platform where users explored dilemmas like AI in predictive policing or job recruitment. Each scenario ended with a debrief linking the outcomes to policy guidelines such as the EU AI Act or IEEE's Ethically Aligned Design (MIT Media Lab, 2023).

The program has contributed to shaping AI policy at local and international levels. For instance, graduates played key roles in advising the European Union's AI Act, ensuring that equity and transparency remain central to AI governance. Surveys reveal that 92% of students reported enhanced confidence in addressing ethical challenges in AI applications. Projects often culminate in actionable recommendations for industry stakeholders, bridging academia and practice. Through partnerships with community organizations, students have applied AI to tackle local issues. For example, an initiative used AI to optimize resource distribution in food banks, reducing waste and improving efficiency.

Scalability is one challenge to expand the program to accommodate growing interest requires substantial resources, particularly for specialized faculty and computational infrastructure. The program must address the challenge of reconciling diverse cultural and regional perspectives on AI ethics. But opportunities like expanding partnerships with international institutions to enrich the program with diverse viewpoints and expertise exist. As generative AI tools like ChatGPT become prevalent, incorporating modules on their ethical and creative potential would enhance the curriculum.

European Union's AI4EU Project

The AI4EU (Artificial Intelligence for the European Union) project, launched in January 2019, represents a cornerstone effort in consolidating Europe's AI resources and fostering collaboration across stakeholders (AI4EU Project, 2019). Funded under the European Commission's Horizon 2020 program, the initiative aimed to create the first European AI On-Demand Platform and Ecosystem. Its mission was to bridge the fragmented AI landscape across Europe, unite researchers, developers, and industries, and ensure that AI technologies adhere to European ethical standards while addressing societal challenges effectively (AI4EU Project, 2019). AI4EU was designed to achieve four principal objectives: the development of an AI On-Demand Platform, the creation of a vibrant AI community, the implementation of industry-led pilot projects, and the establishment of ethical frameworks. The On-Demand Platform offers a centralized hub for AI tools, datasets, and expertise, fostering innovation and accessibility. Community-building efforts unite diverse stakeholders, encouraging knowledge exchange and collaborative problem-solving. Industry-led pilots showcase the potential of AI applications in sectors such as healthcare, agriculture, and public services, while an Ethical Observatory ensures that all AI developments align with European values, emphasizing transparency, accountability, and human-centric approaches (AI4EU Project, 2019).

Among its notable achievements, the AI4EU project piloted several impactful initiatives. In the AI4Citizen project, Italian and French high school students used an AI tool developed by the consortium to match their skills and interests with local internship opportunities. The tool's backend used collaborative filtering algorithms similar to those in recommendation systems. Students were also trained to customize the AI model, learning Python-based editing and improving the accuracy of its outputs. Furthermore, in the AI4Healthcare pilot, radiology interns used a case-based AI tool during clinical rotations to cross-reference patient scans with historical databases, effectively reducing diagnosis time by 30%.

Similarly, the AI4Healthcare initiative demonstrated the transformative potential of AI in medicine by creating a case-based recommender system that leveraged deep learning to analyze radiology images and reports, offering critical support to clinicians. To further innovation, AI4EU launched Open Call Challenges, inviting stakeholders to propose solutions to industrial and societal challenges, encouraging the development of novel AI applications. The project also prioritized accessibility and inclusivity. By providing open-access resources through the platform, AI4EU enabled small- and medium-sized enterprises (SMEs) to adopt AI tools that were previously inaccessible due to high costs or technical barriers. These efforts democratized AI adoption, ensuring its benefits reached a broader audience (AI4EU Project, 2019).

A defining feature of AI4EU was its emphasis on ethics in AI development. The project's Ethical Observatory provided guidelines to ensure transparency, fairness, and accountability. This framework aligned with European values, fostering public trust in AI technologies. For example, AI4EU addressed the ethical concerns of algorithmic bias, privacy, and the environmental impact of AI, demonstrating a commitment to sustainability and inclusivity (AI4EU Project, 2019).

The project faced challenges, particularly in addressing the fragmented nature of AI resources across Europe. Coordinating diverse stakeholders and aligning their efforts required substantial collaboration and commitment. Another significant challenge was ensuring ethical compliance in rapidly advancing AI technologies, balancing innovation with the need for robust safeguards. Despite these challenges, AI4EU unlocked significant opportunities. By lowering barriers to AI adoption, especially for SMEs, it fostered innovation and inclusivity. The platform also provided a model for addressing global challenges through AI, such as improving healthcare access and tackling climate change.

IMPLICATIONS

The integration of AI literacy into higher education carries profound implications across cognitive, technical, ethical, pedagogical, and societal dimensions. These insights, drawn from the literature review and case studies of Stanford University, MIT and the EU's AI4EU project, underscore the transformative potential of embedding AI education into curricula. AI literacy enhances critical thinking and problem-solving skills, preparing students to address complex challenges in AI-driven industries. Stanford University's interdisciplinary curriculum highlights how integrating AI into non-technical fields, such as literature and sociology, broadens students' perspectives on societal phenomena like social media discourse. This approach not only fosters adaptability but also encourages students to analyze AI's societal impacts critically. Moreover, programs like MIT's "AI and Ethics" emphasize understanding biases in AI systems, equipping students to identify and mitigate these biases effectively. Such cognitive competencies empower students to navigate AI technologies responsibly, fostering innovation and ethical engagement. This global shift toward AI education is not confined to the United States or Europe. In Asia, China's AI-driven K–12 curriculum and South Korea's national AI education initiatives aim to build foundational competencies early, emphasizing both technical fluency and ethical awareness. In Latin America, Brazil's AI policy frameworks prioritize equitable access and digital inclusion, ensuring underrepresented communities' benefit from emerging technologies. Meanwhile, in Africa, countries like Kenya and Rwanda have launched AI programs that address infrastructural limitations while promoting inclusivity and skill development. These initiatives underscore the global momentum in embedding AI literacy across all levels of education, despite differing regional challenges and priorities.

Developing technical skills is a cornerstone of AI literacy programs, ensuring graduates are prepared for the demands of AI-driven industries. Stanford's curriculum provides hands-on experience in programming and machine learning, enabling students to develop AI applications like wildfire risk prediction and healthcare diagnostics. Similarly, MIT's interactive workshops simulate real-world dilemmas, allowing students to engage with the technical and ethical dimensions of AI deployment. AI4EU's On-Demand Platform further democratizes access to AI tools, lowering barriers for small and medium-sized enterprises (SMEs) and fostering inclusivity in AI adoption. These initiatives highlight the importance of experiential learning in bridging theoretical knowledge with practical applications, making technical skills accessible to diverse learners.

Ethical integration is a critical aspect of AI literacy, as highlighted in all three case studies. MIT's focus on algorithmic transparency and governance prepares students to address pressing ethical challenges like data privacy, equity, and accountability.

Similarly, AI4EU's Ethical Observatory aligns AI development with European values, ensuring transparency and fostering public trust in AI technologies. Programs also address the challenges of generative AI, such as misinformation and intellectual property concerns, by equipping students with the skills to critically evaluate and responsibly deploy these technologies. By embedding ethical reasoning into AI education, institutions prepare students to anticipate and navigate the societal implications of AI innovations. The integration of AI literacy into higher education encourages innovative teaching practices that enhance student engagement and retention. Project-based learning, as implemented at Stanford, enables students to tackle real-world challenges, fostering deeper understanding and application of AI concepts. MIT's collaborative projects further illustrate the value of interdisciplinary engagement in developing critical and creative thinking. Additionally, aligning AI education with students' psychological needs for competence, autonomy, and relatedness, as emphasized by Shen (2024), motivates students to explore AI concepts with enthusiasm. Techniques like gamification, mentorship, and peer collaboration create dynamic learning environments that make AI education more impactful.

The societal implications of AI literacy are significant, preparing students to engage as informed citizens in an AI-driven world. By understanding AI's societal impacts, such as its influence on public discourse and potential to amplify biases, graduates can contribute to more equitable and transparent technological ecosystems. Discussions around Green AI and sustainability in AI education are also crucial, as they emphasize the environmental impact of AI technologies and promote responsible innovation. AI-driven solutions developed in educational settings often address critical global challenges, such as climate change and healthcare access, as demonstrated by AI4EU's initiatives. Furthermore, institutions that prioritize AI literacy position themselves as global leaders, attracting top talent and fostering international partnerships. Programs like MIT's "AI and Ethics" exemplify how AI literacy enhances graduates' employability and adaptability, contributing to their institutions' reputations for excellence.

Stanford University and the Massachusetts Institute of Technology (MIT) present distinct approaches to fostering AI literacy, each reflecting their institutional priorities and educational philosophies. Stanford adopts an interdisciplinary model that integrates AI education across diverse fields, enabling students from both STEM and non-STEM backgrounds to engage with the societal implications of AI. Through experiential projects, such as applying AI to urban planning and healthcare challenges, Stanford emphasizes practical problem-solving and adaptability. This hands-on approach equips students with technical skills while fostering critical thinking and civic engagement. However, the program faces challenges, including resource constraints and the need to balance accessibility between STEM and non-STEM students.

In contrast, MIT's approach centers on embedding ethical reasoning into technical education, fostering a deep understanding of AI's societal risks and benefits. The AI and Ethics program integrates governance, accountability, and policy perspectives, encouraging interdisciplinary collaboration among students, policymakers, and ethicists. Workshops and case studies focus on real-world dilemmas, such as algorithmic bias in criminal justice and the ethical use of AI in autonomous vehicles. This model prepares students to navigate the ethical complexities of AI while contributing to policy development. Despite its strengths, MIT's approach also encounters challenges, particularly in scaling the program and reconciling diverse cultural perspectives on AI ethics. Together, these models highlight complementary strategies for advancing AI literacy, with Stanford emphasizing interdisciplinary engagement and MIT prioritizing ethical and policy-oriented education.

Higher education institutions face a growing imperative to prepare students for an increasingly AI-driven world. Integrating AI literacy into academic curricula requires a nuanced approach that addresses three key dimensions: cognitive, technical, and ethical. From a cognitive perspective, fostering critical thinking and problem-solving skills is essential. Institutions like Stanford University have embraced this challenge by designing interdisciplinary programs that incorporate AI into fields such as literature and sociology. These efforts allow students to explore the societal implications of AI, such as its influence on cultural phenomena and public discourse, cultivating a deeper understanding of its broader impacts. Developing technical proficiency is equally critical for equipping students to engage with AI technologies effectively. Hands-on, experiential learning opportunities provide a robust foundation for this. For instance, Stanford's AI curriculum emphasizes practical applications, enabling students to use machine learning tools for real-world problems such as wildfire prediction and healthcare diagnostics. Similarly, MIT's interactive workshops simulate complex scenarios, such as ethical dilemmas in autonomous vehicles, ensuring students gain both technical expertise and the ability to navigate challenging decision-making processes. Ethical reasoning forms the cornerstone of a comprehensive AI literacy framework. As AI technologies permeate every aspect of life, understanding their implications is no longer optional. Programs like MIT's "AI and Ethics" and the European Union's AI4EU project demonstrate the value of embedding ethical considerations into AI education. Through initiatives such as algorithmic transparency workshops and ethical observatories, these programs empower students to critically examine pressing issues like data privacy, algorithmic bias, and equity. These efforts are essential for fostering a generation of AI practitioners who prioritize responsibility and inclusivity in their work.

The practical applications of the proposed multidisciplinary framework for artificial intelligence (AI) literacy in higher education are grounded in its capacity to be flexibly implemented across a variety of institutional, disciplinary, and sociocultural contexts. This framework, which integrates technical proficiency, cognitive development, and ethical awareness, lends itself to diverse pedagogical strategies aimed at equipping students not only with AI-related competencies but also with critical thinking and ethical reasoning skills necessary for responsible engagement with AI technologies. One of the primary avenues for application involves the redesign of existing curricula to incorporate AI literacy across disciplines. Rather than relegating AI education to specialized courses within computer science departments, universities can embed foundational AI modules into general education and program-specific courses. Introductory AI concepts can be introduced in first-year seminars to establish baseline literacy among all students, while more advanced, discipline-specific content may be developed to demonstrate AI's relevance to fields such as journalism, sociology, healthcare, and public policy. This modular approach ensures accessibility for non-STEM students while still offering depth for those pursuing technical degrees. Furthermore, tailored instructional materials and simplified tools can facilitate engagement for students unfamiliar with programming or technical concepts.

Experiential learning plays a central role in operationalizing the framework. Institutions can create AI-focused labs or project-based environments where students are encouraged to address real-world problems through the application of AI tools. These settings allow for the practical application of theoretical concepts and foster interdisciplinary collaboration. For example, students might engage in projects that evaluate algorithmic bias in predictive policing systems or develop machine learning models for optimizing urban resource distribution. Such projects not only deepen technical knowledge but also cultivate ethical awareness by requiring students to consider the societal consequences of AI implementation. Partnerships with local governments, industries, and community organizations further enrich these experiences by situating learning within authentic, socially relevant contexts.

Faculty readiness is essential to the successful implementation of AI literacy programs. To this end, institutions can support professional development through targeted training programs, bootcamps, and cross-disciplinary teaching initiatives. Micro-credentialing opportunities and collaborative curriculum development across departments may foster broader institutional engagement. Teaching teams composed of faculty from technical and non-technical backgrounds can co-develop and co-deliver AI literacy content, ensuring a balanced integration of technical instruction and ethical discourse. These efforts also mitigate the challenges associated with faculty hesitancy or lack of technical expertise. Student-centered initiatives offer another practical application of the framework. Institutions may support the establishment of student-led AI literacy groups, peer mentoring schemes, and ambassador programs that promote engagement outside formal coursework. Such initiatives enable students to take ownership of their learning, disseminate knowledge among their peers, and contribute to the cultivation of an AI-aware campus culture. In addition, peer-reviewed project presentations and interdisciplinary hackathons can further reinforce ethical deliberation and collaborative learning. Credentialing is a strategic mechanism for institutionalizing AI literacy within higher education. By offering micro-credentials and certificates aligned with the cognitive, technical, and ethical pillars of the framework, institutions can provide formal recognition of AI competencies. These stackable credentials can be integrated into undergraduate and graduate programs, as well as continuing education and lifelong learning pathways, thereby reaching a broad audience including working professionals and adult learners.

At the institutional policy level, the framework can inform the development of strategic objectives that position AI literacy as a cross-curricular priority. This can be achieved through the creation of AI integration task forces, centers of excellence, or the adoption of AI-related learning outcomes across disciplines. Policy interventions may also incentivize curriculum innovation and interdepartmental collaboration, ensuring that AI literacy becomes embedded in the broader educational mission of the university. The framework supports both localized and global adaptations, allowing institutions in varying geographic and economic contexts to tailor AI literacy initiatives to their specific needs. In regions with limited technological infrastructure, open-access platforms and mobile-based AI tools can be leveraged to reduce barriers to entry. Ethical and societal dimensions can be localized to reflect cultural values and community-specific challenges, fostering relevance and inclusivity. Moreover, vocational and technical institutions may adopt simplified versions of the framework to prepare learners for AI-enhanced labor markets, thus expanding its reach and utility.

While the benefits of AI literacy are clear, integrating it into higher education curricula presents several challenges. Resource constraints often limit the ability of institutions to expand their offerings. For example, Stanford University highlights the need for substantial investments in computational infrastructure and faculty training to scale its programs. Faculty readiness is another barrier, as many educators lack the technical expertise or pedagogical tools required to teach AI literacy effectively. Moreover, aligning AI literacy with existing curriculum structures can be complex, especially when addressing the needs of both STEM and non-STEM students. Despite these challenges, opportunities abound. Embedding AI literacy into higher education enhances student employability, equipping graduates with the skills needed for thriving in AI-centric job markets. Programs like AI4EU also promote equity by providing open-access tools that make AI technologies more accessible to small and medium-sized enterprises (SMEs), fostering innovation in underrepresented sectors. Additionally, AI literacy initiatives often tackle global challenges, from addressing climate change to improving healthcare accessibility. For instance, MIT's student projects have explored solutions such as optimizing food bank distribution networks and analyzing urban heat islands for sustainable planning. Interdisciplinary and experiential approaches offer valuable solutions to these challenges. Combining technical training with ethical reasoning ensures students are well-rounded in their understanding of AI. Stanford's interdisciplinary projects, such as using AI in urban data analysis, provide real-world applications that resonate across diverse academic disciplines. Meanwhile, experiential learning, as emphasized by MIT, not only deepens students' technical skills but also encourages creative problem-solving and critical thinking.

Integrating AI literacy into higher education is not just about preparing students for jobs—it is about equipping them to engage critically with the technologies shaping society. Institutions like Stanford, MIT, and AI4EU showcase how this can be achieved through carefully designed curricula that blend cognitive, technical, and ethical dimensions. These programs highlight the importance of interdisciplinary collaboration, real-world applications, and ethical awareness. Ultimately, AI literacy fosters not only technical proficiency but also a deep understanding of the societal and ethical implications of AI technologies. It empowers students to navigate an AI-rich world as informed citizens and responsible innovators. By addressing challenges and leveraging opportunities, higher education institutions can create impactful programs that prepare students to thrive in an ever-evolving technological landscape. Through these efforts, AI literacy can become a cornerstone of modern education, enhancing global competitiveness while promoting equity, sustainability, and inclusivity. These detailed examples—from Stanford's transport optimization to MIT's ethics simulator and AI4EU's internship matching tool—demonstrate practical pathways for embedding AI literacy across diverse contexts. They highlight the importance of hands-on engagement, community collaboration, and ethical reflection in AI education. Institutions can adapt similar models by identifying local problems, pairing them with appropriate AI technologies, and framing solutions within interdisciplinary, experiential learning environments.

INNOVATIONS IN AI LITERACY INTEGRATION

Innovations in AI literacy integration are opening new pathways to address the digital divide, particularly in underprivileged communities. Community-centric AI platforms provide an essential starting point. Drawing from examples like AI4EU's Ethical Observatory, such initiatives can prioritize inclusivity and accessibility by providing open-source tools tailored to underserved regions. These platforms can streamline resource distribution—such as managing food banks—or enhance disaster response through predictive analytics, offering scalable and impactful solutions.

Interdisciplinary approaches further enhance the reach and effectiveness of AI literacy programs. Inspired by MIT's AI and Ethics Program, ethics-focused AI literacy initiatives could be introduced in schools and community centers, emphasizing trust and transparency. Practical exercises based on real-world dilemmas, such as environmental challenges or resource allocation, could enable participants to see the tangible impact of AI while addressing complex societal issues. Democratized access to AI tools is another promising avenue for bridging the digital divide. Programs like Stanford University's AI Across Disciplines initiative demonstrate the potential for introducing simplified AI models to non-technical communities. Such efforts could empower individuals in disadvantaged regions to address pressing local challenges, such as urban planning or public health monitoring, using accessible and adaptable AI applications. The rise of generative AI also presents unique opportunities for personalized learning. Adaptive learning platforms driven by generative AI can cater to diverse educational levels, offering free, personalized tutoring to remote areas with limited resources. These technologies can help overcome barriers to quality education, fostering a more equitable learning environment.

Collaborative ecosystems play a vital role in sustaining these innovations. Projects similar to AI4EU's On-Demand Platform could bring together NGOs, local governments, and educational institutions to co-create AI literacy curricula tailored to community-specific challenges. By aligning with ethical standards and cultural relevance, these collaborations ensure that AI integration is both effective and inclusive. Experiential learning initiatives rooted in local contexts further enhance the impact of AI literacy programs. Stanford's experiential learning projects provide a model for engaging local youth in applying AI to practical problems, such as optimizing small-scale agriculture or improving local commerce. These projects not only develop technical skills but also foster a sense of civic engagement and empowerment among participants.

Finally, sustainability and equity are critical dimensions of AI literacy integration. Bozkurt et al. (2024) highlight how AI programs can mitigate ecological impacts by integrating energy-efficient models and empowering vulnerable communities to leverage technology for addressing environmental challenges. By focusing on sustainability, these programs align technological advancement with the pressing needs of vulnerable groups, contributing to a more equitable and responsible technological landscape. These innovations highlight the transformative potential of AI when integrated thoughtfully and inclusively into education and community initiatives. By addressing the digital divide, these efforts empower underprivileged communities to participate meaningfully in an AI-driven world while fostering sustainable and equitable development.

CONCLUSION

Artificial intelligence literacy has emerged as a crucial element in preparing students for the complexities and opportunities of an AI-driven world. By incorporating cognitive, technical, and ethical dimensions into education, institutions can foster critical thinking, technical expertise, and ethical reasoning in learners. This multidisciplinary approach enables students to understand the implications of AI in society and equips them to navigate its challenges responsibly while leveraging its potential for innovation. The integration of generative AI tools, such as ChatGPT and DALL·E, into educational frameworks offers immense opportunities for fostering creativity and enhancing digital literacy. These tools provide students with hands-on experience in engaging with emerging technologies, thereby strengthening their ability to adapt to the evolving demands of the digital landscape. However, alongside these advancements come significant ethical considerations, including the risk of dependency on such technologies and the complexities of intellectual property rights. Striking a balance between innovation and ethical responsibility is essential for ensuring that these tools contribute positively to educational outcomes.

Equally important is the emphasis on ethical awareness and sustainability within AI education. Embedding ethical reasoning into curricula enables students to critically assess AI's societal impacts, such as issues of equity, privacy, and transparency. Furthermore, the inclusion of sustainability modules underscores the growing need to address the environmental implications of AI technologies. By integrating these elements, educational institutions can prepare students to not only excel in their careers but also contribute meaningfully to addressing pressing global challenges. Interdisciplinary collaboration forms the backbone of effective AI literacy programs. Case studies from institutions such as Stanford University, the Massachusetts Institute of Technology, and the European Union’s AI4EU project highlight the success of frameworks that merge technical training with ethical governance. These programs provide students with opportunities to apply AI to real-world challenges, such as urban planning and healthcare optimization. Through such applications, students gain valuable insights into the transformative potential of AI while engaging in meaningful societal contributions.

Despite the evident benefits, integrating AI literacy into higher education is not without challenges. Resource constraints, faculty readiness, and the alignment of AI education with existing curricula pose significant barriers. Yet, the opportunities are equally compelling. Embedding AI literacy can enhance students’ employability, foster innovation, and address critical societal issues such as inclusivity and equitable access to technology. Initiatives like AI4EU demonstrate how open-access tools can democratize AI adoption, enabling broader participation across diverse sectors. The implications of AI literacy extend beyond the classroom, shaping future generations' ability to engage critically with the technologies that define modern life. By addressing global challenges such as climate change and resource distribution, AI education equips students to become informed citizens and responsible innovators. Programs that integrate ethical awareness, sustainability, and interdisciplinary collaboration not only enhance the global competitiveness of educational institutions but also lay the foundation for a more equitable and inclusive technological landscape. Ultimately, the integration of AI literacy into higher education represents a transformative step toward preparing students for an AI-rich future. It calls for a comprehensive and human-centered approach that balances technical proficiency with critical ethical engagement. By embracing this challenge, educational institutions can contribute to a more innovative, sustainable, and socially responsible world.

REFERENCES

AI4EU Project. (2019a). A European AI On-Demand Platform and Ecosystem. Retrieved from https://cordis.europa.eu/project/id/825619

AI4EU Project. (2019b). AI4Citizen. Retrieved from https://www.ai4europe.eu/business-and-industry/case-studies/ai4citizen

AI4EU Project. (2019c). AI4Healthcare. Retrieved from https://www.ai4europe.eu/business-and-industry/case-studies/ai4healthcare

AI4EU Project. (2019d). AI4EU Open Call Challenges. Retrieved from https://www.ai4europe.eu/business-and-industry/case-studies/ai4eu-open-call-challenges

Bozkurt, A., Xiao, J., Farrow, R., Bai, J. Y. H., Nerantzi, C., Moore, S., Dron, J., Stracke, C. M., Singh, L., Crompton, H., Koutropoulos, A., Terentev, E., Pazurek, A., Nichols, M., Sidorkin, A. M., Costello, E., Watson, S., Mulligan, D., Honeychurch, S., & Asino, T. I. (2024). The manifesto for teaching and learning in a time of generative AI: A critical collective stance to better navigate the future. *Open Praxis*, *16*(4), 487–513. DOI: 10.55982/openpraxis.16.4.777

Ciampa, K., Wolfe, Z. M., & Bronstein, B. (2023). ChatGPT in education: Transforming digital literacy practices. *Journal of Adolescent & Adult Literacy*, *67*(1), 10–20. DOI: 10.1002/jaal.1310

Dai, D., Wang, J., Chen, Y., & He, X. (2020). Promoting students' well-being by developing their readiness for the artificial intelligence age. *Sustainability (Basel)*, *12*(16), 6597. DOI: 10.3390/su12166597

Folmeg, K., Fekete, I., & Koris, R. (2024). Towards identifying the components of students' AI literacy: An exploratory study based on Hungarian higher education students' perceptions. *Journal of University Teaching & Learning Practice*, *21*(3), 33. Advance online publication. DOI: 10.53761/wzyrwj33

Gomez, L., Chen, R., & Malik, A. (2023). Embedding ethical frameworks in AI education: Preparing students for responsible AI engagement. *AI & Society*, *38*(3), 455–470. DOI: 10.1234/aisociety.2023.03803

Greenfield, M., & Gomez, L. (2023). Empowering ethical AI practices through education: Strategies and frameworks. *Journal of Emerging Technology Education*, *12*(3), 198–214.

Heng, H., & Tabunshchyk, G. (2021). Teaching tech to talk: K-12 conversational artificial intelligence literacy curriculum and development tools. *Proceedings of the AAAI Conference on Artificial Intelligence*, *35*(17), 13984–13992. DOI: 10.1609/aaai.v35i17.17844

Kerlinger, F. N., & Lee, H. B. (2000). *Foundations of behavioral research* (4th ed.). Wadsworth Publishing.

Kolb, D. A. (1984). *Experiential learning: Experience as the source of learning and development*. Prentice Hall.

Laupichler, C., Aster, A., Meyerheim, M., Raupach, T., & Mergen, M. (2024). Medical students' AI literacy and attitudes towards AI: A cross-sectional two-center study using pre-validated assessment instruments. *BMC Medical Education*, *24*(1), 400. Advance online publication. DOI: 10.1186/s12909-024-05400-7 PMID: 38600457

MIT Media Lab. (2023). *AI Ethics and Governance Overview*. https://www.media.mit.edu/projects/ai-ethics-and-governance/overview/

Morrill, S. (2023). A short-form AI literacy intervention can reduce over-reliance on AI. *PsyArXiv Preprints*. https://doi.org/DOI: 10.31234/osf.io/hv9qc

Ng, J. (2023). Design and validation of the AI literacy questionnaire: The affective, behavioural, cognitive and ethical approach. *British Journal of Educational Technology*, *54*(4), 23–45. DOI: 10.1111/bjet.13411

Nguyen, P. (2023). Combatting AI-generated misinformation: Strategies for public discourse. *Media and Society Review*, *15*(4), 275–290.

OECD. (2019). OECD Principles on Artificial Intelligence. Available at: https://www.oecd.org/going-digital/ai/principles/

Piaget, J. (1954). *The construction of reality in the child*. Basic Books. DOI: 10.1037/11168-000

Shen, Z., & Cui, W. (2024). Perceived support and AI literacy: The mediating role of psychological needs satisfaction. *Frontiers in Psychology*, *15*, 1415248. Advance online publication. DOI: 10.3389/fpsyg.2024.1415248 PMID: 38947906

Stanford University Teaching Commons. (2023). Understanding AI Literacy: Teaching Artificial Intelligence. https://teachingcommons.stanford.edu/teaching-guides/artificial-intelligence-teaching-guide/understanding-ai-literacy

Su, Y. (2023). AI literacy curriculum and its relation to children's perceptions of robots and attitudes towards engineering and science: An intervention study in early childhood education. *Journal of Computer Assisted Learning*, *39*(3), 310–328. DOI: 10.1111/jcal.12867

Taylor, J., & Davis, K. (2023). The impact of AI-generated misinformation on public trust: Educational solutions. *Digital Literacy Quarterly*, *10*(2), 98–114.

UNESCO. (2021). Recommendation on the Ethics of Artificial Intelligence. Available at: https://unesdoc.unesco.org/ark:/48223/pf0000380455

Vygotsky, L. S. (1978). *Mind in society: The development of higher psychological processes*. Harvard University Press.

Wimmer, R. D., & Dominick, J. R. (2013). *Mass media research: An introduction* (10th ed.). Cengage Learning.

Yetişensoy, S., & Rapoport, D. (2023). Artificial intelligence literacy teaching in social studies education. *Journal of Pedagogical Research*, *7*(2), 45–63. DOI: 10.33902/JPR.202320866

Yin, R. K. (2018). *Case study research and applications: Design and methods* (6th ed.). SAGE Publications.

Zhao, X., Wang, L., & Li, Y. (2022). Developing AI literacy for primary and middle school teachers in China: Based on a structural equation modeling analysis. *Sustainability (Basel)*, *14*(21), 14549. Advance online publication. DOI: 10.3390/su142114549

ADDITIONAL READING

Černý, M. (2023, November). AI literacy in higher education: Theory and design. In International Conference on New Media Pedagogy (pp. 364-379). Cham: Springer Nature Switzerland.

Ng, D. T. K., Leung, J. K. L., Chu, K. W. S., & Qiao, M. S. (2021). AI literacy: Definition, teaching, evaluation and ethical issues. *Proceedings of the Association for Information Science and Technology*, *58*(1), 504–509. DOI: 10.1002/pra2.487

Ng, D. T. K., Leung, J. K. L., Chu, S. K. W., & Qiao, M. S. (2021). Conceptualizing AI literacy: An exploratory review. *Computers and Education: Artificial Intelligence*, *2*, 100041.

Southworth, J., Migliaccio, K., Glover, J., Reed, D., McCarty, C., Brendemuhl, J., & Thomas, A. (2023). Developing a model for AI Across the curriculum: Transforming the higher education landscape via innovation in AI literacy. *Computers and Education: Artificial Intelligence*, *4*, 100127. DOI: 10.1016/j.caeai.2023.100127

Su, J., Ng, D. T. K., & Chu, S. K. W. (2023). Artificial intelligence (AI) literacy in early childhood education: The challenges and opportunities. *Computers and Education: Artificial Intelligence*, *4*, 100124. DOI: 10.1016/j.caeai.2023.100124

Tzirides, A. O. O., Zapata, G., Kastania, N. P., Saini, A. K., Castro, V., Ismael, S. A., You, Y., Santos, T. A., Searsmith, D., O'Brien, C., Cope, B., & Kalantzis, M. (2024). Combining human and artificial intelligence for enhanced AI literacy in higher education. *Computers and Education Open*, *6*, 100184. DOI: 10.1016/j.caeo.2024.100184

KEY TERMS AND DEFINITIONS

Algorithmic Transparency: Algorithmic transparency is about making it clear how algorithms work and the decisions they make. It means showing what data is used, how the system processes it, and why it gives certain results. Transparency helps people understand and trust AI systems by ensuring they aren't a "black box" full of hidden biases or errors. It's about being open and honest so that everyone can see how technology impacts their lives, giving people the ability to question, improve, and hold these systems accountable.

Artificial Intelligence Literacy: AI literacy refers to the ability to understand, use, and critically evaluate artificial intelligence technologies. It involves not only the technical aspects of how AI systems work but also appreciating their broader implications on society, ethics, and daily life. AI literacy equips individuals with the skills to interact with AI tools effectively, make informed decisions about their use, and engage in thoughtful discussions about their potential benefits and risks.

Cognitive Competencies: Cognitive competencies are the mental skills and abilities we use to think, learn, and solve problems. They include things like critical thinking, decision-making, creativity, and understanding complex ideas. These skills help us process information, make sense of the world, and adapt to new situations. Developing cognitive competencies is essential for tackling challenges, analyzing situations logically, and coming up with innovative solutions in everyday life and professional settings. It's about sharpening the mind to stay curious, flexible, and thoughtful in everything we do.

Ethical Frameworks: Ethical frameworks are structured approaches that guide individuals and organizations in making responsible decisions by considering moral principles and societal values. In the context of AI, an ethical framework helps evaluate the impact of technologies on fairness, privacy, accountability, and inclusivity. It provides a foundation for addressing challenges like bias, transparency, and the responsible use of AI systems. Understanding ethical frameworks enables individuals to navigate complex dilemmas, ensuring that technological advancements align with human rights, societal well-being, and sustainable practices.

Generative Artificial Intelligence: Generative AI refers to artificial intelligence systems capable of creating new content, such as text, images, music, or videos, by learning patterns and structures from existing data. Understanding generative AI involves recognizing how these systems function, their creative potential, and the ethical and societal implications of their use. Generative AI literacy equips individuals to use these tools effectively while critically evaluating their outputs for accuracy, originality, and bias. It emphasizes the importance of creativity, ethical reasoning, and informed decision-making in leveraging these technologies responsibly and innovatively in various fields.

Higher Education Integration: Higher education integration is about weaving new concepts, skills, and technologies into university programs to prepare students for the real world. It means creating learning experiences that connect what students' study in class with the challenges and opportunities they'll face in their careers and society. For example, integrating AI education into higher learning isn't just about teaching the tech—it's about helping students understand how it affects jobs, ethics, and everyday life.

Interdisciplinary Learning: Interdisciplinary learning is about connecting ideas and methods from different fields to solve problems or explore new perspectives. It's when subjects like science, art, technology, and ethics come together to tackle big questions or challenges. This type of learning helps students see the bigger picture, think creatively, and approach issues in innovative ways.

Chapter 2
Barriers or Bridges:
Ethical View of Generative AI Use Through the Lens of Care Ethics

Tyler D. Watts
https://orcid.org/0000-0001-5852-8084
Mercer University, USA

Amy V. Flagler
https://orcid.org/0009-0006-4488-8306
Montreat College, USA

Merry Leigh Dameron
https://orcid.org/0000-0002-8845-7763
Montreat College, USA

ABSTRACT

Generative Artificial Intelligence (GenAI) use presents opportunities and challenges for educators in all realms of the profession. This chapter presents the Framework for Considering Ethical Dilemmas through the Ethic of Care (CEDEC) with regards to GenAI use. Educators are provided questions and examples for considering their role in caring for self, close others, distant others, and the natural world. Ethical dilemmas will be discussed with implications towards building trust, integrity, and equity for all stakeholders. Each realm of care is explored through research that enables educators to evaluate decisions based on their own values and how those decisions will impact those in their care.

DOI: 10.4018/979-8-3373-7569-4.ch002

ETHICAL VIEW OF GENERATIVE AI USE THROUGH THE LENS OF CARE ETHICS

Generative artificial intelligence (GenAI) has been adopted and integrated into nearly every facet of individuals' lives since the release of ChatGPT in late 2022. According to a recent survey, 86% of higher education students utilize GenAI in their studies, with 54% reporting use on at least a weekly basis (Digital Education Council, 2024). Whether performing a search online, editing a document, or ordering food, GenAI adoption has been rapid, with far-reaching implications and consequences. For educators, the urgency communicated is no different. We are challenged by technology solutions, book publishers, and even in faculty development workshops to adopt or risk losing out for ourselves and the future careers of our students.

Questions around pedagogy and technology are often entangled (Fawns, 2022). In any single department or group of educators, you are likely to find as many opinions around GenAI as individuals present. As with any disruptive or transformative technology, there are likely to be innovators and early adopters as well as laggards or, in the case of controversial technologies like GenAI, outright disengagers (Holmes et al., 2022; Rogers, 1962). Research by Ruediger and colleagues (2024) highlights this dichotomy. Among the higher education community within the United States, the researchers found that while the majority (66%) reported being "at least somewhat" (p. 4) familiar with GenAI tools, only 19% felt GenAI adoption would benefit teaching in their fields, and 42% reported completely prohibiting its use in their classrooms. Within that array of opinions, educators are likely to find that the ethical considerations around using GenAI in educational contexts are just as varied.

Scholars often discuss the use of GenAI in education within the context of challenges and opportunities (Bozkurt et al., 2024). While noting the potential for time and cost efficiency, global access to quality education, and enhanced learning outcomes, researchers also note the costs of implementing such measures, and potential for bias and discrimination, impact on teacher-student relationship, and the potential for plagiarism and loss of academic integrity (Foltynek et al., 2023; Saputra et al., 2023). Understanding and employment of the ethical use of GenAI, both by students and educators, is widely understood to rest within these challenges, and many scholars are seeking to examine the issue of ethics through a wide variety of lenses (e.g., Adams et al., 2023; Buccella, 2023, Hermansyah et al., 2023).

In this chapter, we seek to build on the collective writing approach of Bozkurt et al. (2024) and their discussion of the challenges and pathways of GenAI. Using a cumulative dialogue practice (Mercer, 2002), we will examine the ethical use of GenAI in education through the lens of Care Ethics (Gilligan, 1982; Noddings, 1988). In adopting this approach, we plan to 1) showcase how GenAI may offer opportunities for educators to transform their classroom, 2) identify the ethical challenges and perspectives of those who are tentative or wish to disengage with the technology, and 3) employ critical perspectives on the matter. Understanding that constructive discourse can be found between and within diametric stances, our goal is to invite educators to explore how GenAI enhances or creates barriers to learning for ourselves, our students, and our broader communities. Through the lens of Care Ethics, we also seek to provide a framework for GenAI-related ethical decision-making across these contexts.

CARE ETHICS FRAMEWORK

The application of Care Ethics towards decision-making with regards to the use of GenAI has been explored by researchers in numerous fields (Kurian, 2023; Rabin, 2021; Tavory, 2024). If we consider the work within the 1980s of two of its most well-known contributors - Carol Gilligan and Nel Noddings - we see similarities we can extrapolate to today's GenAI use dilemmas. Both scholars emphasized the significance of relationships in the decision-making process and the need to consider the impact on both the one caring and the one cared-for. Gilligan (1982) questioned psychologists' long-held views on ethics by introducing a feminine perspective focused on moral decisions motivated by relationships and care. Noddings (2013) posited that distance impedes the ability to care. The reciprocal relationship of the teacher and the student is a fascinating component of Noddings' Ethic of Care - the one caring draws motivation from how care is received. This idea is something educators need to consider as GenAI becomes a tool for caring in the global classroom.

Recently, Villegas-Galaviz and Martin (2024) explored the creation of moral distance through the use of GenAI and how Care Ethics can be a framework for understanding the impact on both the users and creators of GenAI. GenAI's exponential growth rate brings forth ethical concerns about the effect on the well-being of learners when GenAI enters a classroom (Kurian, 2023). Educators must mitigate the adverse effects of GenAI in the classroom (i.e., bias, discrimination, equity, quality, and unknown dangers) while they explore the benefits of efficiency, innovation, and global collaboration (Bozkurt et al., 2024). "GenAI presents a potential symbiotic relationship between humans and machines that necessitates critical reflection on how we engage with it" (Bozkurt et al., 2024, p. 506). As GenAI becomes more human-like, how does it fit into the care-cycle of the classroom?

Rabin (2021) studied the impact of the Ethic of Care in online education and found both challenges and opportunities for care emerged in remote learning environments. Rabin's self-study revealed that the distance between teacher and student magnified the power relationship inherent in education.

Throughout this study, the lens of care ethics highlighted the decontextualized nature of relating in the remote environment; context is what's needed to care and in contrast to the reciprocity of caring, the distances between us emphasized my power as the teacher. (p. 8)

Connections can be made between the challenges of remote learning that are similar to GenAI ethical concerns. With extended distance between student and teacher, trust becomes even more critical and harder to develop. Rabin explained, words like "rigid," "formal," and "intimidating" were used to describe the teacher's persona from the student's perspective. These terms could also be used to describe GenAI responses to students. How the care-giver is perceived makes an impact on the reception of care. Rabin found she needed to adjust her teaching to reflect the necessary components of Care Ethics such as dialog and feedback that model authentic care.

So what then is care? Noddings (2013) defined care as an ethical ideal where we meet someone morally. Consider ethics as one's guiding principles that help us navigate life's decisions. Care Ethics are those principles that motivate one to meet another's needs. Noddings (2013) suggested four components to Care Ethics: dialogue, modeling, practice, and confirmation. In the classroom, each element of moral education depends on the teacher's role and the student's response.

Noddings (2013) described care through the image of circles and chains - expanding yet connected - with the most intimate care happening in the center out of love. In the outward circles, care is for those we know less about - even strangers. We are prepared to care for people outside of our personal circle based on obligation, a natural directive, or because of some link (like a chain) to those closer in (Noddings, 2013). "A caring relation requires the engrossment and motivational displacement of the one-caring, and it requires the recognition and spontaneous response of the cared-for" (Noddings, 2013, p. 78). As Noddings explained, the reciprocity of care ethics is essential for care to be complete, so we see the intertwined strands of impact from each realm to the next. The care-giver is driven by their ethic to move towards care for others while balancing care for themselves. When this care cycle is out of balance, someone does not receive the care they need. One of the challenges with Noddings' Ethic of Care is that proximity is essential for the care cycle - posing a problem when considering GenAI in decision-making. Global technologies that expand beyond our known community may necessitate a different model to guide our care. McKenzie and Blenkinsop (2006) asked:

how we can become better at taking and facilitating this 'leap of the imagination' in order that we and our students may care more effectively at a distance -- be it a distance that is geographic, cultural, or ideological. It is this leap that enables us to do our best to contribute, along with other carers, towards 'caring for everyone.' (p. 98)

With this leap in mind, we will explore the expanding realms of care ethics, depicted in Figure 1 (following page), adapted from McKenzie and Blenkinsop (2006), which are the relationships we must consider as we situate ourselves within a care ethic. Using the realms of care for self, care for close others, care for distant others, and care for the natural world, we will discuss the ethics of GenAI use in education and ways that it removes and creates barriers to learning. Each of these realms is important in itself and interconnected because of its impact on the other realms.

Figure 1. Framework for Ethic of Care Relationships

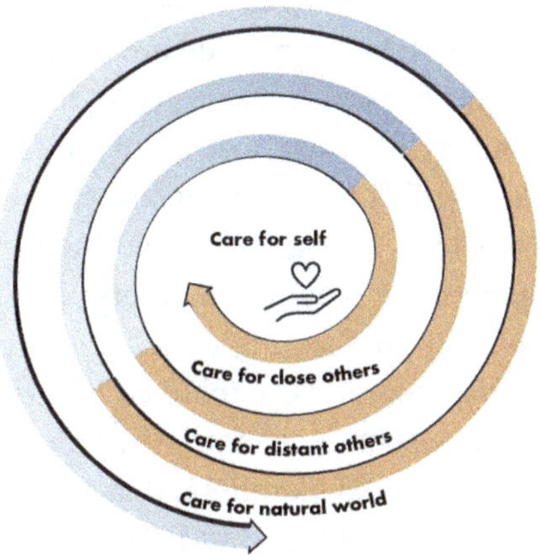

Note. Adapted from "An ethic of care and educational practice," by M. McKenzie & S. Blenkinsop, 2006, Journal of Adventure Education and Outdoor Learning, 6(2), p. 96.

Care for self is viewed more recently as integral to the life of the educator (Collins & Ting, 2014; Barni et al., 2019; Flagler, 2024). For teachers, one can see how care for close others would entail care for students and those within the school building with whom one comes in close contact regularly (e.g., co-teachers). Care for distant others could be defined as those outside the school building, including families in the community or the profession at large. Care for the natural world is an often overlooked realm - seemingly crucial to some who value earth and human impact on it; however, as we look at far-reaching ethical decisions that are impacted by global technologies, care for the natural world becomes increasingly important.

Students are not the only ones who have barriers to learning. Tan et al. (2025) studied 95 research papers on GenAI in education and found that many teachers lack preparation in understanding and using GenAI. This deficit impacts both student learning and teacher success. This is one example of how *care for self* can impact everyone in the classroom. Tan et al. explained how training teachers in GenAI use could positively impact learning. "They illustrate the importance of AI in enhancing teacher professional development, particularly in terms of improving teaching efficiency, student engagement, and overall teacher satisfaction" (Tan et. al, 2025, p.12). Self-efficacy - the belief that one can accomplish one's goals - is a necessary precursor to both teaching and care-giving (Bandura, 1977). Without belief, teacher satisfaction suffers, and the challenges of teaching become overwhelming. Tan et al. suggested professional development in GenAI use could significantly improve teachers' experience and student learning. In this case, the ethical dilemma presents itself to the school district in providing training to its teachers, and in not doing so, one could argue that they are withholding care.

As Figure 1 suggests, the ripple effect of care goes out beyond the immediate one being cared for. As teachers experience care, they are better able to care for others. Teacher self-efficacy in care improves with success (Bandura, 1977). Bandura found that people were willing to put forth more effort when they had initial success with something. How self-efficacy builds on itself for teachers is similar to how trust is fostered in the care relationships. Trust, as defined by Nieldich et al. (2021), is one's willingness to be vulnerable by relying on others. Their study explored trust in three domains - trust in educational settings, educational governance and trust, and generalized trust. Niedlich et al. (2021) explained the benefits of trust for each domain, stating, "In particular, trust has been found to promote collective decision-making and teacher buy-in, increase the likelihood that school improvement will be undertaken, diffuse across schools and result in improved educational outcomes" (p. 125). In their extensive study, Niedlich et al. found that trust is built or removed between people based on relational components. In a world where GenAI is taking the place of human action and decision-making, can and should one be vulnerable to trusting what is not human but human-made? This isn't the first time humans have been faced with trusting in what is human-made. Humans effectively use inventions that increase our efficiency and abilities in every aspect of society, learning to trust in these over time. The difference with GenAI seems to be the speed with which humans need to adapt their trust in the innovation.

Trust and self-efficacy work together to enable and empower teachers to invest their energy, time, and care to those in their classroom, and it is necessary for teachers to invest in GenAI use and implementation. To invest in more professional development to catch the latest educational "craze" can feel self-defeating for many seasoned teachers. For teachers to move towards learning new technologies, they must believe they can understand them and that they are valuable and trustworthy. Nazaretsky et al. (2022) studied teachers' trust and willingness to use AI-EdTech and found that teachers were more open to using AI when they had control over amending the results of it. "This pointed out the importance of designing AI-EdTech systems in which UI/UX does not restrict teachers to a specific pedagogical scenario, but rather provides freedom of choice based on their pedagogical preferences"

(Nazaretsky et al., 2022, p. 929). Professional development that acknowledges the expertise of the teacher, giving them full freedom as a professional to decide how and when to use GenAI, can empower teachers to more efficient practices, allowing more time to care for their students. It also means recognizing that care for their students may involve doing things the long way if that is what their student needs.

The outer realms of Care Ethics stretch the notion of trust beyond those we have familiarity with to those we may have a harder time trusting - including systems and society. The relational structures of our cultures can cause ethical dilemmas for us as we decide how to care for those outside of our immediate reach. Educational leaders tasked with building trust in systems or the profession will be faced with determining how GenAI contributes to or detracts from trust. Gram-Hanssen (2024) argued that Care Ethics should be applied to energy justice issues. Her study showed that evaluating how we use our natural resources and respond to human and world needs could be strengthened through a care approach. "The ethics of care explain connections, mutual obligations and relations of trust, and concern for inclusion, and not only something performed within the walls of the home" (Gram-Hanssen, 2024, p. 2). Recognizing the care needs of communities and the larger natural world can help us determine our ethical obligation towards GenAI use. In this next section, we will present each of the concentric circles of care through examples of how educators act as both the care-giver and care receiver for self, close others, distant others, and the natural world concerning decisions about GenAI use.

CARE FOR SELF

As the innermost circle, care for self is often the most difficult for educators to prioritize. It is challenging to understand how the reciprocity of care ethics even works with care for self, as the one caring is also the one cared for, requiring a unique intentionality. Teachers put aside their own needs to meet the needs of their students, administrators carry the needs of their faculty and institutional stakeholders, and leaders feel pressure from external sources beyond the classrooms and buildings that contend for their attention. Those challenges acknowledged, the necessity to care for oneself is an essential component of being able to care for others. Gilligan (1982) stated, "But if this turning inward is construed against a background of continuing connection, it signals a new responsiveness to the self, an expansion of care rather than a failure of relationship" (p. 10). In looking at the use of GenAI through this lens, educators can explore implications for their own values, pedagogy, effectiveness, efficiency, health, and safety.

Values and GenAI

One of the first areas of exploration when considering the care for self in the context of GenAI is to consider one's values and how we might approach new technologies and consider their place within the context of our worldview. It is important to contextualize the implications of GenAI within our ways of thinking and the values that we hold before we can begin to think about its usage in our lives and in our teaching. While we might look to other sources for guidance on how GenAI might impact our own practices, it is important to take an inventory of our own beliefs and positions before we begin considering the role we want GenAI to play in our lives.

We often view self-care as a process of getting enough sleep, exercising, or eating right. When we isolate the process of self-care into tasks and activities, we miss some of the more foundational elements of self-care. Fiebig et al. (2020) emphasize that "to truly engage in self-care, we must also consider how congruent our values are with our actions in all the other areas of our lives" (p. 560). Therefore, truly practicing self-care requires an examination of the values we wish to emphasize in our lives and a commitment to upholding those values. This examination of our values not only informs us about who we are but also guides how we act (Sayer, 2011). To take concrete actions informed by our values, we need to have a good sense of what is most important to us.

In the context of GenAI, we should consider the following questions to help guide our reflection on the values that determine our actions: What is the role of creativity in our lives, and how important is it? In what ways is writing or generating content valuable to us? What is my relationship with technology, and how do I feel about it? Our ponderings around these questions and our values related to them may lead to even more deeply philosophical questions about knowledge, creation, and sense-making around the world. Karlberg-Granlund and Pastuhov (2024) found that teachers' reflective process impacted their identity, development, and resilience in the field. As they explained, teacher relationships impacted how they found balance in their role, "In all these relationships learning through reflection and dialogue comes to the fore, as the prospective teachers are beginning to see a learning potential in all challenges and changes and start building their practical wisdom as teachers" (p. 383). Through this introspective process, we can begin to think about our role as educators among our myriad of other value-oriented roles and how we wish to respond and engage with GenAI.

Care for Self as Educators

Our notions of self-care do not stop when we consider only our values and personal experiences related to that care. "Self-care requires that we live congruently with our values across many domains" (Fiebig et al., 2020, p. 562). As a result, in our educational practice, it is essential to practice a regular synthesis of self-care in the context of our pedagogical practice. Masland (2023) advocates for the consideration of our values to be centered in our educational practice as pedagogical values. When centered, these values allow us to view our teaching practices through the lens of those same values and drive our pedagogical practice in integrous ways that are consistent with those values. An interesting facet of this that Masland (2023) describes is that when we center ourselves as educators and focus on those values, it consistently puts student-centered practices into place and is not in opposition to those approaches. Holding to our pedagogical values benefits not only us, but also our learners.

Given our understanding of the role our pedagogical values can have on the learning environment and our students, this enables us to ground our perspectives explored through self-care practices to help consider the role of GenAI in our educational roles. As we consider the other dimensions of Care Ethics, our determined values can help us navigate how we want to engage with GenAI as educators in ways that are consistent with our pedagogical values. This may look similar to the types of engagement that are beginning to appear on syllabi to help guide students with options around full engagement with GenAI and engagement in planning and synthesis, but with attribution and original writing required. It may also mean complete disengagement with GenAI for many reasons, which will be explored in other sections. To guide these decisions, we must be clear-eyed about our own values, not only about GenAI but also about our notions of thinking and learning, writing and its purpose, and about the role of technology more broadly in our classrooms.

GenAI and Personal Wellbeing

In addition to considering alignment with our pedagogical values and the ways that our care for self benefits from deeper exploration of our own identities, care for self also needs to consider our personal needs around health, safety, and wellbeing. Part of that calculus around personal well-being is ensuring that our decisions align with our values. When there is a mismatch between our desired values and reality, our personal well-being can suffer. Consideration of alignment to our personal values and our thoughts around GenAI is an important component of seeking to prioritize our health and well-being.

The role of GenAI may differ as we consider our personal and professional roles. There may be use cases for GenAI adoption in our personal lives that we seek to screen from our professional lives or vice versa. The role of privacy and data can factor heavily into our calculus around the role we would like to see GenAI have with wide-ranging considerations around how data is used in large language models (LLM). This can include opting to use GenAI for personal tasks considering our workload while also being sensitive to the information we divulge or what systems we let GenAI access. Professionally, it is also connected to our academic well-being, considering whether we want our intellectual property to be regarded as part of LLM, as many publishers are now seeking, or disengaging from contributing to the data sets that form the backbone of GenAI. All of these decisions ask us to consider our own values and the well-being that we seek through espousing those values with consistency.

Care and Workload

To care for others, we must also feel reciprocal care in our lives, and part of that is ensuring that we have the capacity for both receiving and giving care. We cannot be vessels for this reciprocal care if our workload and capacity for these actions are unbalanced. Faculty consistently report that the workload in their positions is not sustainable and that burnout is a significant factor in well-being and retention (Lo Cascio et al., 2013; Pace et al., 2021). While there is much work to be done at institutional and systemic levels to counter the ongoing workload challenges in educational institutions, is there a role for GenAI?

Proponents of GenAI usage would argue that the technology allows for the off-loading of work that may take up precious time in educators' daily lives (Al Naqbi et al., 2024; Brynjolfsson et al., 2025). Prioritizing emails, performing tasks that are often done regularly, and completing activities that are not central to an educator's main purviews are all areas where GenAI may provide benefit. For example, an educator has been using GenAI to summarize meetings and email threads, elements that are not central to their teaching efforts (Newman, 2025). These time-saving endeavors could be areas where GenAI could help bring additional balance to the workload of individual educators.

On the other hand, data has shown that rather than serving as a time-saving and efficient tool, GenAI actually exacerbates tasks and transforms processes in ways that extend the workload in other ways (Mensik, 2024). Gutmann (2024) compares GenAI to the advent of the vacuum cleaner. With the advent of the device, rather than allowing for less time cleaning, it simply shifted norms around cleaning frequency and standards of living. Rather than saving households more time, it created new standards of expectations around the problems it was meant to solve. Just as email and Zoom meetings before it, what was meant to reduce meetings and in-person necessities has created more work output with the advent of new tools. The Upwork Research Institute (2024) also found that 77% of employees surveyed reported that GenAI has increased their workload rather than reduced it. As we think about care for self and our own values, it's crucial to determine what role we want GenAI to play in our workload and find a balanced space where we are comfortable with how it is providing advantages and fostering our well-being.

CARE FOR CLOSE OTHERS

Within this context, we previously defined close others as those within the school building with whom a teacher comes in close contact on a regular basis (e.g., students, co-teachers). The question of whether to care for others is not usually a difficult one for educators. Most rely on a natural desire to care as a parent does for a child (Noddings, 2013). Care is evidenced in the classroom, in the school, and in the community through educators' service to their students, other teachers, and the broader community. Thayer-Bacon and Bacon (1996) note, "teachers who are about their students are remembered, effect change, stimulate growth, and are more likely to be successful at teaching their students" (p. 255). The question we will explore in this section is: What does it look like to care for close others within the classroom, and school, and what are the ethical implications of GenAI in shaping these interactions?

Personalized Learning and GenAI

It is virtually impossible to be in an educational space and not enter into a conversation about the impact of GenAI on education. Many scholars have cited the opportunities provided by GenAI and the numerous applications to student learning. Understanding the importance of personalized learning, it is understandable that many teachers may feel excited about the myriad of ways GenAI may assist student learning. Scholars have highlighted these potential benefits, including adaptive learning (e.g., intelligent tutoring features, feedback), addressing diverse learning needs, customized/personalized learning experiences (e.g., support systems, scaffolding), novel ways to deliver learning materials, learning evaluation (e.g., automated assessment systems, objective feedback), improved student engagement, self-directed learning (i.e., students taking ownership of their learning), data-driven instruction, flexibility and access (e.g., accessibility for students with special needs), development of life-long learning skills, enhanced learning outcomes, time and cost efficiency, and automation of teachers' duties (e.g., content and lesson plan creation) leading to greater focus on personalized learning (Kamalov et al., 2023, Saputra et al., 2023).

Personalized learning - a step beyond differentiated instruction - could cause educators to panic with the potential added workload. If we needed to personalize education for each student in every subject, we could find ourselves overwhelmed. This is the dichotomy and dilemma: teachers must wrestle with balancing care for self (in this case, potential added workload) with care for others (diminishing the gap I have in caring for a wide range of student needs in one classroom). However, disparity exists in classroom teachers' abilities and resources to do this. Some teachers are better at integrating technology than others, and even within one school, you have teachers who use technology throughout their program design and those who do not. The speed of growth of GenAI makes it a challenge to catch up if you do not catch on quickly.

James and Andrews (2024) agree with many educators' concerns about the misuse of GenAI to replace critical thinking. However, they found numerous benefits for students, including a positive response through engagement with new technological tools. Perifanou and Economides (2025) found benefits to student engagement, explaining, "Students also emphasized the tools' capacity to spark curiosity (e.g., "It can give you food for thought and additional ideas to look into later on your own") and guide further research, suggesting that they could serve as smart encyclopedias, providing instant access to wide-ranging information" (p. 354). To mitigate misuse, James and Andrews suggested a thinking framework for educators to use with students to explore metacognition and take ownership of their thoughts. This model offers educators a way to teach students how to responsibly use GenAI, leaning into the same reflective process that we suggested above on how we must all decide how it fits with our ethos in Care for Self.

We must teach students to evaluate where they get their information, how they develop their ideas, and how tools like GenAI can be part of building knowledge ethically rather than in secret. With these benefits in mind, James and Andrews (2024) warn us, "However, careful consideration and responsible use are crucial to avoid exacerbating the digital divide and potential biases" (p. 257). Responsible use of technology can be an ethical way to care for close others, but it is not without challenges.

Assessment and GenAI

As educators, the pace and breadth of GenAI's impact may feel overwhelming. When looking at the list of opportunities and applications, it can be challenging to see how this can play out in an individual classroom and how we should weigh the risks and benefits for teachers and students, particularly when they may seem diametrically opposed. To make these concepts more tangible, let's examine one particular application: learning evaluation. The automated nature of Gen-AI assessment could potentially lead to reduced teacher workload, but some may hold concerns related to student impact and perception. Recently, Chai and colleagues (2024) examined different evaluators (i.e., AI algorithm vs. teacher) on college students' perceptions of fairness. The results suggest that students view evaluations done by AI algorithms as more fair and impartial than those conducted by human teachers, regardless of whether the assessment is diagnostic, formative, or summative. While other elements could and should be explored, this demonstrates how GenAI can shift students' perceptions of fairness in the classroom–potentially increasing trust in evaluation systems while raising critical questions about the teacher's evolving role. We must not only consider efficiency gains but also how these tools impact the teacher-student relationship, classroom dynamics, and the broader ethical implications of delegating evaluative authority to GenAI.

The question could be: As educators, how do we balance efficiency and fairness in GenAI-assisted grading with our ethical responsibility to care and truly understand our students? Recently, I (the third author) had a group of undergraduate students ask me my opinion on using GenAI in grading. I responded in two ways. First, I acknowledged that I had used GenAI to assist in my grading and cited it as a helpful resource in reducing the time I spend on tasks that can be automated using GenAI. I also noted that I believe that when students put effort into an assignment, they deserve my attention, effort, and feedback. In explaining my hybrid approach, I told them that I will sometimes have GenAI review a paper and provide me with feedback based on a rubric, but that I will also always read a student's paper and provide my own feedback. While I acknowledge that feedback on assignments is just one element in learning evaluation, this is one example of how I personally balance care for self with care for close others (e.g., my students).

Bias and GenAI Impact on Care

Based on the plethora of positive applications to student learning, some authors urge educators to fully embrace GenAI in their teaching. For example, while acknowledging both the positives and drawbacks of GenAI, Kamalov and colleagues (2023) conclude, "the best way forward is to incorporate AI into the educational system and leverage its capabilities to deliver better learning outcomes for the students" (p. 3). Even those who tout the advantages, however, also acknowledge the challenges. Potential challenges impacting students and classrooms include, but are not limited to: data privacy and security, plagiarism and academic integrity, the impact on the student/teacher relationship, and bias and discrimination (Holmes et al., 2022; Kamalov et al., 2023; Saputra et al., 2023). Holmes et al. (2022) examined the decisions educators make daily about the use of student data and how privacy, security, and bias are all at risk with emerging technologies. In addition to these considerations, scholars are urging educators to consider a host of classroom- and institutional-level issues as a matter of social justice (e.g., Buccella, 2023; Healy, 2023; Hermansyah et al., 2023).

Earlier, we described Care Ethics as the principles that motivate one to meet another's needs. A simple yet complicated question that extends from this notion is: How do we weigh the risks and benefits of GenAI to meet students' needs? One particularly salient area to this question is the student/teacher relationship. Supportive student-teacher relationships are related to emotional and behavioral student engagement and predictive of academic performance (Lee, 2012). Some scholars wonder, however, if the permeation of GenAI into the educational environment will reduce the character-shaping capacity of teachers and narrow the role to that of a learning facilitator (Saputra et al., 2023).

Additionally, teachers are no longer students' sole source of information, and since AI systems often have access to a broader range of knowledge, the traditional authority of teachers as knowledge holders is being questioned (Cao, 2024). It is impossible to consider Care Ethics without considering the relational component of education. With the use of GenAI and access to information beyond comprehension, can GenAI care for students? Ultimately, the answer is no – GenAI is not human and therefore, cannot care. It becomes our charge as educators to use it in ways that reflect care for others.

Let's explore, then, the issue of bias and discrimination. Let's imagine a teacher is using a new GenAI tool to provide real-time writing feedback to 7th-grade students. At the end of their writing sessions, students submit a print-out of their writing feedback to the teacher. The teacher decides to review the feedback and notices a pattern: students for whom English is a second language (ESL) are receiving words like "unacademic" and "unclear" even on writing that is clear. How can the teacher follow the Ethic of Care in this situation? To begin with, the teacher can recognize that this GenAI-powered tool may be trained on dominant linguistic norms (i.e., White, Western, academic English). Understanding this potential bias, the teacher may decide to review all feedback provided to ESL students or decide not to use the tool at all, understanding that continuing to use the tool with only non-ESL students may provide non-ESL students with an unfair advantage. Moving forward, the teacher decides to always consider who may be impacted by using a GenAI tool and select tools with inclusivity in mind.

CARE FOR DISTANT OTHERS

Can educators effectively care for distant others with the same kind of respect, responsibility, and reciprocity as we do for those with whom we are in the same room? Does GenAI offer an opportunity to build bridges between distances that could otherwise separate us from ethical care? How do we address GenAI's impact on broader educational equity, including marginalized communities, global disparities, and accessibility? These questions highlight several issues for educators to consider as they think outside of their immediate circle of care. GenAI appears neutral. It is, however, not. Bozkurt et al. (2024) explained the dangers of the "illusion of all-knowing responses" (p. 506). Just as any created curriculum can have unintended bias, we must be aware of how the hidden factors of GenAI can impact how educators care for those outside their physical realms.

Does GenAI allow us to harm other communities unintentionally and who is responsible if we are unaware of the harm? Potential examples include GenAI and questions of access, disparity of implementation, and populations impacted by increasing GenAI usage. Buccella (2023) notes, "a society whose capabilities . . . have been radically transformed by AI is just only if practical and intellectual access to AI is provided to all its members" (p. 1144). The call, then, is to examine and care about the impact of GenAI beyond our immediate circles.

GenAI and Educational Access

One of the most compelling arguments related to the potential positive impact of GenAI is improved access to education. The logic is this: When we, as educators, consider ethical questions related to GenAI, we must consider the implications of our decisions beyond ourselves and our personal classrooms and school buildings. If we reject and rail against using GenAI in classrooms, the reverberations may be felt in distant places and spaces. Kamalov and colleagues (2023) note, "AI has paved the way for significant breakthroughs in worldwide access to high-quality education" (p. 17). Specifically, the scholars add, "AI-powered educational tools and materials can cross geographical, socioeconomic, and linguistic boundaries, allowing for fairer distribution of information" (p. 17). While those who have the privilege of teaching may wonder how GenAI will impact their job security, others may see it as a tool to educate the masses. From a monetary perspective, this can also be performed and scaled at a relatively low cost, particularly when using GenAI reduces the number of teachers or other staff needed (Kamalov et al., 2023). As discussed previously, supportive student-teacher relationships impact student engagement and academic performance (Lee, 2012). If the choice, however, is not between teacher-led education and Gen-AI led education but rather between no education and Gen-AI led education, it seems imperative that we acknowledge the potential positive impact. James and Andrews (2024) explain, "To foster a sense of inclusiveness in HE spaces, there is a critical need for targeted interventions and support mechanisms that address the multifaceted challenges of under-represented groups to promote equitable academic success" (p. 252). Their study gives specific examples of how GenAI can "level the playing field" for students who would otherwise be left out of the game.

Disparity of GenAI Implementation

There are also challenges associated with embracing Gen-AI that impact those outside of our close circles. These challenges include, but are not limited to: 1) the resource-intensive nature of implementation, 2) faculty development and support, 3) curriculum and content adaptation, 4) technical issues, and 5) equity concerns (Kamalov et al., 2023). In relation to the resource-intensive nature of Gen-AI, while use may reduce the number of teachers needed, the necessary investment in infrastructure, technology, and professional development may limit the number of institutions that can fully adopt it. Additionally, faculty development and technical support is needed for those that do embrace GenAI, which comes with financial and personnel costs. Additionally, implementing GenAI into already resource-rich schools may exacerbate achievement gaps when some students face barriers to access (e.g., access to devices and limited connectivity; Kamalov et al., 2023).

Colleagues who work for institutions that provide training and protocols for GenAI use will inevitably be ahead of those who are on their own in making decisions about use and impact. Similarly, colleagues' decisions about using GenAI will inevitably impact others in their institutions and beyond. As one instructor adopts or rejects GenAI, it could have ramifications in other classrooms shared by the same population of students. Considering this dimension, Lee and Low (2024) studied how college students responded to using GenAI in their classrooms. Their feedback was mostly positive in that they like the speed of response. These researchers suggested that "instructors need to model the way in which students could use GenAI meaningfully and ethically" (p. 3). Lee and Low suggested formative assessment emphasizing process over product could reduce misuse of GenAI in writing.

In 2022, when GenAI hit the main media stage, many in academia quickly put out stop signs in their classes for fear of plagiarism, distrust of content, and various other reasons related to the speed at which it took off. Just three years later, and everyone is either exploring its capabilities or waiting to see the challenges get worked out before using it James and Andrews (2024) explained, "Universities are swiftly developing policies and recommendations to strike a balance between upholding academic integrity and empowering educators to seamlessly incorporate

GenAI into their teaching methodologies and curriculum design" (p. 253). Several years from now, our students will be even more comfortable with using it, and if educators are not prepared, they will not be able to care for their educational needs in the same way.

CARE FOR NATURAL WORLD

As members of society, bound by our shared resources and responsibilities to care for them, educators can consider how GenAI use impacts both the natural world and the people living in it. McKenzie and Blenkinsop (2006) note:

> Educators must bridge public and private spheres continuously, and as such, this final leg in our tripartite framework for an ethic of care can help us to think more clearly about the challenge to care: What does it mean to care in and for the public, to care for others not immediately connected to our lives or, even to care for the non-human world? (p. 95)

This question of our responsibility to others and our shared world can come into consideration as educators choose to discover hidden impacts of GenAI on our natural world, considering the environmental impact of data centers, the drain on limited resources from local communities to power GenAI, and the potential for GenAI decision-making to perpetuate environmental harms or foster new unexplored solutions.

Care for the Global Community

While we discussed care for distant others and the impact of GenAI, our considerations primarily focused on the distant others still found within the educational environment and community impacted by our decision-making around GenAI. Because these concentric circles of impact are fluid, it is important to recognize that our decisions also have global ramifications beyond those we might consider to be close or distant others. As a result, it is equally important to consider ethics around GenAI as an area where we can knowingly or unknowingly impact our worldwide community.

One of the first areas of impact for our global community is to consider the digital divide as a concept (Eubanks, 2011). As GenAI progress continues, much like considerations around broadband, computer access, and digital literacy, we must also anticipate that global disparities are going to be perpetuated by the rapid influx of technological change. This often starts with developed countries having access to the technologies and capabilities to leverage GenAI and advances with the technology that may not be afforded our global community in developing countries (OECD, 2024). Consideration of ethical GenAI usage and adoption, particularly in educational contexts, must also be mindful and seek to mitigate these disparities, particularly when our classrooms may have students coming from a wide range of locations and points of access. It is also a call for us as educators to continue to be advocates for ways to reduce the digital divide and provide opportunities for equal access to such technologies.

GenAI adoption also has implications for the labor and environment of global communities we may never encounter. Companies have specifically leveraged developing countries for tasks related to GenAI development because of their low wages and lax employment standards. Perrigo (2023) reported on the use of outsourcing in Kenya, where workers were asked to screen large language model data sets in order to flag inappropriate terms or phrases. These workers, making less than two dollars per day, reported trauma related to the tasks they performed, and little consideration for the scope of the work and its impact on their lives was given. The environmental cost of operating GenAI, an area of discussion below, also tends to impact developing communities more extensively than other communities because of the environmental standards that differ around the world and the possibility that companies from developing countries might leverage these reduced standards for their own purposes (Francisco, 2023). Educators should be aware of how datasets are developed and the hidden labor behind many of the GenAI tools that they are using as part of their critical evaluation of the place of such tools in their lives.

Care for Our Environment

GenAI and its impact on the natural environment is an area of much discussion in considering its usage. We know from recent studies that GenAI uses significant amounts of energy to maintain the datasets and leverage them for algorithmic pattern-making that forms the basis of the results we see when we conduct queries (Ren & Wierman, 2024; Zewe, 2025). Within this year, these energy outputs solely for GenAI are estimated to exceed the energy consumption of small countries like Belgium (Ren & Wierman, 2024) and require water usage estimated to be the equivalent of a single water bottle for every 100-word email generated (Verma & Tan, 2024). There is evidence that the energy required to conduct GenAI queries is significantly affecting the environment, with companies ramping up data center development due to the increased server space needed for GenAI production ("The data-centre investment," 2025).

That said, advances in GenAI efficiency, like developments with Chinese GenAI solutions such as Deepseek, are reducing the energy costs associated with GenAI usage. These efficiencies are likely to continue to develop - following technology trends like Moore's law (1965) that has predicted that the speed of computer processing will continue to increase over time while the costs of the additional computing power continue to decrease. If such assumptions hold true, the extensive costs associated with GenAI are likely to be reduced over time, and the current environmental costs will likely be reduced with it. Some also argue that GenAI might hold the answers to the problems that currently serve as critiques, with solutions to improving productivity and efficiencies in various industries possibly being achieved by GenAI. For example, Google has stated that GenAI algorithms have been used to analyze and find ways to reduce energy usage in their data centers by 30% (Walther, 2024). The potential for GenAI research in other areas that could offset the current output costs is being explored.

For educators, our task is to again consider our values and ethics around GenAI and make a determination around how we can be both responsible stewards of our natural environment while leveraging GenAI tools. For some this may mean a balanced approach while for others the determination might be that the cost of GenAI is simply too costly given the impact on our natural world.

Care for Humanity

The last area of exploration when considering the broader natural world is another that might not be the most immediate thought when we think about this sphere of care - the role of GenAI and our wider humanity. If we consider the scope of humanity and our own contributions to the natural world, the impact of humanity and our imprint on the world is significant. We have transformed the planet in terms of farming and urban development, reshaped waterways and landscapes, but we have also extended the work of humanity through art, scientific inquiry, and countless other achievements that leave our mark on not only the planet but also on ourselves. With this in mind, as educators, it is equally important to consider who we want our learners and ultimately ourselves to be as shaped and in shaping GenAI. What does it mean to be human in the reality of a world where we are surrounded by machine-generated writing, art, and ultimately thinking? Should we embrace this symbiotic relationship as one that enhances our world and ourselves? Or should we question whether part of our humanity and what makes us genuinely alive is lost when we give over some of these elements to GenAI? These questions are ones that we, as educators, can help our learners grapple with as part of our educational discourse.

Implications for Practice

Beyond the challenges and opportunities for living in a GenAI movement, educators need to decide how GenAI will impact their practices. As professionals, teachers' decisions impact many in their environment from self to their students, to the community and the profession. How teachers care for self and others, impacts how the community trusts the profession. Fear is certainly a driver for many as they learn new technologies and can motivate teachers to spend inordinate amounts of time trying to get ahead of a fast moving train. Figure 2 on the next page offers a visual to consider ethical dilemmas as educators face them and can help them decide who is impacted by the decision and whether it builds trust, integrity, and equity for all stakeholders.

Ethical Examples

Using the Framework, *Considering Ethical Dilemmas through the Ethic of Care (CEDEC)*, Figure 2 (next page), we will explore examples of ethical dilemmas in the three domains reported by Nieldich et al. (2021) - trust in educational settings, educational governance and trust, and generalized trust. Care within each domain has an impact on stakeholders beyond the domain. Decision-making, therefore, needs to consider the effect on those within the domain and those outside of it. Fitzpatrick (2024) explained, "Trust emerges when leaders demonstrate reliability, transparency, and follow-through on commitment" (p. 256). Building trust can be an essential first step in caring with integrity and equity for the stakeholders involved. With trust, self-efficacy for ethical use of GenAI can empower educators to make decisions about its use for themselves and those in their care.

Figure 2. Framework for Considering Ethical Dilemmas through the Ethic of Care (CEDEC)

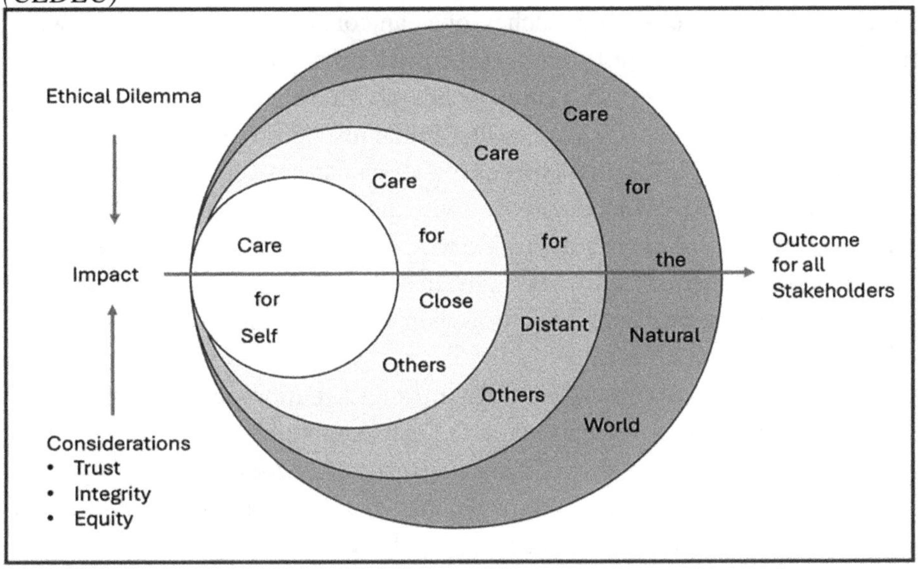

Note. CEDEC Framework modified from Figure 1: Framework for Ethic of Care Relationships. Own work.

Trust in Educational Settings

Trust is a necessary component of care in the classroom. Both the care giver and receiver need to trust each other and the methods of care. Nieldich et al. (2021) emphasize this importance, stating, "studies show that teachers who have low trust in students are more likely to suffer from burnout" (p. 134). Building trust is integral to building relationships and is at the crux of successful teaching. In consideration of GenAI use, there are numerous situations where trust can be compromised. One increasingly frequent dilemma is the question of authorship in essay writing. Many teachers are reading student work that does not sound like their students and has them questioning their integrity. While anti-plagiarism tools exist, it is becoming easier to navigate around those tools, and teachers are left with dilemmas. Do I trust this student, do I engage in a discussion over the mistrust which could potentially cause more distrust, do I ignore the nagging feeling that something is wrong? Each of these questions can be addressed through one's personal beliefs. In using the CEDEC Framework (Figure 2), evaluating the dilemma through the lens of care can help us to identify how trust, integrity, and equity can be considered so that the outcome for all stakeholders feels just.

Trust in the Classroom. As a teacher, one can consider if trust exists between student and teacher or if it needs work. If the trust already exists, then the discussion of the questionable authorship could be an opportunity to solidify that trust by showing how we treat students with respect. Mutual respect is essential for trust and must be established long before difficult conversations can have beneficial outcomes. For both teacher and student to feel satisfied with the reciprocal care, they must both feel heard and believed. This is a delicate dance at times, but when a student feels cared for, outside of performance, they can be honest with their caregiver. Likewise, when a teacher feels the student responds to their care, they can have patience even through a challenging dilemma.

As the teacher explores how to handle a difficult situation, they can remember how they have handled other situations in the classroom and consider if the same level of care is applied to all students. Do they trust each student? Is there equity in their response to questions of authorship? Do they give each student an opportunity to respond to the questions? Each of these questions can help teachers build trust with their class as students see them provide equitable care to each member of the class. This Ethic of Care goes both ways, and the students need to see the teacher as a trustworthy care-giver for them to engage fully in the learning process.

Trust in the School. One hurdle that school administrators face in the advent of the GenAI movement is preparing faculty and staff to adapt to the changes. Fitzpatrick (2024) suggests teachers resist change when they feel unprepared for it. "Innovation requires more than enthusiasm. It demands skills, tools, and resources, and many organizations falter here" (Fitzpatrick, 2024, p. 282). Using the CEDEC Framework (Figure 2), school leaders can assess the dilemma of resistance to change through the three areas of trust, integrity, and equity to seek solutions that all stakeholders can embrace. Building trust through thoughtful considerations of the challenges facing faculty and staff will help administrators build buy-in to the work involved in change. There must be room for faculty and staff to build their capacity for the change to be empowered by it. Fitzpatrick suggests offering specific workshops where faculty can build their self-efficacy and competence in using new tools.

Teachers who feel empowered will lead in the change. Tools, training, and trusting educators as professionals is needed for administrators to build a culture ripe for innovation. Fawns (2022) stated, "Like pedagogy, ethics cannot be the sole responsibility of teachers. Working relationships between University IT staff and commercial providers shape not only broader institutional implementations of technology, but the distribution of pedagogical and ethical knowledge and decision-making" (p. 722). Over time, clear and consistent messaging from administrators can provide the structure faculty and staff need to grow into comfort with ethical decisions around GenAI. Faculty need to be able to express their concerns over GenAI use and make decisions based on their core ethics. This is non-negotiable. Faculty cannot teach what they do not believe is good. Because there are so many uncertainties with GenAI use, there needs to be room for those who would prefer to hold back on its use, leaning into the growing research, before stepping onto the high-speed train platform. The capabilities and challenges we discussed earlier of personalized learning, bias, and assessment will continue to be areas where research will show either a widening margin between benefit and detriment or clearer guidelines.

Educational Governance and Trust

Trust in the larger care circle of the school and community comes under the care for distant others in the Ethic of Care. While there is some overlap in care circles, we have explored distant others and GenAI in large part as how it impacts relationships with people we do not know as well as the close others of our classroom. Those outside our daily interactions may not have the same level of trust in our decision-making as those we care for daily. One area that can be a dilemma in this context is using assessment practices that create distance between those involved in the education. In response to current standardized-test structures, Nieldich et al. (2021) found numerous studies that "recommend placing more trust in the professional judgment of teachers and promote alternative approaches" (p. 134). The challenge for educational institutions then is to trust the judgment of the professionals they have put in place to educate their citizens.

Trust in Leadership. Educational leaders must examine areas impacted by the current performance and assessment systems established to govern. A current area of debate is the lack of evidence that Praxis exams for pre-service teachers accurately measure teacher success. Numerous researchers have suggested using alternative assessment methods for teacher competency (Zelkowski, 2024). Could GenAI provide opportunities for teachers to show their competency and potentially open doors for teachers who may have previously been disqualified? With the current shortage of teachers and the growing rate of alternative licensure routes for educators, having new options available could be a life-line to schools being pinched by short supply and high demand.

Fischer et al. (2024) explained the need for higher education to adjust, "We must now change to a more agile environment and respond with a sense of urgency to remain relevant" (p. 9). This urgency involves creating and testing new systems that allow for more opportunities for new teachers - removing barriers to achieving licensure.

Assessment in higher education plays a pivotal role in shaping both student learning and teaching practices. Both formative and summative assessments play important roles in ensuring that students can engage with GenAI technologies while achieving the learning outcomes required by higher education institutions (Fischer et al., 2024, p. 9).

Fischer et al. suggest that educational leaders take the opportunity to expand GenAI use for the personalization of assessment while establishing clear guidance for appropriate use. Fitzpatrick (2024) explains, "Trust grows from reliability" (p. 269). School systems need to build trustworthiness based on the consistency of operations. Reliable school leaders are transparent, forthright, and base decisions on evidence. The general public needs to see educational leaders do what they do best: teach society how to adapt and use new technology. Leaders can then leverage trust built to innovate school systems.

Generalized Trust and Education

The largest sphere of trust is at the societal level with educational systems. Nieldich et al. (2021) stated, "A common theme in the literature is that the positive association between education and generalised trust is generally found in democratic, non-corrupt countries" (p. 135). Distrust in education is at an all-time high in the United States (Mintz, 2023). While there is some value in skepticism, blatant distrust can erode the good work happening across the spheres of education. Tavory (2024) offered recommendations for robust principles of AI use developed through the lens of the Ethic of Care, stating, "It demands an adaptable and dynamic ethical mechanism aimed at protecting human relationships, emotions, and behavior, which are the core of the human experience" (p. 8). The largest sphere of influence on trust and education will need leaders to work not only on building trust in their districts and schools but with the greater community. Mintz explained, "today's overemphasis on measurable learning objectives, assessment, and accountability has undercut the true value of a college education, which is developmental and transformative and seeks to produce graduates who are self-reflective and able to think critically" (para 13). Higher education isn't alone in needing to build general societal trust. Nadeem (2024) shared several ways to build trust between education's stakeholders, including establishing clear roles and responsibilities, distributive leadership, and collaborative decision-making. As education leaders consider challenges with building support for change, they can consider the CEDEC Framework where integrity, trust, and equity are each elements of the decision-making process.

Fitzpatrick (2024) suggested that educational leaders must envision a future based on identified trends, experimentation, and developing new competencies. "The challenge before us is monumental. To reimagine education for an age where artificial intelligence complements and transforms human capabilities" (Fitzpatrick, 2024, p. 161). Fitzpatrick presents the Speculative Design approach to institutional change where the gap between the future goals and current challenges is bridged. We suggest using the CEDEC Framework to develop principles for GenAI usage so that our institutions can consider each realm of care with integrity, trust, and equity. Again, transparency is key in building trust between those making decisions and those impacted by them.

Trust in Education. Nadeem (2024) recommended, "By actively engaging teachers, students, parents, and community members in the collaborative process of decision-making, schools are poised to achieve a comprehensive array of positive outcomes that resonate across every facet of education" (p. 7). While GenAI is pushing the boundaries in every aspect of work, it is not understood by every stakeholder in the larger education community. In thinking about the ethical dilemmas that can stir up a community, using the CEDEC Framework (Figure 2) can be useful to determine how each stakeholder will be impacted by a decision.

For example, can GenAI be a valuable tool in bridging the communication gap between stakeholders? Will we trust messaging that seems to be given from unknown or distant sources, or can GenAI improve our communication capabilities to speak into cultural divides in new ways? Perifanou and Economides (2025) studied the impact of students who used GenAI as a collaborative tool in project-based learning. "Students generally expressed satisfaction with these communication channels, highlighting their familiarity, ease of use, and effectiveness in enabling real-time communication and collaboration" (Perifanou & Economides, 2025, p. 18). Advantages of using GenAI tools included speed and comprehension of communication between group members. At the same time, disadvantages included accuracy and reliability.

While the tools were not found to be fully effective, they were more effective than not using the tools. Nadeem (2024) shared, "Exploring how digital tools can facilitate collaboration, communication, and decision-making among stakeholders can open new avenues for engagement" (p. 7). In considering the use of GenAI tools with a larger community, leaders need to consider how the GenAI tool will be perceived by the community. As our CEDEC Framework suggests, trust, equity, and integrity are all considerations to consider through the circles of care. Moving from self to close others, to distant others, and then the natural world, can using GenAI as a communication tool improve trust, equity, and integrity for each stakeholder.

Research like that done by Perifanou and Economides (2025) will help educators weigh decisions based not only on their own beliefs but on supported practices. Duckett and Westrick (2024) recommended that students create their own ethical framework to navigate dilemmas. "This comprehensive engagement begins to equip students with the requisite knowledge, skills, and ethical acumen to navigate the dynamic terrain of genAI-powered communication adeptly" (Duckett & Westrick,

2024, p. 37). While educators face ethical decision-making, their students must also confront their choices with consideration of their belief systems.

CONCLUSION

In using a care ethic framework to explore the ethical challenges and opportunities offered by GenAI, our hope is that this chapter provides a lens through which to explore the myriad ways that GenAI impacts our environment. This includes its impact on ourselves and our students most directly, but also on the institutions we inhibit, our broader communities, and the people and natural world that are impacted in ways we may never see.

Questions abound around GenAI use and can feel overwhelming to educators. Using the care ethics framework, we suggest that as educators make decisions around GenAI, they can use the framework for decision-making that addresses the following questions: Does this decision align with my values (self)? Is trust built through the decision (close others)? Who, outside of my community, is impacted by this decision (distant others)? And what is the impact of this decision on the broader environment (natural world)? Our goal was to scaffold the scope of questions around GenAI use into a manageable structure. Given that our decision-making around GenAI might often be fraught with gut reactions and in-the-moment adjustments to technology, providing a systematic approach for considering these ethical decisions will help educators move forward with GenAI in thoughtful, intentional, and engaged ways.

REFERENCES

Adams, C., Pente, P., Lemermeyer, G., & Rockwell, G. (2023). Ethical principles for artificial intelligence in K-12 education. *Computers and Education: Artificial Intelligence, 4*, 100131. Advance online publication. DOI: 10.1016/j.caeai.2023.100131

Al Naqbi, H., Bahroun, Z., & Ahmed, V. (2024). Enhancing work productivity through generative artificial intelligence: A comprehensive literature review. *Sustainability (Basel), 16*(3), 1166. DOI: 10.3390/su16031166

Bandura, A. (1977). Self-efficacy: Toward a unifying theory of behavioral change. *Psychological Review, 84*(2), 191–215. DOI: 10.1037/0033-295X.84.2.191 PMID: 847061

Barni, D., Danioni, F., & Benevene, P. (2019, July). Teachers' self-efficacy: The role of personal values and motivations for teaching. *Frontiers in Psychology, 10*(1645), 1–7. https://www.frontiersin.org/articles/10.3389/fpsyg.2019.01645/full. DOI: 10.3389/fpsyg.2019.01645 PMID: 31354604

Bozkurt, A., Xiao, J., Farrow, R., Bai, J. Y., Nerantzi, C., Moore, S., & Asino, T. I. (Eds.). (2024). The manifesto for teaching and learning in a time of generative AI: A critical collective stance to better navigate the future. *Open Praxis, 16*(4), 487-513. https://doi.org/DOI: 10.55982/openpraxis.16.4.777

Brynjolfsson, E., Li, D., & Raymond, L. (2025). Generative AI at work. *The Quarterly Journal of Economics, 140*(2), qjae044. Advance online publication. DOI: 10.1093/qje/qjae044

Buccella, A. (2023). "AI for all" is a matter of social justice. *AI and Ethics, 3*(4), 1143–1152. DOI: 10.1007/s43681-022-00222-z PMID: 36189174

Cao, M. (2024). Teacher-student relationships in the context of artificial intelligence. *Advances in Educational Technology and Psychology, 8*(4), 75–80. DOI: 10.23977/aetp.2024.080412

Chai, C. S., Liang, S., & Wang, X. (2024). A survey study of Chinese teachers' continuous intentions to teach artificial intelligence. *Education and Information Technologies, 29*(11), 14015–14034. DOI: 10.1007/s10639-023-12430-z

Collins, S., & Ting, H. (2014). The complexity of care. *Complicity: An International Journal of Complexity and Education, 11*(1), 5–19. DOI: 10.29173/cmplct21452

Digital Education Council. (2024). *Global AI student survey 2024.* https://campustechnology.com/articles/2024/08/28/survey-86-of-students-already-use-ai-in-their-studies.aspx

Duckett, D., & Westrick, N. (2025). Exploring the use, adoption, and ethics of generative artificial intelligence in the public relations and communication professions. *Communication Teacher, 39*(1), 33–41. DOI: 10.1080/17404622.2024.2395312

Eubanks, V. (2011). *Digital dead end: Fighting for social justice in the information age*. The MIT Press. DOI: 10.7551/mitpress/8073.001.0001

Fawns, T. (2022). An entangled pedagogy: Looking beyond the pedagogy-technology dichotomy. *Postdigital Science and Education*, *4*(3), 711–728. DOI: 10.1007/s42438-022-00302-7 PMID: 40477872

Fiebig, J. H., Gould, E. R., Ming, S., & Watson, R. A. (2020). An invitation to act on the value of self-care: Being a whole person in all that you do. *Behavior Analysis in Practice, 13*(3), 559–567. DOI: 10.1007/s40617-020-00442-x PMID: 32837703

Fischer, I., Sweeney, S., Lucas, M., & Gupta, N. (2024). Making sense of generative AI for assessments: Contrasting student claims and assessor evaluations. *International Journal of Management Education*, *22*(3), 101081. DOI: 10.1016/j.ijme.2024.101081

Fitzpatrick, D. (2024). *Infinite education: The four-step strategy for leading change in the age of artificial intelligence*. Teacher Goals Publishing.

Flagler, A. V. (2024). Integrated care: Transforming beginning teachers and students with EBD. [ICCTE]. *International Christian Community of Teacher Educators Journal*, *19*(2). Advance online publication. DOI: 10.55221/1932-7846.1336

Foltynek, T., Bjelobaba, S., Glendinning, I., Khan, Z. R., Santos, R., Pavletic, P., & Kravjar, J. (2023). ENAI Recommendations on the ethical use of artificial intelligence in education. *International Journal for Educational Integrity*, *19*(1), 1–4. DOI: 10.1007/s40979-023-00133-4

Francisco, M. (2023). Artificial intelligence for environmental security: National, international, human and ecological perspectives. *Current Opinion in Environmental Sustainability*, *61*, 101250. DOI: 10.1016/j.cosust.2022.101250

Gilligan, C. (1982). *In a different voice: Psychological theory and women's development*. Harvard University Press.

Gram-Hanssen, K. (2024). Beyond energy justice: Ethics of care as a new approach in the energy system. *Energy Issues and Social Science*, *111*, 103470. Advance online publication. DOI: 10.1016/j.erss.2024.103470

Gutmann, M. (2024, November 11). AI's false-time saving promise. Or why AI is like the vacuum cleaner. *Forbes.* https://www.forbes.com/sites/martingutmann/2024/11/11/ais-false-time-saving-promise-or-why-ai-is-like-the-vacuum-cleaner/

Healy, M. (2023). Approaches to generative artificial intelligence, a social justice perspective. *arXiv.* https://arxiv.org/abs/2309.12331

Hermansyah, M., Najib, A., Farida, A., Sacipto, R., & Rintyarna, B. S. (2023). Artificial intelligence and ethics: Building an artificial intelligence system that ensures privacy and social justice. *The International Journal of Science in Society, 5*(1), 154–168. DOI: 10.54783/ijsoc.v5i1.644

Holmes, W., Porayska-Pomsta, K., Holstein, K., Sutherland, E., Baker, T., Buckingham Shum, S., Santos, O., Rodrigo, M., Bittencourt, I., Cukurova, M., & Koedinger, K. (2022). Ethics of AI in education: Towards a community-wide framework. *International Journal of Artificial Intelligence in Education, 32*(3), 504–526. DOI: 10.1007/s40593-021-00239-1

James, T., & Andrews, G. (2024). Leveling the playing field through GenAI: Harnessing artificial intelligence to bridge educational gaps for equity and disadvantaged students. *Widening Participation and Lifelong Learning : the Journal of the Institute for Access Studies and the European Access Network, 26*(3), 250–260. DOI: 10.5456/WPLL.26.3.250

Kamalov, F., Cherukuri, A. K., Sulieman, H., Thabtah, F., & Hossain, A. (2023). Machine learning applications for COVID-19: A state-of-the-art review. In Tyagi, A. K., & Abraham, A. (Eds.), *Data Science for Genomics* (pp. 277–289). Elsevier. DOI: 10.1016/B978-0-323-98352-5.00010-0

Karlberg-Granlund, G., & Pastuhov, A. (2024). Being, becoming and sustaining: Learning professional learning in teacher education. *Professional Development in Education, 50*(2), 372–385. DOI: 10.1080/19415257.2023.2291360

Kurian, N. (2023). Toddlers and robots? The ethics of supporting young children with disabilities with AI Companions and the implications for children's rights. *International Journal of Human Rights Education, 7*(1). https://repository.usfca.edu/ijhre/vol7/iss1/9

Lee, C., & Low, M. (2024). Using genAI in education: The case for critical thinking. *Frontiers in Artificial Intelligence, 1*(7), 1–3. DOI: 10.3389/frai.2024.1452131 PMID: 39554991

Lee, J. S. (2012). The effects of the teacher–student relationship and academic press on student engagement and academic performance. *International Journal of Educational Research*, *53*, 330–340. DOI: 10.1016/j.ijer.2012.04.006

Lo Cascio, V., Guzzo, G., Pace, F., & Pace, U. (2013). Anxiety and self-esteem as mediators of the relation between family communication and indecisiveness in adolescence. *International Journal for Educational and Vocational Guidance*, *13*(2), 135–149. DOI: 10.1007/s10775-013-9243-1

Masland, L. (2023, August 16). *In defense of teacher-centered teaching…and other things I'm not supposed to say* [Conference keynote]. Empowering Teaching Excellence Conference, Logan, UT, United States.

McKenzie, M. & Blenkinsop, S. (2006). An ethic of care and educational practice.

McKenzie, M., & Blenkinsop, S. (2006, January). An ethic of care and educational practice. *Journal of Adventure Education and Outdoor Learning*, *6*(2), 91–105. DOI: 10.1080/14729670685200781

DOI: 10.1080/14729670685200781

Mensik, H. (2024, July 24). AI is actually making workers less productive. *Worklife*. https://www.worklife.news/technology/ai-is-actually-making-workers-less-productive/

Mercer, N. (2002). Developing dialogues. In Wells, G., & Claxton, G. (Eds.), *Learning for life in the 21st century* (pp. 141–153). Blackwell Publishers. DOI: 10.1002/9780470753545.ch11

Mintz, S. (2023, June 2). The trust gap in higher education: How can colleges and universities create cultures built on trust? *Inside Higher Education*. https://www.insidehighered.com/opinion/blogs/higher-ed-gamma/2023/06/02/trust-gap-higher-education

Moore, G. E. (1965). Cramming more components onto integrated circuits. *Electronics (Basel)*, *38*, 114–117.

Nadeem, M. (2024). Distributed leadership in educational contexts: A catalyst for school improvement. *Social Sciences & Humanities Open*, *9*, 100835. DOI: 10.1016/j.ssaho.2024.100835

Nazaretsky, T., Ariely, M., Cukurova, M., & Alexandron, G. (2022). Teachers' trust in AI-powered educational technology and a professional development program to improve it. *British Journal of Educational Technology*, *53*(4), 914–931. DOI: 10.1111/bjet.13232

Newman, M. (2025, March 10). Review: Microsoft Copilot could transform K–12 education for good. *EdTech Magazine*. https://edtechmagazine.com/k12/article/2025/03/review-microsoft-copilot-could-transform-k-12-education-good

Niedlich, S., Kallfaß, A., Pohle, S., & Bormann, I. (2021). A comprehensive view of trust in education: Conclusions from a systematic literature review. *Review of Education*, *9*(1), 124–158. DOI: 10.1002/rev3.3239

Noddings, N. (1988). An ethic of caring and its implications for instructional arrangements. *American Journal of Education*, *96*(2), 215–230.

Noddings, N. (2013). *Caring: A relational approach to ethics and moral education*. University of California Press.

OECD. (2024, November 28). *Generative AI set to exacerbate regional divide in OECD countries, says first regional analysis on its impact on local job markets* [Press release]. https://www.oecd.org/en/about/news/press-releases/2024/11/generative-ai-set-to-exacerbate-regional-divide-in-oecd-countries-says-first-regional-analysis-on-its-impact-on-local-job-markets.html

Pace, F., D'Urso, G., Zappulla, C., & Pace, U. (2021). The relation between workload and personal well-being among university professors. *Current Psychology (New Brunswick, N.J.)*, *40*(7), 3417–3424. DOI: 10.1007/s12144-019-00294-x

Perifanou, M., & Economides, A. (2025). Collaborative uses of GenAI tools in project-based learning. *Education Sciences*, *15*(3), 354. DOI: 10.3390/educsci15030354

Perrigo, B. (2023, January 18). OpenAI used Kenyan workers on less than $2 per hour to make ChatGPT less toxic. *Time*. https://time.com/6247678/openai-chatgpt-kenya-workers/

Rabin, C. (2021). Care ethics in online teaching. *Studying Teacher Education*, *17*(1), 38–56. DOI: 10.1080/17425964.2021.1902801

Ren, S., & Wierman, A. (2024, July 15). The uneven distribution of AI's environmental impacts. *Harvard Business Review*. https://hbr.org/2024/07/the-uneven-distribution-of-ais-environmental-impacts

Rogers, E. M. (1962). *Diffusions of innovations* (1st ed.). Free Press of Glencoe.

Ruediger, D., Blankstein, M., & Love, S. (2024). Generative AI and postsecondary instructional practices: Findings from a national survey of instructors. *Ithaka S+R, 20*. https://doi.org/DOI: 10.18665/sr.320892

Saputra, I., Astuti, M., Sayuti, M., & Kusumastuti, D. (2023). Integration of artificial intelligence in education: Opportunities, challenges, threats and obstacles. A literature review. *The Indonesian Journal of Computer Science*, *12*(4). Advance online publication. DOI: 10.33022/ijcs.v12i4.3266

Sayer, A. (2011). *Why things matter to people: Social science, values and ethical life*. Cambridge University Press. DOI: 10.1017/CBO9780511734779

Tan, X., Chen, G., & Ho Ling, M. (2025). Artificial intelligence in teaching and teacher professional development: A systematic review. *Computers and Education: Artificial Intelligence*, *8*, 1–19. DOI: 10.1016/j.caeai.2024.100355

Tavory, T. (2024). Regulating AI in mental health: Ethics of care perspective. *JMIR Mental Health*, *11*(1), 1–11. DOI: 10.2196/58493 PMID: 39298759

Thayer-Bacon, B., & Bacon, C. S. (1996). Caring professors: A model. *The Journal of General Education*, *45*(4), 255–256.

"The data-centre investment spree shows no signs of stopping." (2025, February 5). *The Economist*. https://www.economist.com/business/2025/02/05/the-data-centre-investment-spree-shows-no-signs-of-stopping

Upwork Research Institute. (2024, July 23). From burnout to balance: AI-enhanced work models. *Upwork Research Institute.* https://www.upwork.com/research/ai-enhanced-work-models

Verma, P., & Tan, S. (2024, September 18). A bottle of water per email: The hidden environmental costs of using AI chatbots. *The Washington Post.* https://www.washingtonpost.com/technology/2024/09/18/energy-ai-use-electricity-water-data-centers/

Villegas-Galaviz, C., & Martin, K. (2024). Moral distance, AI, and the ethics of care. *AI & Society*, *39*(4), 1695–1706. DOI: 10.1007/s00146-023-01642-z PMID: 37358944

Walther, C. C. (2024, November 12). Generative AI's impact on climate change: Benefits and costs. *Forbes*. https://www.forbes.com/sites/corneliawalther/2024/11/12/generative-ais-impact-on-climate-change-benefits-and-costs/

Zelkowski, J. (2024). To Praxis test or not? Mathematics content knowledge tests for teacher licensure and programmatic considerations on moving the preparation field forward. *Investigations in Mathematics Learning*, 1–20. https://doi.org/DOI: 10.1080/19477503.2024.2401728

Zewe, A. (2025, January 17). Explained: Generative AI's environmental impact. *MIT News*. https://news.mit.edu/2025/explained-generative-ai-environmental-impact-0117

KEY TERMS AND DEFINITIONS

Bias in AI Systems: The concept that, because models largely reflect the data sources used in training AI, they inherently carry biases originating from those data sources.

Care Cycle: Different extensions of reciprocal care based on proximity to the individual, including self, close others, distant others, and the natural world.

Digital Divide: The gap between those individuals, communities and societies which have access to both technology and digital literacy and those that do not.

Ethic of Care: A relational theory of care where motivation to care is based on the relationship between those involved on both sides of the care. The caregiver is motivated to care because of their innate capacity to care and the response of the one receiving care.

Ethical Dilemmas: Problems that contradict one's core moral principles and cause conflict with a person's established beliefs.

GenAI: Generative Artificial Intelligence is a term that refers to content that is newly created from technological means, not just collected from search engines.

Moral Distance: The perceived gap between actors in a moral decision with the implication being that the greater the distance, the more difficult it is to exhibit empathy and care.

Pedagogical Values: An educator's beliefs about learning that influence their teaching.

Self-Efficacy: Confidence in one's ability to succeed that is often built on previous success.

Trust: A firm belief in someone or something as reliable and true.

Chapter 3

AI Surveillance in Education: Unpacking Ethical Dilemmas and the Snake-Oil Promises of AI-Infused Technosolutionism

Apostolos Koutropoulos
https://orcid.org/0000-0001-7571-1796
University of Massachusetts, Boston, USA

Sarah Honeychurch
https://orcid.org/0000-0002-9931-6827
University of Glasgow, UK

Maha Bali
https://orcid.org/0000-0002-8142-7262
American University in Cairo, Egypt

Lenandlar Singh
https://orcid.org/0000-0002-8550-4237
University of Guyana, Guyana

Chrissi Nerantzi
University of Leeds, UK

Bonnie Stewart
https://orcid.org/0000-0001-9576-1037
University of Windsor, Canada

Sandra Abegglen
https://orcid.org/0000-0002-1582-9394
University of Calgary, Canada

Sandra Frances Sinfield
https://orcid.org/0000-0003-0484-7623
London Metropolitan University, UK

Chrysoula Lazou
https://orcid.org/0000-0003-2956-9762
Democritus University of Thrace, Greece

Stephanie Moore
University of New Mexico, USA

ABSTRACT

This chapter examines the ethical implications of the increasing integration of AI surveillance technologies within educational settings, including proctoring software,

DOI: 10.4018/979-8-3373-7569-4.ch003

classroom monitoring tools, and behavioral analytics. The swarm approach employed reflects diverse perspectives on this complex issue. It unpacks how AI surveillance reduces multifaceted students and faculty to data points, disproportionately targeting marginalized learners and misreading neurodivergent behaviors. The chapter critiques the snake's oil sales pitch of AI-infused technosolutionist discourse and foregrounds concerns regarding the erosion of student and lecturer autonomy, the alteration of student-lecturer relationships and the erosion of trust, the normalization of surveillance, and the amplification of existing inequalities and biases through algorithmic processes. The chapter concludes by emphasizing the need for educators to foster a learning environment that amplifies human potential.

INTRODUCTION

"Surveillance breeds conformity" - Glenn Greenwald

As new technologies enter our daily lives and take over our daily lexicons, we often see a familiar hype cycle that promises to make obsolete the existing processes and replace them with better, faster, and easier analogs. This trend is nothing new; in fact, in educational settings, it can go back to the dawn of computing itself. In 2022, the latest iteration of this hype entered our lexicons, and it responds to the name Generative Artificial Intelligence. As of this writing, there are more AI-enabled products, not all of which are *generative* in architecture, than you can shake a stick at, whether consumers, educators, and learners want them or not. In this paper we refer to all the variations of AI, from predictive AI to Generative AI, simply as 'AI.' This may seem like imprecise writing, however our aim is to focus on an application-level within personal and organizational practices, rather than smaller, specific, technological nuts-and-bolts approaches to AI. While it is true that different approaches to AI systems are built for different use cases, are trained on different sorts of data, and have different outputs depending on what they were built for, their use as surveillance instruments remains nevertheless either a core feature or a major use case. As surveillance can take different forms, so too AI systems that enable it. Algorithmic surveillance has been framed as a tool for efficiency, security, and safeguarding the academic integrity of the academe. However, such technologies evoke an eerie notion of a *Ghost in the Machine*, an invisible force that watches but does not understand, it judges but does not empathize.

This digital overseer, a capability embedded in proctoring software, classroom monitoring tools, typing fingerprinting, behavioral analytics suites, and workplace "bossware," (cf. Munn, 2024) reduces students and faculty to data points rather than complex and multifaceted individuals engaged in learning. In order for such tools to work, complexity is often bulldozed and replaced by binaries and statistical probabilities that are necessary for the machine to operate. But as those complex realities are essentialized and made unrealistically non-complex, we lose something. The quietly invasive presence of the mechanized gaze disproportionately targets marginalized students, misreads neurodivergent behaviors, and punishes those who fail to conform to an algorithmic ideal of "normal" academic conduct. Anything out of the "norm" is flagged as suspicious and deserving of extra scrutiny. Even student outputs that are a little "off" elicit the question of whether the submission is AI-generated. Thus, one of the dangers is transforming academic spaces where people grow through risk-taking and exploring new ideas into a mechanized surveillance state where human agency is subordinated to the cold binary logic of machine oversight. While it is true that some form of classroom surveillance predates this algorithmic gaze, unexamined practices that lean into the algorithmic gaze risk further alienating learners and teachers, both from each other and from the joy of learning. Learning is a messy endeavor, and surveillance practices don't often acknowledge the messy reality and notyetness of learning (cf, Ross & Collier, 2016).

With this in mind, we ask what are some of the ethical implications that we face as higher education professionals when confronted with the increased prevalence of AI, and by extension AI surveillance, in the products and services that we use? How do they impact our learners and our colleagues? What are some of the risks of being exposed to this ghostly algorithmic gaze? And how do we (re)gain agency and autonomy for ourselves and our learners? This chapter is a space for this epistemic conversation that we, as a field of professionals, need to have.

"*Under observation, we act less free, which means we effectively are less free.*"
- Edward Snowden

A SWARMING METHOD

We are all there in the text not as I, but as i. We lacked a word and made do with what was at hand. We was too unified, a coherent whole, a choir with one voice, and not a swarm. I carries way too much baggage from centuries of coherence and individualism and our own delusions that we exist. i had to do. It worked rather well. i also helps to remind us to check our egos at the door — something that made possible a truly collaborative experience, though collaboration is too stringent a word. Swarm is better. - (Hamon et al., 2015)

We, the authors of this chapter, came together as a collective, a collaboration, perhaps even a "swarm" (Hamon et al., 2015), in a manner similar to the *Writing the Unreadable Untext* (Hamon et al., 2015) which was a collaborative auto-ethnography as a reflection on and a 'mapping' of a rhizomatic cMOOC (Cormier's *The Community is the Curriculum*) from the inside. Since then, the swarm has grown, divided, sub-divided, and come together again in various shapes and iterations, producing a diversity of pieces wrestling with technology and its impact on the educational landscape: drawing strength from our together-writing.

Collective writing brings people — and their thoughts and experiences — together (Burns et al., 2023). It creates larger narratives about who we are and how we see the world. However, while it brings great outcomes and joy, it is a continuous struggle for meaning-making (Jandrić et. al., 2023). It requires negotiating perspectives, voices, and contexts, each shaped by different cultural, social, and ideological frameworks. Moreover, the fluid and dynamic nature of meaning-making means that interpretations shift over time. This ongoing negotiation underscores the transformative potential of collective writing while also revealing its complexities and inherent contradictions.

In this chapter, we used collective, collaborative writing as a method of inquiry where the writing itself is part of the exploration, the research, and the struggle for meaning (Gale & Bowstead, 2013). We do not apologize for straying from the traditional single writerly voice and its traditional and academic authority. Claiming instead a greater authority from our collective positionality, our insider subjectivities, and our multi-authorial voice(s). In this way, producing something "more scholarly, more insightful, and more in touch with the real than the traditional scholarly document we could have written and have written" (Hamon et al., 2015).

We started our collective writerly process by openly brainstorming in a shared, online (Google) document — both synchronously and asynchronously — back and forth. The swarm engaged with this multi-authored 'pattern note', refining and reshaping it into a concrete proposal that was in turn, used to frame a potential chapter introduction. The chapter itself emerged gradually, with all authors writing short pattern notes first that were then again swarmed upon, refined, and finally shaped into arguments. This process and that writing allowed us to each voice our views and experiences, to bounce off and be inspired by the "lightning bolts" (Mazzei & McCoy, 2010) of others, all opened up to the collective for joined meaning-making. This writing as a collective process enabled us to finalize both the individual contributions and the collective chapter: the swarm as an emergent process where individual voices intersect and evolve into something greater. The power of a swarm in motion is that ideas circulated, adapted, and mutated, creating a living text that reflects the diversity and complexity of its creators, creating a generative system and output where voices merge, diverge, and coalesce into shared meaning: not artificial, but human-generated text.

WE MURDER TO DISSECT: GAZING AT CURRENT DIGITAL INEQUALITIES FROM THE PAST *BY SANDRA & SANDRA*

Education itself has always been contested territory (viz. Bourdieu & Passeron, 1977; Blundell & Abegglen, 2017). The word itself oscillates between and bristles with contradictory meanings - from *educere*, which emphasises training and moulding, and where any expression of the self is transgressive (Noble, 2003) - to *educare* which suggests 'leading out', making space for the learner to emerge and grow in more rhizomatic ways (Deleuze & Guattari, 1987; Cormier, 2011). In the UK, education has long engaged in 'class work,' part of the ideological state apparatus (Althusser, 2012) which replicates all the inequalities found in an unequal society - socialising people into accepting their place and their lot, coercing them to internalise the portrait of them held in the ruling classes' loft, stripping away creativity, self-efficacy and love of learning in the process (viz. Ken Robinson on how school strips away creativity, and also Carol Black (n.d.) and 'The Evaluative Gaze' - and whereas Wordsworth (1798) might have said, 'schooling' therefore needs to "murder to dissect" - part of a broader critique of how scientific analysis strips away the beauty and essence of nature). Education was never 'right' and it also was never 'a right' for the majority but a cultural affirmation and finishing school for the privileged classes - preparing them for their professions - turning out socially acceptable bourgeois individuals who knew how to behave in 'civilised' company and who would not 'scare the horses.' For the masses, education trickled in - not to loosen their chains, but to prepare them for the labour, the factories, the clerical work for which they were deemed fit. This education was designed to tame and control the unruly minds and bodies of the great unwashed and assuage the fear of the rising middle and upper classes (viz. Watters, 2025) - increasingly outnumbered: Shaping the internal landscape of the proletariat so that they learned to surveille and manage themselves. Fitting into a cramped habitus (viz. Bourdieu, 1977) not of their own choosing, but egged on by the hidden curriculum: the high windows through which we could not look; the bell that told us when to sit - to stand - to play - to eat - to be silent; the literal big sticks of the Victorian age - and the smaller sticks of the detention, suspension and expulsion of these more 'enlightened' times. Never forgetting the small window in the door through which came the evaluative gaze (Foucault, 1977) of the head teacher. For whilst the learners have been surveilled, the teachers have also been surveilled, more so, drawn into the managerial and bureaucratic workings of an increasing neoliberal education system, from kindergarten to university and beyond.

More recently governments locally and internationally pushed this reductive educational agenda, insisting on the 'harnessing' of digital technology as a fundamental given of the new marketised education landscape - and an unproblematic 'good' serving up 24/7 education anywhere and anytime (viz. Sinfield et al., 2009, critique of 'harnessing' technology, and Kuhn et al., 2023, critique on digital education more generally). Today's rulers proffer an uncritical blueprint for integrating computers, software, and also AI in every aspect of education. Terms like TEL (Technology Enhanced Learning) emerged to shape the imagination of educators and policy makers alike, asserting that technology 'can only,' and 'must' and 'does' enhance learning. Universal technology strategies were imposed on education with little evidence base, whilst requiring vast cash injections to place hardware into every classroom and coincidental with many educators forbidden to print off a module guide or photocopy a handout let alone have pen and paper in the classroom. The bolted down AudioVisualAid (AVA) system locked the teacher as 'the sage on the stage' pronouncing from the front of a 21st century HE classroom where all the chairs are still in rows - the windows are still high - and the VLE (Virtual Learning Environment) surveilles what the staff and students do with their time. All the while rendering invisible or unproblematic that technology itself is neither neutral nor objective (like education itself is neither neutral nor objective, viz. Freire, 1996) - and that wider social and structural inequalities can create, sustain, and even enhance digital inequalities just as they do with educational ones (Abegglen et al, 2025; Althusser, 2012; Bowles & Gintis, 1975).

QUESTIONS TO ASK OURSELVES FIRST *BY MAHA*

Three key concerns I would like to foreground:

First, when we choose to adopt a new technology (surveillance or other), do we carefully consider the potential impact on enhancing learning and/or reproducing or exacerbating inequalities (Daniel, 2024)? We might, for example, use the SAMR (Puentedura, 2015) or PICRAT (Kimmons et al, 2020) models to assess whether this new technology allows us to transform our teaching, or provide more creative and constructive ways for students to learn, or whether the new technology is just reproducing passive ways of learning. For example, so-called "personalized learning" is often more about surveillance and categorizing humans than truly adapting to individual needs (Watters, 2021). Are efficiency gains (if any) offset by reductions or losses in the quality of the learning experience for particular groups (e.g., if we use automated feedback, what happens to students whose writing styles fall outside the norm)? We know that historically, technologies, including AI, have served as

> *"a reflection of who we have let have a voice in the past and that voice was built from and still has large contributions from systems of hierarchy that use academia to further justify their positionality of power and stratification." ('Ofakihevahanoa Fotu, 2024)*

The danger here is that technology tools amplify such power while obfuscating the accountability and transparency of who is wielding this power under the guise of what others may perceive as neutral technologies. We need to resist this, since we know that no technology is politically neutral (Williamson, 2024).

Second, we need to consider the hidden curriculum of our choices. Using something like Turnitin.com, itself meant to show whether students copy/pasted text from somewhere without paraphrasing or citing, misconstrues the act of citation and referencing as one of avoiding the copy/paste thing that Turnitin "catches," rather than truly valuing the behavior of acknowledging where we got ideas from. This made students initially think copying text from AI was not a problem: it was not another human's text, and Turnitin initially could not detect it, and still cannot reliably detect it; but that is beside the point: it is still text that the student did not write, and they need to learn to acknowledge where they get their ideas, and words, from - and this is problematic with AI because some AI tools like ChatGPT don't always acknowledge their sources accurately, if at all (Mills & Bali, 2024). What we should have been doing is helping students internalize a culture of acknowledgment, not because of the (not-so?) hidden curriculum of "catch-me-if-you-can." Instead of teaching students the conventions of citation, a technical skill they can learn, we have been making it a form of academic dishonesty and focusing on how to catch and punish them instead of how to help them grow and learn. That's the hidden curriculum of Turnitin.

Third, what are the macro and long-term implications of the use of surveillance cultures in education for learners as citizens? How might this normalize surveillance as a way of being in the world, restricting people's capacity to think and act freely? Technologies such as AI "cannot be considered inevitable, beneficial, or transformative in any straightforward way… AI in education is highly contested and controversial" (Williamson, 2024).

We should never adopt technologies in education that (Bali, 2025):

1. Go against our teaching philosophies and values, or
2. Have no evidence or potential of truly making a positive impact on learning or teaching, or
3. Could potentially reproduce or exacerbate inequalities or introduce new ones, or reduce trust and care in the classroom or educational community, or
4. Could restrict human agency of teachers or learners, or
5. Have potentially harmful trade-offs that are visible or invisible in their hidden curriculum.

DIMINISHING AGENCY OR SUPPORTING AUTONOMY? *BY STEPHANIE*

Much of the discourse on the use of generative AI in education has focused more on instructor decisions and uses, such as how to re-imagine assessments of learning or what policies to create to shape and guide student use. In a sense, the tendency has been to center instructor and institutional agency over and above student agency. Reflecting this tendency, a crowd-sourced Google sheet was created in January 2023 and maintained through 2024 in which instructors at institutions around the world shared their class policies relating to generative AI in their courses (Eaton, 2024). The rhetorical structure of the large majority of these is revealing. Using Bakhtin's (1989) definitions of closed and open discourse, a quick analysis of these policies illuminates how the vast majority of the syllabus statements reflect a closed discourse. Closed discourse features rhetoric that establishes dichotomous options: one can only accept or reject, comply or defy. Examples of closed language in these policies includes repeated use of words such as "must," "discouraged," and "explicitly prohibited," along with threats to "follow the institution's policy (on academic integrity) to the letter" and deal "severely" with any use of AI that is deemed to be cheating or plagiarism. A centering of instructor (or designer) agency does not necessarily translate into student agency.

In that same collection, a few policies represented more open approaches that centered discourse and decision-making with students. For example, one policy states, "it should be you (the students) that guides, verifies and crafts your ultimate answer … let's leverage the tools as an extension of ourselves." The use of collective nouns and pronouns in particular creates more of a sense of shared agency. Another policy states that part of the goal is to "open up a class dialogue about the role of AI in education" and describes the co-creation of a class agreement on the use of AI tools. The act of creating with students similarly treats agency as something to be distributed and shared.

However well-intended the more closed policies and language may be, these have the unintended impact of denying learners their own autonomy and moral agency. One rather tricky aspect of ethical considerations is that one's ethical analysis may not lead them to the same conclusions as someone else. Additionally, learners in our classes are not limited in their identities to "our students." They are individuals with lives and jobs where they are engaging in a range of decision-making processes on when and how to use or not use generative AI. By prohibiting this technology, we are actually limiting their opportunities to develop reflective practices and decision-making processes that can serve them well in their lives and careers. Centering student agency means making space for their moral agency and supporting their autonomy in their decision-making.

Practices that create more open, dialogic spaces and allow for learner negotiation and construction are reflective of the psychological principle of autonomy support from self-determination theory (Gagné, 2003a; Ryan & Deci, 2000), which we propose as an essential theory for research and practice related to AI in education, as it centers learner autonomy and agency in ways that can also promote learning and learner wellbeing (Calvo et al., 2018; Deci et al., 2006; Gagne, 2003b). I would argue that we can draw on pedagogical practices from the autonomy support literature to better center learner autonomy and agency in learning environments.

In instructional design work, an ethics-as-design (Whitbeck, 1996) framing can turn ethical analysis and critique into courses of action, approaching ethics not just as issues to be named but as complex problems that require creative synthesis. Scholes (2016) provides a good example of this in her treatment of ethics and learning analytics (LA), a technology with uses akin to AI in education. She starts with the question of how students are perceived and treated in one's vision for the technology. If they are individuals and are agentive, then implementation of the technology should afford individual assessment, inform the individual, and present opportunities for students to enact agency in their learning journeys. She brainstorms various ways instructional designers can reframe LA to focus more on individual choices, efforts, and achievements – such as designing instructional supports around needs or gaps that make a difference in learner persistence. She also calls for a distinction between risk factors that are static versus those that are dynamic, i.e., what can be changed over time or through an instructional intervention or support structure. Similarly, we can pose the question of generative AI: How are students perceived and treated in our vision of generative AI? Do we frame their roles as ones where they have agency in their learning? If so, how does that cascade down into implementation decisions and instructional interventions or supports that facilitate learner agency and support them in driving their learning choices and developing their personal decision-making and moral agency?

THE SPIRIT OF THE [AI] AGE *BY SARAH*

"But what then am I? A thing which thinks. What is this thing which thinks? It is a thing which doubts, understands, [conceives], affirms, denies, wills, refuses, which also imagines and feels." Descartes, 1978

The idea that it's our ability to think logically – our rationality – that makes us uniquely human is a prevailing theme throughout Western Philosophy. From Plato's Philosopher Rulers to Star Trek's Mr. Spock, we are given models of logical thinking giants who are far superior to other mere mortals, and we are led to believe that we should aspire to be more like them.

In *The Concept of Mind,* Gilbert Ryle calls the Cartesian version of this philosophy of mind the dogma of The Ghost in the Machine (Ryle, 1949). We might use the Ghost in the Machine as a metaphor for AI – the project of abstracting the 'rational' part of human understanding and calling this 'intelligence.' I think that this metaphor gives a helpful way of understanding what is wrong with a purely rational model of human thought.

So what is going wrong with this model of human intelligence, and why does it matter?

In *Phaedrus,* Plato (2006) paints a picture of the human soul as a charioteer steering two horses – the rational horse which leads us towards truth and the irrational (emotional) one that leads us into error. But we are human beings, not machines, and we can (and do) learn from our passions and emotions as much – maybe even more – than from logic. And reducing all of human thought and human learning to the former is not merely absurd; it is dangerous. As well as our ability to think logically, we need to develop what Aristotle calls *phronesis* (practical wisdom), and to harness the power of our emotions as well as our ability to think logically.

If we turn learning into the set of things that can be counted rather than what counts (matters), into measurable outputs rather than messy looking (complicated) processes, we lose the serendipity of emergent learning. When failure is thought of as a negative, and the space to be different is squeezed out, then we deny learners the autonomy to develop in ways they find authentic. If we allow capitalist forces to redefine what it means to be intelligent, and to be human, then we risk redefining humanity. This is a metaphysical crisis.

Analytical philosophy warns about the perils of rhetoric and the logical perils of falling for slippery slopes fallacies, but sometimes warnings should be heeded. When I taught Descartes to undergraduates, I used to play them a song by the mighty Hawkwind called *The Spirit of the Age*, and this has been playing in my head as I have been writing this:

if you had ever seen us you'd rejoice in your uniqueness
And consider every weakness something special of your own
Being a clone I have no flaws to identify
Even this doggerel that pours from my pen
Has just been written by another twenty telepathic men
Word for word it says
"Oh, for the wings of any bird other than a battery hen"

FORESHADOWING THE 'GHOSTLY ALGORITHMIC GAZE' IN THE BACKGROUND / TOWARDS RECENTERING RELATIONS IN EDUCATION *BY LEN*

In the age of artificial intelligence (AI), educational institutions are increasingly integrating AI-driven tools such as ChatGPT, plagiarism detection systems, and automated grading software into their systems (Bhullar et al., 2024; Gambo et al., 2024; Mphahlele & McKenna, 2019). While these tools promise to enhance efficiency and accessibility, they also introduce background AI surveillance (the 'ghostly algorithmic gaze'), which operates (mostly) invisibly yet significantly in shaping educational processes, cultures, and relationships.

According to Philosopher of Technology Don Ihde's concept of background relations, technologies can function as an unseen or 'barely detectable' (Ihde, 1990, p.109) force shaping human experiences without direct interaction (Ihde, 1990). In the context of higher education, limited memory AI tools like ChatGPT, as well as more specialized AI surveillance tools influence learning, assessment, and other processes, without students and lecturers always realizing their full impact. These hidden AI mechanisms operating within the sphere of 'an absent presence' (Ihde, 1990, p.111) shape the educational experience by filtering what is seen, emphasized, or valued, while leaving other aspects in the periphery raise critical concerns about agency, autonomy, and ethics (Bozkurt, 2024; Bozkurt et al., 2024; Xiao et al., 2025).

Background AI Surveillance and the Erosion of Student and Lecturer Autonomy

Background AI surveillance influences students and lecturers without them actively engaging with it, making autonomy a central ethical concern. For students, AI-driven learning analytics may track their behavior, engagement levels, and academic performance in ways that shape their educational journey without direct input. Universities may use AI-generated predictions to identify students at risk of failing, recommend interventions, or even determine grading curves, often without students fully understanding how these assessments are made. While intended to improve academic outcomes, these systems risk limiting student autonomy by imposing algorithmic decisions on their learning trajectories. For example, if AI predictions label a student as disengaged or struggling, institutions may implement automatic remedial actions, potentially misinterpreting external factors such as limited internet access or personal circumstances as academic deficiencies.

For lecturers, the background AI monitoring of teaching effectiveness may influence their professional autonomy in unintended ways. For example, universities might rely on AI-driven analytics to assess faculty performance based on student engagement metrics, attendance tracking, and automated student feedback analysis. When these AI systems operate without transparency, lecturers may feel pressured to adjust their teaching styles to fit algorithmic expectations rather than focusing on student-centered learning. If AI-generated performance scores dictate promotion opportunities or contract renewals, faculty might continue to lose control over how they teach, prioritizing data-driven metrics over pedagogical creativity. Over time, these behavior hacks may erode academic freedom by reducing lecturers to data points within an AI-driven system rather than active agents of education.

Impact on Student-Lecturer Relationships: Trust vs. Algorithmic Control

Background AI surveillance may subtly alter the power dynamics between students and lecturers, affecting trust, engagement, and the overall educational experience in cases where they are unaware of how AI surveillance operates, how data is collected, and how decisions are made. When AI operates as an invisible arbiter of academic performance, it introduces a third, often unaccountable, influence into this relationship. This is in stark contrast to the traditional student-lecturer relationship built on open communication and mutual respect for intellectual growth.

Conversely, for students, knowing that their engagement, attendance, and even writing patterns are being tracked by AI can create an atmosphere of constant monitoring and passive compliance rather than active learning. Instead of experimenting with ideas, questioning concepts, or engaging in complex problem-solving, students may opt for AI-friendly behaviors that align with what the system rewards, potentially stifling creativity and independent thought. Furthermore, if students perceive that lecturers rely on AI-generated insights rather than direct interaction, they may feel that their unique learning experiences may not be fully understood.

For lecturers, AI surveillance may lead to an unintended shift from being mentors and educators to algorithmic enforcers. If AI tools dictate how assignments should be graded, how student participation is evaluated, or how content should be structured, faculty may feel pressured to conform to AI recommendations rather than exercising professional judgment. Over time, this weakens the student-lecturer connection, replacing dialogue-driven education with AI-mediated interactions that prioritize efficiency over deep learning.

Reclaiming Agency: Ethical AI Integration in Higher Education

To ensure ethical and fair AI integration in higher education, universities must prioritize transparency and consent, ensuring that students and lecturers understand as far as possible how AI surveillance operates, what data is collected, and how decisions are made. AI systems should remain explainable and open to human intervention, preventing blind reliance on automated decisions. Additionally, human oversight and review must be mandatory, ensuring that AI-generated academic decisions, whether in grading, plagiarism detection, or faculty evaluations, are not final without the possibility of critical human judgment and appeals.

CRITICAL DISCOURSE AND NAVIGATION IN AI CONTEXTS *BY CHRYSSA*

As Artificial Intelligence (AI) tools emerge, so do mixed reactions, with either fervent supporters of their adoption in education and training advocating that AI can revolutionize the way we learn, live, and communicate, or others who express skepticism regarding ethical considerations and the overtaking of technology as the primary agency. In the educational field, questions arise regarding AI tool usage implications for Gen Z and Gen Alpha cognitive and socio-emotional dependency on the ever-evolving AI networks and infrastructures. Adams et al. (2023) discuss human-nonhuman agent interactions from the posthumanism perspective. In an effort to unfold the nature of posthuman beings in the AI era, ethical considerations in the context of learners and non-human relational collaborations become complicated. As AI dialogue systems become more sophisticated, learners become more over-reliant, which may lead to the diminishing of cognitive skills development, lack of critical and analytical thinking, and susceptibility to AI hallucinations and misleading content (Zhai et al., 2024), while further deeper ethical considerations include algorithmic bias, plagiarism, privacy breaches, and transparency concerns (Hua et al., 2023). On the premise that algorithmic surveillance operates on preexisting datasets, misidentifying individuals with diverse patterns, concerns about discriminatory flagging and societal inequalities arise. This may involve higher rates of scrutiny for students from underrepresented backgrounds or unfair ratings of neurodivergent students whose behavioral patterns deviate from algorithmic expectations. As AI mechanisms fail to understand human complexity, ethical concerns lie in the dehumanization of original effort and the overshadowing of human processing abilities.

While the adoption of AI tools may decrease instructors' workload and support diverse learners' need for personalized and self-regulated learning addressing specific gaps in knowledge or enriching it, we need to stress the importance of the ethical use of dialogue systems and advocate the establishment of fundamental guidelines for interacting with these systems based on principles of appropriateness, transparency, honesty, and integrity. The advancement in GenAI and its multifaceted uses should be seen as an opportunity rather than a threat, as long as we find a balance and effective solutions that align with the principles of academic integrity (Bozkurt et al., 2024) and critical thinking toward information verification of AI generated responses (Lee et al., 2025). As an educator, I feel that it is my responsibility to cultivate my students' skills and attitudes toward a responsible, critical, and ethical use of AI as a means rather than an end without an a priori suspicion regarding the originality of their work. I feel that assessment methods should develop their skills for strategically using GenAI, embracing its affordances to enhance human-led creativity and unique contributions to authentic work. Nevertheless, I feel that in order to effectively integrate the ever-evolving technology into my teaching and learning practices and reassure all actors' well-being, there is a need for a framework to support mindful integration of AI's affordances and align them with my intended learning outcomes while retaining academic integrity. The TPACK (Mishra & Koehler, 2006) and SAMR (Puentedura, 2015) models have so far led our actions and decisions in enhancing learning outcomes. But is this enough in our new "AI-enhanced" reality? The SETI (social-ecological technology integration) framework, introduced by Crompton et al. (2024), highlights the socio and ecological factors that need to be considered, such as training, tech support, and policy development. While educators and learners are at the center of decision-making for technology integration, the interactions of people within those contexts need to be considered at the micro- (school) and macro- (national) levels of this ecological system.

RELATIONAL PEDAGOGY AS AN ANTIDOTE *BY CHRISSI*

Big Brother is always watching. We are watching Big Brother. We are watching each other. Every breath we take can be monitored if we are with our digital devices or our debit/credit card. We generate a tsunami of data every second. Unless we lock our devices up and stop using them, our steps can be followed very easily. I remember when, during the pandemic, I received a report from Google with the places I visited and very exact information. While this could be useful if I wanted to track where I am going, which I didn't, or when somebody got lost, I understand this, it can also be dangerous if somebody has bad intentions. We have so many different accounts, and so many companies are after our data, even supermarket loyalty cards are not harmless, promising everyday savings and discounts to lure us into saving while spending more and handing them over our data. Like with everything; anything that can be used for good can also be used for bad, to destroy.

Thinking about learning and teaching and my role as an educator. I have no intention to start policing my students. To track what they do and how. I don't want anybody to police me, so why would I police others?

My work focuses on designing stimulating and relevant to my students' learning experiences. Helping students become autonomous and feel empowered to design their own experiences and learn in a way that helps them move forward, overcome blockages, and feel excited are all things that deeply matter to me. I want them to reach out to others and also use tools to experiment responsibly, critically, and creatively. To try different things. To connect with their peers and others and learn together. I am not going to blame my students for using GenAI. However, I also don't want them to grow new dependencies. We have seen how students often rely solely on their tutors for help and support. This was evident during the pandemic (Dunbar-Morris et al., 2023), and all this in a highly connected world. If students have found ways that help them learn, I will support them. I will help them sharpen their criticality and creativity so that they get the maximum out of it and become more autonomous (Nerantzi et al. 2023). Knowing where to find help when we feel helpless is an important skill to learn, and if GenAI can help my students, that is great. Criticality, responsibility, and accountability are key, of course.

Cheating doesn't lead to any learning. Learning means genuine change. If anybody wants to do something that is not genuinely helping them learn, and they are just looking for shortcuts, they are cheating themselves. These days, students seem routinely to be accused of using GenAI to cheat (Gorichanaz, 2023; Dawson et al., 2024), while it seems that not all educators are open and transparent about their own use of GenAI (Luo, 2024). This is unhelpful and damaging for learning relationships and trust. First of all, we need to be mindful of learning that can be surface, strategic, or deep (Säljö, 1979; Entwistle et al., 2001). We all do this at times, depending on the situation. This is not cheating. The problem with GenAI is more acute when we think about assessment, where educators make a judgment on their students' performance on an assessment based on specific criteria. The more remote the educator is from their students, the less they know them, their work, their interests and aspirations, the more the suspicion will grow about the work the student submitted, especially if it is outstanding. There will be mistrust. The value of anonymous marking is such a myth. Often it is mandated as a way for educators to be more objective, more distant as a good strategy to make a better judgement about the student's performance, the final output. In research we often call this "bracketing." Is this really possible and desirable in education? We seem to forget the value of the learning process, the relational aspect of learning. Its value seems to be erased with anonymous marking. That inner motivation to learn can do wonders (Anggraeni et al., 2024), and relational pedagogy can, too. Relational pedagogies can "creates a sense that there is shared commitment and a common good that binds us" (hooks, 1994, p.40), reinforcing those emotional connections between teachers and learners which are important to the enterprise of learning (Quinlan, 2019). This inner motivation is what needs to be awakened and practised. It is our humanity that brings us closer together. Our vulnerability, history, curiosity, and respect for otherness and the desire for togetherness to make a contribution to the world.

Learning is relational. Let's finally acknowledge this more fully. What is our role as educators?

GHOSTS IN THE MACHINE: WE CAN HAVE AGENCY OR WE CAN HAVE AI *BY BONNIE*

In the current moment, as the technocrat billionaires of Silicon Valley appear to have executed a governmental takeover of the most powerful nation on earth without ever appearing on a ballot, my fear is not that AI is the ghost in the machine. Rather, I fear that *we* have been rendered ghosts…our human agency reduced to shadows by systems that enclose us but do not see us. The algorithmic gaze of automated systems registers human beings – like all other inputs – as mere binary representations. It does not, and cannot, see anything more.

After hundreds of years of struggle towards a flawed and still unevenly distributed ideal of human liberty and agency, humans of this 'digital age' are being hyped right out of hard-won democratic protections by an alliance of technology, capital, and increasingly naked power. More, we are being hyped out of our own agency to even comprehend or resist.

The logic of hype is powerful in business and media sectors, and fundamental to the venture capital model on which Silicon Valley runs. When a technology or trend is deemed innovative, it is imbued with a grand promise of inevitable change and accumulating capital. That promise – of an optimized future ever just around the corner, decoupled from any responsibility to the here and now – is freed of the need to actually deliver. There's an actual proprietary company – Gartner – which has very profitably tracked the swells and collapses of innovation expectations in its 'Gartner Hype Cycle' since 1995 (Fenn, 2022). And from the time that what we now call GenAI first burst into public consciousness in late 2022 as ChatGPT, major forces like Forbes (Silver, 2023) and the World Economic Forum (North, 2023) have heralded it as pretty much the biggest hype cycle ever.

Education is not immune to innovation hype: its logic has bled beyond business and media over the past decade, and encroached powerfully into education systems (and their funding). While digital education originally centered on the participatory possibilities of the web and its human-to-human capacities for democratic pedagogy, gradually this space of possibility has been enclosed – and often transactionalized – by its own tools and vendors. Educators interested in developing students' learning and agency through digital methods must rely on data-extractive platforms, whose vendors tend to be far more versed in the logic of capital than they are in pedagogy.

A divide has emerged between the lucrative hype of educational technologies and trends, and the participatory practice roots of digital education (Stewart, 2022).

This divide has only been amplified by the rise of Generative AI. GenAI is not a participatory process in the way the web was, connecting humans in the creation of a commons of knowledge. Rather, AI is a plagiarism machine that trawls the commons we once built, running roughshod over any concept of copyright or even ownership of original ideas. It synthesizes and serves up our own traces to us, blindly, rendering us unseen ghosts even when our words are present. And when or where we are absent, deleted from the narrative by programming bias or by AI's training on the data of the global north, we are again ghosts, unrepresented and unacknowledged.

Now, with Musk suggesting that AI systems can be more 'efficient' at teaching than teachers (Musk, 2025; Figure 1), the digital infrastructure that originated to enhance learning has morphed into one that threatens any vision of human growth or connection within it. This consolidation of power represents an existential threat, not from sentient machines, but from the full debasement of knowledge into commodity, education into credentials, and humans into afterthoughts in the so-called learning process.

GenAI has uses, yes. But in every educational decision made about how it is used in learning, we need to prioritize and foster the idea of human agency over hype. Otherwise, we surrender to automated extraction and surveillance for profit, and become merely ghosts, haunting the educational machine.

Figure 1. Screenshot from Twitter/X where Musk comments on a Luckey post. Screenshot was captured by authors on March 23, 2025.

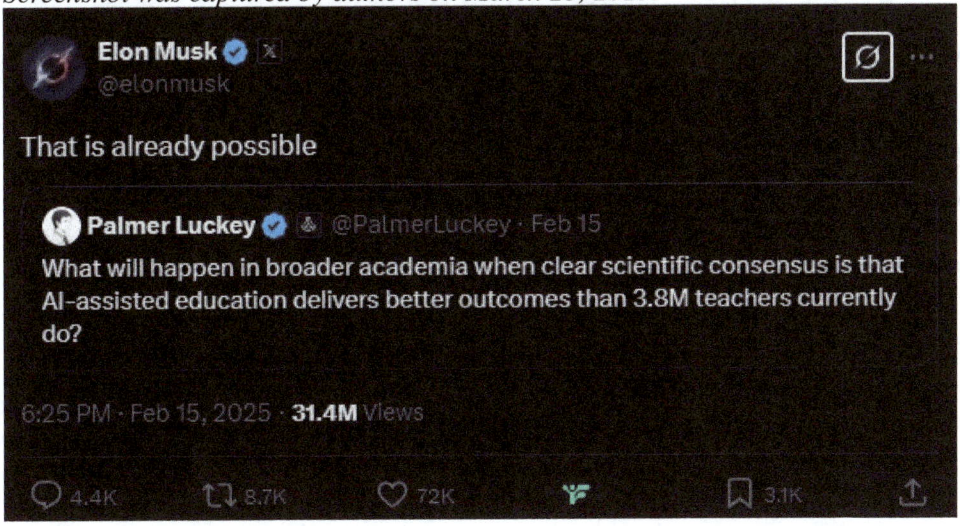

WAS EDTECH ALWAYS SURVEILLANCETECH? *BY AK*

The arc of my professional career has brought me from a young, technology-curious, geek through to a critical instructional designer and, for the last decade, to teacher and academic manager roles. Without technology, what I do would not exist, so I am understandably excited when new developments arise that enable new learning opportunities both for my learners and me. While I am still excited, and perpetually curious, as I've grown, my reaction to any claims about technology is met with a similar reaction reminiscent of Thor's "does it though?" reaction from the movie *Thor: Ragnarok* (Waititi, 2017). The same is true about any sort of AI claims that we've collectively experienced these past few years. The AI narrative has followed a predictable pathway that frames AI-laced products as an inevitability, and this inevitability will improve what we do in the classroom. While it's not wrong to want to use technology to improve our practice, much of that narrative has focused on banishing the drudgery of teaching and administrative tasks rather than improving the actual teaching. This was true of the first computer, when the ENIAC's (Electronic Numerical Integrator and Computer) creators started to think of applications beyond war for their creation (McCartney, 1999); and it remains true when research on algorithmic solutions to attendance-taking evokes a narrative of the inefficiency and error-prone nature of having a human conduct a roll-call at the beginning of class (e.g., Ahila et al., 2024; Gao et al., 2021; Liu & Liu, 2024). The same goes for student engagement. Student engagement is seen as a fundamentally good thing, so algorithmic systems are proposed to monitor that for the teacher (cf. Bala, 2020; Pabba & Kumar, 2022), and as a result of such 'efficiencies', learners need to be constantly monitored by technology to ensure compliance, and instructors need to constantly monitor the student monitor (cf. Selwyn & Cumbo, 2024).

Digging a little deeper, we see that critiques of the surveilled classroom are not a novel idea, but it's not a topic that is at the forefront of practitioners' minds, probably because it's not deemed to be a 'sexy' or exciting topic. Luck (2012) highlights Rodger's (2002, in Luck, 2012) previous work when he highlights that attendance does not ensure that learning takes place; a student may score highly in attendance but low in subject-area comprehension. This means that students may be pressured into a performative activity that earns them high marks for conforming to certain behaviors but doesn't necessarily benefit their learning. Even twenty years before AI was in our daily lexicon and crammed into every conceivable product, these were concerns. The current AI hype has benefited greatly from the Learning Analytics decade that preceded it, and through which we've had increased "dataveillance," a term coined by Clarke (1988), where companies are benefiting from those data exhausts that we leave behind in our day-to-day online learning activities. These exhausts used to be just in the virtual realm; however, as technology advances and our physical classrooms become 'smart,' the number and types of sensors and data recording mechanisms far exceed simple click-stream data (e.g., Zhang et al., 2024; Kwet & Prinsloo, 2020). This isn't just impacting classrooms and students; it has the potential to negatively impact the teaching and administrative staff as well (cf. Charara, 2025; Moore, 2025).

Ultimately, as educational professionals, we have to ask who is benefiting and who is harmed by the use of classroom surveillance. The research and scholarly analysis seem to suggest that both students and teachers are the ultimate losers in this field by experiencing stress and anxiety, experiencing an erosion of trust between teachers and learners (cf. Bala, 2020; Barrett, 2022; Citron, 2024; Madaio et al., 2022), people perform in robotic, conformist, and algorithmic-friendly ways to work with the ghost's programmed logic, rather than exercising their innate creativity and means of self-expression. There is no *intelligence*; there is just *conformity* and *programmed* logic, which is the antithesis of learning and learning spaces characterized by relational and caring connections that epitomize a learning atmosphere.

Figure 2. "Does it though?" meme, adapted from the film "Thor: Ragnarok." Created by authors with imgflip meme generator: https://imgflip.com/memegenerator

A SWARM SYNTHESIS

"Openness and participation are antidotes to surveillance and control." - Howard Rheingold

Over the preceding decades, computers and other information and communication technologies (ICT) have made their way into our classrooms under various guises. The initial dream, and sales pitch, of removing the 'drudgery' from teaching still remains one of the selling points of educational technology, although it's not often framed in such terms. Technological solutions are often marketed as a means of getting personalized attention for individual learners, becoming more efficient, reaching greater crowds, and offering other micro and macro indicators of success. These indicators of success are often based on grains of truth, such as the benefits of attending class, or of having an attentive *agent* that adapts to the learners' needs.

Today, various technological threads extolling the positive sides of technology, including those on personalized learning, adaptive learning, just-in-time learning, chatbots, massified learning (vis-à-vis xMOOCs), and learning analytics, have converged to new focal points. Meanwhile, in this mélange of threads, there are darker-tech threads that have found new focal points, one of which is the so-called 'plagiarism detection' services, which may include text analysis software, and another is the algorithmic, or live, proctoring of learners taking exams and other kinds of assessments. These services predate the pandemic and have been available for the past twenty years. However, the wider availability of broadband has made audio-visual surveillance, whether algorithmic or human, more available and affordable for institutions. The Emergency Remote Teaching era of the COVID pandemic, which immediately precedes our current algorithmic AI era, also brought an additional element of surveillance in our digital classrooms: The requirement to keep your camera on in Zoom, or other synchronous meeting software was amplified during the pandemic era (Barrett, 2022). Instructor discomfort and self-doubt about instructional efficacy became a reason to force learners to bring the world into potentially private spaces.

These threads have started to acquire additional dimensions in our current age of algorithmic decision-making, now powered by various forms of so-called AI. In addition to the predictable cycle of academic angst over 'detecting' AI in student submissions, there is also a movement to incorporate AI into teaching and learning, using an 'evolve or perish' argument that we've experienced in the past as ICTs *du jour* emerge in our collective consciousness and day-to-day professional and personal lives. For instance, data exhaust (cf. Zuboff, 2019) from our learning management systems that were collected under a learning analytics thread are now marketed as AI solutions for determining how learners are performing in class based on an analysis of the learner's data exhaust. This isn't new, of course, universities have experimented with these features, for instance, Purdue's *Signals* (ca. 2009) or various kinds of activity matrices and activity summaries built into the types of reports that learning management systems can produce. The new façade of AI-driven insights may promise to be an oracle into the future without having a complete picture of what's happening in the background outside of the context of learners' data exhausts. Another instance where there's new wall paint on an old product is the threat of 'plagiarism detection,' which now also gets marketed as 'AI detection' despite the demonstrable fact that the nature of large language model outputs can neither be reasonably nor reliably detected. While it is true that traditional plagiarism detection relies on textual pattern matches, and 'AI detection' uses different mechanisms, the promotion of such technologies feeds on the same underlying fears, and amplifies doubt in our learners.

The challenge that we face as educational professionals isn't simply one that is technological in nature. Rather, it's a challenge that is, at its core, one of the ethical and relational duties that we have toward our learners, and toward our colleagues. While education as an enterprise in the modern era does derive from a standardization and compliance model of learning, this doesn't square with our rhetoric of making education available to more people, often framed as *democratizing education.* Such goals are also purported by the EdTech companies that market products to us. However, our goals aren't always compatible. It is important to balance any promissory benefits against any challenges and ethical conflicts that exist with using the various technologies, and this is true with AI. The EdTech coin has two sides, one which presents a sunny, productivity-enhancing, streamlined, personalized learning tutor wundertech; and a darker side that promises to catch those who aren't conforming to the norms that we set. Algorithmic surveillance has been framed as a tool for efficiency, security, and safeguarding the academic integrity of the academe, however, this *Apparition of Intelligence,* along with the illusions that its *security theater* provides, may serve only to stifle creativity and reinforce perceptions of learning rather than encourage authentic and true learning. Perhaps this is to be expected as education was designed to tame and control the unruly minds and bodies; and while the actual mechanism by which AI surveillance works may be invisible to the learner, the *ghost* that powers this machine stays true to the original goals of education. If we want to break out of this mold, to practice emancipatory and liberatory educational and work practices, we need to ask ourselves deep questions about the tools that are available to us.

In our swarm, we approached the ethical implications of AI-powered classroom surveillance from our various perspectives. Our diverse and varied backgrounds have allowed us to come together and explore this topic through different lenses and viewpoints. Despite the multitude of viewing angles and refractions, one thing is clear: we have just scratched the surface, and this is a subject that warrants further exploration and active engagement not just with our colleagues and our institutions but also with our students. Our profession has various models available to us as educators to help us think of technology deployment in the classroom and across the institution, such as SAMR (Puentedura, 2015), PICRAT (Kimmons et al, 2020), TPACK (Mishra & Koehler, 2006), and SECTIONS (Bates, 2019). However, this isn't simply a box-checking exercise. It requires deep engagement with other human actors to determine what is right for our contexts and goals.

Amongst the issues that emerged in our swarm, we find algorithmic surveillance as exacerbating inequalities through algorithmic bias, a normalization of surveillance and its long-term impact, a diminishment of learner and instructor agency and autonomy, an erosion of trust amongst members of a learning community, a focus on surface-level outcomes rather than deep, meaningful, and long-term outcomes, and a transmission a distorted image of academic integrity.

Technology is often billed as something that is neutral and objective; however, it is anything but neutral and objective, and it can serve as a means of exacerbating existing social and structural inequalities. Baked into the core of current generation AI technologies are deep rooted biases. Some biases are visual - in other words who is represented; some biases are textual - in other words what and how things are said; and some biases are behavioral - how someone should behave. Biases exist in the data that informs the AI, the pre-training the algorithm receives, the way the algorithm privileges or depriviledges certain information, and in the kinds of inputs that it receives (Xiao & Bozkurt, 2025). The *belief* that bigger datasets could remove bias and "offer a higher form of intelligence and knowledge that can generate insights that were previously impossible, with the aura of truth, objectivity, and accuracy" is part of the *Big Data Mythology* (boyd & Crawford, 2012, p. 663). Technologies serve as a reflection of dominant ideas, ideologies, and discourses. The danger in uncritically accepting tools and their claims *prima facie* is that technology tools amplify such power while obfuscating the accountability and transparency of who is wielding this power under the guise of what others may perceive as neutral technologies. A reflection of such dominant ideas in AI surveillance includes an increased scrutiny of the behaviors of underrepresented and neurodivergent, and therefore, algorithmic surveillance may be skewed against them; and 'academic dishonesty detection' tools may keep flagging language used by second language learners as they develop increased competency in their additional languages, as well as learners with atypical writing patterns, for instance learners with specific learning disabilities, and more formal writing styles, such as the more formalized writing in journalism.

The normalization of classroom and workplace surveillance has a long-term impact. Learners, and teachers, who are surveilled as a means of recommending behavioral improvements, ostensibly for their own benefit, are rendered servile to an algorithm that is designed to quantify and render simple that which is complex. Using technology to massify or intensify surveillance without questioning it in the first place is so dangerous. Many technologies, including AI applications, rely on behavioral engineering, tracing their origin to B.F. Skinner. The bedrock of Skinnerian approaches appears to be that human behavior can, and should, be controlled (Watters, 2025). This raises urgent ethical questions about who gets to decide which behaviours are desirable, and how such control mechanisms might reinforce power structures under the guise of personalization. While we acknowledge that such power structures and philosophical approaches to education existed before the advent of AI, and its application in classroom surveillance, we question affordance-based view of technology in the classroom and see it as uncritically amplifying existing, unexamined, structures. A more apt approach may be an *entangled view* of technology adoption (cf. Fawns, 2022).

So-called *personalization* imposed by a black box algorithm is a diminishment of learner and teacher agency, a restriction of pathways towards a future that are not built on statistics about the past. Students also find it worrisome and distracting that they are being watched (Barrett, 2022). Technological errors not only interfere with the flow of class (Barrett, 2022), but even when the surveillance technology works unobtrusively, data is subject to misuse, either by intentional data breaches by malevolent actors (e.g., Kelley, 2021) or when the company decides to monetize their collected student (or employee) data in other ways and without the consent of the surveilled. Beyond the unnerving emotional impact, there is a real danger of self-silencing, a kind of 'obey in advance' chilling effect that this has on actual actions and behaviours (Citron, 2024), and by extension human agency. Again, the theme of personalized and adaptive learning is not new. It's been a theme since computers were introduced into learning, and with successive generations of technologies employed to address it we've arrived today at attempts to crack this nut using AI. It's not that personalized learning is bad per se, however technological approaches over the decades have relied on a type of big data mythology (boyd & Crawford, 2012) as a solution rather than alternative, more humanized, more relational approaches.

Related to student surveillance, the surveillance tools that educators deploy against students are the sort of "BossWare" tools that can be turned against the educators. Similar data exhaust can be collected for instructional faculty and university staff, from one's digital footprints in the LMS, to their 'availability' on platforms such as Zoom, Teams, and Slack, and content that is automatically transcribed and summarized, without human interventions, from various meetings that employees attend during the usual run of business. The same sort of algorithms that can track 'learner attention' can be turned back to reflect on staff and faculty attitudes and knowledge; and the results are similar: If knowledge workers, students and faculty, are encouraged to try something new, even if there's a chance that it won't work as expected, they will try it and they will evaluate the results, and adapt accordingly. If they are penalized for experimentations that lead to sub-par results in their work evaluation, they won't even attempt to be innovative, they will repeat what is currently deemed as being sufficient to pass their work evaluations. These perverse incentives are a good example of Goodhart's Law: When a measure becomes a target, it ceases to be a good measure.

Relating to the aforementioned chilling effect, AI surveillance in academic contexts leads to a diminishment of learner and instructor agency and autonomy. Agency in the classroom is a multifaceted problem, but only the issue of dealing with the AI 'menace,' which is creating an unruly learning space, has been taking up discoursal space. This is a natural extension to what has been our "catch me, if you can" attitudes and approaches to academic honesty. In deploying algorithmic detectors on student submissions in the classroom, which don't work, we are treating the symptom and not the cause. Instead of using the opportunity to 'stand on the shoulders of giants' and trace our line of thought, and give credit to, those who walked the path before us, we - as educators - are succumbing to the forces that we warn our students not to succumb to: the easy answer that might be provided by an AI chatbot. An uncritical acceptance and use of such technologies is already changing learner behaviors as they write their paper submissions. Learners, in order to protect themselves from spurious claims of academic dishonesty, write on platforms that can track their progress and develop a digital paper trail. They avoid using language that may *hint* at 'AI-enabled academic dishonesty' even though those words might better express their ideas. This is a downstream example of inappropriate usage, and understanding of, AI surveillance tech.

Examples from further upstream in the learning process may be looming. Another technology, intelligent textbooks (cf. Sosnovsky et al., 2025) has been adapting as new technologies and approaches become available. Tracing its origins to common ancestors with adaptive learning, the evolution of intelligent textbooks has provided the capacity to collect and mine the interaction data of its users. While this may yield interesting insights as to what stands out to learners, surveilling learners as they read, annotate, and process new information may hinder their development as learners if educator and institutional practices prescribe how one should be interacting with learning resources, such as intelligent textbooks, and thus short circuit learner development. The learner may exhibit surface behaviors that the instructor is looking for, but deeper practices and understanding may never develop.

Still, in cases of total prohibition of such technology in the classroom, the pendulum may have also swung too far in the other direction, which also denies learners their agency as autonomous beings in our classrooms. It's important to recognize that AI tools are not an either/or, a use/don't-use, dichotomy. More than two lanes exist in examining technologies used in our classrooms (Curtis, 2025). Smart use of

AI tools entails a critical approach from end users, be they faculty or students. We cannot predict if these tools will have staying power, or whether they might influence our learners in the long term. Technologies that once seemed like they'd be relevant in the long term (e.g., standalone MP3 players such as Apple's iPod or Microsoft's Zune), are all but forgotten by the younger generations and considered *retro*. What does remain relevant, however, are the skills that learners develop by learning to engage in critical, and entangled, ways with new technologies.

Questions we must ask ourselves include whether or not efficiency gains are offset by any losses in the quality of the learning experience, as well as asking ourselves what are the connections between members of a learning community? Much of the discourse around the learning gains of AI treat learning as a purely cognitive act, without taking account of other important elements of learning. For example, when we use AI chatbots instead of human tutors, we may get a quicker response, but we lose the opportunity to build connections with human mentors who can help us beyond answering our immediate questions; we also lose an opportunity for social learning amongst learners themselves, the opportunity to build relationships and cultural and social capital that benefit us beyond the learning moment.

A lack of agency, an unease with surveillance, and the façade of big data objectivity also lead to an erosion of trust amongst members of a learning community. Trust is a multidimensional construct that has cognitive, emotional, and behavioral components (Mishra, 1996). Tshannen-Moran (1999, as cited in Luo, 2024) defines trust in the classroom contexts as "an individual's or group's willingness to be vulnerable to another party based on the confidence that the latter party is benevolent, reliable, competent, honest, and open." When complex human behaviors are algorithmically reduced, we see conformity to those standards and measurements. Learner agency is diminished, and trust in faculty expertise evaporates. When students are accused of wrongdoing, or of exhibiting unconventional behavior, the lack of concrete proof of academic dishonesty "leaves the door open for teacher bias to creep in" (Fowler, 2023), this makes it easier for students to be falsely accused of using AI tools (cf. Sokol, 2023), which makes for learning environments that treat students as potential wrongdoers. Just as with plagiarism detectors, algorithmic proctoring is also ineffective, and virtual proctoring is essentially a placebo for the purposes of academic integrity (Bergmans et al., 2021), but the surveillance harms it causes are real and felt. All of this erodes trust between and among learning community members.

Another area of concern regards the afterlife of our data exhausts. When institutions subscribe to various AI tools, there's little indication as to what happens to that data exhaust. Are chatlogs private when personalized learning chatbots are employed in the classrooms, or is there a danger of these past chatbot-based activities being used for purposes other than the original purpose? In fact, we see these perverse economic incentives at work: Companies have used the data exhaust from one tool for purposes other than the initially stated purposes when economic incentives were sufficient enough to use that data to launch a new tool or service. Another potential harm is that anonymized data can be re-identified rather easily (Barrett, 2022), which is a serious breach of trust. Trust is paramount in a learning environment because learning is *relational*, and that *requires* trust. Furthermore, we need to consider in what ways this kind of data collection and surveillance is placing teachers into policing roles that they never signed up for.

Finally, there is a distorted image presented of what academic integrity and teaching are. Academic surveillance opens the door by enticing users through calls of optimization and efficiency, or outright drudgery elimination. However, along with the so-called drudgery, such as taking attendance, the human-to-human element is eliminated. When you can have an adaptive and personalized AI agent that you can connect with at any time, why wait for the time that you'll meet members of your learning community? Simply regurgitating the 'right' answer becomes the goal rather than understanding why and how something works and being able to derive the answer. This has a beeline to a rationale that if your submission doesn't trigger the 'AI detector' or 'plagiarism detector,' it's fine. What's lost in this mental calculus are the surface-level responses and the kinds of understanding that it might engender. This is not a bug, rather, it is a feature. After all, big data models are trained on massive amounts of data, but their human creators neither care where those data came from nor ask the machine to cite its work. AI appropriates without consent (cf. Hays, 2024; Knibbs, 2025). We must ask ourselves how these technologies are emphasizing what can be observed or counted versus what is truly valuable and meaningful about learning. Algorithmic surveillance, and the constraints it forces upon those being surveilled, gives an *illusion* of "knowing" more about learners when it is only about quantifying learners' observable analog and digital behaviors, which tell us very little about how they are thinking or feeling.

Idea origination, how we know what we know, and how we know it's valid, a core idea in teaching and learning is merely an afterthought, at best, with some of the technologies that are presenting themselves to us. As such, AI surveillance may be thought of not as a tool to improve teaching but rather as an instantiation of managerialism. Managerialism in academic settings over the past twenty years has promoted pathways toward 'more efficient' and 'massive' teaching, but also teaching that is more 'personal' and 'adaptive,' concepts that don't square with one another. That kind of dangerous discourse leads to this kind of problematic attitude towards AI. This discourse misrepresents and undermines what teaching and learning are and dismisses the most important dimensions of teaching and learning while foregrounding the parts AI can *supposedly* do. In this context, agency is appropriated by tech oligarchs to appear as if it is something their extractive tools support rather than reduce.

"A computer can never be held accountable, therefore a computer must never make a management decision." - Often attributed to a 1979 IBM Presentation

CONCLUSION

The consolidation of power over educational systems that has been achieved by corporate digital platforms and their attendant managerial reductionism puts agency in education at risk. In this chapter, we have examined some of the facets that emerge as ethical issues with the use of classroom surveillance, and more specifically with both active and passive "AI-powered" surveillance of learning environments. Background AI surveillance is a powerful yet often invisible force in higher education, though not altogether in the "backstage of reality" (Wellner & Levin, 2024, p. 664). They shape student and lecturer experiences in ways that challenge autonomy, ethics, and educational relationships. While AI tools like ChatGPT can enhance learning and teaching, their unseen surveillance mechanisms risk reducing students and lecturers to algorithmic subjects rather than independent thinkers. If universities prioritize efficiency over ethical AI governance, they risk creating an education system dictated by invisible AI forces rather than human-driven inquiry.

Hype is a powerful thing in the business and media sectors. Technologies, such as AI, that are promoted as innovative are imbued with a grand promise of inevitable change and accumulating capital. As highlighted in the sections above, there are no clear and ethical firewalls between products. If a company decides that it has enough user data from its educational chatbot to connect to LinkedIn recruiter listings, will it be tempted to pursue that revenue-generating lead? *Privacy be damned.* It is our duty to resist hype and the snake-oil promises. As part of this resistance, we, as educators, need to talk openly and overtly about the power structures we are enclosed by, with digital systems, as we are trying to model in this chapter. Both as individuals and as groups of responsible and responsive educators, we build the muscle of agency and autonomy even by just insisting on naming the algorithmic and managerial 'ghosts of the machine' whose power to turn us into powerless ghosts is reinforced when we cannot see or address them.

To reclaim agency and autonomy, institutions must adopt transparent, equitable, and human-centered AI policies that empower students and lecturers to engage critically with technology rather than be controlled by it. The goal should not be to replace human judgment with AI surveillance but to use AI as a tool that amplifies rather than restricts human potential in education. To do so would mean a 'foreshadowing' of the 'ghostly algorithmic gaze.' The focus must shift from an uncritical acceptance of technological hype and classroom policing using automated surveillance and control toward a focus that empowers human agency, fostering relational pedagogies, and ensuring that technology serves to amplify, rather than restrict, human potential in education.

Finally, while this chapter mainly focuses on algorithmic surveillance in, and adjacent to, learning environment settings, we'd be remiss if we did not highlight surveillance that is enacted upon our learners both on-campus and off-campus (cf. Taft, 2025). Surveillance of learners in broader society, as we've seen in early 2025 in the USA, reverberates onto school campuses and creates a chilling effect. These power structures need to be fought both inside and outside of the walls of the academy.

REFERENCES

Abegglen, S., Burns, T., & Sinfield, S. (2025, March 31). Critical pedagogy and digital liberation: A Freirean debate for SoTL. *Open Scholarship of Teaching and Learning Journal.*, *4*(1). Advance online publication. DOI: 10.56230/osotl.116

Adams, C., Pente, P., Lemermeyer, G., & Rockwell, G. (2023). Ethical principles for artificial intelligence in K-12 education. *Computers and Education: Artificial Intelligence*, *4*, 100131. DOI: 10.1016/j.caeai.2023.100131

Ahila, A., Poonguzhali, A., Deepa, M., Arthy, A., & Saravanakumar, R. (2024, August). Artificial Intelligence For Realtime Face Recognition Attendance Using College Classrooms and Buses. In *2024 International Conference on Electrical Electronics and Computing Technologies (ICEECT)* (Vol. 1, pp. 1-6). IEEE. DOI: 10.1109/ICEECT61758.2024.10738995

Althusser, L. (2012). *Ideology and ideological state apparatuses: Notes towards an investigation*. Critical Quest.

Anggraeni, D., Wardani, D. K., & Noviani, L. (2024). Self-Regulated Learning, Grit, and Learning Motivation in Developing Learning Achievement: A Review. *Formosa Journal of Multidisciplinary Research*, *3*(1), 135–148. DOI: 10.55927/fjmr.v3i1.7908

Aristotle, . (1999). *Nicomachean ethics* (Irwin, T., Ed.; 2nd ed.). Hackett Pub. Co.

Bakhtin, M. (1989). Discourse in the novel. In Richter, D. (Ed.), *The critical tradition: Classic texts and contemporary trends* (pp. 781–791). St. Martin's Press. (Original work published 1934)

Bala, N. (2020). The Danger of Facial Recognition in Our Children's Classrooms. *Duke Law & Technology Review, 18*, 249-267. https://scholarship.law.duke.edu/dltr/vol18/iss1/19/

Bali, M. (2025, January). Five questions to ask before adopting a new technology. *London School of Economics Higher Education Blog*. https://blogs.lse.ac.uk/highereducation/2025/01/08/five-questions-to-ask-before-adopting-a-new-technology/

Bates, A. W. (2019). *Teaching in a digital age: Guidelines for designing teaching and learning* (2nd Ed.). BCcampus. https://pressbooks.bccampus.ca/teachinginadigitalagev2/

Bergmans, L., Bouali, N., Luttikhuis, M., & Rensink, A. (2021). On the efficacy of online proctoring using proctorio. In 13th *International Conference on Computer Supported Education, CSEDU 2021* (pp. 279-290). Scitepress. DOI: 10.5220/0010399602790290

Bhullar, P. S., Joshi, M., & Chugh, R. (2024). ChatGPT in higher education-a synthesis of the literature and a future research agenda. *Education and Information Technologies, 29*(16), 21501–21522. DOI: 10.1007/s10639-024-12723-x

Bourdieu, P. (1977). *Outline of a theory of practice*. Cambridge University Press. DOI: 10.1017/CBO9780511812507

Bourdieu, P., & Passeron, J.-C. (1977). Reproduction in education, society and culture. *Sage (Atlanta, Ga.).*

Bowles, S., & Gintis, S. (1975). The problem with human capital theory: A Marxian critique. *The American Economic Review, 65*(2), 74–82. https://www.jstor.org/stable/1818836

Boyd, D. & Crawford, K. (2012) Critical Questions for Big Data. *Information, Communication & Society, 15*(5), 662–679. https://doi.org/10.1080/1369118X.2012.678878

Black, C. (n.d.). *Children, learning, and the 'evaluative gaze' of school: How we watched pot loses the desire to boil.* Carol Black. https://carolblack.org/the-gaze

Blundell, D., & Abegglen, S. (2017). European ideals, schooling and modern childhood: Deploying the template child. In Isaacs, S. (Ed.), *European social problems* (pp. 131–148). Routledge. DOI: 10.4324/9781315687513-8

Bozkurt, A. (2024). GenAI et al.: Cocreation, Authorship, Ownership, Academic Ethics and Integrity in a Time of Generative AI. *Open Praxis, 16*(1), 1–10. DOI: 10.55982/openpraxis.16.1.654

Bozkurt, A., Xiao, J., Farrow, R., Bai, J. Y., Nerantzi, C., Moore, S., & Asino, T. I. (Eds.). (2024). The manifesto for teaching and learning in a time of generative AI: A critical collective stance to better navigate the future. *Open Praxis, 16*(4), 487-513.

Burns, T., Sinfield, S., & Abegglen, S. (2023). Postdigital academic writing. In Jandrić, P. (Ed.), *Encyclopedia of postdigital science and education*. Springer., DOI: 10.1007/978-3-031-35469-4_27-1

Calvo, R., Peters, D., & Ryan, R. (2018). Autonomy in AI systems. Input paper for the Horizon Scanning Project "*The effective and ethical development of artificial intelligence: An opportunity to improve our wellbeing*" on behalf of the Australian Council of Learned Academies. https://acola.org/wp-content/uploads/2019/07/acola-ai-input-paper_human-autonomy-in-ai-systems_calvo-peters-ryan.pdf

Charara, S. (2025, February, 26). Your Boss Wants You Back in the Office. This Surveillance Tech Could Be Waiting for You. *WIRED*. https://www.wired.com/story/your-boss-wants-you-back-in-the-office-this-surveillance-tech-could-be-waiting-for-you

Citron, D. K. (2024). The surveilled student. *Stanford Law Review*, *76*(7), 1439–1472.

Clarke, R. (1988). Information technology and dataveillance. *Communications of the ACM*, *31*(5), 498–512. DOI: 10.1145/42411.42413

Cormier, D. (2011, November 05). *Rhizomatic learning - why we teach?* Dave Cormier. https://davecormier.com/edblog/2011/11/05/rhizomatic-learning-why-learn/

Crompton, H., Burke, D., Nickel, C., & Chigona, A. (2024). The SETI framework and technology integration in the digital age. *Asian Journal of Distance Education*, *19*, 167–176. https://www.asianjde.com/ojs/index.php/AsianJDE/article/view/771

Curtis, G. J. (2025). The two-lane road to hell is paved with good intentions: Why an all-or-none approach to generative AI, integrity, and assessment is insupportable. *Higher Education Research & Development*, •••, 1–8. DOI: 10.1080/07294360.2025.2476516

Daniel, T. (2024). Foreword. In B. Buyserie and T. N. Thurston (Eds.), *Teaching and generative AI*. https://uen.pressbooks.pub/teachingandgenerativeai/front-matter/forweword/

Dawson, P., Bearman, M., Dollinger, M., & Boud, D. (2024). Validity matters more than cheating. *Assessment & Evaluation in Higher Education*, *49*(7), 1–12. DOI: 10.1080/02602938.2024.2386662

Deci, E., La Guardia, J., Moller, A., Scheiner, M., & Ryan, R. (2006). On the benefits of giving as well as receiving autonomy support: Mutuality in close friendships. *Personality and Social Psychology Bulletin*, *32*(3), 313–327. DOI: 10.1177/0146167205282148 PMID: 16455859

Deleuze, G., & Guattari, F. (1987). *A thousand plateaus: Capitalism and schizophrenia*. University of Minnesota Press.

Descartes, R. (1978). *The philosophical works of Descartes*. 1 (Repr). Univ. Press.

Dunbar-Morris, H., Nerantzi, C., Sharp, L., & Sidiropoulou, M. (2023). (In) dependent learning as explored in a cross-institutional collaborative project studying the perceptions of learning of ethnically diverse students. In Fitzgerald, R., Huijser, H., Altena, S., & Armellini, A. (Eds.), *Addressing the 'challenging' elements of learning at a distance* (Special Edition). Distance Education., DOI: 10.1080/01587919.2023.2198492

Eaton, L. (2024). *Syllabi / Policies for AI Generative Tools* https://docs.google.com/document/d/1RMVwzjc1o0Mi8Blw_-JUTcXv02b2WRH86vw7mi16W3U/edit#heading=h.1cykjn2vg2wx

Entwistle, N., McCune, V., & Walker, P. (2001). Conceptions, styles and approaches within higher education: analytic abstractions and everyday experience. In Sternberg, R. J., & Zhang, L.-F. (Eds.), *Perspectives on Thinking, Learning and Cognitive Styles*. Lawrence Erlbaum.

Fawns, T. (2022). An entangled pedagogy: Looking beyond the pedagogy—technology dichotomy. *Postdigital Science and Education*, *4*(3), 711–728. DOI: 10.1007/s42438-022-00302-7 PMID: 40477872

Fenn, J. (2022). *The first hype cycle: An origin story*. LinkedIn Pulse. https://www.linkedin.com/pulse/first-hype-cycle-origin-story-jackie-fenn/

Foucault, M. (1977). *Discipline and punish: The birth of the prison*. Pantheon Books.

Fowler, A. G. (2023, April 3). We tested a new ChatGPT-detector for teachers. It flagged an innocent student. *The Washington Post*. https://www.washingtonpost.com/technology/2023/04/01/chatgpt-cheating-detection-turnitin/

Freire, P. (1996). *Letters to Cristina: Reflections on my life and work*. Routledge.

Gagné, M. (2003a). The role of autonomy support and autonomy orientation in prosocial behavior engagement. *Motivation and Emotion*, *27*(3), 199–223. DOI: 10.1023/A:1025007614869

Gagné, M. (2003b). Autonomy support and need satisfaction in the motivation and well-being of gymnasts. *Journal of Applied Sport Psychology*, *15*(4), 372–390. DOI: 10.1080/714044203

Gale, K., & Bowstead, H. (2013). Deleuze and collaborative writing as a method of inquiry. *Journal of Learning Development in Higher Education*, *6*(6), 1–15. https://journal.aldinhe.ac.uk/index.php/jldhe/article/view/222/147. DOI: 10.47408/jldhe.v0i6.222

Gambo, I., Abegunde, F. J., Gambo, O., Ogundokun, R. O., Babatunde, A. N., & Lee, C. C. (2024). GRAD-AI: An automated grading tool for code assessment and feedback in programming course. *Education and Information Technologies*, •••, 1–41. DOI: 10.1007/s10639-024-13218-5

Gao, Z., Huang, Y., Zheng, L., Li, X., Lu, H., Zhang, J., Zhao, Q., Diao, W., Fang, Q., & Fang, J. (2021). A student attendance management method based on crowdsensing in classroom environment. *IEEE Access : Practical Innovations, Open Solutions*, *9*, 31481–31492. DOI: 10.1109/ACCESS.2021.3060256

Gorichanaz, T. (2023). Accused: How students respond to allegations of using ChatGPT on assessments, Learning. *Research and Practice*, *9*(2), 183–196. DOI: 10.1080/23735082.2023.2254787

Hamon, K., Hogue, R. J., Honeychurch, S., Johnson, S., Koutropoulos, A., Ensor, S., . . . Bali, M. (2015). Writing the unreadable untext: A collaborative autoethnography of #rhizo14. *Hybrid Pedagogy*. https://hybridpedagogy.org/writing-the-unreadable-untext/

Hays, L. (2024, June 21). OpenAI and Anthropic are ignoring an established rule that prevents bots scraping online content. *Business Insider*. https://www.businessinsider.com/openai-anthropic-ai-ignore-rule-scraping-web-contect-robotstxt

hooks, b. (1994) *Teaching to transgress, Education as the practice of freedom*. Oxon: Routledge.

Hua, S., Jin, S., & Jiang, S. (2023). The limitations and ethical considerations of ChatGPT. *Data Intelligence*, *6*(1), 201–329. DOI: 10.1162/dint_a_00243

Ihde, D. (1990). *Technology and the lifeworld: From garden to earth*. Indiana University Press. DOI: 10.2979/3108.0

Jandrić, P., Luke, T. W., Sturm, S., McLaren, P., Jackson, L., MacKenzie, A., Tesar, M., Stewart, G. T., Roberts, P., Abegglen, S., Burns, T., Sinfield, S., Hayes, S., Jaldemark, J., Peters, M. A., Sinclair, C., & Gibbons, A. (2023). Collective writing: The continuous struggle for meaning-making. In Jandrić, P., MacKenzie, A., & Knox, J. (Eds.), *Postdigital research. Postdigital science and education* (pp. 249–293). Springer., DOI: 10.1007/978-3-031-35469-4

Kelley, J. (2021, June 22). A Long Overdue Reckoning For Online Proctoring Companies May Finally Be Here. *Electronic Frontier Foundation*. https://www.eff.org/deeplinks/2021/06/long-overdue-reckoning-online-proctoring-companies-may-finally-be-here

Kimmons, R., Graham, C. R., & West, R. E. (2020). The PICRAT model for technology integration in teacher preparation. *Contemporary Issues in Technology & Teacher Education, 20*(1), 176–198.

Knibbs, K. (2025, January 9) Meta Secretly Trained Its AI on a Notorious Piracy Database, Unredacted court documents reveal. *WIRED.* https://www.wired.com/story/new-documents-unredacted-meta-copyright-ai-lawsuit/

Kuhn, C., Khoo, S. M., Czerniewicz, L., Warren, L., Bute, S., Crean, A., Abegglen, S., Burns, T., Sinfield, S., Jandrić, P., Knox, J., & MacKenzie, A. (2023). Understanding digital inequality: A theoretical kaleidoscope. In Jandrić, P., Knox, J., & MacKenzie, A. (Eds.), *Constructing postdigital research: Method and emancipation* (pp. 333–373). Springer., DOI: 10.1007/978-3-031-35411-3_17

Kwet, M., & Prinsloo, P. (2020). The 'smart' classroom: A new frontier in the age of the smart university. *Teaching in Higher Education, 25*(4), 510–526. DOI: 10.1080/13562517.2020.1734922

Lee, H. P. H., Sarkar, A., Tankelevitch, L., Drosos, I., Rintel, S., Banks, R., & Wilson, N. (2025). The Impact of Generative AI on Critical Thinking: Self-Reported Reductions in Cognitive Effort and Confidence Effects From a Survey of Knowledge Workers. *CHI, 2025*, 1–22. Advance online publication. DOI: 10.1145/3706598.3713778

Liu, X., & Liu, C. (2024, September). The application of artificial intelligence to classroom attendance. In *Proceedings of the International Conference on Image Processing, Machine Learning and Pattern Recognition* (pp. 583-590). https://doi.org/DOI: 10.1145/3700906.3701000

Luck, M. (2012). Surveillance in the virtual classroom. In Khosrow-Pour, M. (Ed.), *Virtual Learning Environments: Concepts, Methodologies, Tools and Applications* (pp. 1676–1685). IGI Global Scientific Publishing. DOI: 10.4018/978-1-4666-0011-9.ch808

Luo (Jess), J. (. (2024). How does GenAI affect trust in teacher-student relationships? Insights from students' assessment experiences. *Teaching in Higher Education*, •••, 1–16. DOI: 10.1080/13562517.2024.2341005

Madaio, M., Blodgett, S. L., Mayfield, E., & Dixon-Román, E. (2022). Beyond "fairness": Structural (in) justice lenses on ai for education. In Holmes, W., & Porayska-Pomsta, K. (Eds.), *The ethics of artificial intelligence in education* (pp. 203–239). Routledge. DOI: 10.4324/9780429329067-11

Margolis, E. (2001). The Hidden Curriculum in Higher Education *1st Edition*, Kindle Edition. NY: Routledge.

Mazzei, L. A., & McCoy, K. (2010). Thinking with Deleuze in qualitative research. *International Journal of Qualitative Studies in Education : QSE, 23*(5), 503–509. DOI: 10.1080/09518398.2010.500634

McCartney, S. (1999). *ENIAC: The triumphs and tragedies of the world's first computer*. Walker & Company.

Mills, A., & Bali, M. (2024). Don't trust AI to cite its sources. In A. Mills (Ed.), *How arguments work: A guide to writing*. https://human.libretexts.org/Bookshelves/Composition/Advanced_Composition/How_Arguments_Work_-_A_Guide_to_Writing_and_Analyzing_Texts_in_College_(Mills)/16%3A_Artificial_Intelligence_and_College_Writing_(Under_Construction)/Don't_Trust_AI_to_Cite_Its_Sources

Mishra, A. K. (1996). Organizational responses to crisis: The centrality of trust. In Kramer, R. & Tyler, T. (Eds.), *Trust in Organizations*. Sage

Mishra, P., & Koehler, M. J. (2006). Technological pedagogical content knowledge: A framework for teacher knowledge. *Teachers College Record, 108*(6), 1017–1054. DOI: 10.1111/j.1467-9620.2006.00684.x

Moore, K. (2025, February 28). UAlbany Professor Develops AI to Give Teachers Feedback. *Government Technology*. https://www.govtech.com/education/k-12/ualbany-professor-develops-ai-to-give-teachers-feedback

Morozov, E. (2013). *To save everything, click here: The folly of technological solutionism*. Public Affairs.

Mphahlele, A., & McKenna, S. (2019). The use of turnitin in the higher education sector: Decoding the myth. *Assessment & Evaluation in Higher Education, 44*(7), 1079–1089. DOI: 10.1080/02602938.2019.1573971

Munn, L. (2024). Expansive and Invasive: Mapping the "Bossware" Used to Monitor Workers. *Surveillance & Society, 22*(2), 104–119. DOI: 10.24908/ss.v22i2.16179

Musk, E. [@elonmusk] (2025, February 15) *That is already possible QT @PalmerLuckey What will happen in broader academia when clear scientific consensus is that AI-assisted education delivers better outcomes than 3.8M teachers currently do?* Twitter/X. https://x.com/elonmusk/status/1890905182516461608?lang=en

Nerantzi, C., Sidiropoulou, M. P., Dunbar-Morris, H., Sharp, L., Farrell-Savage, K., Heard-Lauréote, K., Speight, S., Nawaz, R., & Ali, M. (2023) There are other fish in the sea: Open-up and connect. In: M. Harrison, I. DeVries, T. Morgan, & M. Paskevicious (Eds.), *Re-think learning design. Critical learning design and the untextbook*. https://rethinkld.trubox.ca/chapter/activation-there-are-other-fish-in-the-sea-open-up-and-connect/

Noble, D. (2003). Digital diploma mills. In Johnson, B., Kavanagh, P., & Mattson, K. (Eds.), *Steal this university: The Rise of the Corporate University and the Academic Labor Movement* (pp. 39–54). Routledge.

North, M. (2023). Generative AI has disrupted education. Here's how it can be used for good – *UNESCO. World Economic Forum.* https://www.weforum.org/stories/2023/09/generative-ai-education-unesco/

'Ofakihevahanoa Fotu, B. (2024). Rude Reflections: Current AI Acts as a Mirror of Our Flawed Society. In B. Buyserie & T. N. Thurston (Eds.), *Teaching and generative AI.* https://uen.pressbooks.pub/teachingandgenerativeai/chapter/rude-reflections-current-ai-acts-as-a-mirror-of-our-flawed-society/

Pabba, C., & Kumar, P. (2022). An intelligent system for monitoring students' engagement in large classroom teaching through facial expression recognition. *Expert Systems: International Journal of Knowledge Engineering and Neural Networks, 39*(1), e12839. Advance online publication. DOI: 10.1111/exsy.12839

Plato, . (2006). *Phaedrus*. Penguin Books.

Plato, . (2019). *Republic* (Waterfield, R., Ed.). Oxford University Press., DOI: 10.1093/actrade/9780199535767.book.1

Puentedura, R. (2015, October 14). SAMR: A brief introduction. *Ruben Puentedura's Blog*. https://hippasus.com/blog/archives/227

Quinlan, K. M. (2019). What triggers students' interest during higher education lectures? personal and situational variables associated with situational interest. *Studies in Higher Education, 44*(10), 1781–1792. DOI: 10.1080/03075079.2019.1665325

Ross, J., & Collier, A. (2016). 2 Complexity, Mess, and Not-Yetness Teaching Online with Emerging Technologies. In Veletsianos, G. (Ed.), *Emergence and Innovation in Digital Learning: Foundations and Applications* (pp. 17–34). Athabasca University Press., DOI: 10.15215/aupress/9781771991490.004

Ryle, G. (1949). *The concept of mind*. Hutchinson's University Library.

Sætra, H. S., & Selinger, E. (2024). Technological Remedies for Social Problems: Defining and Demarcating Techno-Fixes and Techno-Solutionism. *Science and Engineering Ethics, 30*(6), 1–17. DOI: 10.1007/s11948-024-00524-x PMID: 39621170

Säljö, R. (1979). Learning about learning. *Higher Education, 8*(4), 443–451. DOI: 10.1007/BF01680533

Scholes, V. (2016). The ethics of using learning analytics to categorize students on risk. *Educational Technology Research and Development*, *64*(5), 939–955. DOI: 10.1007/s11423-016-9458-1

Selwyn, N., & Cumbo, B. (2024). "We've Tried to Keep the Beast on a Leash": The Domestication of Digital Classroom Surveillance. *Surveillance & Society*, *22*(2), 88–103. DOI: 10.24908/ss.v22i2.15791

Silver, N. (2023, June 5). The future of education – disruption caused by AI and ChatGPT: Artificial Intelligence Series 3/5. *Forbes*. https://www.forbes.com/sites/nicolesilver/2023/06/05/the-future-of-educationdisruption-caused-by-ai-and-chatgpt-artificial-intelligence-series-3-of-5/

Sokol, D. (2023, July 10). It is too easy to falsely accuse a student of using AI: A cautionary tale. *Times Higher Education*. https://www.timeshighereducation.com/blog/it-too-easy-falsely-accuse-student-using-ai-cautionary-tale

Sosnovsky, S., Brusilovsky, P., & Lan, A. (2025). Intelligent Textbooks. *International Journal of Artificial Intelligence in Education*, *35*(3), 1–20. DOI: 10.1007/s40593-024-00451-9

Stewart, B. (2022). The problem of the web: Can we prioritize both participatory practices and privacy? *Contemporary Educational Technology*, *15*(1), ep402. DOI: 10.30935/cedtech/12668

Taft, I. (2025, March 29). How Colleges Are Cracking Down on Students Now. *The New York Times*. https://www.nytimes.com/2025/03/29/us/universities-students-search-warrants.html

Waititi, T. (Director). (2017). *Thor: Ragnarok*. Marvel Studios

Watters, A. (2021/2023). *Teaching machines: The history of personalized learning*. MIT Press. DOI: 10.7551/mitpress/12262.001.0001

Watters, A. (2025, March 10). Agents versus Agency. *Second Breakfast*. https://2ndbreakfast.audreywatters.com/agents-versus-agency/

Wellner, G., & Levin, I. (2024). Ihde meets Papert: Combining postphenomenology and constructionism for a future agenda of philosophy of education in the era of digital technologies. *Learning, Media and Technology*, *49*(4), 656–669. DOI: 10.1080/17439884.2023.2251388

Whitbeck, C. (1996). Ethics as Design: Doing Justice to Moral Problems. *The Hastings Center Report*, *26*(3), 9–16. DOI: 10.2307/3527925 PMID: 8736668

Williamson, B. (2024). Code acts in education: AI in education is a public problem. *National education policy center blog*. https://nepc.colorado.edu/blog/ai-public

Wordsworth, W. (1798). *The tables turned.* Poetry Foundation. https://www.poetryfoundation.org/poems/45557/the-tables-turned

Xiao, J., & Bozkurt, A. (2025). Prophets of progress: How do leading global agencies naturalize enchanted determinism surrounding artificial intelligence for education? *Journal of Applied Learning and Teaching*, *8*(1). Advance online publication. DOI: 10.37074/jalt.2025.8.1.19

Xiao, J., Bozkurt, A., Nichols, M., Pazurek, A., Stracke, C. M., Bai, J. Y., Farrow, R., Mulligan, D., Nerantzi, C., Sharma, R. C., Singh, L., Frumin, I., Swindell, A., Honeychurch, S., Bond, M., Dron, J., Moore, S., Leng, J., Slaghter van Tryon, P. J., & Themeli, C. (2025). Venturing into the unknown: Critical insights into grey areas and pioneering future directions in educational generative AI research. *TechTrends*, *69*(3), 1–16. DOI: 10.1007/s11528-025-01060-6

Zhai, C., Wibowo, S., & Li, L. D. (2024). The effects of over-reliance on AI dialogue systems on students' cognitive abilities: A systematic review. *Smart Learning Environments*, *11*(1), 28. DOI: 10.1186/s40561-024-00316-7

Zhang, X., Ding, Y., Huang, X., Li, W., Long, L., & Ding, S. (2024). Smart classrooms: How sensors and AI are shaping educational paradigms. *Sensors (Basel)*, *24*(17), 5487. Advance online publication. DOI: 10.3390/s24175487 PMID: 39275398

Zuboff, S. (2019). *The Age of Surveillance Capitalism: The Fight for a Human Future at the New Frontier of Power*. Public Affairs.

KEY TERMS AND DEFINITIONS

Agency: Agency is the capacity to make choices and decisions, large or small, about one's practices, responsibilities, and participation within a broader group system such as education or society. Democratic approaches to systems generally allow for exercises of agency by individuals that extend to some level of resistance *to* the system itself, while more authoritarian approaches tend not to.

Artificial Intelligence (AI): The capability of computational systems to perform tasks typically associated with human intelligence, such as reasoning and problem-solving. There are many types of AI that could be used in education.

Autonomy Support: The perception of choice in learning, along with the opportunity to take initiative in one's own learning such that it scaffolds an individual's ability to enact their own agency in decisions

Contested Education: Refers to the ongoing debates, disagreements, and power struggles over the purpose, content, and delivery of education. It encompasses conflicts over curriculum design, access, equity, pedagogical approaches, and the influence of political, cultural, and economic forces on learning systems. These disputes often reflect broader societal tensions and differing visions of knowledge, authority, and the role of education in shaping individuals and societies.

Ethics as Design: A reframing of ethics from an act of analysis to a more applied approach of synthesizing insights into creative problem solving

Hidden Curriculum: Aspects of curriculum design or curriculum-in-practice that are either intentionally or unintentionally not revealed to stakeholders such as students, parents, or teachers. There are many perspectives on the hidden curriculum, some of which perceive it as functional and needed for schooling to work; others are Marxist and more critical, viewing it as "the elements of socialization that take place in school, but are not part of the formal curricular content. These include the norms, values, and belief systems embedded in the curriculum, the school, and classroom life, and imparted to students through daily routines, curricular content, and social relationships" (Margolis, 2001). While some may intentionally create or influence these norms, "because we humans tell ourselves lies and come to believe them, meanings can be hidden from us" (Margolis, 2001). Additionally, "many kinds of socialization are indeed covert, will not work if made visible, and in fact will produce resistance if revealed. Here we are thinking of intentionally produced forms of subordination, discrimination, and hegemony that benefit some at the expense of others" (Margolis, 2001). While some, building on Bourdieu's theory of cultural and social reproduction, see the hidden curriculum as just how societal hierarchies are reproduced in school, others believe there is space for resistance and that teachers and students are not passive recipients but potentially active players in their own socialization (Margolis, 2001).

Phronesis: A term from Ancient Greek Philosophy. In Aristotelian philosophy, phronesis means practical wisdom, or prudence. It is contrasted with intellectual intelligence (*episteme* and *sophia*) by having a practical nature - it is what allows us to turn our moral judgements into action (Aristotle, 1999).

Recentering Relationships: in the context of human-technology relations refers to a shift in focus from viewing technology as merely tools or systems to be optimized, toward prioritizing the relational dynamics between humans and technology. It emphasizes the ways technologies mediate, shape, and are shaped by human values, emotions, identities, and social practices. This perspective calls for a more ethical, empathetic, and reflexive engagement with technology, one that foregrounds care, mutual influence, and the broader sociocultural contexts in which these relationships unfold. Rather than centering efficiency or innovation alone, recentering relationships invites us to design, use, and critique technology with a deep awareness of how it affects and reflects our connections with ourselves, others, and the world.

Relational Pedagogy: A social way of learning in which others play an active and participatory role in learning. Where students and educators come together in a learning community and share experiences, thoughts, ideas, perspectives, and their vulnerabilities to genuinely learn with and from each other. Relational pedagogy and practice there is respect to otherness and acceptance and a recognition that this diversity is enriching and helps individuals and the collective work through challenges, grow and flourish.

Surveillance: The practice of monitoring individuals' behaviour and activities to gather data for the purpose of control or regulation. Our use here is informed by Michel Foucault, who argued that surveillance has become a pervasive force in contemporary society, moving beyond formal institutions like prisons to influence behaviour in a wide range of settings. This is achieved through the "panoptic gaze," where the constant threat of being observed encourages self-discipline and self-regulation.

Technosolutionism: Technosolutionism is derived from Dobbin's *solutionism*, whereby a problem is presumed to have a "right" answer, and rather than investigating and asking the necessary questions to determine the appropriate course of action, a "correct" solution is picked (Morozov, 2013). In technosolutionism, technology often provides that "correct" solution to whatever the problem is, however in a setup where the right questions have not been asked, we risk the proverbial problem of "If all you have is a hammer, everything looks like a nail." This isn't a particularly new concept, other authors have used similar terms going back to the 1960s and it has several terms that mean roughly the same thing, such as "techno-fix," "technology fix," and "techno-solutionism" (Sætra & Selinger, 2024). What these have in common are claims that social problems can be alleviated by turning them into technical engineering issues. In the context of this chapter, flattening the complexity world into binaries so that AI systems can give us the "right" solution.

Transparency for Well-Being: In the practice of AI-human discourse, transparency for well-being refers to the clear communication of how AI systems operate, ensuring trust and ethical use with the intent to safeguard the individual's cognitive, social, and emotional well-being.

Chapter 4
Artificial Intelligence–Supported Education Policies:
New Paradigms in Management

Murat Polat
https://orcid.org/0000-0002-2921-7831
Niğde Ömer Halisdemir University, Turkey

Nurgün Varol
https://orcid.org/0000-0002-6282-1926
Independent Researcher, Turkey

ABSTRACT

The advent of Artificial Intelligence (AI), specifically Generative AI (GenAI), has had a profound impact on various sectors, including education. As AI technologies rapidly evolve, educational management must adapt to these shifts by rethinking traditional policies and embracing new paradigms.This paper explores how AI-supported education policies can transform the governance, decision-making and strategic planning processes in educational institutions. By analysing the implications of AI on education management, the study provides a comprehensive framework for navigating the challenges and opportunities brought about by this technological revolution.

INTRODUCTION

The advent of Artificial Intelligence (AI), particularly Generative AI (GenAI), has precipitated a profound transformation in various sectors, including education.

DOI: 10.4018/979-8-3373-7569-4.ch004

As these technologies rapidly evolve, the field of educational management must adapt by rethinking traditional policies and embracing innovative paradigms. AI technologies, including machine learning, intelligent tutoring systems, and personalised learning environments, are transforming educational practices, enabling tailored and efficient learning experiences (Chen et al., 2020; Nykonenko, 2023; Tapalova et al., 2022). These advancements enable the customisation of curriculum and content to meet individual student needs, thereby improving engagement and learning outcomes (Chen et al., 2020; Tapalova et al., 2022).

Beyond classroom applications, AI's integration into educational governance has introduced transformative approaches to decision-making and strategic planning. By leveraging data-driven insights, educational institutions are able to design personalised education pathways and address systemic challenges, such as resource allocation and equity (Filgueiras, 2023; Paek & Kim, 2021). However, the rapid adoption of AI in education brings significant challenges, including concerns about data privacy, ethical implications, and the potential for increased socioeconomic disparities due to unequal access to technology (Kamalov et al., 2023; Nykonenko, 2023; Popenici & Kerr, 2017).

In this context, the "Manifesto for Teaching and Learning in a Time of Generative AI" by Bozkurt et al. (2024) provides a critical and actionable perspective for educators and policymakers. The manifesto underscores pivotal domains necessitating prompt consideration, including the ethical implementation of GenAI, the potential to amplify biases embedded in AI systems, and the imperative to preserve human agency in educational settings. The authors argue that while GenAI has the potential to personalise learning and streamline administrative processes, its adoption must be grounded in ethical frameworks that prioritise equity and inclusivity. The authors emphasise the necessity of cultivating critical digital literacy among educators and students alike, equipping them with the skills to navigate GenAI-enhanced environments responsibly.

This viewpoint is in alignment with the broader discourse within the field, where the dual emphasis on innovation and ethical considerations is becoming increasingly imperative. For instance, while Chen et al. (2020) and Tapalova et al. (2022) emphasise the role of AI in improving engagement and learning outcomes, Bozkurt et al. (2024) adopt a cautionary stance, examining the long-term implications of GenAI in education systems. This balanced approach contributes to the discourse by advocating for strategies that integrate technological advancements without compromising the foundational values of education.

The role of AI in educational management also extends to the optimisation of institutional operations. These opportunities are manifold, ranging from the automation of administrative tasks to the enhancement of curriculum development and the optimisation of resource allocation. However, it is imperative for educational institutions to adopt adaptive, forward-thinking strategies that are aligned with the evolving technological landscape if they are to fully harness these benefits.

Recent contributions in the field (Dai et al., 2024; Holmes et al., 2023; Kangwa et al., 2025) emphasise the shifting landscape of academic writing due to AI-assisted technologies. The present studies explore the manner in which tools such as generative text models and semantic search platforms are redefining literature synthesis, paraphrasing, and research design—key components of final degree projects. The findings of the study highlight the necessity of both technical proficiency and ethical awareness among students and faculty members.

This chapter examines how AI-supported education policies are transforming governance, decision-making, and strategic planning processes in educational institutions. By analysing the implications of AI on education management, it provides a comprehensive framework for navigating the challenges and opportunities brought about by this technological revolution. A balanced approach that integrates innovation with ethical considerations is recommended for policymakers and educators, to ensure that AI-driven solutions contribute equitably and meaningfully to the future of education. While a comprehensive understanding of the technical capacities of AI tools is imperative, their integration into educational contexts must be meticulously framed within pedagogical and ethical considerations. These include the preservation of academic integrity, the development of critical literacy, and the evolving role of the tutor in guiding students through AI-assisted inquiry. A list of key terms and definitions is appended to the end of the chapter with a view to facilitating conceptual clarity.

AI-DRIVEN DECISION-MAKING IN EDUCATION

The integration of Artificial Intelligence (AI) in educational management has been demonstrated to hold significant transformative potential, facilitating data-driven decision-making through the analysis of extensive datasets. AI empowers educational leaders to discern trends, generate actionable insights, and predict outcomes, thereby enhancing strategic planning, optimising resource allocation, and refining institutional strategies. For instance, AI algorithms can analyse enrolment patterns, forecast attrition rates, and recommend targeted interventions for specific student demographics. These capabilities empower educational leaders to proactively address challenges, enhancing institutional efficiency and effectiveness (Badmus et al., 2024; Murugesan & Kadalmani, 2023).

The capacity of AI to adapt and learn over time is instrumental in ensuring that decision-making processes remain pertinent and efficacious in rapidly evolving educational landscapes (Badmus et al., 2024; Murugesan & Kadalmani, 2023). At the level of the classroom, AI tools provide detailed insights into student performance, identifying areas of difficulty and enabling educators to design targeted interventions. By nurturing a culture of continuous improvement, AI shifts the basis of decision-making from being solely based on historical data to incorporating real-time analytics, thereby rendering educational practices more dynamic and responsive (Murwaningsih et al., 2024; Nguyen et al., 2020). In this context, the examination of the dimensions presented in Figure 1 on AI-supported decision-making in education may be a valuable contribution.

Figure 1. Balancing AI Integration in Education

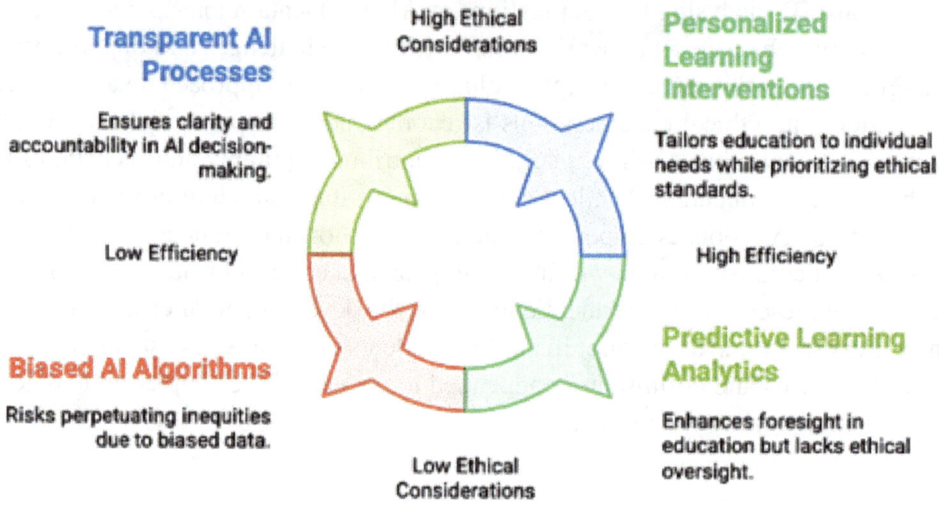

Comparative Analysis of AI Academic Tools

The academic use of AI has evolved beyond the domain of general-purpose tools and now encompasses platforms designed for specific scholarly functions. The purpose of Table 1 is to present a comparative overview of four widely-used academic AI tools: Grammarly, Turnitin AI, Elicit and Scite.

Table 1. Comparative Overview of Four Widely-Used Academic AI Tools

Tool	Primary Function	Benefits	Limitations
Grammarly	Grammar and style aid	Real-time feedback, clarity tools	May overlook academic tone or discipline-specific usage
Turnitin AI	Plagiarism detection	Institutional integration	Black-box algorithms raise interpretability concerns
Elicit	Literature review tool	Semantic paper search, summaries	Limited to indexed databases
Scite	Citation analysis	Contextual citation network	Incomplete coverage of recent publications

The objective of this comparative analysis is to provide clearer guidance for both students and tutors navigating the integration of AI into research workflows.

Enhancing Educational Outcomes with AI

AI-driven systems have been demonstrated to offer substantial benefits in terms of personalising education. By leveraging insights derived from individual student characteristics and historical performance, AI can tailor learning interventions to diverse needs, ultimately enhancing student engagement and academic success (Chen et al., 2020; Maghsudi et al., 2021). Predictive applications, such as forecasting student success metrics like graduation rates, enable institutions to develop targeted interventions that improve outcomes (Nieto et al., 2019; Teng et al., 2022). The integration of various data analysis approaches, facilitated by learning analytics and educational data mining, provides a comprehensive framework for understanding and modelling pedagogical processes (Elfeky et al., 2024; Nguyen et al., 2020).

The utilisation of big data in learning management systems (LMS) has also been demonstrated to have a significant impact on academic success, as data-driven insights allow students to perform better compared to their peers (Elfeky et al., 2024). Reports generated from big data analytics enable educators to effectively address learning gaps and implement personalised interventions (Ling, 2024). Furthermore, predictive learning analytics powered by AI can provide more accurate forecasts of student success compared to traditional methods and enable early interventions for at-risk students (Murwaningsih et al., 2024). *Case Vignette:* A master's student in education utilised Elicit to identify literature on formative assessment strategies. Initially overwhelmed by traditional database interfaces, the student found Elicit's semantic summarisation function helpful in narrowing down relevant studies. Under the supervision of a faculty advisor, the student validated the tool's outputs against conventional sources, leading to a more efficient and critically robust literature review process (Kruiper et al., 2022).

Ethical Challenges and Pedagogical Implications

Notwithstanding the numerous advantages of AI's integration into education, critical ethical challenges are raised. A significant concern pertains to the possibility of algorithms, trained on biased or unrepresentative datasets, perpetuating inequities and resulting in unfair treatment of marginalised groups (Wang, 2020; Viberg et al., 2024). In educational settings where the principles of equity and inclusion are fundamental, such biases have the capacity to undermine efforts to create fair learning environments. The opacity of complex AI models, such as deep learning systems, poses difficulties in explaining and justifying AI-driven decisions, potentially eroding trust and accountability among stakeholders (McConvey et al., 2023).

Another critical issue is the tension between data-driven AI decisions and value-based moral considerations. A significant concern in the realm of AI-assisted research pertains to the absence of transparency, as numerous tools function as "black boxes," providing outputs without disclosing the underlying processes (Longo, et al., 2024). This opacity complicates the validation and academic scrutiny of AI-generated content. In order to address this issue, universities are increasingly requiring students to disclose the tools that were used, to provide a justification for the outputs, and to reflect critically on the reliability and limitations of AI assistance in their projects. These practices support both explainability and accountability in AI-driven research. While AI demonstrates proficiency in analytical tasks, it is deficient in the empathy and ethical reasoning necessary to navigate the nuanced social and moral dimensions of education. Consequently, the integration of AI within educational settings necessitates meticulous oversight to ensure that technological efficiency is balanced with ethical, human-centred decision-making (Wang, 2021; Zeide, 2016).

Furthermore, data governance practices in educational institutions, at both the governmental and institutional levels, give rise to concerns regarding data security, transparency, and the ethical implementation of AI (Selwyn, 2016). As academic institutions adapt to the increasing presence of artificial intelligence in research, institutional policies on academic integrity are evolving rapidly. Bridgeman et al. (2024) stipulates that students must disclose any utilisation of generative AI in their academic submissions. In a similar vein, Stanford University prohibits the use of uncredited AI-generated content in academic work (Stanford, 2023), while Oxford University provides guidelines that encourage critical human oversight when using AI tools in research (University of Oxford, 2024). These policy developments underscore a mounting consensus on the imperative for transparency, ethical boundaries, and institutional responsibility in overseeing AI implementation in final degree projects. For instance, the University of Sydney mandates the disclosure of any AI tools used in assessments, while Stanford University prohibits the uncredited use of generative AI in student submissions. These institutional stances are intended to achieve a balance between academic integrity and the pedagogical benefits of emerging technologies. Tutors play a vital role in interpreting these policies for students and ensuring alignment between educational objectives and responsible AI use (OEI, 2025). These issues have prompted a re-evaluation of the manner in which educators provide assistance to students in the navigation of AI tools.

A Balanced, Human-Centered Approach

In order to address the challenges identified, it is imperative to adopt a human-centred approach to the integration of AI. This approach positions AI as a tool that augments rather than replaces human judgment, ensuring that ethical considerations and human values remain central to decision-making processes (McConvey et al., 2023). By integrating AI's analytical capabilities with the moral reasoning and contextual understanding of educational leaders, institutions can formulate balanced and informed decisions that prioritise fairness and inclusivity.

Educational leaders must implement strategies to reduce biases in AI systems through rigorous evaluation of training data, continuous monitoring of AI outputs, and iterative refinement of algorithms to align with equity and inclusion goals (Wang, 2020; Wang, 2021). Transparent AI processes and clear explanations of AI-driven decisions are also crucial for enhancing trust and accountability among stakeholders.

Real-time analytics and adaptive decision-making frameworks that are powered by machine learning enable educational institutions to respond rapidly to changing conditions (Panian, 2009; Kridel et al., 2015). The integration of deep reinforcement learning models into decision-making structures has been shown to enhance the ability of AI-driven systems to improve resource allocation and institutional efficiency (Gong et al., 2024; van der Schaar, 2014). Furthermore, decentralised reinforcement learning models have the capacity to optimise individual devices in wireless networks, thereby enhancing scalability and autonomy (Shalini et al., 2024).

The integration of AI-driven decision-making systems has the potential to transform educational management by enhancing efficiency, personalisation, and strategic foresight. However, to realise this potential, it is imperative to address ethical considerations and maintain human judgment at the core of decision-making. Adopting a balanced, human-centred approach is therefore paramount for educational leaders, enabling them to harness the transformative power of AI while safeguarding the principles of fairness, equity, and accountability that underpin effective educational leadership. It is therefore the responsibility of educational leaders to ensure that the implementation of AI technologies is both thoughtful and responsible, thus ensuring that these technologies serve to advance the quality and inclusivity of education.

POLICY INNOVATION IN EDUCATION MANAGEMENT

The integration of Artificial Intelligence (AI) into educational management has been shown to drive significant policy innovation. This is due to the fact that it addresses the limitations of conventional frameworks and enables the design of dynamic, adaptive, and data-driven policies. This transformation facilitates real-time adjustments, responsive governance, and streamlined decision-making processes, setting the stage for a more efficient and inclusive approach to education management.

The integration of technology, the development of leadership, and the establishment of a supportive organisational culture are among the key factors that are shaping policy innovation in education management. The rapid advancement of information and communication technologies necessitates their continuous integration into educational practices to meet the evolving needs of 21st-century students (Dwi, 2024). The integration of technology in education management is further compounded by the necessity for continuous professional development, fostering an environment conducive to innovation (Moreira et al., 2024). Policies that promote inclusivity and sustainability play a crucial role in enhancing collaboration within schools (Wang, 2024). To encourage innovation, educational systems must maintain flexibility (Ellison, 2009) and align public policies with innovative practices, ensuring a holistic approach to equitable education (Aidl et al., 2012).

Addressing the Limitations of Traditional Education Policies

Conventional educational policies are frequently characterised by rigid and inflexible structures that are unable to keep pace with technological advancements and the evolving needs of educational systems. These frameworks are often criticised for their failure to accommodate diverse learning needs, resulting in inequitable resource distribution, outdated pedagogical practices, and limited capacity to address systemic issues such as inclusion and equity (Chan, 2023). Moreover, the infrequency with which such policies are updated hinders the ability to respond in a timely manner to emerging challenges, thus underscoring the necessity for innovative solutions that can adapt dynamically to the complexities of modern education.

AI-driven systems have been shown to mitigate these limitations by enabling real-time policy updates and responsive governance. For instance, AI technologies can automate the alignment of institutional policies with regulatory changes, reducing redundancies and streamlining bureaucratic processes. The integration of these capabilities within educational institutions would facilitate a rapid response to emerging trends, thereby optimising resource allocation and fostering a more equitable and effective educational environment.

Conventional education policies also face challenges in addressing technological advancements, systemic inequalities, and barriers to social mobility. Issues such as inadequate policy resources, structural inequalities, economic barriers, and discrimination have been shown to disproportionately impact marginalised groups, including low-income families, immigrants, and ethnic minorities (Guimarães et al., 2024). Furthermore, an exclusive emphasis on individualised solutions, as opposed to systemic reforms, results in an oversight of broader socio-economic structures, thereby constraining the capacity for substantial social mobility (Barker & Hoskins, 2021).

Case Studies of AI-Supported Policy Reforms

The integration of AI into education has had a considerable impact on policy reforms, with a focus on inclusivity, transparency, and operational efficiency. In the United States, academic institutions have adopted governance frameworks that address the ethical and operational complexities of AI deployment. Ghimire and Edwards (2024) emphasise the significance of role-specific governance structures that facilitate streamlined operations while addressing concerns regarding accountability and transparency. Another example involves the use of AI-driven analytics to refine resource allocation policies. By analysing extensive datasets, AI empowers policymakers to align resources more effectively with student needs, promoting equitable outcomes. Spaniol and Rowland (2023) demonstrate how targeted AI applications can address inefficiencies and enhance policy impact, particularly in underserved areas where traditional methods fall short.

The utilisation of AI-driven data analytics and simulations empowers governments to analyse extensive datasets, identify trends, and predict outcomes, thereby facilitating evidence-based policymaking (EIDM). AI assists policymakers in intuitively visualizing data and assessing the impacts of various policy options. Furthermore, AI enhances citizen participation in policymaking by personalising services and fostering democratic engagement (Manias et al., 2023; Upreti et al., 2023). However, it is imperative to address challenges such as algorithmic bias, ethical concerns, and the protection of individual rights to ensure that AI-driven governance remains transparent and accountable (Yar et al., 2024). Explainable AI (XAI) enhances the interpretability of complex models, making data-driven insights accessible and actionable while promoting transparency in policy implementation (Carvalho & Silva, 2021).

Designing Dynamic and Responsive Policies with AI

AI has been demonstrated to play a pivotal role in the development of dynamic and responsive educational policies by leveraging predictive capabilities and real-time data analysis. These tools empower policymakers to proactively anticipate challenges and adjust strategies accordingly. For instance, AI can monitor enrolment trends or student performance metrics, providing actionable insights that inform timely policy adaptations (Chan, 2023). Furthermore, the utilisation of predictive modelling facilitates the execution of scenario simulations, thereby empowering policymakers to appraise the potential consequences of diverse interventions prior to their implementation (Spaniol & Rowland, 2023). Furthermore, AI has been demonstrated to enhance the iterative refinement of policies by collecting and analysing stakeholder feedback, ensuring that policies evolve to remain relevant and effective in educational management (Ghimire & Edwards, 2024).

The field of policy analysis has evolved into a critical discipline within education governance, especially with the rise of evidence-based policymaking (Newman & Mintrom, 2023). The contemporary policy landscape is characterised by escalating intricacy and unpredictability (Haag & Kaupenjohann, 2001; Nilsson et al., 2008), engendering a heightened sense of uncertainty among policymakers. In this context, Kolkman (2020) underscores the use of algorithmic tools by governments to enhance policy design and to explore the potential of artificial intelligence in the realm of public administration.

The integration of AI-driven policy modelling and analytics within governance structures is poised to enhance the quality of governance, by ensuring that it is more informed, responsive, and effective. The capacity of AI to analyse extensive datasets facilitates the identification of patterns, the forecasting of future scenarios, and the development of proactive strategies, thereby facilitating the streamlining of administrative processes and the optimisation of resource allocation (Arora et al., 2024). However, it is important to note that the application of AI in policymaking also raises significant ethical concerns. To address these concerns, robust governance frameworks must be established to ensure that algorithmic bias and transparency issues are addressed (Saxena, 2024).

Ethical Considerations in AI Policy Development

The accelerated integration of AI technologies within educational settings has surpassed the formulation of comprehensive ethical frameworks, giving rise to concerns regarding privacy, bias, and algorithmic transparency. A significant number of institutions have been found to be deficient in the provision of detailed guidelines for the responsible deployment of AI, thus giving rise to a number of ethical questions concerning fairness and accountability (Ghimire & Edwards, 2024). Addressing these concerns necessitates the establishment of interdisciplinary frameworks that integrate ethical, operational, and pedagogical dimensions. In the contemporary higher education landscape, there is an observable trend of universities formalising their governance structures pertaining to artificial intelligence (AI). The primary objective of this governance is to establish a framework that delineates the permitted applications of AI, to ensure transparency, and to safeguard the integrity of academic pursuits. For instance, the University of Melbourne mandates the disclosure of AI usage in student research reports (University of Melbourne, 2025), while Harvard University differentiates between assistive and generative AI usage in graduate-level work (Harvard University, 2025). These governance models illustrate the range of institutional approaches in setting clear boundaries around ethical AI adoption in final degree projects. Similarly, Goosen and Mugumo (2024) propose an AI education policy framework that emphasises responsible AI use, balancing innovation with inclusivity and security. Holmes et al. (2021) emphasise the significance of fostering fairness, accountability, and transparency in AI applications. The establishment of robust ethical guidelines and the fostering of multidisciplinary collaboration by policymakers can ensure that AI-driven policies promote equity and effectiveness in educational practices.

The advent of AI-driven policy innovation signifies a transformative opportunity for education management. By addressing the rigidity of traditional frameworks and leveraging AI's capabilities for predictive analytics, real-time adjustments, and stakeholder engagement, educational institutions can enhance equity, efficiency, and responsiveness. However, the realisation of this potential is predicated on the establishment of comprehensive governance structures, the implementation of robust ethical oversight mechanisms, and the cultivation of AI literacy among policymakers. Through judicious and conscientious implementation, AI has the potential to propel improvements in educational quality and inclusivity, thereby paving the way for a more equitable and innovative future in education. Institutional responses are increasingly incorporating proactive educator training as a key component of their strategy. It is evident that prestigious academic institutions such as the Massachusetts Institute of Technology (MIT) (2025) and the University of Toronto (2025) have initiated the implementation of AI integrity protocols. The primary objective of these protocols is to provide a framework for faculty members, guiding them in the supervision of AI-assisted academic work. These include academic misconduct scenarios involving AI, strategies to teach AI citation ethics, and tools for auditing student submissions. The objective of these efforts is to ensure that AI serves learning purposes rather than circumventing them.

It is evident that several universities have implemented governance frameworks for AI use that mandate disclosure, clarify boundaries for AI-assisted writing, and establish training responsibilities for faculty (Stanford, 2023; University of Oxford, 2025; University of Sydney, 2025). This development signifies a transition towards the adoption of structured and transparent AI in higher education.

LEADERSHIP AND GOVERNANCE

The integration of Artificial Intelligence (AI) into educational leadership and governance is having a profound impact on traditional roles and management practices, creating unprecedented opportunities to address complex challenges. AI has been demonstrated to empower leaders by automating routine administrative tasks, enhancing strategic foresight, and fostering meaningful stakeholder engagement. However, this transformation also necessitates the development of new leadership skills and ethical frameworks to ensure equitable and responsible implementation. The underlying rationale for this phenomenon can be elucidated by referring to Figure 2.

Figure 2. Transforming Educational Leadership with AI

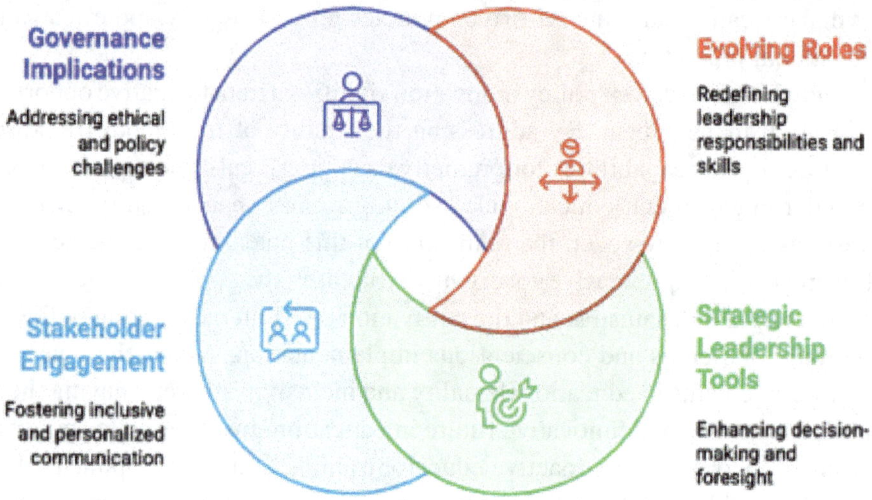

Evolving Roles and Responsibilities of Educational Leaders

The concept of artificial intelligence (AI) has profoundly impacted the responsibilities of educational leaders, equipping them with tools for data-driven, evidence-informed decision-making. Wang (2021) characterises AI as an "extended brain", thereby facilitating leaders' ability to process complex datasets and make strategic decisions with greater efficiency. These tools enable leaders to transition their focus from routine administrative functions, such as scheduling or performance evaluations, to more strategic initiatives like fostering innovation and collaborative cultures. However, the integration of AI also introduces challenges related to data privacy, algorithmic transparency, and ethical dilemmas. It is incumbent upon leaders to strike a balance between the technical advantages of AI and broader social and moral considerations, ensuring that decisions are aligned with institutional values and community needs (Wang, 2020; Wang, 2021). The necessity of human oversight in maintaining accountability and trust in AI-driven decision-making processes is paramount.

AI Tools for Strategic Leadership and Scenario Planning

AI-powered tools have the potential to transform strategic leadership by enhancing scenario planning and predictive decision-making. Predictive analytics, simulation models, and AI-enabled chatbots furnish leaders with actionable insights that optimise resource allocation, anticipate challenges, and design proactive strategies. For instance, as Dai et al. (2024) demonstrate, AI systems can simulate various outcomes of policy decisions, allowing leaders to assess long-term implications and adapt strategies accordingly. This enhanced capacity for foresight not only streamlines decision-making but also strengthens institutional resilience in uncertain educational landscapes. The transformative capacity of AI is evident in the development of forward-thinking leadership training programmes. To this end, educational managers must evolve to equip themselves with the necessary skills to navigate the complexities of AI effectively. By integrating AI literacy and ethical considerations into leadership development, educational institutions can prepare leaders to meet the demands of AI-driven change.

Enhancing Stakeholder Engagement Through AI

The utilisation of artificial intelligence (AI) has been demonstrated to enhance stakeholder engagement by fostering personalised, efficient, and inclusive communication. Technologies such as chatbots and virtual assistants facilitate real-time updates and support tailored interactions with staff members, students, and parents. These technological solutions ensure that all stakeholders are actively involved in decision-making processes and that their voices are reflected in institutional goals (Karakose & Tülübaş, 2024). Furthermore, AI-driven communication platforms enable educational leaders to build participatory environments, where diverse perspectives are integrated into governance frameworks. Such inclusivity strengthens institutional cohesion and aligns policies with the needs of the broader educational community (Karakose & Tülübaş, 2024).

Broader Implications for Leadership and Governance

The influence of AI on governance is twofold. Firstly, it can be used to enhance operational efficiencies. Secondly, it has the potential to transform policy development and implementation. The advent of "automated governance," wherein AI systems assume a pivotal role in decision-making, necessitates the development of novel frameworks that emphasise technological literacy, ethical responsibility, and collaboration (Gulson & Witzenberger, 2020). Du et al. (2023) emphasise the necessity of innovative pedagogical approaches to equip leaders with the necessary skills to navigate these shifts, while also maintaining principles of equity and inclusivity. Furthermore, the integration of AI necessitates a re-evaluation of leadership theories, particularly those concerning distributed leadership models, which emphasise shared responsibility and collaboration. The integration of AI into these models, as posited by Burke (2010), has the potential to engender a more integrated and adaptive governance structure within educational institutions.

The integration of AI with educational leadership and governance presents both transformative opportunities and complex challenges. The enhancement of decision-making processes, the facilitation of strategic foresight, and the cultivation of stakeholder engagement, are all enabled by AI, thereby empowering educational institutions to navigate the intricacies of modern education with greater efficacy. However, it is imperative for educational leaders to adopt transparent policies, develop ethical frameworks, and cultivate new skills to manage AI's integration responsibly. By addressing these challenges thoughtfully, leaders can harness AI's potential to drive innovation while upholding values of equity, accountability, and inclusivity.

ETHICS AND EQUITY IN AI IMPLEMENTATION

The integration of Artificial Intelligence (AI) into educational management brings with it both transformative opportunities and significant ethical challenges. Concerns such as data privacy, algorithmic bias, and equitable access underscore the necessity for meticulous and inclusive implementation strategies. By prioritising fairness, accountability, transparency, and inclusivity, educational institutions can harness the potential of AI while safeguarding the rights and well-being of all stakeholders. This section explores the key ethical concerns and offers strategies for addressing them effectively.

Addressing Algorithmic Bias and Data Privacy

Algorithmic bias and data privacy represent critical challenges in the ethical deployment of AI systems in education. Algorithmic bias occurs when flawed or non-representative datasets produce inequitable outcomes, disproportionately disadvantageous to specific student groups (Mehrabi et al., 2021). For instance, biases embedded in AI-driven decision-making processes can unfairly affect admissions, resource allocation, or performance evaluations. In order to mitigate these risks, it is recommended that educational institutions implement the following measures; *Diverse and Representative Datasets:* The training of AI systems on datasets that reflect diverse demographics is recommended in order to minimise bias and ensure equitable outcomes. *Algorithmic Transparency*: The development of AI systems with explainable decision-making processes is essential to enhance accountability and build trust. *Regular Audits Are Also Recommended:* The establishment of continuous monitoring mechanisms to identify and address biases in AI algorithms is paramount. Additionally, data privacy remains paramount, as AI systems frequently process extensive amounts of sensitive student information. Robust data protection measures, adherence to privacy regulations, and clear policies for data use are necessary to maintain trust and safeguard individual rights (Schiff, 2021).

Policies for Bridging the Digital Divide

The digital divide, defined as a disparity in access to technology, poses a significant barrier to the equitable implementation of AI in education. This discrepancy serves to compound existing socio-economic inequalities, particularly for students hailing from marginalised communities. The following policies have been identified as effective measures to bridge this divide:

- *Equitable Access:* The provision of adequate technological infrastructure, inclusive of hardware, software, and internet connectivity, to all students irrespective of their socioeconomic background, is imperative.
- *Digital Literacy Programs:* These programs should equip educators and students with the skills to effectively utilise digital tools and navigate AI-powered systems.
- *Inclusive AI Design:* The creation of AI tools that are accessible and responsive to the needs of historically underserved groups is also recommended.

These strategies have the potential to ensure that all students benefit from AI-powered educational tools, fostering greater equity and inclusivity in education (Van Deursen & Helsper, 2015).

Building Trust in AI Systems Through Transparency

The acceptance and effectiveness of AI systems in education is contingent upon the establishment of trust among relevant stakeholders. Transparency and explainability are considered to be pivotal in establishing this trust. It is imperative that stakeholders, encompassing educators, students, and parents, possess a comprehensive understanding of the decision-making processes underlying AI systems to ensure effective engagement and confidence in their utilisation (Doshi-Velez & Kim, 2017). Key strategies to facilitate this process include:

- *Explainable AI:* The design of systems with clear, understandable frameworks for decision-making to enhance stakeholder confidence.
- *Ethical Frameworks:* Adopting guidelines that align AI applications with institutional values and ethical standards.
- *Stakeholder Engagement:* The active involvement of educators, parents and students in the development and implementation of AI systems is recommended, with a view to ensuring that their needs are reflected.

Addressing these dimensions proactively can engender an environment where AI systems are trusted, effective, and aligned with educational goals.

Fostering an Ethical AI Ecosystem

The establishment of an ethical AI ecosystem necessitates a collaborative effort among various stakeholders, including educators, students, parents, and policymakers. This collaborative approach is pivotal in ensuring that AI systems reflect diverse values and priorities, thereby promoting fairness and inclusivity. Adversarial learning techniques have been shown to address intersectional biases, thereby enhancing fairness in educational outcomes (Mangal & Pardos, 2024). Furthermore, the establishment of platforms for dialogue and collaboration can facilitate the alignment of AI applications with the values of the educational community. Ethical frameworks are instrumental in ensuring the safeguarding of student rights and the establishment of inclusive learning environments. By integrating these frameworks into the design and implementation of AI systems, educational institutions can ensure that AI tools support transparency, equity, and accountability (Durães et al., 2024; Hong et al., 2022). Furthermore, sustained collaboration among educators, developers, and policymakers is imperative for cultivating a socio-technical approach that integrates technical innovation with cultural and ethical considerations (Klimova et al., 2023; Kousa & Niemi, 2022).

The integration of AI within educational settings presents significant potential for transformative change; however, this must be executed with meticulous consideration for ethical implications, encompassing concerns such as data privacy, algorithmic bias, and ensuring equitable access. By prioritising transparency, inclusivity, and fairness, educational institutions can foster trust and ensure that AI-driven solutions enhance educational quality and equity. In order to create a sustainable and inclusive future for AI in education, it is essential that educational institutions proactively engage with relevant stakeholders and adhere to robust ethical frameworks.

CHALLENGES AND RISKS

Whilst the implementation of Artificial Intelligence (AI) in education management offers significant opportunities for transformation, the challenges associated with its integration must be addressed through strategic and ethical approaches. Key obstacles institutions must address to ensure successful and sustainable adoption of AI technologies include resistance to change, technical limitations, financial constraints, and evolving educational roles.

Resistance to Technological Change

Resistance to AI adoption is a significant barrier, often rooted in fears of job displacement, scepticism about AI's effectiveness, and a lack of familiarity with the technology. Educators may perceive AI as undermining their professional autonomy, reducing their roles to facilitators of automated content delivery (Zawacki-Richter et al., 2019). Likewise, administrators and policymakers may hesitate due to the perceived complexities of implementation and financial burdens (Holmes et al., 2022; Luckin, 2018). Addressing these concerns necessitates the implementation of targeted capacity-building initiatives. Professional development programs have been shown to equip educators with the skills needed to integrate AI into their teaching practices effectively. Transparent communication about AI's role as a complementary tool, rather than a replacement for traditional methods, is equally critical (Means et al., 2021). These efforts can cultivate a culture of innovation and alleviate concerns about AI's impact on educational roles.

Technical and Financial Barriers

The integration of artificial intelligence within educational administration necessitates the establishment of a robust infrastructure, encompassing high-speed internet, cloud computing, and cybersecurity systems. These requirements pose significant challenges, particularly in resource-limited settings where such infrastructure is often unavailable (Chen et al., 2020). The financial constraints experienced by institutions in developing regions further compound the issue, as educational priorities often take precedence over investments in emerging technologies (Ge & Hu, 2020). The absence of technical expertise to design, deploy, and maintain AI systems further complicates implementation efforts (Goosen & Mugumo, 2024). To address these challenges, there is a need for collaborative efforts between educational institutions, governments, and private sector organisations. Partnerships can provide financial support, scalable technologies, and tailored solutions for diverse educational environments (Luckin & Cukurova, 2019). For instance, shared funding models and open-source AI tools can serve to lower entry barriers, thus enabling broader access to AI-driven innovations.

Ethical Dilemmas

The integration of AI into education management gives rise to significant ethical concerns, particularly with regard to data privacy, algorithmic bias, and transparency. AI systems frequently necessitate the utilisation of substantial personal data, thereby giving rise to critical inquiries concerning surveillance and fundamental human rights (Berendt et al., 2020; Klimova et al., 2023). Algorithmic bias, resulting from flawed or non-representative datasets, can disproportionately impact marginalised groups, leading to inequitable outcomes (Mehrabi et al., 2021). In order to mitigate these risks, it is essential that institutions establish ethical frameworks and regulatory guidelines that prioritise fairness, accountability, and transparency (Zhang & Aslan, 2021). The regular auditing of AI systems, in conjunction with clear and comprehensible decision-making processes, has the potential to enhance stakeholder confidence and to safeguard the rights of students. Ensuring compliance with data protection standards is also critical to maintaining stakeholder confidence in AI technologies.

Evolving Educational Roles

The integration of AI into education management is having a profound impact on traditional roles, influencing the manner in which educators and students interact with technology. The integration of AI tools has the potential to alter the teacher-student dynamic, thereby reducing opportunities for social learning and collaborative interactions (Reiss, 2021; Zhai et al., 2021). In order to adapt to these changes, educators must acquire new skills and embrace innovative methodologies in order to strike a balance between AI-driven autonomy and human-centred educational experiences (Luan et al., 2020). Institutional support, encompassing ongoing training and resources, is imperative for facilitating this transition.

Strategies for Sustainable AI Adoption

In order to facilitate the sustainable integration of AI into education management, it is essential that institutions adopt strategies that ensure the future-proofing of AI systems and their alignment with evolving educational needs:

- *Modular AI Frameworks:* Systems that allow for continuous updates and integration with emerging technologies ensure adaptability and relevance (Holmes et al., 2022).
- *Ethical Guidelines:* The establishment of policies that address data privacy, fairness, and transparency is essential to ensure that AI applications are aligned with institutional values (Zhang & Aslan, 2021).
- *Interdisciplinary Collaboration:* Collaborations between educators, policymakers, and AI developers can result in the creation of tools that are pedagogically relevant and culturally sensitive (Zawacki-Richter et al., 2019).
- *Regular Evaluation and Feedback:* Continuous assessments of AI systems, informed by stakeholder feedback, can enhance their effectiveness and alignment with educational goals (Ge & Hu, 2020).

The integration of AI into education management presents both opportunities and challenges. Addressing resistance to change, overcoming technical and financial barriers, and resolving ethical dilemmas are critical to ensuring successful adoption. By fostering collaboration, prioritising ethical considerations, and investing in continuous learning, educational institutions can harness the transformative potential of AI while maintaining equity and inclusivity. Through strategic planning and the implementation of adaptive policies, AI has the potential to serve as a powerful tool for advancing the quality and accessibility of education.

AI AND PEDAGOGICAL INNOVATION

The field of Artificial Intelligence (AI) is undergoing a paradigm shift that is set to transform pedagogical practices. This transformation is characterised by the emergence of personalised learning environments, the fostering of curriculum innovation, and the enhancement of formative assessments. Beyond its administrative applications, AI has the potential to fundamentally reshape teaching and learning, promoting inclusivity, engagement, and innovation in education.

Building AI Literacy in Higher Education

The increasing prevalence of AI-assisted academic work has led to a growing need for structured AI literacy programmes for both students and academic staff. It is imperative that students are equipped with the necessary skills to critically evaluate AI-generated outputs, correctly cite AI-assisted work, and comprehend its limitations. Institutions such as the University of Helsinki have incorporated AI literacy into research methodology courses (Mannila, 2024), while the University of Edinburgh offers workshops on evaluating large language model outputs (University of Edinburgh, 2025). Concurrently, faculty members are undergoing training to identify AI-generated content, adapt assessment rubrics, and provide guidance on ethical use. These initiatives are indicative of an emerging consensus that AI literacy constitutes a fundamental competency within the context of higher education.

The Role of Tutors in Ethical AI Integration

Tutors are the primary mediators of ethical AI use in student research (Sofologi et al., 2025). They play a pivotal role in assisting students to discern between AI-generated suggestions and original thought, thereby ensuring that AI tools serve to support rather than substitute academic reasoning. By guiding students through the process of validating AI-assisted findings, offering structured critique of AI-generated content, and promoting reflective documentation, tutors help maintain both academic rigor and integrity (Everson, 2025). It is incumbent upon tutors to guide students in navigating the thin line between support and substitution when using AI tools. The facilitation of reflective discussions, the provision of examples of appropriate citation of AI contributions, and the modelling of critical interrogation of AI outputs are all strategies that tutors can employ to ensure that students' academic work remains original, ethical, and analytically rich. Strategies such as the scaffolding of AI use through the utilisation of annotated logs or reflection papers have been demonstrated to facilitate the documentation and regulation of student engagement with AI tools.

Personalized Learning and Student Engagement

AI-powered learning platforms have redefined personalisation by adapting content and pacing to individual student needs (Jones et al., 2022). Machine learning algorithms analyse performance data, learning styles and preferences in order to deliver tailored instruction and real-time feedback (Chen et al., 2020; Zawacki-Richter et al., 2019). Systems such as Carnegie Learning and DreamBox Learning offer dynamic curriculum adjustments, addressing knowledge gaps effectively and enhancing student engagement (Means et al., 2021). These platforms have been shown to cater to diverse learning requirements (Means et al., 2021), as well as empowering students to set personal goals and track progress, thus cultivating habits for lifelong learning (Luckin, 2018). Furthermore, the provision of personalised learning environments is conducive to inclusivity, inasmuch as it ensures that every student, irrespective of background, has access to quality educational resources. The integration of AI into teaching practices has the potential to address learning disparities and promote equity within the classroom environment. While AI tools enhance personalisation and efficiency in academic work, scholars have raised concerns about their potential to diminish students' critical thinking skills. Kangwa et al. (2025) hypothesise that excessive reliance on AI-generated summaries may diminish individuals' engagement with primary sources. In contrast, Dai et al. (2024) posit that when employed in a reflective manner, AI has the capacity to facilitate metacognitive abilities by encouraging students to assess the validity and relevance of insights generated by machines. Consequently, educators must judiciously balance the utilisation of tools with the provision of structured opportunities for independent inquiry and argumentation.

Innovation in Curriculum Design

AI also plays a pivotal role in curriculum development, emphasising collaboration and inclusivity. The utilisation of advanced Natural Language Processing (NLP) systems facilitates the analysis of existing educational materials, the identification of gaps, and the provision of assistance to educators in the creation of contextually relevant and culturally sensitive curricula (Luckin & Cukurova, 2019). These systems have been shown to incorporate input from diverse stakeholders, thereby ensuring that curricula reflect a range of cultural perspectives and address biases (Luckin & Cukurova, 2019). For instance, AI models such as those developed by OpenAI have been shown to generate inclusive content, thereby enhancing cultural representation in educational materials (Holmes et al., 2022). By promoting equitable educational practices, AI-driven tools ensure that curriculum development meets the needs of all learners (Holmes et al., 2022).

Enhancing Formative Assessments

In the domain of formative assessment, AI has exhibited considerable promise. Tools such as Gradescope and Turnitin AI evaluate student submissions efficiently, providing detailed, personalised feedback that supports student development (Zawacki-Richter et al., 2019). These technologies enable educators to identify performance trends, target interventions, and make data-driven instructional adjustments (Means et al., 2021). Furthermore, the utilisation of AI-enhanced assessment tools serves to mitigate the presence of grading biases, thereby ensuring a fair and consistent evaluation process. Furthermore, gamified assessments that are powered by AI have been shown to increase student motivation and engagement (Holmes et al., 2022). By rendering the evaluation process interactive and meaningful, these tools transform assessments into opportunities for both learning and enjoyment (Holmes et al., 2022).

New Teaching Methodologies and Administrative Efficiencies

The advent of AI has precipitated the emergence of innovative pedagogical methodologies, a salient example of which is the embodied, analogical, and disruptive (EAD) approach to teaching. This approach integrates human-AI interactions and analogical reasoning, thereby helping students to grasp complex concepts more effectively (Dai et al., 2023). Research indicates that AI-enhanced teaching methods significantly outperform traditional approaches, highlighting their potential to transform classroom practices (Dai et al., 2023). Administratively, AI has been shown to streamline tasks such as enrolment, grading, and resource allocation, thereby reducing educators' workloads and enhancing institutional efficiency (Ge & Hu, 2020; Goosen & Mugumo, 2024). Adaptive learning systems analyse extensive datasets to identify learning patterns and predict student performance, enabling timely and precise interventions (Bozkurt et al., 2021; Yin, 2022). By reducing bureaucratic burdens, AI enables educators to focus more on teaching and student engagement (Smith et al., 2023).

Ethical Considerations and Implementation Challenges

Notwithstanding the numerous advantages inherent in the integration of AI within educational settings, concerns regarding ethical implications must be given due consideration. Concerns have been raised regarding issues such as data privacy, fairness, and transparency, which must be addressed in order to ensure responsible implementation. AI-driven tools frequently depend on substantial datasets, which can give rise to concerns regarding surveillance and the misappropriation of personal data (Holmes et al., 2021). Furthermore, biases embedded in AI algorithms have the potential to engender inequitable outcomes, underscoring the necessity for robust ethical frameworks (Zhang & Aslan, 2021). Comprehensive guidelines are essential for guiding the ethical use of AI in education. These frameworks must prioritise fairness, accountability, and inclusivity, ensuring that AI applications enhance learning outcomes while protecting student rights and interests.

As demonstrated in Figure 3, the visual presentation offers a comprehensive overview of the pivotal impacts of AI in the educational sector. It elucidates the following: Personalised learning, enhanced assessments, curriculum innovation, novel teaching methodologies, and ethical considerations. These dimensions demonstrate the multifaceted ways in which AI is shaping educational environments and underscore the importance of a balanced approach to its integration.

Figure 3. Key Dimensions of AI's Impact on Education

The advent of artificial intelligence has precipitated a profound pedagogical innovation, ushering in a paradigm shift towards personalised learning methodologies, the augmentation of formative assessments, and the cultivation of inclusive curriculum design. It also introduces new teaching methodologies and administrative efficiencies, significantly improving the quality and accessibility of education. However, it is imperative to acknowledge the necessity of addressing ethical concerns and establishing robust implementation frameworks to realise the full potential of AI. By prioritizing fairness, transparency, and inclusivity, educational institutions can leverage AI to create transformative and equitable learning environments on a global scale.

FUTURE IMPLICATIONS

The integration of Artificial Intelligence (AI) in education management is a dynamic and ongoing process with transformative implications for teaching, learning, and administration. As AI technologies evolve, it is anticipated that their applications will expand, driving innovation across all levels of the education sector. However, the realisation of the full potential of AI necessitates a collaborative effort among policymakers, educators, and technology developers to balance opportunities with challenges, including ethical considerations and cultural diversity.

Transformative Potential of AI in Education Management

The role of artificial intelligence (AI) in education is multifaceted, impacting teaching methodologies, learning processes, and administrative functions. AI-powered platforms, including intelligent tutoring systems and automated assessments, facilitate personalised and collaborative learning, thereby enabling tailored instruction and enhancing student outcomes (Bozkurt et al., 2021; Kamalov et al., 2023). These technologies enhance efficiency by automating routine tasks, such as grading and scheduling, allowing educators to focus on more strategic initiatives (Paek & Kim, 2021). Another significant trend in the realm of AI-driven education management is the emergence of virtual and hybrid educational models. Virtual institutions leverage adaptive AI technologies to provide accessible learning experiences for diverse student populations, including those in remote or underserved areas (Zawacki-Richter et al., 2019). Hybrid models combine online and in-person instruction, offering flexible pathways to accommodate evolving learner needs (Zawacki-Richter et al., 2019). Initiatives such as the University of the People and micro-credentialing programs are demonstrative of the manner in which virtual education is effecting a transformation of conventional paradigms (Means et al., 2021). These models enhance accessibility and support lifelong learning through modular and scalable approaches.

Addressing Global Disparities and Promoting Inclusivity

The accelerated integration of artificial intelligence (AI) within educational institutions underscores the imperative for global standardisation and policy harmonisation. Organisations such as UNESCO and the OECD are at the forefront of endeavours to establish international frameworks that promote the ethical and equitable use of AI in education (UNESCO, 2021). These initiatives seek to address the digital divide between technologically advanced and resource-constrained regions, aiming to mitigate disparities in infrastructure and expertise (Holmes et al., 2022). A coordinated approach emphasising capacity-building programmes and ethical standards can ensure that AI technologies contribute to global educational goals of equity and inclusivity. However, challenges persist in ensuring that AI respects cultural diversity while fostering global connectivity (Holmes et al., 2022). Many AI systems are designed using data and pedagogical principles rooted in specific cultural contexts, potentially marginalizing underrepresented groups (Luckin, 2018; Holmes et al., 2022). The development of culturally adaptive AI systems that reflect local traditions, languages, and values is imperative. Inclusivity and cultural sensitivity in educational practices can be promoted by engaging diverse stakeholders in the design and implementation of AI technologies (Zawacki-Richter et al., 2019).

Ethical Considerations and Professional Development

The integration of AI into education gives rise to ethical concerns, particularly with regard to data privacy and algorithmic bias. Inadequate management of these issues has the potential to erode public confidence in AI systems and to intensify pre-existing disparities (Bozkurt et al., 2021; Zhang & Aslan, 2021). In order to ensure the safeguarding of student data and the establishment of fairness in algorithmic decision-making, there is a necessity for the implementation of robust ethical frameworks and transparent governance structures. Furthermore, the development of systematic professional development programmes is imperative to equip educators and students with the competencies required for AI-driven education (Cox, 2021; Lester, 2021). Addressing these challenges necessitates interdisciplinary collaborations among policymakers, educators, and technologists. The integration of pedagogical expertise with technical innovation is pivotal in the development of AI applications that align with ethical and educational standards (Zawacki-Richter et al., 2019; Zhang & Aslan, 2021).

Future Directions for AI in Education Management

In contemplating the future of AI in education management, it is anticipated that its applications will undergo expansion, whilst concomitantly addressing the challenges that are associated with this development. The following emerging trends are worthy of note; *Predictive Analytics and Intelligent Systems:* The implementation of AI-driven predictive models will empower educational institutions to proactively anticipate the needs of students, identify those who may be at risk of underperformance, and implement timely interventions to address these issues. *Virtual Institutions and Hybrid Models:* The sustained growth of AI-driven virtual and hybrid educational systems is poised to enhance accessibility and flexibility, catering to a diverse range of learner demographics. The global standardisation of educational metrics is another key trend. AI will play a central role in developing standardized metrics for evaluating educational quality, fostering greater international collaboration. *Culturally Adaptive AI:* Institutions will prioritize the development of AI systems that respect local values and traditions while promoting global understanding. In order to achieve these advancements, it is essential that institutions adopt a dynamic approach to AI integration, ensuring that systems remain adaptable and future-proof. Continuous updates, interdisciplinary collaboration, and stakeholder engagement will be critical in navigating the complexities of AI-driven education.

AI is poised to revolutionize education management by enhancing efficiency, accessibility, and learning outcomes. However, this transformative potential is accompanied by significant challenges, including ethical dilemmas, global disparities, and cultural considerations. By adopting a collaborative and inclusive approach, educational stakeholders can leverage the potential of AI to create equitable and innovative educational systems. As AI technologies continue to evolve, their role in shaping the future of education will be pivotal, offering new opportunities to improve global educational practices and outcomes.

CASE STUDIES AND PRACTICAL APPLICATIONS

The advent of Artificial Intelligence (AI) has precipitated a paradigm shift within the domain of education management, effecting a transformation that is characterised by the optimisation of administrative efficiency, the personalisation of learning experiences, and the augmentation of instructional processes. Institutions worldwide are leveraging AI technologies to address challenges, optimise resources, and improve educational outcomes. However, it is important to acknowledge the challenges that accompany these opportunities, including concerns regarding data privacy, a shortage of technical expertise, and the necessity for strategic scaling. This section explores the multifaceted contributions of AI to education, illustrated by case studies, best practices, and the insights from Figure 4, while addressing the challenges and strategies for effective implementation.

Figure 4. AI's Role in Transforming Education Management

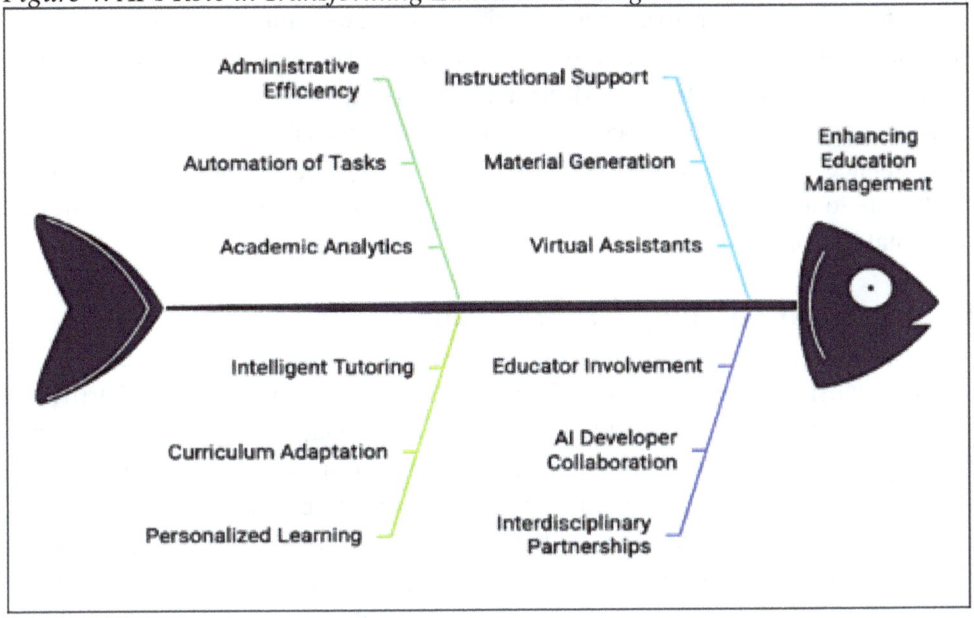

Institutional Models of AI Integration

It is evident that several universities have initiated the systematic integration of AI tools into their academic support services. For instance, the Open University (UK) has piloted AI-based recommendation systems that assist students in structuring final projects (The Open University, 2025). Tampere University (Finland) has embedded AI literacy components into research methods courses, thus enabling students to navigate AI-enhanced literature reviews and data analysis tools (Tampere University, 2025). Furthermore, institutions such as Arizona State University and the University of Michigan have adopted Turnitin AI in conjunction with formative feedback mechanisms to ensure both academic integrity and learning efficacy in undergraduate theses (ASU, 2025; University of Michigan, 2025). These illustrations elucidate a variety of institutional methodologies for the conscientious integration of AI within academic workflows.

Enhancing Administrative Efficiency

AI technologies have been found to have a significant impact on the streamlining of administrative tasks in educational institutions, thereby enabling educators and administrators to allocate more time to strategic initiatives and instructional duties.

The automation of routine tasks, including grading, scheduling, and resource allocation, has been instrumental in reducing workloads while enhancing accuracy and timeliness (Chen et al., 2020). As demonstrated in Figure 2, the automation of tasks and the integration of AI-driven academic analytics have been shown to enhance decision-making processes by providing actionable insights into student performance and institutional operations (Kloos et al., 2024). These advancements contribute to a more efficient and data-driven approach to the management of educational institutions.

Personalized Learning Experiences

Personalisation represents one of the most significant contributions of artificial intelligence to the domain of education management. Machine learning algorithms empower AI systems to adapt curricula and learning materials to the individual needs of students, catering to their learning pace and style (Chen et al., 2020; Sekli et al., 2024). Intelligent tutoring systems, for instance, offer customised guidance and feedback, thereby promoting engagement and retention (see Figure 2). These systems facilitate curriculum adaptation, ensuring that students receive personalised learning experiences that address knowledge gaps and build on their strengths. The integration of personalised learning platforms has yielded significant outcomes in various educational systems (see, for example, Sahlberg, 2022). Finland's adoption of AI-driven adaptive learning tools in K-12 education, which customises teaching materials to individual students, exemplifies the manner in which these technologies contribute to educational equity and excellence (Sahlberg, 2022). Furthermore, platforms such as Carnegie Learning and DreamBox Learning empower students to set personal goals and track their progress, cultivating habits for lifelong learning (Luckin, 2018).

Supporting Instructional Processes

AI also plays a critical role in supporting teachers by generating educational materials and facilitating classroom activities. As demonstrated in Figure 2, material generation tools assist educators in preparing lesson plans and problem sets that align with specific learning objectives (Kloos et al., 2024). AI-powered chatbots and virtual assistants function as supplementary tutors, offering on-demand support to students outside the classroom (Sekli et al., 2024). The enhancement of instructional quality and the creation of opportunities for more individualised and flexible learning experiences are further advantages of these tools. The contribution of AI to instructional support extends beyond the confines of the classroom. Generative AI systems aid in developing culturally inclusive curricula, ensuring that educational materials reflect diverse perspectives and address biases (Holmes et al., 2022). These advancements underscore the potential of AI to enrich teaching methodologies and foster innovation.

Interdisciplinary Partnerships and Collaboration

The development and implementation of AI in education are significantly enhanced by interdisciplinary partnerships, as illustrated in Figure 2. Collaboration between educators, AI developers and researchers is vital to ensure that AI technologies are designed with a deep understanding of educational needs and learning sciences (Luckin & Cukurova, 2019). Initiatives such as the EDUCATE Educational Technology programme are demonstrative of the manner in which such partnerships drive innovation in the field of educational AI. Educator involvement is particularly critical in aligning AI applications with pedagogical goals. The integration of educators within the design process ensures the creation of user-friendly and contextually relevant tools, thereby enhancing their impact on teaching and learning outcomes (Zawacki-Richter et al., 2019). Furthermore, partnerships with technology companies facilitate the development of scalable and impactful AI solutions tailored to diverse educational settings (Zawacki-Richter et al., 2019).

Addressing Challenges in AI Integration

Notwithstanding its considerable transformative potential, the integration of AI in education management is not without challenges. Key issues include:

- *Data Privacy Concerns*: Ensuring the secure storage and anonymisation of sensitive student information is critical. Institutions are obliged to adhere to strict privacy standards if they are to build trust in AI systems (Woolf et al., 2021). Additionally, there is a lack of technical expertise among educators and administrators. A paucity of adequate training for educators and administrators hinders the effective utilisation of AI technologies. Studies have revealed that many teachers feel unprepared to integrate AI into their classrooms (Holmes et al., 2022). The necessity for comprehensive professional development programs is therefore paramount in order to address these deficiencies.
- *Scaling and Infrastructure:* Institutions in resource-constrained settings encounter challenges in scaling AI solutions due to limited infrastructure and financial constraints (Ge & Hu, 2020). Collaborative efforts between educational institutions and technology providers are necessary to ensure equitable access.

Strategies for Effective AI Implementation

In order to surmount the challenges identified and to reap the maximum benefits of AI, it is recommended that educational institutions adopt the following strategies:

- *Pilot Projects:* The testing of AI tools on a smaller scale prior to broader implementation enables institutions to refine their approaches. For instance, a school network in the Netherlands initiated a pilot programme involving the implementation of AI-based learning platforms in select classrooms, yielding favourable outcomes. Subsequent to this, the network expanded the utilisation of these platforms to encompass the entire network (van der Zwaan et al., 2021). In addition, professional development initiatives should be considered. The continuous training of teachers and administrators is vital for the effective integration and utilisation of AI technologies by stakeholders (Luckin, 2018).
- *Cross-Sector Collaborations:* Partnerships between educational institutions and technology companies facilitate the development of user-friendly and impactful AI applications (Zawacki-Richter et al., 2019).
- *Culturally Adaptive AI:* Ensuring that AI systems respect local values and traditions while promoting global inclusivity is essential for equitable adoption. The integration of diverse stakeholders in the design of AI technologies has been identified as a key factor in the development of tools that are both culturally sensitive and pedagogically relevant (Sahlberg, 2022; Holmes et al., 2022).

The integration of AI into education management holds immense potential to enhance administrative efficiency, personalise learning experiences, and support instructional processes. As Figure 2 illustrates, the diverse applications of AI – spanning automation, personalised learning, instructional support, and interdisciplinary collaboration – underscore its transformative impact on education. However, in order to ensure successful implementation, it is critical to address challenges such as data privacy, technical expertise gaps, and scaling limitations. By adopting best practices, such as pilot projects, professional development, and cross-sector collaborations, institutions can harness AI's transformative power while mitigating risks. As AI technologies continue to evolve, their role in shaping the future of education management will be pivotal, driving innovation and equity across global education systems.

CONCLUSION AND RECOMMENDATIONS

The integration of artificial intelligence (AI) into educational policies signifies a substantial paradigm shift in the management of educational institutions. By adopting AI-driven technologies, educational leaders can promote innovation, enhance operational efficiency, and address longstanding challenges in education. However, it is imperative to recognise that the seamless integration of AI into educational institutions necessitates meticulous planning, ethical oversight, and a unwavering commitment to equity. Institutions must allocate resources to infrastructure, capacity-building, and trust-building initiatives to support AI-driven educational transformations effectively. This paper provides a foundation for future research and practical applications, outlining how AI can be leveraged to develop more resilient, inclusive, and future-oriented educational systems.

Summary of Key Insights

The integration of AI within educational administration has evidenced its transformative influence across a variety of domains, ranging from personalised learning and curriculum innovation to strategic decision-making and institutional governance. AI technologies enhance institutional efficiency, improve learning outcomes, and promote inclusivity. Through the utilisation of predictive analytics and adaptive learning systems, AI facilitates early intervention strategies, thereby assisting students who are at risk of academic failure. Furthermore, AI optimises resource allocation, ensuring that institutional policies align with real-time data and emerging educational trends.

However, it is important to acknowledge the challenges that come with the adoption of AI in education. These include ethical concerns regarding algorithmic bias and data privacy, as well as structural challenges such as the digital divide. Addressing these issues necessitates the establishment of ethical frameworks that uphold transparency, fairness, and accountability. The successful implementation of AI in education is predicated on interdisciplinary collaboration among policymakers, educators, and AI developers. The proactive governance measures that are required for the successful implementation of AI in education include the following: the enhancement of educational accessibility; the fostering of stakeholder engagement; and the support of the continuous improvement of learning environments.

Framework for Responsible AI Integration in Final Degree Projects

The proposal of a structured framework for guiding AI use in final degree projects is the foundation of this study, which is informed by institutional case studies and policy analysis. The following elements are to be considered: The following four points are to be considered in order to ensure effective AI usage within an institutional context:

- The implementation of disclosure policies regarding the use of AI.
- The introduction of mandatory modules on AI ethics and literacy.
- The establishment of supervision protocols that necessitate the discussion of AI tool usage.
- The creation of assessment rubrics that differentiate between human-generated content and content supported by AI.

A framework of this nature has the capacity to engender transparency, academic rigour, and equitable outcomes across a range of institutional contexts.

Ethical and Practical Strategies for Tutors

These ethical challenges, including AI-generated plagiarism, opaque algorithmic decision-making, and overreliance on automated content, necessitate targeted pedagogical responses. The subsequent section delineates the manner in which tutors can address these risks through the provision of structured guidance, transparent assessment, and critical dialogue with students.

It is imperative that students include an "AI Use Statement" in their final project submissions.In order to distinguish between human-generated and AI-assisted components, departmental rubrics must be developed.In addition, staff should be provided with workshops on assessing AI-influenced work (e.g. ChatGPT-assisted synthesis).Furthermore, it should be encouraged that students validate AI content using peer-reviewed sources. Finally, reflective writing components should be integrated, asking students to explain how AI shaped their research process. Students should be invited to consider the reasons for their selection of particular AI tools and the manner in which they understood the outputs generated by these tools.In conjunction with students, "AI Usage Agreements" should be developed in order to establish acceptable limits for tool assistance.Student drafts should be reviewed with a focus on identifying instances of overuse or uncritical adoption of AI-generated text.Exemplars of appropriate AI citations (e.g., OpenAI, 2023) should be provided within annotated bibliographies.

Assessment Framework for AI-Aided Academic Work

In addition to the imperative of responsible usage, the evaluation of academic work influenced by artificial intelligence presents a distinctive challenge for educators. In order to facilitate consistent and equitable evaluation practices, a pragmatic framework is hereby proposed, predicated upon four fundamental criteria:

- It is imperative to ascertain whether the student has explicitly articulated the AI tools employed, along with their intended function within the research process.
- Originality: The question to be answered here is whether the submission evidences independent reasoning, synthesis and critical engagement that extends beyond the capabilities of the AI tool.
- Validation: It is imperative to ascertain whether the student has verified the accuracy, appropriateness and relevance of AI-generated content through academic sources.
- Reflection: It is imperative to ascertain whether the student incorporates a reflective component that discusses how AI shaped their research, along with its limitations and implications.

This framework is designed to promote ethical practice, pedagogical transparency, and the development of student autonomy in AI-supported academic work.

Policy Recommendations for AI Adoption

In order to ensure that the full potential of AI in education is realised whilst concomitantly mitigating the risks associated with its implementation, the following policy recommendations are proposed:

1. *Ethical AI Frameworks:* Institutions must establish comprehensive ethical guidelines for AI deployment in education. These frameworks should address issues such as algorithmic bias, data privacy, and equity concerns to ensure that AI-driven policies remain fair and inclusive.
2. *Transparency and Accountability Measures:* AI decision-making processes should be explainable and accessible to all stakeholders, including educators, students, and parents. The implementation of Explainable AI (XAI) models and routine AI audits has been identified as a means to achieve this objective.
3. *Teacher Training and AI Literacy:* Professional development programs should be designed to equip educators with the necessary skills to integrate AI into

teaching and administration effectively. The training curriculum should encompass AI ethics, data interpretation, and adaptive teaching methodologies.

4. *Bridging the Digital Divide:* It is incumbent upon policymakers to ensure equitable access to AI-powered educational tools, particularly for underrepresented communities. This necessitates the provision of digital infrastructure, affordable technology, and AI-driven learning resources in low-income and rural areas.
5. *Collaborative AI Development:* The establishment of interdisciplinary partnerships between education policymakers, AI researchers, and technology developers is imperative to ensure that AI systems are pedagogically relevant and culturally sensitive.
6. *Real-Time Policy Adaptation:* The utilisation of AI to monitor emerging trends and facilitate flexible policy adjustments is imperative. Predictive modelling can assist policymakers in anticipating challenges and implementing timely interventions.
7. *Student-Centered AI Policies:* AI tools should prioritize student well-being by promoting personalised learning while safeguarding individual rights. Regulations should ensure that AI applications enhance, rather than replace, human engagement in education.

Directions for Future Research

As artificial intelligence continues to evolve, future research should focus on the following areas to further enhance its application in education management:

1. *AI in Adaptive Learning Environments:* This field should involve investigation into how AI-driven adaptive learning systems can enhance differentiated instruction for diverse student populations.
2. *Algorithmic Fairness and Bias Mitigation:* Exploration of advanced techniques to identify and eliminate biases in AI-driven decision-making within education.
3. *AI-Powered Governance Models:* The assessment of the impact of AI-driven policy making in educational institutions and its influence on governance and accountability.
4. *Long-Term AI Impact on Student Outcomes:* Conducting longitudinal studies to measure how AI influences academic success, student engagement, and career readiness.
5. *Culturally Adaptive AI Models:* The development of AI systems that reflect diverse cultural, linguistic, and pedagogical traditions is essential to ensure global applicability and inclusivity.

6. *Human-AI Collaboration in Education:* The examination of optimal models of human-AI interaction is undertaken to achieve a balance between automation and human-centred pedagogical strategies.
7. *Sustainable AI Implementation Strategies:* Evaluating cost-effective and scalable AI adoption frameworks for different educational contexts, including resource-constrained environments.

It is vital that the education sector addresses these critical areas if it is to maximise the potential of AI while minimising the risks involved. In this way, an ethical, equitable, and impactful future for AI-driven education management can be ensured. The formulation of thoughtful AI policies, the establishment of transparent governance structures, and the continuation of interdisciplinary research will be essential in shaping the next generation of education systems. These systems will effectively integrate AI innovations while prioritising human values and inclusivity.

Glossary of Key Terms in AI-Assisted Academic Research

To improve accessibility for readers unfamiliar with technical terminology, the following glossary is added at the end of the chapter:

Term	**Definition**
Artificial Intelligence (AI)	The ability of machines to perform tasks that typically require human intelligence, such as problem-solving or language processing.
Machine Learning (ML)	A subfield of AI that involves algorithms that learn from data to improve performance over time.
Large Language Models (LLMs)	AI models trained on massive amounts of text to generate human-like responses, such as ChatGPT.
Semantic Search	Search that understands meaning and context rather than just matching keywords.
Plagiarism Detection	The process of identifying content similarities using AI algorithms to detect potential academic misconduct.
Explainability	The degree to which the inner workings of an AI system can be understood and interpreted by humans.
Generative AI	AI that can create new content, such as text or images, based on learned patterns in data.

This glossary is intended to support diverse readers in understanding key concepts and terminology used throughout the chapter.

REFERENCES

Aidla, A., Irs, R., & Türk, K. (2012). Creating innovation in the education sector: Policy implications. In Carayannis, E., Varblane, U., & Roolaht, T. (Eds.), *Innovation systems in small catching-up economies* (pp. 267–284). Springer., DOI: 10.1007/978-1-4614-1548-0_19

Arizona State University (ASU). (2025). *Artificial Intelligence (AI) resources and guidelines.* https://instruction.thecollege.asu.edu/AIguidelines

Arora, A.. (2024). Towards intelligent governance: The role of AI in policymaking and decision support for e-governance. In So In, C., Londhe, N. D., Bhatt, N., & Kitsing, M. (Eds.), *Information systems for intelligent systems* (pp. 231–245). Springer., DOI: 10.1007/978-981-99-8612-5_19

Badmus, O., Anas, S., Arogundade, J. B., & Williams, M. (2024). AI-driven business analytics and decision making. *World Journal of Advanced Research and Reviews, 24*(1), 616–633. DOI: 10.30574/wjarr.2024.24.1.3093

Baker, R., & Yacef, K. (2009). The state of educational data mining in 2009: A review and future visions. *Journal of Educational Data Mining, 1*(1), 3–17.

Balachandar, S. K., Kumara, I. V., Godavari, A., Marieswari, S., & Karthikeyan, T.Sanjay Kanth Balachandar. (2024). Dynamic adaptive resource allocation for edge computing in big data analytics using GBDT, DQN, and GA algorithms. *Journal of Electrical Systems, 20*(5), 2158–2165. DOI: 10.52783/jes.2561

Barker, B., & Hoskins, K. (2021). Education, inequality and social mobility: Key findings from three case studies. *Forum for Promoting 3-19 Comprehensive Education, 63*(1), 107–114. DOI: 10.3898/forum.2021.63.1.12

Berendt, B., Littlejohn, A., & Blakemore, M. (2020). AI in education: Learner choice and fundamental rights. *Learning, Media and Technology, 45*(3), 312–324. DOI: 10.1080/17439884.2020.1786399

Berland, M., Baker, R. S., & Blikstein, P. (2014). Educational data mining and learning analytics: Applications to constructionist research. *Technology. Knowledge and Learning, 19*(1-2), 205–220. DOI: 10.1007/s10758-014-9223-7

Bozkurt, A., Karadeniz, A., Bañeres, D., Guerrero-Roldán, A., & Rodríguez, M. (2021). Artificial intelligence and reflections from educational landscape: A review of AI studies in half a century. *Sustainability (Basel), 13*(2), 800. DOI: 10.3390/su13020800

Bozkurt, A., Xiao, J., Farrow, R., Bai, J. Y. H., Nerantzi, C., Moore, S., Dron, J., Stracke, C. M., Singh, L., Crompton, H., Koutropoulos, A., Terentev, E., Pazurek, A., Nichols, M., Sidorkin, A. M., Costello, E., Watson, S., Mulligan, D., Honeychurch, S., & Asino, T. I. (2024). The manifesto for teaching and learning in a time of generative AI: A critical collective stance to better navigate the future. *Open Praxis, 16*(4), 487–513. DOI: 10.55982/openpraxis.16.4.777

Brans, M., Geva-May, I., & Howlett, M. (2017). Policy analysis in comparative perspective: An introduction. In Brans, M., Geva-May, I., & Howlett, M. (Eds.), *Routledge handbook of comparative policy analysis* (pp. 1–23). Routledge. DOI: 10.4324/9781315660561-1

Bridgeman, A., Weeks, R., & Liu, D. (2024). *Aligning our assessments to the age of generative AI*. Teaching@Sydney. https://educational-innovation.sydney.edu.au/teaching@sydney/aligning-our-assessments-to-the-age-of-generative-ai/

Burke, K. (2010). Distributed leadership and shared governance in post-secondary education. *Management in Education, 24*(2), 51–54. DOI: 10.1177/0892020610363088

Campbell, J. P., DeBlois, P. B., & Oblinger, D. G. (2007). Academic analytics: A new tool for a new era. *EDUCAUSE Review, 42*(4), 41–57.

Carvalho, M. S. d., & Silva, G. L. d. (2021). Inside the black box: Using explainable AI to improve evidence-based policies. *2021 IEEE 23rd Conference on Business Informatics (CBI)*, 57–64. DOI: 10.1109/CBI52690.2021.10055

Chan, C. K. Y. (2023). A comprehensive AI policy education framework for university teaching and learning. *International Journal of Educational Technology in Higher Education, 20*(1), 38. DOI: 10.1186/s41239-023-00408-3

Chen, L., Chen, P., & Lin, Z. (2020). Artificial intelligence in education: A review. *IEEE Access : Practical Innovations, Open Solutions, 8*, 75264–75278. DOI: 10.1109/ACCESS.2020.2988510

Cox, A. (2021). Exploring the impact of artificial intelligence and robots on higher education through literature-based design fictions. *International Journal of Educational Technology in Higher Education, 18*(1), 1–22. DOI: 10.1186/s41239-020-00237-8

Dai, R., Thomas, M. K. E., & Rawolle, S. (2024). The roles of AI and educational leaders in AI-assisted administrative decision-making: A proposed framework for symbiotic collaboration. *Australian Educational Researcher*. Advance online publication. DOI: 10.1007/s13384-024-00771-8

Dai, Y., Lin, Z., Liu, A., & Wang, W. (2023). An embodied, analogical and disruptive approach of AI pedagogy in upper elementary education: An experimental study. *British Journal of Educational Technology*, *55*(2), 417–434. DOI: 10.1111/bjet.13371

De Rosa, R. (2017). Governing by data: Some considerations on the role of learning analytics in education. In Lauro, N., Amaturo, E., Grassia, M., Aragona, B., & Marino, M. (Eds.), *Data science and social research* (pp. 87–98). Springer., DOI: 10.1007/978-3-319-55477-8_7

Deshpande, L., Agarwal, A., Haripriya, V., Jain, R., Choudhary, S., & Kumar, S. C. (2024). Investigating novel machine learning approaches to enhance real-time data analysis. *2024 2nd World Conference on Communication & Computing (WCONF)*, 1–7. DOI: 10.1109/WCONF61366.2024.10691969

Doshi-Velez, F., & Kim, B. (2017). Towards a rigorous science of interpretable machine learning. *arXiv preprint arXiv:1702.08608*.

Du, X., Alghowinem, S., Taylor, M., Darling, K., & Breazeal, C. (2023). Innovating AI leadership education. *2023 IEEE Frontiers in Education Conference (FIE)*, 1–8. DOI: 10.1109/FIE58773.2023.10343238

Durães, D., Bezerra, R., & Novais, P. (2024). AI-driven educational transformation in secondary schools: Leveraging data insights for inclusive learning environments. *2024 IEEE Global Engineering Education Conference (EDUCON)*, 1–9. DOI: 10.1109/EDUCON60312.2024.10578910

Dwi, S. (2024). The role of education management in improving learning innovation. *Gestion Educativa*, *1*(1). Advance online publication. DOI: 10.62872/ntf4c997

Elfeky, A. I. M., Najmi, A. H., Yasien, M., & Elbyaly, H. Abdellah Ibrahim Mohammed ElfekyAli Hassan NajmiMarwa Yasien Helmy Elbyaly. (2024). Effects of big data analytics in learning management systems for improving learners' academic success. *El Profesional de la Información*, *33*(1), e330016. DOI: 10.3145/epi.2024.0016

Ellison, S. (2009). Hard-wired for innovation? Comparing two policy paths toward innovative schooling. *International Education*, *39*(1). https://trace.tennessee.edu/internationaleducation/vol39/iss1/2

Everson, K. K. (2025). *Enhancing doctoral dissertations ethically with AI: A comprehensive guide*. Stylus Publishing, LLC.

Ferreira, S. A., & Andrade, A. (2014). Academic analytics: Anatomy of an exploratory essay. *Education and Information Technologies*, *20*(1), 1–15.

Filgueiras, F. (2023). Artificial intelligence and education governance. *Education, Citizenship and Social Justice*. Advance online publication. DOI: 10.1177/17461979231160674

Ge, Z., & Hu, Y. (2020). Innovative application of artificial intelligence (AI) in the management of higher education and teaching. *Journal of Physics: Conference Series*, *1533*(3), 032089. DOI: 10.1088/1742-6596/1533/3/032089

George, B., & Wooden, O. (2023). Managing the strategic transformation of higher education through artificial intelligence. *Administrative Sciences*, *13*(9), 196. DOI: 10.3390/admsci13090196

Ghimire, A., & Edwards, J. (2024). From guidelines to governance: A study of AI policies in education. *arXiv preprint arXiv:2403.15601*. DOI: 10.1007/978-3-031-64312-5_36

Gong, Y., Huang, J., Liu, B., Xu, J., Wu, B., & Zhang, Y. (2024). Dynamic resource allocation for virtual machine migration optimization using machine learning. *Applied and Computational Engineering*, *57*(1), 1–8. DOI: 10.54254/2755-2721/57/20241348

Goosen, W., & Mugumo, P. (2024). A framework for the application of AI in higher education in association with APPETD and Swiss Institute for Management and Innovation. *Proceedings of SPIE - the International Society for Optical Engineering*, *13188*, 1318808. DOI: 10.1117/12.3030740

Gulson, K., & Witzenberger, K. (2020). Repackaging authority: Artificial intelligence, automated governance and education trade shows. *Journal of Education Policy*, *37*(2), 145–160. DOI: 10.1080/02680939.2020.1785552

Gunjal, A., Pednekar, R. S. K., & Ruke, S. (2024). Dynamic resource allocation in edge computing environments: A machine learning approach. *Journal of Trends and Challenges in Artificial Intelligence*, *1*(4), 133–138. DOI: 10.61552/JAI.2024.04.003

Gupta, B., Dusane, A., Patil, N. P., Mane, Y. D., Raut, S., & Agrawal, A. (2024). Enhancing adaptive learning and decision-making systems using swarm intelligence and deep learning for advanced AI applications. *ICTACT Journal on Soft Computing*, *15*(2), 3482–3490. DOI: 10.21917/ijsc.2024.0486

Haag, D., & Kaupenjohann, M. (2001). Parameters, prediction, post-normal science and the precautionary principle—A roadmap for modelling for decision-making. *Ecological Modelling*, *144*(1), 45–60. DOI: 10.1016/S0304-3800(01)00361-1

Hannan, E., & Liu, S. (2021). AI: New source of competitiveness in higher education. *Competitiveness Review*. Advance online publication. DOI: 10.1108/CR-03-2021-0045

Harvard University. (2025). *Initial guidelines for the use of Generative AI tools at Harvard*. https://www.huit.harvard.edu/ai/guidelines

Hawksey, M., Baker, R., Jeffery, N., Behrens, J. T., & Pea, R. (2013). Educational data scientists: A scarce breed. *Proceedings of the Third International Conference on Learning Analytics and Knowledge*, 278–281.

Holmes, W., Bialik, M., & Fadel, C. (2022). *Artificial intelligence in education: Promises and implications for teaching and learning*. Center for Curriculum Redesign.

Holmes, W., Porayska-Pomsta, K., Holstein, K., Sutherland, E., Baker, T., Shum, S., Santos, O. C., Rodrigo, M. T., Cukurova, M., Bittencourt, I. I., & Koedinger, K. (2021). Ethics of AI in education: Towards a community-wide framework. *International Journal of Artificial Intelligence in Education, 32*(3), 504–526. DOI: 10.1007/s40593-021-00239-1

Hong, Y., Nguyen, A., Dang, B., & Nguyen, B. (2022). Data ethics framework for artificial intelligence in education (AIED). *2022 International Conference on Advanced Learning Technologies (ICALT)*, 297–301. DOI: 10.1109/ICALT55010.2022.00095

Kamalov, F., Calonge, D., & Gurrib, I. (2023). New era of artificial intelligence in education: Towards a sustainable multifaceted revolution. *Sustainability (Basel), 15*(16), 12451. DOI: 10.3390/su151612451

Kanchetti, D., Munirathnam, R., & Thakkar, D. (2024). Integration of machine learning algorithms with cloud computing for real-time data analysis. *Journal for Research in Applied Sciences and Biotechnology, 3*(2), 301–306. DOI: 10.55544/jrasb.3.2.46

Kangwa, D., Msafiri, M. M., & Fute, A. (2025). Balancing innovation and ethics: Promote academic integrity through support and effective use of GenAI tools in higher education. *AI and Ethics, 5*(4), 3497–3530. Advance online publication. DOI: 10.1007/s43681-025-00689-6

Karakose, T., & Tülübaş, T. (2024). School leadership and management in the age of artificial intelligence (AI): Recent developments and future prospects. *Educational Process: International Journal, 13*(1), 7–14. DOI: 10.22521/edupij.2024.131.1

Klimova, B., Pikhart, M., & Kacetl, J. (2023). Ethical issues of the use of AI-driven mobile apps for education. *Frontiers in Public Health, 10*, 1118116. Advance online publication. DOI: 10.3389/fpubh.2022.1118116

Kloos, C., Alario-Hoyos, C., Estévez-Ayres, I., Callejo-Pinardo, P., Hombrados-Herrera, M., Muñoz-Merino, P., & Ibáñez, M. (2024). How can generative AI support education? *2024 IEEE Global Engineering Education Conference (EDUCON)*, 1–7. DOI: 10.1109/EDUCON60312.2024.10578716

Kolkman, D. (2020). The usefulness of algorithmic models in policy making. *Government Information Quarterly*, *37*(3), 101488. DOI: 10.1016/j.giq.2020.101488

Kousa, P., & Niemi, H. (2022). AI ethics and learning: EdTech companies' challenges and solutions. *Interactive Learning Environments*, *31*(7), 6735–6746. DOI: 10.1080/10494820.2022.2043908

Kridel, D. J., Dolk, D. R., & Castillo, D. G. (2015). Adaptive modeling for real-time analytics: The case of "big data" in mobile advertising. *2015 48th Hawaii International Conference on System Sciences (HICSS)*, 887–896. DOI: 10.1109/HICSS.2015.111

Kruiper, S. M., Leenknecht, M. J., & Slof, B. (2022). Using scaffolding strategies to improve formative assessment practice in higher education. *Assessment & Evaluation in Higher Education*, *47*(3), 458–476. DOI: 10.1080/02602938.2021.1927981

Leimanis, A. (2020). Self-imposed ethical guidelines for AI in education. *International Scientific Conference "Society, Integration, Education-SIE2020"*. DOI: 10.17770/sie2020vol1.5048

Lester, J. (2021). AI and the future of education. *Proceedings of the 29th ACM International Conference on Multimedia*. DOI: 10.1145/3474085.3475715

Lim, C. P., & Tan, C. Y. (2020). Technology-enhanced learning: Using AI to address diverse learning needs. *Educational Technology Research and Development*, *68*(4), 541–555. DOI: 10.1007/s11423-020-09789-6

Ling, N. Y. (2024). Educational big data analytics: Machine learning-based academic performance predictive modelling. *Pakistan Journal of Life and Social Sciences*, *22*(2). Advance online publication. DOI: 10.57239/PJLSS-2024-22.2.00562

Longo, L., Brcic, M., Cabitza, F., Choi, J., Confalonieri, R., Del Ser, J., & Stumpf, S. (2024). Explainable Artificial Intelligence (XAI) 2.0: A manifesto of open challenges and interdisciplinary research directions. *Information Fusion*, *106*, 102301. DOI: 10.1016/j.inffus.2024.102301

Luan, H., Géczy, P., Lai, H., Gobert, J., Yang, S., Ogata, H., Baltes, J., Guerra, R., Li, P., & Tsai, C. (2020). Challenges and future directions of big data and artificial intelligence in education. *Frontiers in Psychology*, *11*, 580820. Advance online publication. DOI: 10.3389/fpsyg.2020.580820

Luckin, R. (2018). *Machine learning and human intelligence: The future of education for the 21st century*. UCL Institute of Education Press.

Luckin, R., & Cukurova, M. (2019). Designing educational technologies in the age of AI: A learning sciences-driven approach. *British Journal of Educational Technology*, *50*(6), 2824–2838. DOI: 10.1111/bjet.12861

Maghsudi, S., Lan, A., Xu, J., & Van Der Schaar, M. (2021). Personalized education in the artificial intelligence era: What to expect next. *IEEE Signal Processing Magazine*, *38*(3), 37–50. DOI: 10.1109/MSP.2021.3055032

Mangal, M., & Pardos, Z. (2024). Implementing equitable and intersectionality-aware ML in education: A practical guide. *British Journal of Educational Technology*, *55*(5), 2003–2038. DOI: 10.1111/bjet.13484

Manias, G., ... (2023). AI4Gov: Trusted AI for transparent public governance fostering democratic values. *2023 19th International Conference on Distributed Computing in Smart Systems and the Internet of Things (DCOSS-IoT)*, 548–555. DOI: 10.1109/DCOSS-IoT58021.2023.00090

Mannila, L. (2024). *AI literacy is part of modern education*. https://www.helsinki.fi/en/news/donation/ai-literacy-part-modern-education

Massachusetts Institute of Technology (MIT). (2025). *Guidance for use of Generative AI tools*. https://ist.mit.edu/ai-guidance

McConvey, K., Guha, S., & Kuzminykh, A. (2023). A human-centered review of algorithms in decision-making in higher education. *Proceedings of the 2023 CHI Conference on Human Factors in Computing Systems*. DOI: 10.1145/3544548.3580658

Means, B., Toyama, Y., Murphy, R., & Baki, M. (2021). The effectiveness of online and blended learning: A meta-analysis of the empirical literature. *Teachers College Record, 115*(3), 1–47. DOI: 10.1177/016146811311500307

Mehrabi, N., Morstatter, F., Saxena, N., Lerman, K., & Galstyan, A. (2021). A survey on bias and fairness in machine learning. *ACM Computing Surveys*, *54*(6), 1–35. DOI: 10.1145/3457607

Mohaghegh, M. (2020). The role of artificial intelligence in the future of education. *International Journal of Virtual Learning and Medical Sciences*, *11*(1), 65–67. DOI: 10.30476/IJVLMS.2020.85472.1021

Moreira, A. S., Borges, T. S. S., Souto, P. F., Araujo, P. Q., Cellin, J., Gois, A. M., . . . Araújo, A. M. (2024). Innovation in educational management: Challenges and opportunities. In *Seven Editora Acadêmica* (pp. 195–206). DOI: 10.56238/sevened2024.024-014

Murugesan, S., & Kadalmani, A. (2023). A strategic framework of artificial intelligence in integrated decision making: A systematic review. *Proceedings - Academy of Management*, *2023*(1), 17111. DOI: 10.5465/AMPROC.2023.17111abstract

Murwaningsih, T., Sasmini, S. S., Rahardjo, S., Suwandi, K., Saddhono, K., & Nurhasanah, F. (2024). A well-structured strategy development via AI integrated analytics systems to improve performance of education. *2024 4th International Conference on Advance Computing and Innovative Technologies in Engineering (ICACITE)*, 873–878. DOI: 10.1109/ICACITE60783.2024.10617260

Newman, J., & Mintrom, M. (2023). Mapping the discourse on evidence-based policy, artificial intelligence, and the ethical practice of policy analysis. *Journal of European Public Policy*, *30*(9), 1839–1859. DOI: 10.1080/13501763.2023.2193223

Nguyen, A., Gardner, L., & Sheridan, D. (2020). Data analytics in higher education: An integrated view. *Journal of Information Systems Education*, *31*(1), 61–71.

Nieto, Y., Gacía-Díaz, V., Montenegro, C., Gonzalez, C., & Crespo, G. (2019). Usage of machine learning for strategic decision making at higher educational institutions. *IEEE Access : Practical Innovations, Open Solutions*, *7*, 75007–75017. DOI: 10.1109/ACCESS.2019.2919343

Nilsson, M., Jordan, A., Turnpenny, J., Hertin, J., Nykvist, B., & Russel, D. (2008). The use and non-use of policy appraisal tools in public policy making: An analysis of three European countries and the European Union. *Policy Sciences*, *41*(4), 335–355. DOI: 10.1007/s11077-008-9071-1

Nykonenko, A. (2023). The impact of artificial intelligence on modern education: Prospects and challenges. *Artificial Intelligence*, *2*(AI.2023.28(2))), 10–15. DOI: 10.15407/jai2023.02.010

Office of Educational Integrity (OEI). (2025). Using Artificial Intelligence tools responsibly in your studies and assessments. The University of Sydney. https://www.sydney.edu.au/students/responsible-ai-use.html

Open, A. I. (2023). *ChatGPT* (May 24 version) [Large language model]. https://chat.openai.com/chat

Paek, S., & Kim, N. (2021). Analysis of worldwide research trends on the impact of artificial intelligence in education. *Sustainability (Basel), 13*(14), 7941. DOI: 10.3390/su13147941

Panian, Z. (2009). Just-in-time business intelligence and real-time decisioning. *Recent Advances in Applied Informatics and Communications, Proceedings of AIC, 9*, 106–111.

Popenici, S., & Kerr, S. (2017). Exploring the impact of artificial intelligence on teaching and learning in higher education. *Research and Practice in Technology Enhanced Learning, 12*(1), 22. Advance online publication. DOI: 10.1186/s41039-017-0062-8

Reiss, M. (2021). The use of AI in education: Practicalities and ethical considerations. *London Review of Education, 19*(1). Advance online publication. DOI: 10.14324/LRE.19.1.05

Romero, C., & Ventura, S. (2013). Data mining in education. *Wiley Interdisciplinary Reviews. Data Mining and Knowledge Discovery, 3*(1), 12–27. DOI: 10.1002/widm.1075

Sahlberg, P. (2022). *Finnish lessons 3.0: What can the world learn from educational change in Finland?* Teachers College Press.

Saxena, A. (2024). AI in governance and policy making. *International Journal of Science and Research (Raipur, India), 13*(5), 1218–1223. DOI: 10.21275/SR24519015426

Schiff, D. (2021). Out of the laboratory and into the classroom: The future of artificial intelligence in education. *AI & Society, 36*(1), 331–348. DOI: 10.1007/s00146-020-01033-8

Sekli, G., Godo, A., & Véliz, J. (2024). Generative AI solutions for faculty and students: A review of literature and roadmap for future research. *Journal of Information Technology Education, 23*, 14. DOI: 10.28945/5304

Selwyn, N. (2015). Data entry: Towards the critical study of digital data and education. *Learning, Media and Technology, 40*(1), 64–82. DOI: 10.1080/17439884.2014.921628

Selwyn, N. (2016). 'There's so much data': Exploring the realities of data-based school governance. *European Educational Research Journal, 15*(1), 54–68. DOI: 10.1177/1474904115602909

Shalini, K. S., Kopperundevi, N., Rajkumar, R., Radhika, A., Gopianand, M., & Preethi, M.K.Shantha Shalini. (2024). Decentralized machine learning for dynamic resource optimization in wireless networks using reinforcement learning. *Journal of Electrical Systems*, *20*(5), 2025–2033. DOI: 10.52783/jes.2539

Sofologi, M., Katsarou, D. V., Tsirides, A., & Efthymiou, E. (2025). The synergy of artificial ıntelligence and education: new perspectives of an ınnovative artificial tutoring in school settings. In *Prompt Engineering and Generative AI Applications for Teaching and Learning* (pp. 189–202). IGI Global Scientific Publishing. DOI: 10.4018/979-8-3693-7332-3.ch012

Spaniol, M. J., & Rowland, N. J. (2023). AI-assisted scenario generation for strategic planning. *Futures & Foresight Science*, *5*(2), e148. DOI: 10.1002/ffo2.148

Stanford University. (2023). *Generative AI policy guidance*. https://communitystandards.stanford.edu/generative-ai-policy-guidance

Tampere University. (2025). *Use of AI-based applications*. https://www.tuni.fi/en/students-guide/handbook/uni/studying-0/academic-integrity-and-study-regulations/use-ai-based-applications

Tang, K., Chang, C., & Hwang, G. (2021). Trends in artificial intelligence-supported e-learning: A systematic review and co-citation network analysis (1998–2019). *Interactive Learning Environments*, *31*(7), 2134–2152. DOI: 10.1080/10494820.2021.1875001

Tapalova, O., Zhiyenbayeva, N., & Gura, D. (2022). Artificial intelligence in education: AIEd for personalised learning pathways. *Electronic Journal of e-Learning*, *20*(5), 639–653. Advance online publication. DOI: 10.34190/ejel.20.5.2597

Teng, Y., Zhang, J., & Sun, T. (2022). Data-driven decision-making model based on artificial intelligence in higher education system of colleges and universities. *Expert Systems: International Journal of Knowledge Engineering and Neural Networks*, *40*(1), e12820. Advance online publication. DOI: 10.1111/exsy.12820

The Open University. (2025). *Generative AI for students*. https://about.open.ac.uk/policies-and-reports/policies-and-statements/gen-ai/generative-ai-students

UNESCO. (2021). *AI in education: Challenges and opportunities for sustainable development*. UNESCO Publishing.

University of Edinburgh. (2025). *Case study: Ethical and effective use of large language models*. https://gail.ed.ac.uk/research/case-studies/case-study-ethical-and-effective-use-of-large-language-models

University of Melbourne. (2025). *Acknowledging AI tools and technologies*. https://students.unimelb.edu.au/academic-skills/resources/academic-integrity/acknowledging-AI-tools-and-technologies

University of Michigan. (2025). *U-M guidance for students*. https://genai.umich.edu/resources/students

University of Oxford. (2024). *Advice on using artificial intelligence (AI) tools to support your learning*. https://www.ox.ac.uk/students/news/2024-01-08-advice-using-artificial-intelligence-ai-tools-support-your-learning

University of Toronto. (2025). *Use artificial intelligence intelligently*. https://security.utoronto.ca/governance/guidelines/use-ai-intelligently/

Upreti, K., Verma, A., Mittal, S., Vats, P., Haque, M., & Ali, S. (2023). A novel framework for harnessing AI for evidence-based policymaking in e-governance using smart contracts. In Shaw, R. N., Paprzycki, M., & Ghosh, A. (Eds.), *Advanced communication and intelligent systems* (pp. 231–245). Springer., DOI: 10.1007/978-3-031-45124-9_18

van der Schaar, M. (2014). Real-time discovery and decision making from big data. *2014 IEEE International Conference on Consumer Electronics-Taiwan*, 1–3. DOI: 10.1109/ICCE-TW.2014.6903996

van der Zwaan, J. M., Bruijne, M., & Kester, L. (2021). Scaling adaptive learning technologies in the Dutch education system: Insights from pilot studies. *European Journal of Educational Research, 10*(2), 287–302. DOI: 10.12973/eu-jer.10.2.287

Viberg, O., Kizilcec, R., Wise, A., Jivet, I., & Nixon, N. (2024). Advancing equity and inclusion in educational practices with AI-powered educational decision support systems (AI-EDSS). *British Journal of Educational Technology, 55*(5), 1974–1981. DOI: 10.1111/bjet.13507

Walton, R. B., Ciarallo, F. W., & Champagne, L. E. (2024). A unified digital twin approach incorporating virtual, physical, and prescriptive analytical components to support adaptive real-time decision-making. *Computers & Industrial Engineering, 193*, 110241. DOI: 10.1016/j.cie.2024.110241

Wang, Y. (2020). When artificial intelligence meets educational leaders' data-informed decision-making: A cautionary tale. *Studies in Educational Evaluation, 66*. Advance online publication. DOI: 10.1016/j.stueduc.2020.100872

Wang, Y. (2021). Artificial intelligence in educational leadership: A symbiotic role of human-artificial intelligence decision-making. *Journal of Educational Administration, 59*(3), 256–270. DOI: 10.1108/JEA-10-2020-0216

Wang, Z. (2024). Innovation in education management from the perspective of sustainable development. *Industrial Engineering and Innovation Management*, *7*(2), 139–148. DOI: 10.23977/ieim.2024.070219

Wilson, R. (2006). Policy analysis as policy advice. In R. Goodin, M. Moran, & M. Rein (Eds.), *The Oxford handbook of public policy* (pp. 152–168). Oxford University Press.

Woolf, B. P., Lane, H. C., Chaudhri, V., & Kolodner, J. L. (2021). AI for educational technologies: Emerging research and opportunities. *International Journal of Artificial Intelligence in Education*, *31*(1), 1–14. DOI: 10.1007/s40593-020-00227-6

Yar, M. A., Hamdan, M., Anshari, M., Fitriyani, N. L., & Syafrudin, M. (2024). Governing with intelligence: The impact of artificial intelligence on policy development. *Information (Basel)*, *15*(9), 556. DOI: 10.3390/info15090556

Yedatkar, A. S.Anju Santosh Yedatkar. (2024). Real-time data analytics in distributed systems. *International Journal of Scientific Research in Modern Science and Technology*, *3*(6), 9–16. DOI: 10.59828/ijsrmst.v3i6.215

Yin, W. (2022). Personalized hybrid education framework based on neuroevolution methodologies. *Computational Intelligence and Neuroscience*, *2022*, 1–16. Advance online publication. DOI: 10.1155/2022/6925668

Zawacki-Richter, O., Marín, V., Bond, M., & Gouverneur, F. (2019). Systematic review of research on artificial intelligence applications in higher education – Where are the educators? *International Journal of Educational Technology in Higher Education*, *16*(1), 39. Advance online publication. DOI: 10.1186/s41239-019-0171-0

Zhai, X., Chu, X., Chai, C., Jong, M., Istenič, A., Spector, M., Liu, J.-B., Yuan, J., & Li, Y. (2021). A review of artificial intelligence (AI) in education from 2010 to 2020. *Complexity*, *8812542*(1), 8812542. Advance online publication. DOI: 10.1155/2021/8812542

Zhang, K., & Aslan, A. (2021). AI technologies for education: Recent research & future directions. *Computers and Education: Artificial Intelligence*, *2*, 100025. DOI: 10.1016/j.caeai.2021.100025

Zheng, H., Xu, K., Zhang, M., Tan, H., & Li, H. (2024). Efficient resource allocation in cloud computing environments using AI-driven predictive analytics. *Applied and Computational Engineering*, *82*(1), 6–12. DOI: 10.54254/2755-2721/82/2024GLG0055

KEY TERMS AND DEFINITIONS

Academic Integrity: A commitment to honesty, responsibility, and ethical behavior in all aspects of academic work.

AI Literacy: The knowledge and skills required to critically understand, evaluate, and ethically use AI technologies in academic or professional settings.

Artificial Intelligence (AI): Computer systems capable of performing tasks that typically require human intelligence, such as reasoning, learning, or language processing.

Generative AI: A type of AI designed to create new content—text, images, or data—by learning from existing patterns.Plagiarism Detection: The process of identifying overlapping or unattributed content in academic work using automated tools.

Large Language Models (LLMs): Advanced AI systems trained on large datasets to generate human-like text responses.

Tutor Guidance in AI Use: The role of educators in helping students use AI tools ethically, critically, and as part of a sound academic process.

Chapter 5
The Policy Landscape: Charting a Course for Ethical AI Integration in Turkish Higher Education

Hatice Bilgin
https://orcid.org/0000-0003-0020-2051
İstanbul Technical University, Turkey

ABSTRACT

This chapter provides a comprehensive analysis of generative artificial intelligence (GenAI) policies in Turkish higher education institutions, exploring institutional responses to AI integration. Through qualitative document analysis of policy documents from nine major Turkish universities and the Council of Higher Education, the study identifies common elements, such as ethical principles and user responsibility, alongside significant gaps in enforcement and support mechanisms. These findings highlight uneven governance practices that challenge responsible AI adoption. This study offers targeted suggestions to guide higher education institutions in developing effective GenAI policies that uphold academic integrity, equity, and ethical standards. By addressing local and global ethical challenges, these recommendations aim to support stakeholders in fostering innovative yet responsible AI integration in Türkiye's higher education system, contributing to a more inclusive and ethically grounded approach to GenAI governance.

INTRODUCTION

Artificial Intelligence (AI) has emerged as a transformative force in higher education, reshaping teaching, learning, as well as research, and within this broader

DOI: 10.4018/979-8-3373-7569-4.ch005

context, generative AI (GenAI), a subset of AI capable of creating original content such as text, images, and code, has gained prominence. Tools like ChatGPT (OpenAI), Claude (Anthropic), and Gemini (Google) facilitate rapid content generation for academic writing, research, and creative tasks, unlocking substantial potential for education. GenAI's ability to personalize learning (Chaika, 2023; Chen et al., 2023; ColMOOC, 2019; Fitria, 2021; Hu et al., 2023; Jian-hua et al., 2019; Pogorskiy & Beckmann, 2023; Sajja et al., 2023; Shan et al., 2020; Sumakul et al., 2022), enhance assessment (Crompton & Burke, 2023), and democratize access to knowledge (Chaika, 2023; Neha et al., 2024; Sajja et al., 2023; The Institute for Ethical AI in Education, 2020) presents immense opportunities. However, significant challenges exist for higher education institutions, including ethical concerns about bias (Holstein & Doroudi, 2022; Ivanov, 2023; Kizilcec & Lee, 2022; Madaio et al., 2022), transparency (Smuha, 2022; Conijn et al., 2023), privacy (Hagendorff, 2020; Jobin et al., 2019; Lu et al., 2024) and academic integrity (Maslej et al., 2024; National Institute of Standards and Technology, 2024; Yeo, 2023). These challenges demand careful consideration to ensure responsible integration of AI in educational settings. In response to this imperative, the scholarly community is actively seeking to develop guiding principles, with significant contributions like Bozkurt et al. (2024) articulating a critical collective stance to better navigate this evolving educational future.

The deployment of GenAI requires careful planning and ethical frameworks, as most universities currently lack clear guidelines, leaving critical issues like student privacy, algorithmic transparency, and bias unaddressed (Ghimire & Edwards, 2024). Ethical governance and policy development for AI in higher education relates to the principles, rules and decision-making processes put in place to ensure that AI systems and practices used in educational institutions comply with ethical standards, protect the rights of stakeholders and promote responsible innovation. In order to build an ethical foundation for AI in higher education, it is important to establish a comprehensive approach to establish clear ethical guidelines and principles specific to AI in education, ensuring that key aspects, including transparency, privacy, and accountability, are protected (Hagendorff, 2020; Jobin et al., 2019; Lu et al., 2024). It is essential to emphasize basic principles in the context of policies to be created for the implementation of AI in higher education with an ethical foundation (Jobin et al., 2019; Nguyen et al., 2022). The principles of openly sharing how AI algorithms work and what data is used, protecting student information and sensitive data, and ensuring that individuals and institutions responsible for the use of AI systems are accountable for the consequences of their practices are interconnected and, when applied together, can foster trust in and ethical use of AI by students, educators and other stakeholders. It can also contribute to preventing the misuse of AI systems and reducing potential harm. Thus, a more equitable, trustworthy and responsible implementation of AI in higher education will be possible.

The literature reveals that higher education institutions worldwide are responding to rise of GenAI through diverse approaches, priorities, and stages of policy development. There is a growing recognition of the need for policies and guidelines to navigate this integration effectively (An et al., 2025; Chaka et al., 2024; Holmes et al., 2022; Jin et al., 2025; McDonald et al., 2025; Mendigutxia, 2025; Schiff, 2022; Stracke et al, 2025; Symeou et al., 2025; Ullah et al., 2024; Vidal et al., 2023). However, ethical considerations are inconsistently addressed across institutional policies. Schiff (2022) notes that while national AI strategies overwhelmingly prioritize workforce development and AI expertise, they largely neglect the ethical implications of AI in education (AIED), despite the broader AI ethics discourse. Ullah et al. (2024) find that most universities address academic integrity and data privacy, but few tackle algorithmic transparency, AI detection tools, or reporting mechanisms. Similarly, McDonald et al. (2025) highlight that fewer than half of leading United States (U.S.) research universities address research-related privacy or ethical concerns, despite promoting GenAI for productivity. European studies (Stracke et al., 2025; Symeou et al., 2025) integrate ethical frameworks more systematically, referencing principles like fairness, transparency, and human rights. The European University Cyprus framework (Symeou et al., 2025), for instance, explicitly addresses General Data Protection Regulation (GDPR) compliance, data protection, and iterative guideline improvement. The contrast between instrumentalist approaches (e.g., AI for productivity, workforce readiness) and values-driven frameworks (e.g., fairness, autonomy, human-centricity) reflects broader ideological tensions in AI policy discourse.

GenAI policy development in higher education is evolving at varying paces globally, with notable disparities between regions. In a study offering a comprehensive overview of how different countries approach the governance of GenAI in education, Vidal et al. (2023) note that none of the 18 Organisation for Economic Co-operation and Development (OECD) countries have specific regulations on the use of GenAI in education although countries such as France and Korea are poised to introduce relevant policies. About half of the countries in the study have issued non-binding guidance on the use of GenAI in educational settings. This study noted that in the absence of centralized regulations, many decisions on integrating GenAI into education are made at the school level, subject to broader national rules on data protection and digital resources. An et al. (2025) found that 94% of the top 50 U.S. universities had faculty guidelines for GenAI use, indicating a proactive approach in high-resource institutions. Similarly, McDonald et al. (2025) reported that 63% of leading research universities in the U.S. actively encourage GenAI use. In contrast, Chaka et al. (2024) discovered that only five of 26 South African higher education institutions had published GenAI policies, highlighting significant regional differences in policy readiness. These disparities reflect broader patterns identified by Jin et al. (2025), whose global analysis of 40 universities across six regions revealed that institutions in the Global North generally demonstrated more developed policies than those in the Global South. This finding aligns with Schiff's (2022) earlier observation that national AI strategies in economically advanced countries tend to be more comprehensive, though often with limited focus on AI applications in education. In a global higher education sector grappling with both the promises and perils of GenAI, while institutions in high-resource contexts are more likely to have formalized and comprehensive guidelines, emerging and resource-constrained settings are often innovating out of necessity, drawing on local values and collaborative governance models.

The analyzed literature reveals varying approaches to stakeholder targeting in GenAI policies. An et al. (2025) note that in U.S. universities, 94% provided faculty guidelines, while far fewer offered guidance for researchers (18%) or administrators (14%). This imbalance is echoed by Stracke et al. (2025), who find that European AI policies predominantly target teachers and students, with limited attention to education managers and policymakers. Symeou et al. (2025) describe a more inclusive approach at European University Cyprus, where guideline development involved multiple stakeholders, including faculty from all academic schools, IT experts, instructional designers, students, and GDPR officers. This aligns with Spivakovsky et al.'s (2023) case study of Kherson State University, which emphasizes stakeholder discussions despite wartime challenges, suggesting that comprehensive stakeholder engagement may be achievable even in adverse circumstances. Mendigutxia (2025) calls for governments to involve higher education institutions in shaping national AI strategies, recognizing universities' unique capacities for ethical governance and interdisciplinary collaboration.

GenAI policies are in early stages of development, with frequent updates and iterative refinement being critical. An et al. (2025) and Ullah et al. (2024) stress the importance of updating policies to match GenAI's rapid evolution and avoiding reliance on outdated or unreliable AI detection tools. Several studies identify notable policy gaps, including inconsistent ethical integration (Mendigutxia, 2025), limited attention to non-faculty stakeholders (Stracke et al., 2025), and insufficient monitoring and enforcement mechanisms (Ullah et al., 2024). Jin et al. (2025) calls for improved evaluation of GenAI's impact and recommend capacity-building through training and stakeholder collaboration. There is also a call for greater alignment between institutional policies and national strategies. Schiff (2022) and Mendigutxia (2025) argue that higher education can play a more active role in shaping responsible AI governance by embedding ethics, research, and skills development into national AI agendas.

As educators and institutions are experimenting with GenAI technologies, a comprehensive understanding of existing policies and the development of future-oriented ethical frameworks remains crucial. This chapter contributes to this effort by examining the current policy landscape for GenAI in Turkish higher education institutions, identifying key areas of focus, and proposing pathways for ethically grounded and effective policies. In Türkiye, where higher education is shaped by centralized governance under the Yükseköğretim Kurulu (YÖK, Council of Higher Education) and a culturally diverse student population, the rapid adoption of GenAI amplifies these challenges, yet the landscape of GenAI-specific policies remains underexplored. This study addresses this gap by analyzing GenAI policies across ten Turkish higher education institutions, examining their scope, ethical principles, governance mechanisms, and cultural considerations to identify commonalities, divergences, and unique Turkish contextual factors. By doing so, it aims to inform the development of consistent, culturally sensitive GenAI policies, contributing to ethical AI integration in Türkiye's higher education system. The aim of this study is:

- To analyze and compare existing GenAI policies across Turkish higher education institutions
- To identify common elements, divergences, and gaps in current policy approaches
- To identify unique considerations emerging in the Turkish context

METHODOLOGY

This study employed a qualitative research design, utilizing document analysis to explore the emerging landscape of GenAI policies in Turkish higher education institutions. Document analysis was selected as the primary methodological approach because it allows for a systematic and in-depth examination of publicly available institutional policies and guidelines, providing insights into the formal approaches adopted by universities to address the use of GenAI. As a non-reactive method, document analysis allows for the examination of policies in their natural context, without influencing the content or implementation of those policies (Bowen, 2009; Morgan, 2022; Wach & Ward, 2013).

Data collection involved a multi-stage process. First, a comprehensive list of Turkish universities was compiled using the website of YÖK. According to Yükseköğretim Bilgi Yönetim Sistemi (2025), there are 127 public universities, 74 foundation universities, and 4 foundation vocational schools, which makes 205 higher education institutions in total in Türkiye. Next, as some universities may have English versions of their policies, a keyword search using both Turkish and English terms such as "yapay zeka" (artificial intelligence), "üretken yapay zeka" (generative artificial intelligence), "politika" (policy), and "etik rehber," (ethical guidelines) was conducted in Google, utilizing Boolean operators (AND, OR, NOT) to refine the search. The websites of each university were then systematically searched, focusing on "Hakkında" (About) section. Data collection continued until no new themes or policy approaches were emerging from the analysis of additional documents between January 1, 2025, and February 1, 2025. Officially published documents by a Turkish higher education institution (university, institute, or a recognized body like YÖK) which explicitly address the use of GenAI (or closely related terms like "large language models," "AI-powered tools") in an academic context (teaching, learning, research, assessment, etc.) were included. Document types were formal policies, ethical guidelines, recommendations/guidance documents, handbooks for students or faculty, directives/regulations, and official statements or announcements. Only finalized, officially approved documents were included while documents from private training centers, or other non-university institutions were excluded. The initial search yielded 39 potential documents, which were then screened for relevance based on their explicit mention of GenAI or related technologies in the context of academic policies. Along with blog posts, news articles, opinion pieces, or other documents that are not officially endorsed by the institution, documents that discuss AI in a very broad sense without specific reference to GenAI or its use in education/research were not included. Also, guidelines or policy documents published by different units of universities such as faculties, departments or research centers were excluded as the focus of the study is to understand institutional policies at the university level. This screening process resulted in a final dataset of 15 documents from 10 different institutions. All identified documents were managed using a spreadsheet logging key information about each document, including the institution, title of the document, and web address.

The collected data comprising publicly accessible policy documents, guidelines, and official statements related to GenAI from Turkish higher education institutions were analyzed using a thematic analysis approach. Thematic analysis was employed to identify recurring patterns, similarities, and differences in the approaches taken by Turkish institutions to address GenAI (Clarke & Braun, 2017; Maguire & Delahunt, 2017). Coded data were grouped into broader themes, and relationships between themes were explored to develop a comprehensive understanding of the GenAI policy landscape. *Taguette* (Rampin & Rampin, 2021), a free and open-source qualitative data analysis software, was used to manage and analyze the collected documents as it has a user-friendly interface, and is suitable for coding and thematic analysis. A comparative analysis was then performed to identify commonalities, divergences, and gaps in GenAI policies across different Turkish universities, which provided a nuanced understanding of how Turkish higher education institutions formally conceptualize and regulate GenAI, laying the groundwork for critical discussions about policy coherence, ethical governance, and the future of AI integration in academia.

As this study analyzed publicly available documents, ethical approval from an Institutional Review Board was not required. However, the researcher adhered to ethical principles of research integrity, ensuring accurate representation of the data and avoiding any misrepresentation or distortion of the content of the documents.

FINDINGS

This section presents the findings of a document analysis examining 15 policy documents from 10 Turkish higher education institutions, focusing on institutional-level policies and regulatory approaches. Table 1, organized alphabetically by institution, illustrates the institutional guidance and regulation efforts across Türkiye's higher education sector by listing central policies approved and published by governing bodies as GenAI technologies gain prominence. The analysis includes five foundation (private) universities (Bilkent, İstanbul Bilgi, Kadir Has, Koç, and MEF) and four public universities (Burdur Mehmet Akif Ersoy, Gazi, Hacettepe, İzmir Institute of Technology), along with the national public entity YÖK, reflecting distinct governance structures that shape their GenAI policies and highlight the interplay of institutional type and national oversight in addressing ethical AI integration.

*Table 1. List of Documents Analyzed in the Study**

Institution	Title of the document	Language(s)	Web address**
Bilkent University	Guidelines for the Use of Generative Artificial Intelligence (GenAI) Tools at Bilkent	English	https://w3.bilkent.edu.tr/bilkent/generative-artificial-intelligence-genai-guideline/
Burdur Mehmet Akif Ersoy University	Burdur Mehmet Akif Ersoy Üniversitesi Üretken Yapay Zekâ Kullanımı Etik Rehberi	Turkish	https://gs.mehmetakif.edu.tr/upload/gs/74-form-2031-38290621-yapay-zeka-etik-rehber-tasla-senato-gndem-son.pdf
Gazi University	Üretken Yapay Zekâ Araçlarının Kullanımına İlişkin Etik İlkeler ve Öneriler Rehberi (Sürüm 1.0)	Turkish	https://aicenter.gazi.edu.tr/files/etik-ilkeler.pdf

continued on following page

Table 1. Continued

Institution	Title of the document	Language(s)	Web address**
Hacettepe University	Eğitim ve Öğretim Süreçlerinde Üretken Yapay Zeka Kullanım Politikası	Turkish	https://gazete.hacettepe.edu.tr/fs_/HABERLER/2025/Ocak/YapayZeka.pdf
İstanbul Bilgi University	İstanbul Bilgi Üniversitesi Yükseköğretim ve Araştırma için Yapay Zeka (YZ) Politikası	Turkish	https://www.bilgi.edu.tr/media/uploads/2024/04/05/yapayzekapolitikasi.pdf
	Istanbul Bilgi University Artificial Intelligence (AI) Policy for Higher Education and Research	English	https://www.bilgi.edu.tr/media/uploads/2024/04/05/artificialintelligencepolicy.pdf
İzmir Institute of Technology (İzmir Yüksek Teknoloji Enstitüsü)	İzmir Yüksek Teknoloji Enstitüsü Yapay Zekâ Politikası	Turkish	https://yks-karartakip.iyte.edu.tr/files/KararDevamDosyasi/ykstdd-1156-1-250115155514.pdf
Kadir Has University	Üretken Yapay Zekâ (ÜYZ) Araçları Kullanımı Hakkında Etik Rehber	Turkish	https://www.khas.edu.tr/uretken-yapay-zeka-uyz-araclari-kullanimi-hakkinda-etik-rehber/
	Ethical Guidance on the Use of Generative Artificial Intelligence (GENERATIVE AI) Tools	English (only the title of the document available in English, but the content in Turkish)	https://www.khas.edu.tr/en/ethical-guidance-on-the-use-of-generative-artificial-intelligence-generative-ai-tools/
Koç University	Koç Üniversitesi'nde Yapay Zeka Araçlarının Kullanımına İlişkin Prosedürler	Turkish	https://kolt.ku.edu.tr/tr/yapay-zeka/
	Koç University Policy Statement Regarding the Use of Artificial Intelligence Tools (ChatGPT or other similar tools)	English	https://kolt.ku.edu.tr/artificial-intelligence/

continued on following page

Table 1. Continued

Institution	Title of the document	Language(s)	Web address**
MEF University	MEF Üniversitesi Yapay Zeka Politikası Versiyon 2.0	Turkish	https://www.datocms-assets.com/99182/1726134331-mef-universitesi-yapay-zeka-politikasi-versiyon-2-0.pdf
	MEF University AI Policy Version 2.0	English	https://www.datocms-assets.com/99182/1726134331-mef-university-ai-policy-version-2-0.pdf
Council of Higher Education (Yükseköğretim Kurulu, YÖK)	Yükseköğretim Kurumları Bilimsel Araştırma ve Yayın Faaliyetlerinde Üretken Yapay Zekâ Kullanımına Dair Etik Rehber	Turkish	https://www.yok.gov.tr/Documents/2024/yapay-zeka-kullanimina-dair-etik-rehber.pdf
	Ethics Guide of Generative Artificial Intelligence Use in the Scientific Research and Publication Process of Higher Education Institutions	English	https://www.yok.gov.tr/en/Documents/2024/ethics-guide-of-generative-ai-use-in-the-scientific-research-and-publication-process.pdf

*See Appendix for the full reference of the analyzed documents in Table 1
**All web addresses listed in Table 1 were accessed on February 16, 2025.

These policies, titled variably (e.g., "ethical guide," "usage policy," "ethical principles and recommendations guide"), generally provide frameworks for integrating GenAI tools into education, research, and administrative processes, aligning with their respective missions. The variability in document titles may reflect the different stages of policy maturity and institutional cautiousness in a rapidly evolving technological landscape. For instance, guidelines or recommendations might suggest a more flexible, less binding approach suitable for initial explorations, whereas formal policies imply a more established and enforceable stance. This terminological diversity could also indicate varying levels of perceived urgency or differing philosophies on how prescriptive institutional directives should be in this nascent area. Furthermore, the general aim of these documents to provide frameworks for GenAI integration, while positive, requires scrutiny to determine if they are comprehensive enough to move beyond broad principles to actionable guidance. While most documents are originally drafted in Turkish, reflecting the national language, several institutions and YÖK have published English versions to enhance international accessibility and align with global standards. Specifically, İstanbul Bilgi University, Koç University, MEF University, and YÖK offer bilingual (Turkish and English) versions. Across all these four institutions, the English and Turkish texts align closely in structure, content, and intent. The English and Turkish versions of AI-related policy and ethics documents from these four Turkish institutions demonstrate a high degree of consistency between their bilingual iterations, substantive equivalence between English and Turkish versions, with differences limited to natural linguistic adaptations (e.g., Turkish elaboration for emphasis). Kadir Has University's English-titled document, however, contains Turkish content, limiting its utility as a fully bilingual resource. While Bilkent University provides its policy exclusively in English, catering to its internationalized community, Burdur Mehmet Akif Ersoy, Gazi, Hacettepe, and İzmir Institute of Technology offer their documents only in Turkish, emphasizing national accessibility. These linguistic variations highlight differing institutional priorities and audiences, influencing the accessibility and reach of GenAI policy frameworks within Türkiye's higher education landscape. The provision of English versions by several institutions and YÖK not only caters to international faculty and students but also positions these Turkish higher education institutions within the global discourse on AI ethics and governance, facilitating international comparison and collaboration. Conversely, policies offered exclusively in Turkish, while ensuring national accessibility, might limit their international visibility and the ease with which non-Turkish speaking researchers can engage with them. The instance of a document with an English title but Turkish content further highlights potential inconsistencies in multilingual strategy. Ultimately, these language choices have direct implications for knowledge dissemination, inclusivity for diverse campus populations, and Türkiye's broader engagement with international standards and debates on GenAI in education.

Building on the diverse institutional contexts and linguistic approaches of Turkish higher education entities, the scope and focus of their GenAI policies reveal distinct priorities shaped by governance structures and missions. Table 2 provides a structured overview of these policies.

Table 2. Overview of Scope and Focus of GenAI Policies Across Turkish Higher Education Institutions

Institution	Scope	Primary Focus	Unique Emphasis
Bilkent University	GenAI	Education	Classroom integration, use cases
Burdur Mehmet Akif Ersoy University	GenAI	Education, research, administration, society	Accessibility, sustainability
Gazi University	GenAI	Education, research, administration	Practical policy, citation specificity
Hacettepe University	GenAI	Education, administration	Ecosystem, GenAI literacy

continued on following page

Table 2. Continued

Institution	Scope	Primary Focus	Unique Emphasis
İstanbul Bilgi University	Broad AI	Education, research, administration	Innovation, monitoring
İzmir Institute of Technology	Broad AI	Education, research, administration, society	Research leadership, AI Commission
Kadir Has University	GenAI	Education, research	Instructor autonomy, YÖK alignment
Koç University	AI (GenAI focus)	Education	Student use, reflection requirement
MEF University	Broad AI	Education, research, administration, society	AI-integrated vision, AI Café
YÖK	GenAI	Research, publication	Ethical climate, FAQs

As it is seen in Table 2, revealing distinct institutional approaches, seven policies specifically target GenAI, reflecting a focused response to tools like ChatGPT, while three encompass broader AI technologies, indicating a wider technological ambition. This distinction in scope (explained in Table 5 below) offers insight into institutional foresight and regulatory philosophy. While a broader scope might future-proof policies, a GenAI-specific focus allows for more targeted and immediately relevant guidance. Education is the predominant focus, present in nine policies, followed by research in seven, administration in six, and societal benefits in three. The predominance of education as a primary focus in nearly all policies logically reflects the core mission of these institutions and the immediate impact of GenAI on teaching and learning. The relatively widespread attention to research and administration also signals an understanding of GenAI's broader utility. However, the comparatively limited focus on societal benefits (addressed in only three policies) might indicate an early stage of policy development where internal operational and academic concerns take precedence. This could represent a missed opportunity for Turkish higher education institutions to explicitly articulate their role in leveraging AI for broader societal good, a key aspect of a university's third mission. The extent to which these focus areas are deeply integrated versus superficially mentioned also warrants consideration, as a policy might list research but lack substantive guidance on AI use in scholarly publication or data analysis. Beyond the primary areas of application, the analyzed policies are further differentiated by a diverse range of unique institutional emphases. These specific priorities signal varied strategic directions, which can represent strategic institutional investments and priorities that differentiate them in the national higher education landscape. For instance, an emphasis on an AI Commission might signal a commitment to robust governance and expert oversight, while an AI Café suggests a focus on community building, experimentation, and practical support. The presence or absence of such unique, actionable initiatives within policy documents can thus be an indicator of how deeply an institution is planning to embed GenAI support into its operational fabric, beyond mere compliance statements. The collective pattern of these unique elements further reinforces the observation of a system where institutional autonomy in addressing specific nuances of AI integration is evident, despite a centralized governance structure. This wide array of unique focal points suggests that while common themes exist, institutions are also tailoring their GenAI responses to their specific missions, resources, and perceived needs within the Turkish higher education landscape. Such diversity, however, may also point to a lack of a unified national strategy on these specific nuances of AI integration, potentially leading to varied levels of preparedness or focus across the system.

Examination of the diverse scopes and focuses of GenAI policies across Turkish higher education institutions reveals a unifying framework of shared elements, underscoring a collective commitment to ethical AI integration. Table 3 synthesizes these commonalities, identifying four core elements present across the policies, collectively signifying a concerted effort by Turkish higher education institutions to establish a foundational ethical posture navigating the complexities of AI integration.

Table 3. Common Elements Across GenAI Policies in Turkish Higher Education

Element	Institutions Exhibiting Element	Description
Ethical principles/ values	All (explicitly mentioned or implied)	See Table 4 below for details
Risk awareness	All	Inaccuracies (e.g., hallucinations), bias, privacy, and misconduct risks noted
User responsibility	All	Users accountable for verifying outputs and adhering to guidelines
Citation requirement	Bilkent, Gazi, Kadir Has, Koç, MEF, YÖK (implied in Burdur Mehmet Akif Ersoy, Hacettepe, İstanbul Bilgi, İzmir Institute of Technology)	Explicit requirement to acknowledge GenAI use in academic work; varies in specificity. See Table 5 below for details

GenAI is generally viewed as a tool to aid learning and research, not a replacement for original thought and work, and the ethical and responsible use of GenAI tools is emphasized in all policies analyzed. The universal emphasis on ethical principles like transparency, integrity, and accountability (detailed in Table 4 below) is a significant finding, indicating a recognized need across Turkish higher education institutions to ground GenAI use within an ethical framework. This widespread adoption likely stems from both national directives (e.g., YÖK's guidance) and an awareness of international best practices in responsible AI. However, while the mention of these principles is universal, their operationalization and the depth of their integration into actionable policy measures may vary (as explored further in the discussion of Table 4 and Table 5). The mere presence of these terms does not automatically guarantee a deeply embedded ethical culture, but it does provide a critical starting point for fostering one. Secondly, the fact that all analyzed policies address risk awareness, highlighting issues such as inaccuracies, bias, and privacy, signals a mature initial understanding that GenAI tools are not without their perils. This 'cautious stance' is vital for preempting potential harms and fostering critical user engagement rather than uncritical adoption. Analytically, this widespread risk awareness is a positive indicator, but its practical impact will depend on whether this awareness translates into specific mitigation strategies, robust support mechanisms for users navigating these risks, and clear protocols for addressing incidents. Acknowledging risk is foundational, but mitigating it requires further institutional commitment beyond mere mention in policy. Thirdly, across analyzed policies, a key strategy is the strong emphasis on user responsibility, requiring students and faculty to validate AI-generated content and comply with usage rules. This is intended to cultivate critical digital literacy and ensure human judgment remains central to academic work. However, while promoting individual accountability is crucial, an excessive reliance on users for verification risks shifting the burden away from institutions, potentially excusing them from providing adequate training, resources (as noted in Table 6), and technically sound systems. Consequently, the effectiveness of this user-focused approach is directly contingent on the level of institutional backing and the AI proficiency within its community Finally, the focus on citation requirements for GenAI use, explicit in a majority of policies and implied in others, underscores the perceived threat to traditional notions of authorship and the importance of transparency in scholarly communication. This reflects a direct attempt to integrate GenAI use into existing academic integrity frameworks. However, the distinction between explicit and merely implied citation requirements in nearly half the institutions warrants analytical attention. An implied requirement may create ambiguity for users and could lead to inconsistent application, potentially undermining the goal of universal transparency. This variance suggests that consensus on the precise mechanisms for ensuring disclosure in AI-assisted work is still developing within the Turkish higher education system, a point further elaborated in the divergences noted in Table 5.

Building on the shared ethical commitments identified across GenAI policies in Turkish higher education, a deeper examination of specific ethical principles articulated by each institution reveals both uniformity and diversity. Unlike Bilkent, Hacettepe, and Koç, which embed ethical concepts within broader policy sections rather than dedicating distinct sections to them, seven institutions, detailed in Table 4, explicitly delineate principles and values in separate, dedicated sections within their policies.

Table 4. Ethical Principles Stated in GenAI Policies

Institution	Ethical Principles
Burdur Mehmet Akif Ersoy University	Inclusivity (Kapsayıcılık), Accessibility (Erişebilirlik), Stakeholder Participation (Paydaş Katılımı), Security and Privacy (Güvenlik ve Gizlilik), Transparency and Explainability (Şeffaflık ve Açıklanabilirlik), Responsibility and Auditability (Sorumluluk ve Denetlenebilirlik), Academic Integrity (Akademik Dürüstlük), Critical Thinking (Eleştirel Düşünme)
Gazi University	Responsibility (Sorumluluk), Disclosure Obligation (Açıklama Yükümlülüğü), Transparency (Şeffaflık), Academic Integrity (Akademik Dürüstlük), Critical Thinking (Eleştirel Düşünme), Accuracy and Reliability (Doğruluk ve Güvenilirlik),
İstanbul Bilgi University	Ethical Use, Privacy and Data Protection, Academic Integrity, Access and Equity, Innovation and Continuous Learning, Adaptability
İzmir Institute of Technology	Human Rights (İnsan Hakları), Academic Ethics (Akademik Etik), Environmental Sustainability (Çevresel Sürdürülebilirlik), Inclusivity (Kapsayıcılık), Impartiality (Tarafsızlık), Transparency (Şeffaflık)
Kadir Has University	Stated the same principles within the framework of the ethical values specified in the Higher Education Council Guidelines: Transparency (Şeffaflık), Honesty (Dürüstlük), Care (Özen/Diligence), Justice and Respect (Adalet ve Saygı), Privacy and Protection of Confidentiality (Gizlilik ve Mahremiyetin Korunması), Accountability and Responsibility (Hesap Verebilirlik ve Sorumluluk Üstlenme), Contributing to Ethical Climate (Etik İklime Katkıda Bulunma)
MEF University	Respect for Human Rights, Democracy and Rule of Law, Enhancing the Environment and Biological Ecosystem, Diversity and Inclusivity, Living in Peaceful, Just and Interconnected Societies, Proportionality, Safety and Security, Impartiality, Privacy, Transparency and Explainability, Responsibility and Accountability, Data Sovereignty, Multi-stakeholder Governance
YÖK	Transparency, Integrity, Diligence, Justice and Respect, Privacy and Protection of Confidentiality, Accountability and Responsibility, Contributing to Ethical Climate

As shown in Table 4, the ethical principles articulated in the policies reveal distinct institutional priorities, reflecting institutions' efforts to tailor their frameworks to specific missions and contexts. For instance, direct alignment with YÖK's framework by some institutions, such as Kadir Has University, promotes national consistency, though it may risk diluting institution-specific ethical considerations or overlooking unique regional and cultural risks. Other unique priorities highlighted by various institutions include environmental sustainability, a focus on innovation, a comprehensive global orientation in ethical thought, and a drive to cultivate an ethical climate, each reflecting tailored institutional values beyond the more commonly cited principles. This divergence in explicitly stated unique ethical priorities, while allowing for institutional differentiation, could complicate efforts to establish a uniformly understood and applied ethical standard for GenAI use across all Turkish higher education institutions. Also, the lack of a separate, distinct section on ethical principles in some policies may suggest less emphasis on isolating ethics as a standalone topic and could potentially affect user clarity. Despite this diversity, the observed divergence in institutional policies, including the notable absence of key principles like data privacy in some cases, raises questions about the consistency and comprehensiveness of ethical safeguards. This inconsistency not only suggests potential vulnerabilities in ethical safeguards but also hinders the development of a shared understanding of responsible AI practices within the Turkish higher education system, suggesting a need for more robust and nationally consistent standards to foster a unified approach to GenAI/AI ethics.

Following the identification of shared ethical commitments and principles in GenAI policies across Turkish higher education, significant variations emerge, reflecting the diverse priorities and approaches of individual institutions. Table 5 outlines these divergences.

Table 5. Divergences in GenAI Policies

Institution	Scope Specificity	Detail Level	Unique Governance/ Support	Citation/ Documentation
Bilkent University	GenAI	Rich examples	Syllabus guidance	Citation
Burdur Mehmet Akif Ersoy University	GenAI	Broad principles	Accessibility focus	Implied citation
Gazi University	GenAI	Citation specifics	None specified	APA/MLA, prompts
Hacettepe University	GenAI	Literacy/assessment focus	Detection tools (e.g., *Turnitin*)	Implied citation
İstanbul Bilgi University	Broad AI	High-level principles	Monitoring, training	Implied citation
İzmir Institute of Technology	Broad AI	Strategic goals	AI Commission, training	Implied citation
Kadir Has University	GenAI	Specific uses	Ethics committee	Bibliography, prompts/ evaluation
Koç University	AI (GenAI focus)	Actionable rules	Disciplinary link	APA/MLA, prompts/ outputs/reflection
MEF University	Broad AI	Pedagogical framework	AI Committee, AI Cafe, CELT	Citation, prompts/outputs in appendix
YÖK	GenAI	Ethical climate focus	Ethical climate training	Method section disclosure

The analyzed policies reveal a fragmented landscape characterized by inconsistencies in different areas. Seven policies are GenAI-specific while three encompass broader AI technologies, reflecting differing technological emphases that complicate a unified approach. This divergence in technological scope could reflect varying levels of institutional ambition, available expertise, or perhaps different interpretations of the most pressing regulatory needs. A focused GenAI scope allows for immediate, targeted responses to the most prominent new tools like ChatGPT. However, this narrower focus might necessitate frequent policy updates as new AI paradigms emerge. Conversely, policies addressing broad AI may exhibit greater technological ambition and aim for more enduring relevance, but they risk becoming too general to provide clear, actionable guidance for specific GenAI applications, potentially diluting their impact if not accompanied by detailed, tool-specific addendums or resources. This strategic choice could also reflect institutional capacity, where developing comprehensive broad AI policies might require more extensive expertise and resources than formulating guidelines for currently prevalent GenAI tools. The divergence in scope is further compounded by a lack of consistent definitions for Generative AI or AI tools. While Kadir Has and Bilkent provide a section on the definition of GenAI, MEF adheres to the OECD's definition of AI systems and the remaining policies offer no definitions, potentially undermining clarity for users. Beyond user clarity, the absence of common definitions (or any definition in many cases) creates ambiguity in policy application and enforcement. For instance, faculty and students may struggle to determine if a particular AI tool falls under the policy's purview, potentially leading to inconsistent adherence or disputes. This lack of foundational consensus also complicates inter-institutional collaboration and the development of national benchmarks for responsible AI use in Türkiye. Significant divergence was also evident in the level of practical implementation guidance offered within the policies. While some institutions provided rich, actionable examples or specific rules for documentation and use, many others offered only broad principles. This variation in the detail of implementation guidance may stem from differing institutional capacities to develop comprehensive resources, diverse pedagogical philosophies regarding the use of GenAI, or simply the early and iterative stage of policy development across the sector. This unevenness in the granularity and specificity of guidance suggests that users across the Turkish higher education system may experience varied levels of clarity and support in applying these policies to their daily academic activities, potentially impacting consistent and effective GenAI integration. More specifically, students at institutions with vague guidelines might be disadvantaged or inadvertently commit academic misconduct, while faculty may hesitate to integrate GenAI innovatively without clear institutional backing or examples of good practice. Such disparities could also hinder efforts to cultivate a shared understanding and baseline competency in ethical AI use across the national academic community. Accountability mechanisms, crucial for policy effectiveness, also showed considerable variation across institutions, ranging from establishing dedicated AI or ethics committees and utilizing detection tools to implementing monitoring processes or developing innovative support resources like AI Cafés and specialized teaching and learning centers. The adoption of such varied accountability mechanisms might reflect different institutional cultures (e.g., emphasizing developmental support versus punitive enforcement) or varying assessments of the primary risks associated with GenAI use. However, the absence of clearly articulated formal oversight or enforcement procedures in several policies is a significant finding. This particular divergence points to potential inconsistencies in ensuring compliance and addressing violations across the Turkish higher education landscape, potentially weakening the overall governance framework for GenAI. A lack of clear and consistently applied accountability measures can erode trust in the policies themselves and may fail to establish clear expectations for behavior. For the Turkish higher education system, this could mean an inconsistent approach to upholding academic integrity and managing AI-related risks, making it difficult to assure quality and ethical standards uniformly. Finally, the specific practices, requirements, or methods outlined in each policy for acknowledging, reporting, or documenting the use of GenAI tools in academic or research work also reveal significant variation, reflecting diverse institutional priorities within the nation's higher education landscape. The considerable variation in citation requirements likely reflects the ongoing global debate and lack of universal consensus on how to appropriately acknowledge AI contributions, coupled with the rapid pace of technological development outstripping slower academic norm-setting processes. These inconsistencies highlight the need for standardized practices to enhance consistency and address the fragmented nature of GenAI policy implementation across Türkiye's higher education landscape. This lack of standardization can create significant confusion for students and researchers, particularly those collaborating across institutions or submitting work to different forums. It also complicates the task of educators in teaching and assessing responsible AI use and may impede the establishment of a clear national standard for academic transparency in the age of AI, a critical component for maintaining scholarly credibility within Türkiye and internationally.

Following the examination of the diverse approaches and divergences in GenAI policies across different Turkish higher education institutions, significant gaps emerge that challenge their effective implementation and relevance. Table 6 identifies these gaps.

Table 6. Gaps in GenAI Policies

Institution	Enforcement Mechanisms	Practical Guidance	Faculty Support
Bilkent University	Unspecified	Examples	Syllabus focus
Burdur Mehmet Akif Ersoy University	Unspecified	No examples	Unspecified
Gazi University	Unspecified	Citation	Unspecified
Hacettepe University	Detection tools	No examples	Vague training
İstanbul Bilgi University	Monitoring	No examples	Training implied
İzmir Institute of Technology	AI Commission	No examples	Training implied

continued on following page

Table 6. Continued

Institution	Enforcement Mechanisms	Practical Guidance	Faculty Support
Kadir Has University	Ethics committee	Uses	Unspecified
Koç University	Disciplinary link	Rules	Unspecified
MEF University	Committee audits	Framework	AI Café, CELT, training
YÖK	Disciplinary mention	FAQs	Training suggested

The existence of the gaps detailed in Table 6 is perhaps unsurprising given the nascent stage of GenAI policy development in Türkiye. However, their specific nature and prevalence carry significant implications for the successful, ethical, and equitable integration of these technologies across the Turkish higher education system. Understanding these omissions is crucial for charting a course towards more robust and effective AI governance. Enforcement mechanisms are present in seven policies, with specific approaches like detection tools, monitoring, and AI Commission, but none provide detailed violation detection or penalty processes, revealing a significant gap in accountability. This general lack of detailed violation detection protocols or clearly stipulated penalty processes across all analyzed documents reveals a critical gap in accountability, which may inadvertently indicate that policies are aspirational rather than strictly enforceable, potentially diminishing their deterrent effect on academic misconduct. Furthermore, without transparent procedures, institutions may struggle to apply consequences consistently and fairly, which could lead to perceptions of inequity or arbitrariness, thereby undermining trust in the entire governance framework. The absence of such details also leaves faculty and administrative staff without clear guidance on how to proceed when suspected violations occur, potentially leading to inaction or inconsistent responses. Policies often do not provide specific guidance on using particular GenAI tools, indicating uneven applicability across the system. This disparity in practical guidance has profound implications. For faculty, a lack of concrete examples or pedagogical frameworks can stifle innovative teaching with GenAI and create uncertainty about how to guide students responsibly. For students, unclear or absent guidance on specific tools or use-cases can lead to confusion, unintentional misuse, or an uneven playing field where students at better-resourced or more proactive institutions receive more support. This guidance gap may therefore not only hinder effective GenAI integration but also exacerbate existing digital literacy and equity divides within Turkish higher education. Faculty support is specified in only five policies often vaguely, lacking detailed training programs, while others omit it entirely. The widespread lack of detailed, concrete commitments to faculty support and training is particularly concerning. Faculty are at the forefront of AI integration in pedagogical settings, yet without adequate institutional support, ranging from technical training to pedagogical consultations and resources for assessment redesign, they may feel unprepared, overwhelmed, or unsupported in navigating these complex new tools. This gap could significantly slow down meaningful pedagogical innovation and the development of AI literacy within the academic community. Moreover, it implicitly places a substantial burden on individual academics to self-skill, which is neither equitable nor sustainable, and may reflect an underestimation of the institutional resources required for effective change management in the era of AI. These identified gaps in enforcement, practical guidance, and faculty support are not isolated shortcomings; collectively, they highlight systemic weaknesses in the current GenAI policy landscape within Turkish higher education. Such omissions suggest that while foundational ethical principles may be acknowledged (as seen in Table 3), the translation of these principles into robust, actionable, and supportive governance frameworks is still significantly underdeveloped. Addressing these gaps through targeted policy enhancements is therefore crucial not just for ensuring compliance, but for building institutional capacity, fostering user trust, and ultimately realizing the potential for effective, ethical, and contextually relevant GenAI integration across Türkiye's universities.

Following the identification of gaps in the implementation of GenAI policies across Turkish higher education institutions, it is essential to examine the unique contextual factors that shape these policies within Türkiye's specific socio-educational landscape. Table 7 highlights these key considerations.

Table 7. Unique Considerations in the Turkish Context Across GenAI Policies

Institution	Legal/National Ties
Bilkent University	Internal (Academic Integrity Policy)
Burdur Mehmet Akif Ersoy University	KVKK*, Higher Education Law, Intellectual and Artistic Works Law, Graduate Education and Examination Regulations, Higher Education Institutions Scientific Research and Publication Ethics Directive, Ethics Guide of Generative Artificial Intelligence Use in The Scientific Research and Publication Process of Higher Education Institutions
Gazi University	None explicitly stated
Hacettepe University	Ethics Guide of Generative Artificial Intelligence Use in The Scientific Research and Publication Process of Higher Education Institutions
İstanbul Bilgi University	Implied (Privacy Laws and Regulations, Higher Education Regulations)
İzmir Institute of Technology	The laws and regulations of the Republic of Türkiye, EU AI Act
Kadir Has University	Ethics Guide of Generative Artificial Intelligence Use in The Scientific Research and Publication Process of Higher Education Institutions

continued on following page

Table 7. Continued

Institution	Legal/National Ties
Koç University	Internal (Student Code of Conduct)
MEF University	KVKK, EU AI Act, National AI Strategy, Ethics Guide of Generative Artificial Intelligence Use in The Scientific Research and Publication Process of Higher Education Institutions
YÖK	KVKK, Higher Education Law, Intellectual and Artistic Works Law, Graduate Education and Examination Regulations, Higher Education Institutions Scientific Research and Publication Ethics Directive

*KVKK: Türkiye's Personal Data Protection Law

A key unique consideration in the Turkish context is the varying extent of explicit legal and national framework alignment within institutional GenAI policies, detailed in Table 7. A discernible pattern indicates that public institutions and the national YÖK guidance tend to demonstrate more extensive and explicit ties to Turkish national laws (such as KVKK, the Higher Education Law, and intellectual property laws) and YÖK's own ethical directives. Some institutions, both public and foundation, also referenced international frameworks like the EU AI Act or Türkiye's National AI Strategy, signaling a forward-thinking approach. In contrast, other policies, particularly from some foundation universities, showed less explicit connection to these overarching national legal frameworks, sometimes relying more on internal codes of conduct or making only implied reference to broader regulations. This fragmentation in explicit legal grounding across policies, ranging from comprehensive national legal integration to more autonomous internal referencing, highlights a complex regulatory landscape. Such variation could impact the uniformity of legal compliance and ethical oversight in GenAI use across Türkiye, potentially creating challenges for developing a cohesive national strategy that balances institutional autonomy with centralized governance objectives.

In summary, the emerging landscape of GenAI policies in Turkish higher education reflects a dynamic interplay of ethical caution, practical innovation, and national alignment, shaped by institutional priorities and Türkiye's unique context. The policies analyzed demonstrate a proactive and serious approach to harnessing GenAI's potential while mitigating its risks, emphasizing ethical and responsible use through shared values of integrity and accountability. However, despite a shared commitment to ethical GenAI use, divergences in scope ranging from GenAI-specific to broader AI frameworks as well as gaps in enforcement and practical guidance reflect a rapidly developing policy area, shaped by differing institutional priorities. Moreover, critical gaps such as inconsistent attention to some risks, limited enforcement mechanisms, and insufficient practical guidance point to a framework still in transition, requiring further refinement to effectively address Türkiye's diverse and evolving context. Addressing these gaps, while leveraging Türkiye's centralized governance, legal frameworks, and technological ambitions, can position its universities as leaders in ethical AI integration, marking these policies as a critical step toward raising awareness and providing guidance for GenAI use in Turkish higher education.

DISCUSSION

The findings presented in the previous section reveal a dynamic and evolving landscape of GenAI policies within Turkish higher education, characterized by both shared commitments and significant divergences. Understanding the implications of this landscape requires a deeper dive into the specific challenges and ethical questions these policies attempt to address, often reflecting broader global dialogues. The discussion will now situate these findings within the broader international literature, exploring the key challenges and ethical considerations that emerge. The rapid advancement of GenAI has indeed globally prompted higher education institutions to develop policies and guidelines to manage its integration into teaching, learning, research, and administration. This analysis reveals that Turkish higher education institutions are at various stages of developing and implementing GenAI policies. While some progress has been made, there is still significant work needed to create comprehensive, effective, and standardized approaches across Turkish higher education institutions.

The Shifting Sands: Definitional Challenges in AI Governance

The integration of AI into higher education presents significant opportunities but also poses challenges, particularly due to the lack of a clear, unified definition of AI, specifically GenAI, itself. Schuett (2021) identifies this definitional ambiguity as a primary obstacle in AI regulation, noting that the absence of a standardized scope complicates the establishment of ethical and legal frameworks. This challenge is compounded by AI's complex nature, which Scherer (2016) describes as hidden (requiring minimal physical infrastructure), discrete (involving uncoordinated components), diffuse (developed across dispersed locations), and opaque (obscuring potentially harmful features from external observers), making consensus on a single definition elusive. Such ambiguity creates uncertainty in determining which regulations such as those concerning data privacy, algorithmic neutrality, and accountability apply to AI applications like AI-based learning platforms, potentially leading to implementation challenges that hinder AI's full potential in higher education settings. This definitional ambiguity is not merely theoretical but manifests concretely in the GenAI policies of Turkish higher education institutions, where the lack of consistent definitions for Generative AI or AI tools undermines policy clarity and effective implementation. Specifically, among the 10 institutions analyzed, only Kadir Has and Bilkent provide a dedicated section defining GenAI, while MEF adopts the OECD's broader definition of AI systems, and the remaining policies including those from Mehmet Akif Ersoy, Gazi, Hacettepe, İstanbul Bilgi, İzmir Institute of Technology, Koç, and YÖK offer no definitions, potentially undermining clarity for users such as faculty and students (Table 5). This inconsistency mirrors the broader definitional challenges outlined by Schuett (2021) and Scherer (2016), as the absence of a standardized GenAI definition within these policies creates ambiguity about their scope, complicating the application of ethical principles like transparency and accountability, which are universally emphasized (Table 4). For instance, without a clear definition, it remains uncertain whether a GenAI tool used in academic writing should comply with privacy regulations like KVKK or ethical guidelines like YÖK's *Ethics Guide*, exacerbating implementation challenges in Türkiye's centralized higher education system, where uniform standards are critical for effective governance (Table 7).

Navigating Academic Integrity

The lack of consistent GenAI definitions across Turkish higher education, as previously discussed, naturally complicates the establishment of clear ethical and legal frameworks. Beyond these foundational definitional ambiguities, however, lies another critical domain profoundly impacted by GenAI's rise: academic integrity. The practical application of these powerful tools raises immediate and pressing concerns regarding traditional notions of authorship, originality, and responsible use in scholarly work. With their capacity to generate human-like texts, GenAI tools pose a significant, transformative challenge to traditional notions of academic integrity, authorship, and assessment in higher education (Kopp & Gröblinger, 2024; Kotsis, 2025; Rasul et al., 2024; Ward et al., 2024; Yusuf et al., 2024; Zlotnikova et al., 2025). A major concern is the potential for misuse, where students submit AI-generated work as their own, undermining learning and assessment validity, which blurs the lines of authorship and originality. Although the scoping review by Moya et al. (2024) demonstrates that concerns about AI's impact on academic integrity, including issues of plagiarism, authorship, and the limits of acceptable assistance, predate the widespread availability of sophisticated GenAI tools like ChatGPT, the advent of GenAI has significantly amplified these concerns and accelerated the urgency for institutional response (Kopp & Gröblinger, 2024; Kotsis, 2025; Ward et al., 2024). Beyond the deliberate misuse of GenAI for academic dishonesty, institutions must also contend with the inherent unreliability of these tools. For example, one issue with GenAI tools is that they can hallucinate, meaning that they could confidently produce inaccurate information, non-existent citations, or flawed reasoning (Kopp & Gröblinger, 2024; Kotsis, 2025; Moya et al., 2024; Yusuf et al., 2024; Zlotnikova et al., 2025). Relying on this flawed output for academic work raises serious ethical issues regarding scholarly rigor and the dissemination of misinformation. This underscores the need for verification, a challenge in higher education. Users (students and faculty) must remain responsible for the work they submit, even if AI-assisted. This includes verifying the accuracy of AI-generated content, checking for bias, ensuring proper attribution (where required by policy), and critically evaluating the output (Kopp & Gröblinger, 2024; Kotsis, 2025; Zlotnikova et al., 2025).

A key component of this responsible and critical engagement involves transparently acknowledging the use of AI. Consequently, the integration of AI, particularly GenAI tools like ChatGPT, into academic research and writing has necessitated the development of citation practices to ensure transparency, academic integrity, and proper attribution. Citation practices vary by style, reflecting the evolving nature of AI in academia. Different style guides, such as APA, MLA, and Chicago, provide guidelines, but the approach can vary based on how AI is used. The American Psychological Association (American Psychological Association, 2023) treats AI tools as software or computer programs, requiring in-text citations and reference list entries as well as disclosing use in the methods section. This approach ensures transparency but may challenge researchers to verify AI-generated citations, given risks of hallucinations. The Modern Language Association (The MLA Style Center, 2023) uses its core elements template, citing AI tools in the works-cited list with details and in-text citations for transparency. This method is flexible but may struggle with non-retrievable AI outputs, treated as personal communication, limiting bibliographic inclusion and raising questions about verifiability. The Chicago Manual of Style (The Chicago Manual of Style Online, n.d.) treats AI as the author and its developer as the publisher, recommending footnotes rather than bibliography entries for non-retrievable content. This approach suits notes-bibliography systems but may confuse author-date users, highlighting a need for style-specific clarity in AI citation. This variation underscores the need for researchers to choose styles based on assignment requirements, with APA offering robust disclosure and MLA/Chicago providing flexibility but potential verifiability challenges. The evolving nature of AI citation norms suggests potential future changes, with publishers and institutions likely to refine their guidelines. Future developments in citation norms and national standards will be essential to maintain academic integrity amid AI's rapid integration. Also, continued exploration is needed to define concepts like authorship, originality, and plagiarism in the context of human-AI collaboration, as highlighted even pre-ChatGPT (Moya et al., 2024) and amplified now (Kopp & Gröblinger, 2024; Kotsis, 2025).

These evolving international norms and debates around AI-assisted authorship and citation provide a backdrop against which national and institutional responses, such as those in Türkiye, are being formulated. In the Turkish context, while standard citation styles are followed, additional guidelines from YÖK or institutions may apply. YÖK requires researchers to "explain in the method section" the stages where GenAI is used, aligning with APA's disclosure but lacking specific citation formats. Institutions like Gazi and Koç specify APA/MLA styles and prompt documentation (Table 5), suggesting a blend of international and national practices, yet along with this, the lack of uniform definitions (Table 5) may hinder consistency. Parallel to these citation concerns are questions of accountability. The findings on accountability mechanisms in Turkish higher education institutions reveal a varied landscape of governance approaches. Governance approaches varied, including the use of AI Committees, detection tools, ethics committees, or innovative support structures (see Table 5 for institutional examples), while others lack formal oversight, exposing enforcement gaps. These findings align with the literature's consensus that relying solely on technical detection tools, such as those used by Hacettepe, is unreliable and inadequate as a primary strategy for managing AI use (Kopp & Gröblinger, 2024; Rasul et al., 2024; Ward et al., 2024; Yusuf et al., 2024; Zlotnikova et al., 2025). The absence of robust oversight in some institutions underscores the need for more comprehensive, multi-faceted accountability frameworks that move beyond technical solutions to ensure ethical and effective GenAI integration.

Bridging the Gaps: Ethical Imperatives

Ensuring academic integrity in the age of GenAI thus requires more than just clear rules on use and citation; it necessitates robust accountability and a foundational ethical compass. Fortunately, the analysis of GenAI policies in Turkish higher education institutions (Table 3) reveals a promising, unified framework in this regard, emphasizing core ethical principles, risk awareness, user responsibility, and citation requirements. These commonalities resonate strongly with the concerns highlighted in the broader literature and provide a crucial starting point for ethical AI integration. All institutions underscore ethical principles like transparency, integrity, and accountability, alongside a cautious approach to risks such as hallucinations, bias, and privacy issues, aligning with the literature's warnings about GenAI's potential to produce inaccurate or flawed outputs (Kopp & Gröblinger, 2024; Kotsis, 2025; Moya et al., 2024; Yusuf et al., 2024; Zlotnikova et al., 2025). The universal emphasis on user responsibility, requiring students and faculty to verify AI outputs and adhere to guidelines, mirrors the literature's call for critical evaluation and accountability to maintain scholarly rigor and prevent misinformation (Kopp & Gröblinger, 2024; Kotsis, 2025; Zlotnikova et al., 2025). Additionally, the citation requirement, explicitly mandated by six institutions and implied in others, supports the literature's advocacy for proper attribution to ensure transparency in academic work. These shared elements indicate a sound ethical foundation across Turkish institutions, addressing the literature's concerns about GenAI's risks while fostering responsible integration in higher education.

While this shared ethical foundation provides a strong starting point, the rapidly evolving nature of GenAI brings forth a wider spectrum of ethical challenges that demand ongoing attention. These include concerns such as bias in AI, data privacy, accuracy, and potential deskilling, which are also frequently mentioned in different studies (Kotsis, 2025; Rasul et al., 2024; Yusuf et al., 2024; Zlotnikova et al., 2025). Also, there are studies highlighting ethical dimensions, including security, algorithmic bias, transparency, and environmental impact, as crucial considerations in GenAI integration (Beckingham et al., 2024; Gupta, 2024; Slimi & Villarejo-Carballido, 2024). Concerns about digital equity, including access to tools (especially paid versions) and potential biases disadvantaging certain student groups, are raised in multiple articles (Beckingham et al., 2024; Davis, 2024; Gupta, 2024). Davis (2024) centers inclusion as a primary concern for policy development. The findings from Tables 4 and Table 6 on GenAI policies in Turkish higher education institutions reveal significant gaps in enforcement, guidance, and faculty support, which align with broader ethical concerns identified in the literature, such as bias, transparency, and digital equity. While Table 4 highlights a commitment to ethical principles like transparency, academic integrity, and inclusion across several institutions, the inconsistent articulation and integration of these principles, evident in the absence of dedicated ethics sections at Bilkent, Hacettepe, and Koç, mirror ethical concerns. Addressing these multifaceted ethical challenges effectively requires more than just policy statements; it necessitates a supportive institutional environment. To fully exploit the potential of AI, higher education institutions should create an environment that encourages exploration and testing of these new technologies by investing in training to improve the AI literacy of both faculty and students, and by actively supporting and rewarding those who are willing to experiment with AI tools in their work at universities (Tarisayi, 2024). The GenAI policies of Turkish higher education institutions reveal significant gaps in providing the necessary training, support, and resources to foster such an environment, potentially limiting the responsible and effective integration of GenAI tools (Table 6). Also, the uneven emphasis on inclusivity and accessibility, particularly strong at Burdur Mehmet Akif and MEF but less explicit elsewhere, underscores Davis's (2024) focus on inclusion as a policy priority to address digital equity. These gaps suggest that Turkish institutions struggle to translate ethical commitments into actionable frameworks, potentially undermining responsible GenAI integration and highlighting the need for more consistent, comprehensive policies to ensure ethical standards and equitable access.

Charting the Course: Towards Responsible and Equitable GenAI Integration

The identified policy gaps and ethical considerations underscore the complexities facing Turkish higher education institutions. However, these challenges also pave the way for proactive strategies. Drawing upon the insights from the literature and the current policy analysis, several pathways can be identified to foster a more responsible, equitable, and pedagogically sound integration of GenAI. A cornerstone of responsible AI integration is the establishment of robust ethical frameworks and clear institutional policies as Zlotnikova et al. (2025) and Rasul et al. (2024) advocate for institutions to be proactive in establishing frameworks and policies, rather than reacting defensively after issues arise. There is an urgent need for higher education institutions to develop, revise, and/or clarify policies regarding the acceptable and unacceptable use of GenAI (Beckingham et al., 2024; Davis, 2024; Gupta, 2024; Kopp & Gröblinger, 2024; Kotsis, 2025; Luo, 2024; Rasul et al., 2024; Slimi & Villarejo-Carballido, 2024; Ward et al., 2024; Yusuf et al., 2024; Zlotnikova et al., 2025;). GenAI tools introduce capabilities that existing academic integrity policies, which are often focused on traditional plagiarism or contract cheating, do not adequately address (Kotsis, 2025; Ward et al., 2024; Zlotnikova et al., 2025). There is ambiguity about what constitutes acceptable assistance versus misconduct when using these tools, necessitating clear definitions and guidelines (Kopp & Gröblinger, 2024; Kotsis, 2025), with Moya et al. (2024) demonstrating that this need for clarity was recognized even before ChatGPT. Kopp and Gröblinger (2024) push for a progressive perspective that reassesses misconduct definitions rather than relying on outdated standards. The policies should be adaptable, context-specific, and focus on ethical use rather than just prohibition. In order to achieve this during the development, revision and clarification of policies, open discussions and collaboration among students, staff, administrators, and policymakers need to be encouraged to develop shared understandings and effective strategies. Beckingham et al. (2024) suggest “collaborative sandpits” for experimentation (pp. 132-134). This is envisioned as a dynamic, participatory environment where the university community can collectively explore, test, evaluate, and learn about emerging GenAI technologies and their pedagogical potential, contributing to the ongoing development of institutional strategy and practice.

There is also a need to educate students and staff about AI capabilities, limitations, and ethical considerations (Moya et al., 2024; Rasul et al., 2024; Yusuf et al., 2024; Zlotnikova et al., 2025). The critical need for faculty preparedness, as emphasized in the literature, finds a stark contrast in the analyzed Turkish GenAI policies. As demonstrated in the findings (Table 6), specific commitments to faculty support and comprehensive training programs were often vague or entirely absent in the majority of institutional documents. This policy gap suggests that Turkish universities may face significant challenges in equipping their academic staff to navigate the pedagogical shifts and ethical considerations GenAI necessitates, potentially hindering effective and responsible AI integration in teaching practices. Multiple studies recommend prioritizing AI literacy education (Beckingham et al., 2024; Gupta, 2024; Jin et al., 2024; Luo, 2024; Slimi & Villarejo-Carballido, 2024), including training for both staff and students on capabilities, limitations, and ethical use. Students and faculty need clear guidance on how they can ethically and effectively use these powerful tools (Rasul et al., 2024; Zlotnikova et al., 2025), and policies should provide the necessary framework for incorporating AI literacy training and establishing expectations for transparency and disclosure (Yusuf et al., 2024; Zlotnikova et al., 2025). While Kotsis (2025) stresses the need for explicit structures to handle this complexity, Jin et al. (2024) specifically focus on the need for objective assessment of this literacy and provide a tool ("GenAI Literacy Assessment Test") to assess this. Davis (2024) strongly advocates for designing policies and guidance using "Universal Design for Learning" (UDL), which supports all students, particularly those potentially vulnerable to academic integrity issues.

Furthermore, it is necessary to consider the pedagogical implications of GenAI, including concerns that excessive reliance may erode foundational academic skills like critical thinking and research (Gupta, 2024; Smith & Francis, 2024). The advent of GenAI necessitates a fundamental rethinking and redesign of assessment practices, moving away from tasks easily completed by AI towards those requiring higher-order thinking, process evaluation, or authentic application (Beckingham et al., 2024; Gupta, 2024; Luo, 2024; Slimi & Villarejo-Carballido, 2024; Smith & Francis, 2024). Additionally, as traditional detection methods such as text-matching software are ineffective against sophisticated GenAI outputs, making policy shifts is crucial (Kopp & Gröblinger, 2024; Ward et al., 2024). Since detection is unreliable, policies need to adapt, perhaps focusing more on assessment design, process evaluation, or defining responsible use rather than solely on prohibition and detection (Kopp & Gröblinger, 2024; Rasul et al., 2024; Ward et al., 2024). Smith and Francis (2024) strongly advocate for process assessment, Davis (2024) focuses on transparency (declaration forms) and UDL in guidance, while others offer broader suggestions like authentic tasks or vivas (Beckingham et al., 2024; Gupta, 2024; Luo, 2024). As educators are encouraged to revise assessment methods to be more AI-resilient (Rasul et al., 2024; Ward et al., 2024; Zlotnikova et al., 2025), institutional policies must support and align with these pedagogical shifts (Rasul et al., 2024).

Finally, equity and ethical concerns are also critical issues that need to be addressed in policies. While some Turkish policies incorporate principles like 'inclusivity' or 'accessibility', the general lack of detailed strategies within these documents to address potential biases in AI tools or ensure equitable access to GenAI resources across diverse student populations (as highlighted by Davis, 2024) could exacerbate existing digital divides within Türkiye's higher education system. Disparities in access to GenAI tools, particularly premium versions, risk creating a digital divide that disadvantages students from lower socioeconomic backgrounds or those with limited digital literacy, a concern emphasized by Beckingham et al. (2024) and Davis (2024), who advocate for institutional provisions to ensure equitable access and counteract digital poverty. Additionally, the potential for GenAI to perpetuate biases in training data, as noted by Kotsis (2025), and Rasul et al. (2024) poses a threat of producing discriminatory outcomes that amplify societal inequities (Smith & Francis, 2024). These challenges are compounded by ethical issues such as data privacy, transparency, and environmental sustainability, which require robust data protection measures and critical evaluation of AI tools for fairness (Beckingham et al., 2024; Gupta, 2024; Slimi & Villarejo-Carballido, 2024). By prioritizing inclusive policies (Kotsis, 2025; Rasul et al., 2024; Yusuf et al., 2024), digital literacy programs (Beckingham et al., 2024; Davis, 2024; Jin et al., 2024; Kopp & Gröblinger, 2024; Slimi & Villarejo-Carballido, 2024; Rasul et al., 2024; Zlotnikova et al., 2025), and bias mitigation strategies (Kotsis, 2025; Moya et al., 2024; Rasul et al., 2024; Yusuf et al., 2024; Zlotnikova et al., 2025), institutions can address these concerns, ensuring that GenAI enhances educational equity rather than exacerbating existing disparities.

In summary, while navigating the era of GenAI, higher education institutions, including those in Türkiye whose policies formed the basis of this chapter's initial analysis, stand at a critical juncture. Higher education institutions must develop flexible, evidence-based, and inclusive policies to responsibly integrate AI. It is also critical to cultivate AI literacy and critical thinking skills among students and faculty to navigate AI's complexities effectively. Furthermore, there is an urgent need to address ethical concerns such as bias, privacy violations, and accountability, to ensure safe and equitable use of AI. Clearly, no single model fits all, but best practices can be adapted across contexts through international dialogue, interdisciplinary collaboration, and continuous learning. Effective GenAI policies require regular updates, stakeholder involvement, alignment with broader frameworks, and concurrent investments in capacity building. As AI technologies continue to evolve, higher education institutions will need to develop increasingly sophisticated, flexible, and inclusive policy approaches that preserve core academic values while leveraging AI's potential to enhance teaching, learning, and research.

CONCLUSION

The integration of GenAI into higher education is reshaping the sector's pedagogical, administrative, and ethical foundations. This chapter examines the evolving landscape of institutional responses to AI integration in Turkish higher education through a comprehensive analysis of GenAI policies from YÖK and nine major universities. With the rapid integration of GenAI in higher education prompting Turkish universities to develop institutional policies and ethical guidelines, it is evident that Turkish universities are in the early stages of developing and implementing AI use policies. This nascent phase reflects the challenges of adapting to fast-evolving technology, as seen in the varied policy. Common elements, such as ethical principles and user responsibility, underscore a commitment to academic integrity, yet gaps in enforcement mechanisms and faculty support highlight uneven governance. These inconsistencies risk undermining responsible AI adoption. To address this, Turkish institutions must prioritize collaborative policy development, robust training, and alignment with global ethical standards. By doing so, they can foster equitable and innovative GenAI integration, positioning Türkiye's higher education system as a leader in responsible AI governance.

Aiming to guide policymakers, administrators, and leaders within Turkish higher education institutions in navigating the ethical implications of GenAI integration, this chapter serves as a valuable resource for educators, researchers, and students in Türkiye who are interested in the responsible implementation of GenAI within their learning environments. By analyzing the current policy landscape and proposing a roadmap for ethical AI integration, this chapter seeks to empower Turkish policymakers to leverage GenAI's potential while upholding core human values in higher education. However, this study acknowledges several limitations. Firstly, while document analysis reveals the intent of policy, it cannot assess the impact of those policies on the ground. This limitation is significant, as a policy's effectiveness hinges on its successful implementation. Future research employing qualitative methods, such as case studies or ethnographic approaches should investigate the implementation challenges and potential discrepancies between stated policy and actual practice, exploring factors that contribute to or hinder successful adoption. Secondly, the study's reliance on publicly available documents may offer a limited view of the complex and nuanced policy landscape surrounding GenAI in Turkish higher education. Future research could benefit from incorporating qualitative data, such as interviews with university administrators and faculty, to gain a deeper understanding of the informal practices and internal discussions shaping AI policy. Finally, the analysis is constrained by the policies available at the time of data collection, reflecting the inherent challenge of capturing the rapidly evolving nature of AI policy in higher education. Future studies should consider longitudinal approaches or regular policy updates to track the development and adaptation of ethical guidelines in response to technological advancements.

This study's analysis of GenAI policies in Turkish higher education reveals critical gaps and shared ethical commitments, offering actionable suggestions for responsible AI integration. As AI technologies evolve, institutions must adopt agile, inclusive policies that prioritize equity and academic integrity. Future research should explore longitudinal impacts, cross-institutional comparisons, and co-created global standards to align local practices with international benchmarks. By fostering ethical, innovative governance, Turkish universities can lead in shaping a future where AI enhances education while upholding core academic values.

REFERENCES

American Psychological Association. (2023, November). *APA Journals policy on generative AI: Additional guidance*. https://www.apa.org/pubs/journals/resources/publishing-tips/policy-generative-ai

An, Y., Yu, J. H., & James, S. (2025). Investigating the higher education institutions' guidelines and policies regarding the use of generative AI in teaching, learning, research, and administration. *International Journal of Educational Technology in Higher Education*, *22*(10), 1–23. DOI: 10.1186/s41239-025-00507-3

Beckingham, S., Lawrence, J., Powell, S., & Hartley, P. (2024). Sustainable and ethical GenAI for the common good: Looking back and forward. In *Using Generative AI Effectively in Higher Education* (pp. 127–138). Routledge., DOI: 10.4324/9781003482918-18

Bowen, G. A. (2009). Document analysis as a qualitative research method. *Qualitative Research Journal*, *9*(2), 27–40. DOI: 10.3316/QRJ0902027

Bozkurt, A., Xiao, J., Farrow, R., Bai, J. Y., Nerantzi, C., Moore, S., Dron, J., Stracke, C. M., Singh, L., Crompton, H., Koutropoulos, A., Terentev, E., Pazurek, A., Nichols, M., Sidorkin, A. M., Costello, E., Watson, S., Mulligan, D., Honeychurch, S., & Asino, T. I. (2024). The manifesto for teaching and learning in a time of generative AI: A critical collective stance to better navigate the future. *Open Praxis*, *16*(4), 487–513. DOI: 10.55982/openpraxis.16.4.777

Chaika, O. (2023). The role of artificial intelligence in higher education. *Молодь і ринок, 6–7*(214–215), 69-74. DOI: 10.24919/2308-4634.2023.287898

Chaka, C., Shange, T., Nkhobo, T., & Hlatshwayo, V. (2024). An environmental review of the generative artificial intelligence policies and guidelines of South African higher education institutions: A content analysis. *International Journal of Learning. Teaching and Educational Research*, *23*(12), 487–511. DOI: 10.26803/ijlter.23.12.25

Chen, Y., Jensen, S., Albert, L. J., Gupta, S., & Lee, T. (2023). Artificial intelligence (AI) student assistants in the classroom: Designing chatbots to support student success. *Information Systems Frontiers*, *25*(1), 161–182. DOI: 10.1007/s10796-022-10291-4

Clarke, V., & Braun, V. (2017). Thematic analysis. *The Journal of Positive Psychology*, *12*(3), 297–298. DOI: 10.1080/17439760.2016.1262613

ColMOOC. (2019). ColMOOC. https://colmooc.eu/

Conijn, R., Kahr, P., & Snijders, C. C. (2023). The effects of explanations in automated essay scoring systems on student trust and motivation. *Journal of Learning Analytics*, *10*(1), 37–53. DOI: 10.18608/jla.2023.7801

Crompton, H., & Burke, D. (2023). Artificial intelligence in higher education: The state of the field. *International Journal of Educational Technology in Higher Education*, *20*(1), 22. DOI: 10.1186/s41239-023-00392-8

Davis, M. (2024). Supporting inclusion in academic integrity in the age of GenAI. In *Using Generative AI Effectively in Higher Education* (pp. 21–29). Routledge., DOI: 10.4324/9781003482918-4

Fitria, T. N. (2021). The use technology based on artificial intelligence in English teaching and learning). *ELT Echo: The Journal of English Language Teaching in Foreign Language Context*, *6*(2). Advance online publication. DOI: 10.24235/eltecho.v6i2.9299

Ghimire, A., & Edwards, J. (2024). From guidelines to governance: A study of AI policies in education. *arXiv preprint arXiv:2403.15601*. DOI: 10.1007/978-3-031-64312-5_36

Gupta, A. (2024, August). *When generative artificial intelligence meets academic integrity: Educational opportunities & challenges in a digital age*. BERA Report Series: Education in a Digital Age. British Educational Research Association. https://www.bera.ac.uk/publication/when-generative-artificial-intelligence-meets-academic-integrity

Hagendorff, T. (2020). The ethics of AI ethics: An evaluation of guidelines. *Minds and Machines*, *30*(1), 99–120. DOI: 10.1007/s11023-020-09517-8

Holmes, W., Porayska-Pomsta, K., Holstein, K., Sutherland, E., Baker, T., Shum, S. B., Santos, O. C., Rodrigo, M. T., Cukurova, M., Bittencourt, I. I., & Koedinger, K. R. (2022). Ethics of AI in education: Towards a community-wide framework. *International Journal of Artificial Intelligence in Education*, *32*(3), 1–23. DOI: 10.1007/s40593-021-00239-1

Holstein, K., & Doroudi, S. (2022). Equity and artificial intelligence in education. In *The Ethics of Artificial İntelligence in Education* (pp. 151–173). Routledge., DOI: 10.4324/9780429329067-9

Hu, Y., Fu, J. S., & Yeh, H. (2023). Developing an early-warning system through robotic process automation: Are intelligent tutoring robots as effective as human teachers? *Interactive Learning Environments*, •••, 1–14. DOI: 10.1080/10494820.2022.2160467

Ivanov, S. (2023). The dark side of artificial intelligence in higher education. *Service Industries Journal, 43*(15-16), 1055–1082. DOI: 10.1080/02642069.2023.2258799

Jian-hua, H., Zhao, W., Jiang, Q., Oubibi, M., & Hu, X. (2019). Intelligent tutoring system trends 2006-2018: A literature review. In *2019 Eighth International Conference on Educational Innovation through Technology (EITT)* (pp. 153-159). IEEE. DOI: 10.1109/EITT.2019.00037

Jin, Y., Martinez-Maldonado, R., Gašević, D., & Yan, L. (2024). GLAT: The generative AI literacy assessment test. *arXiv preprint arXiv:2411.00283.* /DOI: 10.48550

Jin, Y., Yan, L., Echeverria, V., Gašević, D., & Martinez-Maldonado, R. (2025). Generative AI in higher education: A global perspective of institutional adoption policies and guidelines. *Computers and Education: Artificial Intelligence, 8*, 100348. Advance online publication. DOI: 10.1016/j.caeai.2024.100348

Jobin, A., Ienca, M., & Vayena, E. (2019). The global landscape of AI ethics guidelines. *Nature Machine Intelligence, 1*(9), 389–399. DOI: 10.1038/s42256-019-0088-2

Kizilcec, R. F., & Lee, H. (2022). Algorithmic fairness in education. In *The Ethics of Artificial Intelligence in Education* (pp. 174-202). Routledge. /arXiv.2007.05443DOI: 10.48550

Kopp, M., & Gröblinger, O. (2024). Generative AI and academic integrity-a contradiction. In European Association of Distance Teaching Universities, *Leading the Future of Learning. Proceedings of the Innovating Higher Education Conference* (pp. 101-114). DOI: 10.5281/zenodo.14220974

Kotsis, K. T. (2025). Legality of employing artificial intelligence for writing academic papers in education. *Journal of Contemporary Philosophical and Anthropological Studies, 3*(1). Advance online publication. DOI: 10.59652/jcpas.v3i1.375

Lu, Q., Zhu, L., Xu, X., Whittle, J., Zowghi, D., & Jacquet, A. (2024). Responsible AI pattern catalogue: A collection of best practices for AI governance and engineering. *ACM Computing Surveys, 56*(7), 1–35. DOI: 10.1145/3626234

Luo, J. (2024). A critical review of GenAI policies in higher education assessment: A call to reconsider the "originality" of students' work. *Assessment & Evaluation in Higher Education, 49*(5), 651–664. DOI: 10.1080/02602938.2024.2309963

Madaio, M., Blodgett, S. L., Mayfield, E., & Dixon-Román, E. (2022). Beyond "fairness": Structural (in) justice lenses on AI for education. In *The Ethics of Artificial Intelligence in Education* (pp. 203-239). Routledge. DOI: 10.48550

Maguire, M., & Delahunt, B. (2017). Doing a thematic analysis: A practical, step-by-step guide for learning and teaching scholars. *All Ireland Journal of Higher Education, 9*(3), 3351–3364. https://ojs.aishe.org/index.php/aishe-j/article/view/335

Maslej, N., Fattorini, L., Perrault, R., Parli, V., Reuel, A., Brynjolfsson, E., Etchemendy, J., Ligett, K., Lyons, T., Manyika, J., Niebles, J. C., Shoham, Y., Wald, R., & Clark, J. (2024). *The AI Index 2024 annual report*. AI Index Steering Committee, Institute for Human-Centered AI, Stanford University. https://hai.stanford.edu/ai-index/2024-ai-index-report

McDonald, N., Johri, A., Ali, A., & Hingle Collier, A. (2025). Generative artificial intelligence in higher education: Evidence from an analysis of institutional policies and guidelines. *Computers in Human Behavior: Artificial Humans, 3*, 100121. Advance online publication. DOI: 10.1016/j.chbah.2025.100121

Mendigutxia, A. (2025). *The role of higher education in national artificial intelligence strategies: A comparative policy review*. UNESCO International Institute for Higher Education in Latin America and the Caribbean (IESALC), *HE Policy Brief Series*. Document Code: ED/HE/IESALC/IP/2024/73 REV

Morgan, H. (2022). Conducting a qualitative document analysis. *The Qualitative Report, 27*(1), 64–77. DOI: 10.46743/2160-3715/2022.5044

Moya, B., Eaton, S., Pethrick, H., Hayden, A., Brennan, R., Wiens, J., & McDermott, B. (2024). Academic integrity and artificial intelligence in higher education (HE) contexts: A rapid scoping review. *Canadian Perspectives on Academic Integrity, 7*(3), 1–19. DOI: 10.55016/ojs/cpai.v7i3.78123

National Institute of Standards and Technology. (2024). *Artificial intelligence risk management framework: Generative artificial intelligence profile* [NIST AI 600-1]. https://airc.nist.gov/docs/NIST.AI.600-1.GenAI-Profile.ipd.pdf#page=67.47

Neha, K., Kumar, R., & Sankat, M. (2024). AI wizards: Pioneering assistive technologies for higher education inclusion of students with learning disabilities. In Kaluri, R., Mahmud, M., Gadekallu, T. R., Rajput, D. S., & Lakshmanna, K. (Eds.), *Applied Assistive Technologies and Informatics for Students with Disabilities. Applied Intelligence and Informatics*. Springer., DOI: 10.1007/978-981-97-0914-4_4

Nguyen, A., Ngo, H. N., Hong, Y., Dang, B., & Nguyen, B. T. (2022). Ethical principles for artificial intelligence in education. *Education and Information Technologies, 28*(4), 4221–4241. DOI: 10.1007/s10639-022-11316-w PMID: 36254344

Pogorskiy, E., & Beckmann, J. F. (2023). From procrastination to engagement? An experimental exploration of the effects of an adaptive virtual assistant on self-regulation in online learning. *Computers and Education: Artificial Intelligence*, *4*, 100111. DOI: 10.1016/j.caeai.2022.100111

Rampin, R., & Rampin, V. (2021). Taguette: Open-source qualitative data analysis. *Journal of Open Source Software*, *6*(68), 3522. DOI: 10.21105/joss.03522

Rasul, T., Nair, S., Kalendra, D., Balaji, M. S., de Oliveira Santini, F., Ladeira, W. J., Rather, R. A., Yasin, N., Rodriguez, R. V., Kokkalis, P., Murad, M. W., & Hossain, M. U. (2024). Enhancing academic integrity among students in GenAI Era: A holistic framework. *International Journal of Management Education*, *22*(3), 101041. DOI: 10.1016/j.ijme.2024.101041

Sajja, R., Sermet, Y., Cikmaz, M., Cwiertny, D., & Demir, I. (2023). Artificial intelligence-enabled intelligent assistant for personalized and adaptive learning in higher education. *arXiv preprint arXiv:2309.10892*. DOI: 10.3390/info15100596

Scherer, M. U. (2016). Regulating artificial intelligence systems: Risks, challenges, competencies, and strategies. *SSRN*, *29*(2), 354–400. DOI: 10.2139/ssrn.2609777

Schiff, D. (2022). Education for AI, not AI for education: The role of education and ethics in national AI policy strategies. *International Journal of Artificial Intelligence in Education*, *32*(3), 527–563. DOI: 10.1007/s40593-021-00270-2

Schuett, J. (2021). Defining the scope of AI regulations. *Law, Innovation and Technology*, *15*(1), 60–82. DOI: 10.1080/17579961.2023.2184135

Shan, T., Tay, F., & Gu, L. Q. (2020). Application of artificial intelligence in dentistry. *Journal of Dental Research*, *100*(3), 232–244. DOI: 10.1177/0022034520969115 PMID: 33118431

Slimi, Z., & Villarejo-Carballido, B. (2024). Unveiling the potential: Experts' perspectives on artificial intelligence integration in higher education. *European Journal of Educational Research*, *13*(4), 1477–1492. DOI: 10.12973/eu-jer.13.4.1477

Smith, D., & Francis, N. (2024). Process not product in the written assessment. In *Using Generative AI Effectively in Higher Education* (pp. 115–126). Routledge., DOI: 10.4324/9781003482918-17

Smuha, N. A. (2022). Pitfalls and pathways for trustworthy artificial intelligence in education. In *The Ethics of Artificial Intelligence in Education* (pp. 113–145). Routledge., DOI: 10.4324/9780429329067-7

Spivakovsky, O. V., Omelchuk, S. A., Kobets, V. V., Valko, N. V., & Malchykova, D. S. (2023). Institutional policies on artificial intelligence in university learning, teaching and research. *Information Technologies and Learning Tools*, *97*(5), 181–201. DOI: 10.33407/itlt.v97i5.5395

Stracke, C. M., Griffiths, D., Pappa, D., Bećirović, S., Polz, E., Perla, L., Di Grassi, A., Massaro, S., Skenduli, M. P., Burgos, D., Punzo, V., Amram, D., Ziouvelou, X., Katsamori, D., Gabriel, S., Nahar, N., Schleiss, J., & Hollins, P. (2025). Analysis of artificial intelligence policies for higher education in Europe. *International Journal of Interactive Multimedia and Artificial Intelligence*, *9*(2), 124–137. DOI: 10.9781/ijimai.2025.02.011

Sumakul, D. T. Y. G., Hamied, F. A., & Sukyadi, D. (2022). Students' perceptions of the use of AI in a writing class. *Proceedings of the 67th TEFLIN International Virtual Conference*; The 9th ICOELT 2021 (TEFLIN ICOELT 2021). DOI: 10.2991/assehr.k.220201.009

Symeou, L., Louca, L., Kavadella, A., Mackay, J., Danidou, Y., & Raffay, V. (2025). Development of evidence-based guidelines for the integration of generative AI in university education through a multidisciplinary, consensus-based approach. *European Journal of Dental Education*, *29*(1), 1–19. DOI: 10.1111/eje.13069 PMID: 39949032

Tarisayi, K. S. (2024, March). Strategic leadership for responsible artificial intelligence adoption in higher education. In *CTE Workshop Proceedings*, 11, 4-14. DOI: 10.55056/cte.616

The Chicago Manual of Style Online. (n.d.). *Citation, documentation of sources.* https://www.chicagomanualofstyle.org/qanda/data/faq/topics/Documentation/faq0422.html

The Institute for Ethical AI in Education. (2020). *Interim report: towards a shared vision of ethical AI in education.* https://www.buckingham.ac.uk/wp-content/uploads/2020/02/ The-Institute-for-Ethical-AI-in-Educations-Interim-Report-Towards-a-Shared-Vision-of-Ethical-AI-in-Education.pdf

The MLA Style Center. (2023, March). *How do I cite generative AI in MLA style?* https://style.mla.org/citing-generative-ai/

Ullah, M., Bin Naeem, S., & Kamel Boulos, M. N. (2024). *Assessing the Guidelines on the Use of Generative Artificial Intelligence Tools in Universities: Results of a Survey of the World's Top 50 Universities.*

Vidal, Q., Vincent-Lancrin, S., & Yun, H. (2023). Emerging governance of generative AI in education. In *OECD Digital Education Outlook 2023: Towards an Effective Digital Education Ecosystem*. https://www.oecd-ilibrary.org/sites/2a73a245-en/index. html?itemId=/content/component/2a73a245-en DOI: 10.1787/c74f03de-en

Wach, E., & Ward, R. (2013). Learning about qualitative document analysis. *IDS Practice Paper in Brief*, 13, 1-11. https://hdl.handle.net/20.500.12413/2989

Ward, A., Manoharan, S., & Ye, X. (2024, November). Exploring Academic Integrity in the Age of Generative AI. In *2024 21st International Conference on Information Technology Based Higher Education and Training (ITHET)* (pp. 1-5). IEEE. DOI: 10.1109/ITHET61869.2024.10837603

Yeo, M. A. (2023). Academic integrity in the age of artificial intelligence (AI) authoring apps. *TESOL Journal*, *14*(3), e716. DOI: 10.1002/tesj.716

Yükseköğretim Bilgi Yönetim Sistemi. (2025, January 19). *Türlerine göre birim sayıları raporu*. https://istatistik.yok.gov.tr/

Yusuf, A., Pervin, N., & Román-González, M. (2024). Generative AI and the future of higher education: A threat to academic integrity or reformation? Evidence from multicultural perspectives. *International Journal of Educational Technology in Higher Education*, *21*(1), 21. DOI: 10.1186/s41239-024-00453-6

Zlotnikova, I., Hlomani, H., Mokgetse, T., & Bagai, K. (2025). Establishing ethical standards for GenAI in university education: A roadmap for academic integrity and fairness. *Journal of Information. Communication and Ethics in Society*, *23*(2), 188–216. DOI: 10.1108/JICES-07-2024-0104

KEY TERMS AND DEFINITIONS

AI Governance in Higher Education: The framework of rules, decision-making processes, oversight mechanisms, and ethical considerations established by higher education institutions to guide the development, deployment, and use of artificial intelligence technologies, including GenAI, in a responsible and aligned manner.

AI Literacy in Higher Education: The essential knowledge and skills that enable students, faculty, and staff to understand the capabilities and limitations of artificial intelligence, use GenAI tools effectively and ethically, critically evaluate AI-generated content, and comprehend the societal and pedagogical implications of AI integration within the academic environment.

Enforcement Mechanisms for AI Policies: The specific procedures, processes, and consequences established by higher education institutions to ensure compliance with GenAI policies, address violations, and maintain the standards of academic integrity and ethical conduct in the use of these technologies.

Ethical Principles in AI Application: Fundamental moral values and standards such as fairness, transparency, accountability, privacy, and non-maleficence that steer the design, implementation, and oversight of AI systems within the academic environment to ensure they serve human well-being and uphold societal values.

Policy Landscape for GenAI: The overall environment and array of existing formal guidelines, regulations, ethical frameworks, and institutional responses which are developed by higher education institutions such as universities and national councils like YÖK to govern the integration and use of generative AI technologies within their specific contexts.

Responsible AI Adoption: An approach by higher education institutions to integrate generative AI technologies in a manner that is ethically sound, aligns with academic values, promotes equitable access and outcomes, including mechanisms for accountability and continuous evaluation of consequences.

User Responsibility in GenAI Use: The obligation of individuals within the higher education setting (students, faculty, staff) to utilize generative AI tools ethically, transparently, critically, and in accordance with institutional policies, including appropriately acknowledging AI assistance and ensuring the integrity of their academic or professional output.

APPENDIX

Bilkent Üniversitesi. (n.d.). *Guidelines for the use of generative artificial intelligence (GenAI) tools at Bilkent.* https://w3.bilkent.edu.tr/bilkent/generative-artificial-intelligence-genai-guideline/

Burdur Mehmet Akif Ersoy Üniversitesi. (2024, June 04). *Burdur Mehmet Akif Ersoy Üniversitesi üretken yapay zekâ kullanımı etik rehberi.* https://gs.mehmetakif.edu.tr/upload/gs/74-form-2031-38290621-yapay-zeka-etik-rehber-tasla-senato-gndem-son.pdf

Council of Higher Education. (2024, May). *Ethics guide of generative artificial intelligence use in the scientific research and publication process of higher education institutions.* https://www.yok.gov.tr/en/Documents/2024/ethics-guide-of-generative-ai-use-in-the-scientific-research-and-publication-process.pdf

Gazi Üniversitesi. (n.d.). *Üretken yapay zekâ araçlarinin kullanımına ilişkin etik ilkeler ve öneriler rehberi (Sürüm 1.0).* https://aicenter.gazi.edu.tr/files/etik-ilkeler.pdf

Hacettepe Üniversitesi. (2025, January 17). *Eğitim ve öğretim süreçlerinde üretken yapay zeka kullanım politikası.* https://gazete.hacettepe.edu.tr/fs_/HABERLER/2025/Ocak/YapayZeka.pdf https://ait.hacettepe.edu.tr/yapayzekarehber210125.pdf

İstanbul Bilgi Üniversitesi. (2024, March 19). *Istanbul Bilgi University artificial intelligence (AI) policy for higher education and research.* https://www.bilgi.edu.tr/media/uploads/2024/04/05/artificialintelligencepolicy.pdf

İstanbul Bilgi Üniversitesi. (2024, March 19). *İstanbul Bilgi Üniversitesi yükseköğretim ve araştırma için yapay zeka (YZ) politikası.* https://www.bilgi.edu.tr/media/uploads/2024/04/05/yapayzekapolitikasi.pdf

İzmir Yüksek Teknoloji Enstitüsü. (2024, December, 17). *İzmir Yüksek Teknoloji Enstitüsü Yapay Zekâ Politikası.* https://yks-karartakip.iyte.edu.tr/files/KararDevamDosyasi/yksktdd-1156-1-250115155514.pdf

Kadir Has Üniversitesi. (n.d.). *Ethical guidance on the use of generative artificial intelligence (GENERATIVE AI) tools.* https://www.khas.edu.tr/en/ethical-guidance-on-the-use-of-generative-artificial-intelligence-generative-ai-tools/

Kadir Has Üniversitesi. (n.d.). *Üretken yapay zekâ (ÜYZ) araçları kullanımı hakkında etik rehber.* https://www.khas.edu.tr/uretken-yapay-zeka-uyz-araclari-kullanimi-hakkinda-etik-rehber/

Koç Üniversitesi. (n.d.). *Koç Üniversitesi'nde yapay zeka araçlarının kullanımına ilişkin prosedürler.* https://kolt.ku.edu.tr/tr/yapay-zeka/

Koç Üniversitesi. (n.d.). *Koç University policy statement regarding the use of artificial intelligence tools (ChatGPT or other similar tools).* https://kolt.ku.edu.tr/artificial-intelligence/

MEF University (2024, September 04). *AI policy (Version 2.0).* https://www.datocms-assets.com/99182/1726134331-mef-university-ai-policy-version-2-0.pdf

MEF University (2024, September 04). *MEF Üniversitesi yapay zeka politikası versiyon 2.0.* https://www.datocms-assets.com/99182/1726134331-mef-universitesi-yapay-zeka-politikasi-versiyon-2-0.pdf

Yükseköğretim Kurulu. (2024, May). *Yükseköğretim kurumları bilimsel araştırma ve yayın faaliyetlerinde üretken yapay zekâ kullanımına dair etik rehber.* https://www.yok.gov.tr/Documents/2024/yapay-zeka-kullanimina-dair-etik-rehber.pdf

APPENDIX

Chapter 6

The Silent Erosion: How AI in Education Undermines Essential Skills

Hakan Altinpulluk
https://orcid.org/0000-0003-4701-1949
Anadolu University, Turkey

ABSTRACT

The purpose of this study is to obtain insights into the effects of artificial intelligence (AI) technologies on essential skills in education through the perspectives of graduate students enrolled in distance learning programs at the graduate level. The study was conducted using the case study model, one of the qualitative research designs. The perspectives of 31 participants were obtained through structured open-ended questions, providing a multi-dimensional perspective. The findings obtained through content analysis reveal that AI offers significant opportunities in areas such as access to information, efficiency, and personalized learning; however, it may also lead to a "silent erosion" of essential skills such as critical thinking, problem-solving, and creativity. The study demonstrates that AI is not merely a technical tool but an innovative technology that necessitates the updating of learning environments. The findings also provide guidance and insight for future interdisciplinary and longitudinal research.

INTRODUCTION

In the world of artificial intelligence (AI), which is witnessing a new development every day, the field of education is also experiencing its share of changes. AI-based learning environments provide potential benefits in a wide variety of ways and play a leading role in the creation of personalised learning platforms. AI integration of

DOI: 10.4018/979-8-3373-7569-4.ch006

learning analytics and the use of big data also contribute to the preparation and monitoring of more customised and more effective learning processes.

These developments increase the impact of AI technology on educational environments and learning processes are radically changing. Open, distance and online learning environments, which provide learners with activities in various subjects and whose usage rates have increased with easy access to the internet, (Kılınç, 2019; Tse & Wise, 2005) are one of the first educational environments to be affected by AI technologies. In addition to its many benefits, facilitating role and potential, it is also seen that AI technologies are questioned within the scope of some dimensions. Especially in the context of cognitive, affective and behavioural skills, it has recently been discussed in academic environments that it contains some threats. It is argued that the convenience and comfort zone brought by such easy and instant access to information can negatively affect cognitive skills in particular. At this point, new concepts such as AI addiction have emerged. AI addiction may interrupt students' learning process and weaken their metacognitive skills. It is thought that students may slow down in subjects such as information processing, critical literacy, creativity, innovative thinking, quick comprehension, analysing information, bringing instant solutions to problems and synthesising information.

The danger of silent erosion discussed in this chapter attempts to shed light on how AI in education undermines these essential skills. It discusses why this danger occurs and its possible consequences in the context of the dimensions mentioned above. Some suggestions are made on how innovative approaches such as AI technologies can be used effectively and efficiently without harming essential skills.

Within the scope of this research, some questions were asked to distance learning graduate students. These questions are given below:

1. As a graduate student, how do you perceive the impact of AI on the development of your essential skills?
2. In what ways does AI in education undermine the development of critical thinking, problem solving and creativity?
3. In what ways does AI in education support the development of critical thinking, problem solving and creativity?
4. What strategies can be implemented to mitigate the negative effects of AI on essential skills development?

LITERATURE REVIEW

The use of AI in education is a popular topic in recent years. Especially with the popularisation of ChatGPT, interest in this topic has intensified and has been discussed in academic communities. The impact of AI on the education sector has led to mixed reactions. While some educators have heralded it as a progressive step, others have warned about its potential to reduce analytical skills and encourage cognitive laziness (Grassini, 2023).

AI has strengths in saving time, efficiency and effectiveness in learning, personalised learning and personal guidance, self-education, informal and lifelong learning, preparing students for future workplaces, reliable assessment, innovation in education, student autonomy, supporting critical thinking, accessibility and inclusiveness, supporting faculty and institutional capacity, enhancing creativity and innovation, cross-disciplinary and interdisciplinary learning, collaborative learning and improving cognitive capacity (Bozkurt et al., 2024). Although there are many studies in the literature examining the various benefits of using AI in educational settings, it is also known that it may reduce some cognitive, analytical and essential skills. In this context, there are many studies in the literature on how these skills can be weakened in various dimensions (Bozkurt et al., 2024; Bozkurt & Sharma, 2024; Eden, Chisom & Adeniyi, 2024; Frick, 2023; Ifelebuegu, Kulume & Cherukut, 2023; Selwyn, 2024).

AI has been criticised for providing students with ready-made information and increasing dependency, weakening individuals' essential skills. This shows that AI can lead to cognitive laziness. Lack of utilisation of mental muscles may cause laziness in neurons after a while. Prentzas and Sidiropoulou (2023) state that the use of AI tools such as ChatGPT eliminates imagination due to the fact that it provides ready-made information and students will not personally engage in the process of information seeking. Pleios and Tastsoglou (2025), on the other hand, emphasise that AI represents the automation of online content management, content aggregation and combining them, saying that AI tools are a collection of ready-made information available on the Internet.

There are various contrasting approaches that AI enriches critical thinking or, on the contrary, blunts it. Muthmainnah, Ibna Seraj and Oteir (2022) revealed in their study that AI improves students' critical thinking abilities. According to the authors, AI-based education can help students develop critical thinking skills as it increases their self-confidence, open-mindedness and maturity. However, some studies specifically focus on the fact that AI does not realise in-depth learning with superficial knowledge acquisition. Students' superficial learning can cause them to quickly forget the knowledge they have acquired and cause the learning process to be unhealthy and inefficient. Spector and Ma (2019) emphasise that the use of AI, especially in children and young people, affects the four skills of the 21st century: communication, collaboration, critical thinking and creativity. It is pointed out that more emphasis should be placed on the development of human intelligence as well as the value given to AI, especially in young children. According to the authors, although a lot of funding and support goes into the development of AI, this should not be at the expense of human intelligence. It is also emphasised that the use of AI in learning environments requires new curricula and that critical thinking should be redefined in these curricula. Critical thinking should not be allowed to atrophy and children's developmental processes should be recognized.

There are many arguments that AI increases creativity. It is seen that AI tools are used to obtain unpredictable creative outputs, especially in text and visual production processes. However, there are also some limitations. Excessive use of these tools may prevent the emergence of original artefacts or products. In addition, as a personal assistant, AI tools, which answer students' questions anytime, anywhere and develop their creative thinking skills, can also blunt their creativity abilities by easily accessing this ready information. According to Runco (2025), recent developments in AI necessitate the updating of the 'standard definition of creativity'. It is stated that various measures should be taken to ensure that artificial creativity does not prevent and hinder human creativity. According to the author, even if artificial creativity is original and impressive, it lacks the originality and purposefulness that are evident in human creativity. According to Davis (2024), although AI is on the rise, it should not be forgotten that there are inherent limits to what machines can achieve when compared to human capabilities. An android can at most achieve 'weak AI', i.e. it can be intelligent but is likely to lack awareness or empathy. At this point, it can be said that the ability of AI tools to think creatively is limited and the creative ideas they can give to human beings may be blocked at some point.

The dependency on the results produced by AI tools interferes with students' creative problem-solving processes. Prawiti et al. (2025) underline the potential for over-dependence on AI, especially among students with low motivation and information literacy. Especially with AI dependency, resorting to AI tools every time there is a problem leads to the lack of effort used in searching for information. Students are unable to produce their own problem-solving strategies and their reasoning skills decline. Students who resort to AI tools while making decisions also decrease their ability to take responsibility (Boussioux et al., 2024; Memarian & Doleck, 2023; Mustofa, Bilad & Grendis, 2024).

It is obvious that AI tools also have an impact on information literacy. It is known that Generative AI tools can produce inaccurate, biased or biased information (Ferrara, 2023; Nwoyibe, 2025; Wach et al., 2023). This situation negatively affects students' feelings of confidence during information research. Information literacy is needed to understand whether the information is correct or not. It is of great importance to question the validity and reliability of the texts, visuals and videos produced by AI tools and to reach the correct information (Tian, 2023).

One of the biggest challenges in accessing the right information is AI literacy, which is a new type of literacy. Unlike digital literacy or information literacy, low

AI literacy is associated with not using AI tools correctly and not producing correct outputs. The concept of digital literacy is crucial in terms of teaching learners the capabilities of computer and internet technologies and how to use the obtained knowledge effectively (Ayduğ & Altınpulluk, 2025). Prawati et al. (2025) emphasised the need for a careful and supportive approach in AI integration by emphasising AI literacy, which is a subtype of digital literacy, and pointed out that it should serve as a tool to improve rather than hinder educational outcomes.

The impact of AI technologies on essential skills should be examined not only at the pedagogical level but also at the cognitive, social, behavioural, ethical and institutional level. At this point, frameworks related to AI literacy are important. Developing critical awareness of learners and using technology more effectively brings the concept of AI literacy to the fore. The guidance of educators and the regulatory role of institutions can be important in mitigating the silent and profound negative effects that AI can create. Besides, socioeconomic and cultural differences have a direct impact on access to and use of AI. The digital divide created by digital inequalities may reflect negatively on the development of essential skills. Accordingly, it is necessary to develop innovative and original pedagogical approaches that encourage critical thinking, learner-centred and blend human-AI interactions.

The fact that AI tools affect creativity leads to positive or negative effects on innovative thinking skills. While AI tools can improve innovation skills in many dimensions, there may be limitations in some dimensions. The fact that Generative AI tools provide instant and various outputs does not challenge the cognitive capacities of students. The possibilities offered by AI tools to their users and easy access to information cause students to produce fewer ideas and original thoughts to disappear. It should not be forgotten that cognitive laziness will weaken innovative thinking abilities and may cause uniformity in idea generation (Broekhuizen et al, 2023; Verganti, Vendraminelli & Iansiti, 2020).

METHODOLOGY

Research Design

In this research, case study, one of the qualitative research designs, was employed. Case study research involves the intensive examination of a single unit in order to understand a class of similar units observed at a single point in time or in a specific time period (Gerring, 2004). Therefore, case studies provide the researcher with the opportunity to gain a deep and holistic perspective on the research problem and make it easier to define, understand and explain a research problem or situation (Baskarada, 2014; Baxter & Jack, 2008).

This research is a case study because it aims to provide a framework for the dimensions in which AI can weaken essential skills and the views of distance learning master's students are used. Thus, the dimensions of silent erosion that AI may create, especially in graduate education, will be tried to be understood and a holistic perspective will be obtained.

Study Group

Table 1. Study Group

Gender	f
Female	16
Male	15
Employment Status	
I work in the public sector	15
I work in the private sector	6
I do not work	6
I am self-employed	2
I am retired	2
Daily Technological Device Usage Time	
Between 4-6 hours	16
7 hours and above	7
1-3 hours	7
Less than 1 hour	1
AI Usage Frequency	
I use it very little	16
I use it a lot	9
I use it all the time	3
I do not use it at all	2
I have no idea	1
AI Usage Purpose	
I use it to translate.	10
I use it to produce written text.	8
I use it to produce visuals.	5

continued on following page

Table 1. Continued

Gender	f
I do not use any AI tools.	2
I use it to plan and get information.	1
I use it together with translation activities during research.	1
I use it to correct and improve texts.	1
I use it to get information in the form of questions and answers.	1
I use it to design products.	1
I use it to get general information.	1

The study group of this research consists of non-thesis master's degree students studying at a distance. When the gender distribution of 31 participants is analysed, 16 of them are female (51,6%) and 15 of them are male (48,4%). Considering the employment status of the participants, 48.4% of them work in the public sector, 19.4% work in the private sector, and 19.4% do not work in any job. In addition, 6.5% are self-employed and 6.5% are retired. When the distribution of the participants' daily use of technological devices is analysed, 51.6% of them reported 4-6 hours of use, 22.6% reported 7 hours or more, and 22.6% reported 1-3 hours of use. Only 3.2% stated that they used the device for less than 1 hour. Data on the frequency of use of AI tools show that 51.6% of the participants use these tools very rarely, 29.0% use them frequently and 9.7% always use them. 6.5% of the participants stated that they never use these tools, while 3.2% stated that they have no idea about this issue. The purposes of using AI tools are quite diverse. The most frequently mentioned areas of use by the participants were translation (32.3%) and written text production (25.8%). In addition, more specific purposes such as visual production (16.1%), planning, correction, and information acquisition were also mentioned. Two participants (6.5%) stated that they did not use any AI tools. These findings show that the participant group interacted with technology and especially with AI tools at different levels.

Data Collection Tool and Process

In this study, a structured open-ended interview form developed by the researcher was used as a data collection tool. As the name suggests, a structured open-ended interview consists of forms structured in a certain sequence and order that apply a systematic procedure to collect ideas, information and opinions from participants (Monroe, 2002).

In the form used in this study, preliminary information such as gender, employment status, average daily usage time of technological devices, frequency of using AI tools and purpose of using AI tools were obtained, and then 4 open-ended questions were asked on the Google Forms platform for the purpose of the research. Before the open-ended questions were directed to the participants, opinions were obtained from 2 faculty members in terms of content validity. The data were collected between 21 December 2024 - 23 January 2025.

Data Analysis

Content analysis was used to analyse the data. Content analysis, a qualitative analysis technique, is a systematic and objective way of describing and quantifying phenomena (Downe-Wamboldt, 1992; Krippendorff, 1980; Sandelowski, 1995). It is also known as a method of analysing documents and forms. Through content analysis, it is possible to categorise words into fewer content-related categories (Elo & Kyngas, 2008).

In the study, the questions prepared about how AI creates an erosion in essential skills were answered by 31 participants and these answers were processed into tables with theme, sub-theme, sample expression and frequency columns by content analysis. The opinions of the participants were coded anonymously without giving their names, based on the principle of confidentiality.

FINDINGS

The Impact of AI on the Development of Essential Skills

Table 2. The Impact of AI on the Development of Essential Skills

Theme	Sub-Theme	Sample Expression	f
Time Saving and Efficiency	Speed and efficiency in research processes	"It allows me to do research faster and more effectively."	5
	Time saving and increased efficiency	"I save time by completing administrative tasks in a short time."	4
Information Acquisition and Solution Support	Help with complex issues	"When I get help on complex issues, I have fewer questions."	1
	Alternative perspectives and problem solving	"It helps me find solutions by bringing different perspectives to problems."	1
	Summarizing the topic and easy understanding	"It explains certain topics in a summary manner, helping me understand the subject faster."	1
Language and Communication Support	Foreign language translation and writing support	"It makes my language practice easier by suggesting translations and synonyms."	2

continued on following page

Table 2. Continued

Theme	Sub-Theme	Sample Expression	f
Creativity and Critical Thinking	Time for creative thinking	"When I leave labor-intensive tasks to AI, I can spend more time on creative thinking."	1
	Critical thinking development	'Conscious use strengthens my critical thinking skills.'	1
Self-confidence and Motivation	Gaining self-confidence	'I can handle difficult operations in a short time, which increased my self-confidence.'	1
Negative Impact	Skill dulling and laziness	'It does not improve my essential skills, on the contrary, it dulls my problem-solving ability.'	2
	Priority of individual work	'Although it helps, one-to-one research is more effective.'	1
No Effect / Neutral Perception	Only helpful, effect on skills	'It does not affect my essential knowledge much, it only supports me.'	3
	No effect due to low use	'I think it has no effect because I haven't used it much yet.'	2
Future Potential	Increased role in daily life	'It is limited for now, but I believe it will be more effective in daily life in the future.'	1
	Personal development tool	'It is an important technology; when I learn it, I will use it for language practice and translation.'	1
Ethical and Responsible Use	Benefit in ethical conditions	'When the principles of science ethics are followed, AI is very useful for research.'	1
General Attitude	General positive view	'AI is very useful when used correctly.'	1

In line with the views of the participants, the impact of AI on the development of graduate students' essential skills was analysed under various themes. The findings show that the participants largely emphasised the positive contributions of AI technologies on time management, access to information, language skills and thinking processes. The statements with the highest frequency under the title of "time saving and efficiency" are that AI provides speed and efficiency in research processes (f=5) and saves time by completing administrative work in a shorter time (f=4). This situation reveals that AI applications play a role in increasing academic scientific productivity. The statements in the "knowledge acquisition and solution support" theme show that the participants perceive AI as a supportive tool in the processes of understanding complex issues, developing alternative perspectives and summarising the subject. These findings indicate that AI plays a complementary role in learning processes. Within the scope of "language and communication support", it was stated that AI tools that provide translation and spelling support in a foreign language offer a facilitating effect in terms of language practice (f=2). In the "creativity and critical thinking" category, the participants stated that they could spend more time for creative thinking thanks to AI's undertaking routine tasks and that conscious use strengthened their critical thinking skills. These statements show that technology can have an indirect but positive effect on cognitive skills. In the "self-confidence and motivation" theme, it was stated that the ability to easily solve difficult tasks with AI increased self-confidence in the user (f=1). On the other hand, some participants emphasised negative effects. In this context, opinions were expressed that excessive use of AI blunts essential skills (f=2) and that individual work is still more effective (f=1). In addition, some participants stated that technology has an ineffective or neutral role. In this context, it was evaluated that AI is only a supportive tool (f=3) or that it does not have an impact because it is not used enough (f=2). In addition, some participants emphasised that AI has potential for the future and stated that AI will play a more active role in daily life in the future (f=1) and can be used for personal development (f=1). Finally, under the theme of "ethical and responsible use", one participant stated that AI can make a great contribution to research when used within the framework of the principles of scientific ethics; another participant expressed that AI can be very useful when used correctly (f=1).

How AI Weakens Critical Thinking, Problem Solving, and Creativity

Table 3. How AI Weakens Critical Thinking, Problem Solving, and Creativity

Theme	Sub-Theme	Sample Expression	f
Laziness and the Deterioration of Essential Skills	Preparedness (orientation towards ready-made solutions)	'It is preferred to get ready answers to questions instead of thinking about them.'	8
	Laziness / Easy Avoidance (decreased desire to work)	'It leads to laziness.'	5
	Copy-Paste tendency	'If AI is used only as copy-paste, our own skills will not develop.'	1
	Decrease in analytical/research skills	'I think AI weakens the mechanism of research.'	3
	Decreased problem solving skills	'It can dull my problem solving skills by taking the easy way out.'	2
Decline in Critical Thinking and Creativity	Lack of critical thinking (one-way thinking)	'It may cause us to think in one direction.'	1
	Decreased creativity	'It prevents creativity and free development of the individual in education.'	2
	Weakening of imagination / interpretation ability	'It makes us think less, weakens our imagination and interpretation ability.'	1
Dependency and Disclaimer	Excessive reliance on vehicles (addiction)	'Dependency; over-reliance on AI tools, constant recourse.'	2
	Quitting completely / Avoiding responsibility	'Leaving things entirely to AI is like having your parents do your homework.'	1
Skipping the Learning Process	Process skipping / Lack of time management	'It can weaken skills such as learning and time management without the necessary experiences.'	1

When the answers of the participants to the second question were analysed, most of the answers pointed out that AI feeds simplistic approaches. Especially the issue of readiness (searching for ready-made answers) came to the fore; 8 responses expressed this sub-theme. The emphasis on laziness or taking the easy way out was also seen frequently (f=5). In addition, it was stated that the use of copy-paste prevents skill development and reduces the analytical/researching power of AI. The atrophy of problem solving ability (f=2) is also included in this theme.

When the theme of Decline in Critical Thinking and Creativity was analysed, some participants stated that AI narrowed the critical perspective and significantly decreased creativity. For example, the statement 'it may cause us to think in one direction' shows a lack of critical thinking. Opinions on the weakening of imagination and interpretation ability (f=1) were also categorised under this theme.

In the context of Dependency and Denial of Responsibility, it was stated that excessive reliance on AI can indirectly develop dependency (f=2) and that completely delegating tasks to AI (avoiding responsibility) can negatively affect the learning process (f=1). For example, the statement 'Leaving things entirely to AI is like having your parents do your homework.' summarises this situation.

Under the theme of Skipping the Learning Process, one participant stated that focusing only on the result without going through the necessary experiences and processes (for example, without developing time management skills) can have negative effects. The above findings clearly reveal the participants' concerns about the development of critical thinking, problem solving and creativity in education. The most frequently mentioned sub-themes are concerns about simplifying learning processes (readiness, laziness) and loss of skills. Lack of creativity and narrowing of critical perspective were also emphasised.

How AI Supports Critical Thinking, Problem Solving, and Creativity

Table 4. Ways AI Supports Critical Thinking, Problem Solving and Creativity

Theme	Sub-Theme	Sample Expression	f
Advanced Information Access and Processing	Broad Data Access and Synthesis	'It supports students to analyse information and gain a critical perspective with various resources and big data tools.'	7
	Efficiency and Time Savings	'It provides speed and convenience in obtaining information.'	5
Encouraging New Perspectives and Ideas	Diverse Perspectives and Alternative Solutions	'With ChatGPT suggestions, we can have the chance to look at things from perspectives that we had not thought of before.'	6
	Idea Generation and Creative Stimulation	'It improves students' design and production skills with innovative tools that increase creativity and enable the expression of ideas.'	6

continued on following page

Table 4. Continued

Theme	Sub-Theme	Sample Expression	f
Personalized Learning and Skill Development Support	Personalized Learning Paths and Feedback	'Strengthens critical thinking by creating programmes tailored to student levels and needs through personalised learning.'	4
	Facilitating Problem Solving	'Develops students' solution-oriented and analytical thinking skills through interactive scenarios and challenges that encourage problem solving and discovery.'	5
	Support for Diverse Learners	'AI in education supports the development, problem solving and creativity of individuals with disabilities such as dyslexia, individuals with autism, hearing, visually impaired individuals, individuals with disabilities with various applications.'	1
Critical Engagement and Analytical Skills	Analysis and Evaluation	'By improving data analysis skills, it provides new thinking methods through the interpretation and evaluation of data.'	3
Concerns and Limitations	Inhibition of Critical Thinking (Echo Chamber Effect)	'I do not think that AI supports critical thinking, because it is obvious that it often prioritises giving the answer the other person wants instead of providing real information. In such a situation, the echo chamber cannot support critical thinking.'	2
	Potential for Skill Deterioration	'I think that AI in education does not support the development of critical thinking, problem solving and creativity. On the contrary, it even causes the loss of one's abilities.'	3

In this part of the study, participant perceptions of how AI supports the development of critical thinking, problem solving and creativity in education are examined. When the responses of 31 participants were evaluated using content analysis techniques, it was found that AI could provide certain advantages in areas such as increasing access to information, offering new perspectives, encouraging personalized learning, and developing analytical skills. However, it was also determined that AI has some limitations, such as potentially reducing critical thinking and leading to a decline in core skills. Upon examining the findings, it can be stated that AI has a multifaceted impact on education. In particular, it can be said that policymakers, educators, researchers, academics, and AI developers need to work together and increase AI literacy.

According to participants, AI significantly enriches access to information and information processing in education. According to participants, AI provides comprehensive information, synthesizes large data sets, and offers extensive resources. AI's capabilities in these areas are frequently mentioned.

AI's easy access to extensive information resources also democratizes learning environments. It can be said that this situation shifts new educational paradigms from information acquisition to the analysis and synthesis of information. With AI, the burden of information acquisition on learners is now reduced. It has become apparent that learners should now focus their cognitive efforts on critical thinking and creativity.

It can be said that AI has the ability to provide learners with previously unconsidered original perspectives and alternative approaches. Thus, it stands out as an important theme in the context of critical thinking and problem-solving skills.

Participants often emphasized the idea that AI pushes students to find original ideas and new approaches.

Participants noted the role of AI in triggering new ideas, inspiring and acting as a catalyst for creative outputs, especially when individuals experience conceptual blockages. One participant stated that AI could "maybe have a spark effect". The role of AI as a "spark" or idea generator suggests a shift in the creative process from pure idea generation to iterative refinement. AI may initiate the process, but the final creative act remains human-centred, involving the selection, adaptation and integration of the ideas generated by the AI. This suggests that AI acts as a co-creator or muse, rather than a creative agent in its own right, emphasising the centrality of human action in creativity.

Strategies to Reduce the Negative Effects of AI on Essential Skills

Table 5. Strategies That Can Be Used To Mitigate The Negative Effects Of AI On Essential Skills Development

Theme	Sub-Theme	Sample Expression	f
Positioning AI as an Assistive Tool	Emphasis on Assistant/ Consultant Role	'In this way, we get counselling from him/her and we do the work again, he/she can only act as an assistant and guide us by offering ideas when we are lost.'	10
	Idea Generation and Critical Analysis-Oriented Use	"Group chats can be organised that encourage these by analysing, interpreting and thinking critically about the data provided by AI."	11
Ethical Awareness and Legal Infrastructure	Importance of Ethics and Moral Education	"In education, firstly, people should be taught ethics and morality well, and then detailed information should be given about the conditions of use and content of AI."	10
	Plagiarism and Fake Researcher Problem	"The biggest problem is to show the skills that the researcher does not already have in ethical issues as if they exist with AI tools. Therefore, fake researchers who do not have researcher skills and competences may emerge."	4
Promoting Human-Centered Skills	Focus on Essential Skills	"Human-centred activities should be emphasised, technology dependency should be reduced, and we should focus on essential skills such as reading or analytical thinking."	17
	Active Learning and Creative Problem Solving	"Encourage students to participate in projects that develop their thinking and creative problem-solving skills without relying on ready-made solutions."	14
Regulations and Limitations in the Education System	Curriculum and Teacher Equipment	"Equipping educators to be one step ahead of students in AI can also mitigate the negative aspects of AI."	5
	Limits to the Use of AI and Conscious Use	"Setting clear limits on the use of AI, especially in activities that require intellectual endeavour."	11

The views of 31 participants on strategies to mitigate the negative effects of AI on essential skill development in educational settings were examined through content analysis. These views highlight a widespread social concern about the debilitating potential of AI on human intellectual abilities. Participants expressed concerns that silent erosion could occur in the form of the failure to protect intellectual capital. In summary, participants noted that the greatest challenge lies in the philosophical and existential dimensions of being human in an increasingly AI-focused world. It is understood that what is meant by "essential skills" is a perceived threat to the core human characteristics that are considered indispensable for personal development and social sustainability.

Participants emphasized that AI should be positioned as a helpful tool. They stressed that a philosophical shift and update is needed in how AI is perceived and used today. Participants stated that AI should be seen as a tool that empowers humans and facilitates their work, rather than a tool that replaces human intelligence.

Participants consistently advocate for AI to serve as a supportive tool rather than a comprehensive solution provider. For example, the statement 'People can be taught to think that AI can help instead of thinking that it can solve everything' indicates that AI should be positioned as a counsellor or assistant.

The sub-theme Idea Generation and Critical Analysis Focused Use emphasises the strategy of clearly separating human and AI roles in order to preserve and develop high-level cognitive skills such as critical thinking and creativity. Participants tacitly recognise the strengths of AI in processing data and performing routine tasks ('app-style jobs'). However, they explicitly state that 'idea finding and thought generation' are uniquely human domains that are vital for intellectual development. The causal link here is that by strategically delegating mundane or data-intensive tasks to AI, people can devote more mental energy and focus to more complex, interpretive and innovative work. This prevents cognitive 'laziness' and actively encourages the development of more challenging, skill-building activities, thus ensuring that human intelligence remains sharp and adaptive.

The Ethical Awareness and Legal Infrastructure theme emphasises the critical necessity of a sound ethical foundation and regulatory mechanisms to prevent misuse and promote responsible AI engagement. The strong and repeated emphasis on the concepts of 'ethics' and 'morality' suggests that the impact of AI extends far beyond technical functionality to fundamental human values, academic integrity and personal responsibility.

CONCLUSION

This research was shaped by the opinions of distance learning master's students. The aim was to examine the effects of AI on the development of essential skills in education from the perspective of graduate students. The findings show that AI's role in education offers significant opportunities and strengths, but also weaknesses and potential threats.

The study demonstrates that AI offers potential benefits in areas such as access to information, efficiency, providing new perspectives, and personalized learning. However, it also brings serious negative aspects such as the ease of ready-made information, the deterioration of essential skills, cognitive laziness, and a decrease in critical thinking and creativity. Based on these results, AI can be redefined not only as a technological tool but also as a facilitator that updates learning and research paradigms. Participants emphasized the positive contributions of AI technologies to time management, access to information, language skills, and thinking processes, drawing attention to AI's potential to increase efficiency in academic processes.

Alongside all these positive aspects, participants provided some responses regarding the silent erosion that AI may cause on essential skills. Perceptions that AI encourages a lazy approach are noteworthy. Significant concerns have been raised that this could lead to a decline in essential skills in education. In connection with this, it has been found that the unconscious and uncontrolled use of AI could have negative consequences on learning outcomes. In summary, the visual created in the Napkin tool, which shows how AI is causing a silent erosion in education, is shown in Figure 1 below.

Figure 1. How the use of AI in education is eroding essential skills

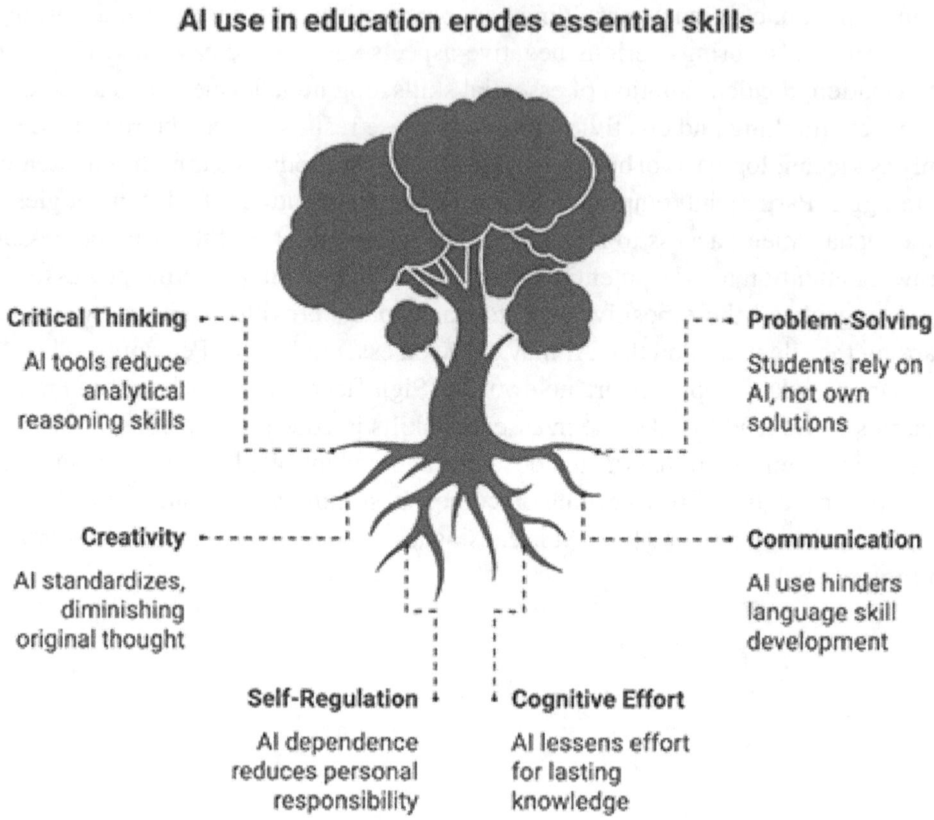

The findings show that the impact of AI on education is not limited to a single perspective. It has been determined that AI does not have a uniform effect on education, but rather produces different results depending on the context in which it is applied and how it is used. At this point, it can be said that strategic integration and the development of AI literacy are necessary for educators, policymakers, and AI developers.

It would not be accurate to describe the impact of AI on education as either "good" or "bad." The impact of AI on education is a dynamic process that is shaped by how it is used, pedagogical approaches, and users' level of AI literacy. This shows that AI is becoming an active component of the educational ecosystem rather than a 'tool'. The fact that the participants experienced both positive and negative effects at the same time shows that there is no neutrality in the nature of AI, on the contrary, its effect is determined by the user and the system. If AI is used in a conscious and ethical framework, its positive effects come to the fore; otherwise, negative consequences are inevitable. This means that the success of AI in education largely depends on 'how' it is used, emphasising that AI integration in education is not only a technological issue but also a pedagogical and ethical responsibility.

Limitations

This research was conducted within the framework of some limitations. Firstly, a qualitative case study design was adopted in the research and the data were collected from a specific group of participants such as non-thesis master's degree students studying at a distance. Therefore, the results obtained do not claim generalisability, but aim to provide an in-depth understanding of similar contexts.

Secondly, data were collected through structured open-ended questions on the Google Forms platform. Although this method allows participants to express their thoughts in detail, it may lead to limited reflection of some meanings due to the lack of verbal and bodily cues that can be obtained in face-to-face interviews.

Thirdly, the limited size of the participant group (n=31) and voluntary participation is another factor that may affect the diversity of the sample. Since the participants' experience and usage levels of technology and AI tools vary, this may limit the homogeneity of the responses.

Finally, the scope and language of the open-ended questions used in the research may have created limitations in terms of depth and diversity in the responses depending on the participants' awareness and expression skills. In addition, although the risk of subjectivity in the coding and theme determination process in the content analysis conducted by the researcher was tried to be reduced with systematic approaches, it could not be completely eliminated.

FUTURE RESEARCH DIRECTIONS

In future research, long-term longitudinal studies should be conducted to understand the effects of AI on essential skills in more depth. These studies should track cognitive and behavioural changes at different stages of AI use and reveal causal relationships more clearly. Although this study focused on graduate students, the effects of AI on the skill development of students from different disciplines (engineering, social sciences, arts, etc.) should be comparatively examined. Interdisciplinary differences may offer important insights for the adaptation strategies of AI. The quantitative and qualitative effects of specific pedagogical models in which AI is integrated (e.g. personalised learning platforms, AI-supported feedback systems) on critical thinking, problem solving and creativity should be evaluated. This will help to identify best practices. Research should be conducted on educators' competencies and needs for AI integration and the effectiveness of professional development programmes. Educators' ability to use AI effectively and ethically is critical to the success of AI integration. Field research should be conducted on the applicability and effectiveness of the developed ethical guidelines and legal regulations in educational settings. This allows to evaluate the practical implications of the theoretical frameworks. The effects of AI use on students' intrinsic motivation, self-regulation skills and learning strategies should be further investigated. While this qualitative study revealed perceptions, future research needs to bridge the gap between these perceptions and empirical reality. The concerns identified (echo chamber, skill degradation) are hypotheses derived from participant feelings and require rigorous testing. Quantitative and mixed-methods studies should be conducted to empirically measure the actual impact of AI on critical thinking, problem solving and creativity in various educational settings.

REFERENCES

Ayduğ, D., & Altınpulluk, H. (2025). Are Turkish pre-service teachers worried about AI? A study on AI anxiety and digital literacy. *AI & Society*, •••, 1–12. DOI: 10.1007/s00146-025-02348-0

Baskarada, S. (2014). Qualitative case study guidelines. *The Qualitative Report*, *19*(40), 1–25. DOI: 10.46743/2160-3715/2014.1008

Baxter, P., & Jack, S. (2008). Qualitative case study methodology: Study design and implementation for novice researchers. *The Qualitative Report*, *13*(4), 544–559. www.nova.edu/ssss/QR/QR13-4/baxter.pdf

Boussioux, L., Lane, J. N., Zhang, M., Jacimovic, V., & Lakhani, K. R. (2024). The crowdless future? Generative AI and creative problem-solving. *Organization Science*, *35*(5), 1589–1607. DOI: 10.1287/orsc.2023.18430

Bozkurt, A., Xiao, J., Farrow, R., Bai, J. Y., Nerantzi, C., Moore, S., & Asino, T. I. (Eds.). (2024). The manifesto for teaching and learning in a time of generative AI: A critical collective stance to better navigate the future. *Open Praxis, 16*(4), 487-513. DOI: 10.55982/openpraxis.16.4.777

Bozkurt, A., & Sharma, R. C. (2024). Trust, credibility and transparency in human-AI ınteraction: Why we need explainable and trustworthy AI and why we need it now. *Asian Journal of Distance Education*, *19*(2). https://www.asianjde.com/ojs/index.php/AsianJDE/article/view/819

Broekhuizen, T., Dekker, H., de Faria, P., Firk, S., Nguyen, D. K., & Sofka, W. (2023). AI for managing open innovation: Opportunities, challenges, and a research agenda. *Journal of Business Research*, *167*, 114196. DOI: 10.1016/j.jbusres.2023.114196

Davis, A. J. (2024). AI rising in higher education: Opportunities, risks and limitations. *Asian Education and Development Studies*, *13*(4), 307–319. DOI: 10.1108/AEDS-01-2024-0017

Downe-Wamboldt, B. (1992). Content analysis: Method, applications and issues. *Health Care for Women International*, *13*, 313–321. DOI: 10.1080/07399339209516006

Eden, C. A., Chisom, O. N., & Adeniyi, I. S. (2024). Integrating AI in education: Opportunities, challenges, and ethical considerations. *Magna Scientia Advanced Research and Reviews, 10*(2), 006-013. https://doi.org/DOI: 10.30574/msarr.2024.10.2.0039

Elo, S., & Kyngäs, H. (2008). The qualitative content analysis process. *Journal of Advanced Nursing*, *62*(1), 107–115. DOI: 10.1111/j.1365-2648.2007.04569.x

Ferrara, E. (2023). Fairness and bias in artificial intelligence: A brief survey of sources, impacts, and mitigation strategies. *Sci*, *6*(1), 1–15. DOI: 10.3390/sci6010003

Frick, T. W. (2023). *Are we dupes? Limitations of AI systems: What should educators do with them? TechTrends: Online first*. Association for Educational Communications and Technology., DOI: 10.1007/s11528-023-00893-3

Gerring, J. (2004). What is a case study and what is it good for? *The American Political Science Review*, *98*(2), 341–354. DOI: 10.1017/S0003055404001182

Grassini, S. (2023). Shaping the future of education: Exploring the potential and consequences of AI and ChatGPT in educational settings. *Education Sciences*, *13*(7), 692. DOI: 10.3390/educsci13070692

Ifelebuegu, A. O., Kulume, P., & Cherukut, P. (2023). Chatbots and AI in Education (AIEd) tools: The good, the bad, and the ugly. *Journal of Applied Learning and Teaching*, *6*(2), 332–345. DOI: 10.37074/jalt.2023.6.2.29

Kılınç, H. (2019). Açık ve uzaktan öğrenme ortamlarında çevrimiçi grup tartışması tekniğinin kullanılması. *Açıköğretim Uygulamaları ve Araştırmaları Dergisi AUAd*, *5*(2), 87-106. https://dergipark.org.tr/en/download/article-file/734331

Krippendorff, K. (1980). *Content analysis: An introduction to its methodology*. Sage Publications.

Memarian, B., & Doleck, T. (2023). ChatGPT in education: Methods, potentials, and limitations. *Computers in Human Behavior: Artificial Humans*, *1*(2), 100022. DOI: 10.1016/j.chbah.2023.100022

Monroe, M. C. (2002). Evaluation s friendly voice: The structured open-ended interview. *Applied Environmental Education and Communication: An International Journal*, *1*(2), 101–106. DOI: 10.1080/15330150213993

Mustofa, H. A., Bilad, M. R., & Grendis, N. W. B. (2024). Utilizing AI for physics problem solving: A literature review and ChatGPT experience. *Lensa: Jurnal Kependidikan Fisika*, *12*(1), 78–97. DOI: 10.33394/j-lkf.v12i1.11748

Muthmainnah, I. S. (2022). P. M., & Oteir, I. (2022). Playing with ai to investigate human-computer interaction technology and improving critical thinking skills to pursue 21st century age. *Education Research International*, *6468995*(1), •••. DOI: 10.1155/2022/6468995

Nwoyibe, O. I. (2025). Deploying AI technology for effective teaching and learning: The need to always verify information gathered from generative AI tools. *Caliphate Journal of Science and Technology*, *7*(1), 22–29. DOI: 10.4314/cajost.v7i1.3

Pleios, G., & Tastsoglou, M. (2025). AI and the news: Challenges arisen from the adoption of ai in news production. *Postmodernism Problems, 15*(1), 3–24. DOI: 10.46324/PMP2501003

Pratiwi, H., Riwanda, A., Hasruddin, H., Sujarwo, S., & Syamsudin, A. (2025). Transforming learning or creating dependency? Teachers' perspectives and barriers to AI integration in education. *Journal of Pedagogical Research*, 1-16. DOI: 10.33902/JPR.202531677

Prentzas, J., & Sidiropoulou, M. (2023, July). Assessing the use of open AI chat-GPT in a University Department of Education. In *2023 14th international conference on information, intelligence, systems & applications (iisa)* (pp. 1-4). IEEE. DOI: 10.1109/IISA59645.2023.10345910

Runco, M. A. (2025). Updating the standard definition of creativity to account for the artificial creativity of AI. *Creativity Research Journal*, *37*(1), 1–5. DOI: 10.1080/10400419.2023.2257977

Sandelowski, M. (1995). Qualitative analysis: What it is and how to begin? *Research in Nursing & Health*, *18*, 371–375. DOI: 10.1002/nur.4770180411

Selwyn, N. (2024). On the limits of artificial intelligence (AI) in education. *Nordisk tidsskrift for pedagogikk og kritikk, 10*(1), 3-14. https://pedagogikkogkritikk.no/index.php/ntpk/article/view/6062/9573

Spector, J. M., & Ma, S. (2019). Inquiry and critical thinking skills for the next generation: From artificial intelligence back to human intelligence. *Smart Learning Environments*, *6*(1), 1–11. DOI: 10.1186/s40561-019-0088-z

Tian, Y. (2023). Limitations and advancements of AI teachers in classroom instruction. *Education and Teaching Research, 3*, 66-72. http://www.fspress.net/static/upload/file/20230801/1690903421713331.pdf

Tse, J. ve Wise, L. (2005). Peer learning, lectures and online learning-putting it all together. *Australian Family Physician, 34*(12). https://search.informit.org/doi/abs/10.3316/informit.363983128361834

Verganti, R., Vendraminelli, L., & Iansiti, M. (2020). Innovation and design in the age of artificial intelligence. *Journal of Product Innovation Management*, *37*(3), 212–227. DOI: 10.1111/jpim.12523

Wach, K., Duong, C. D., Ejdys, J., Kazlauskaitė, R., Korzynski, P., Mazurek, G., & Ziemba, E. (2023). The dark side of generative artificial intelligence: A critical analysis of controversies and risks of ChatGPT. *Entrepreneurial Business and Economics Review*, *11*(2), 7–30. DOI: 10.15678/EBER.2023.110201

KEY TERMS AND DEFINITONS

Artificial Intelligence: Artificial intelligence (AI), as a concept that focuses on the development of systems that mimic human intelligence, refers to a wide range of research areas and technological terms that aim to realise many cognitive processes through information systems.

AI in Distance Education: It refers to the integration of AI-based tools and applications in order to personalise the learning process in distance and online learning environments, to optimise teaching processes and, in summary, to improve the learner experience.

Essential Skills: Core cognitive and social skills such as problem solving, communication, critical thinking, self-regulation, self-regulation, digital literacy, which are necessary for individuals to live and work effectively and efficiently in their family, academic, professional and social lives.

Silent Erosion: Despite the apparent benefits and strengths of AI technologies in education, in the long run it refers to the slow, subtle but profoundly effective decline in individuals' essential skills.

Graduate Education: It covers academic studies at higher education level following a bachelor's degree and generally includes master's (with/without thesis), doctorate and specialisation programmes.

Qualitative Research: It is a research method that adopts an interpretive approach to analyse and understand individuals' experiences and interpretations of social phenomena in depth. Data is collected through techniques such as observation, interview and document analysis.

Case Study: Case study is a qualitative research design that allows in-depth and comprehensive examination of a specific individual, group, event or phenomenon and the data collected are supported by multiple data sources.

Content Analysis: Content analysis is a qualitative data analysis technique that aims to systematically divide the data in written, audio or visual materials into themes and categories.

Chapter 7
Redefining Student Engagement in the Age of AI:
Engagement With AI (EWAI) Model

Gökhan Hınız
https://orcid.org/0000-0003-3569-0198
Çanakkale Onsekiz Mart University, Turkey

ABSTRACT

Generative Artificial Intelligence (GenAI) is transforming student engagement, requiring the reconsideration of traditional models. While engagement theories like Expectancy-Value and Self-Determination provide valuable insights, GenAI's personalized learning and automation call for a new perspective. This chapter introduces the Engagement with AI (EWAI) model, integrating AI research with existing theories. It explores engagement at micro (learner traits) and macro (institutional) levels, highlighting curiosity, analytical thinking, and ethics. The role of AI-supportive environments, including infrastructure and educator training, is emphasized. GenAI enhances engagement through personalized feedback but poses risks like overreliance, academic integrity issues, and algorithmic bias. AI-enhanced tasks should align with autonomy support and collaboration for meaningful learning. The EWAI model provides a structured framework for AI integration, ensuring ethical and equitable use.

DOI: 10.4018/979-8-3373-7569-4.ch007

INTRODUCTION

Generative artificial intelligence (GenAI) is advancing faster than any previous educational technology, forcing scholars and practitioners to re-examine what it means for students to be "engaged." Earlier waves of innovation, such as projectors, smartboards, and Web 2.0. tools, learning-management systems, and other digital platforms, primarily supplemented, augmented, modified teaching and learning or redefined traditional methods (Puentedura, 2013). However, GenAI tools now co-regulate learning because they can provide feedback, offer suggestions and ideas, draft essays, curate data sets, and even initiate peer/tutor-like dialogues in real time. Such capabilities may promise unprecedented personalisation, efficiency and engagement with learning, yet they simultaneously raise profound concerns about autonomy, equity, ethics, and the very nature of scholarly work. This explores the AI's impact on student engagement by introducing the Engagement with AI (EWAI) Model, a framework that reconceptualises engagement for an age in which technology is no longer a peripheral aid but an active partner in teaching and learning.

To appreciate why a new conceptualisation is necessary, it is helpful to recall how the engagement construct itself has evolved. Early work in the 1980s and 1990s equated engagement with behaviour: attendance, participation, time on task (Astin, 1984; Finn, 1989). By the early 2000s, research had expanded to include emotional (belonging, enjoyment) and cognitive (strategy use, self-regulation) dimensions, culminating in the widely cited behavioural–emotional–cognitive tripartite model (Fredricks et al., 2004). A decade later, Reeve and colleagues introduced agentic engagement—students' proactive efforts to shape the learning environment—reflecting a growing emphasis on autonomy and voice. Today, student engagement is defined as a multidimensional performance construct that refers to learners' active, focused, effortful, and willing involvement in meaningful, relevant, and sufficiently challenging learning experiences (Hınız & Çelik, 2024).

GenAI further extends our understanding and measurement of engagement into new frontiers. Its capacity to generate content, monitor performance, and participate in dialogue appears to blur traditional boundaries between teacher, medium, and learner. While these capabilities may extend existing dimensions of engagement, they also introduce new vulnerabilities related to bias, surveillance, and over-reliance.

The EWAI Model offered in this chapter builds on that lineage but adds two potentially valuable insights. First, engagement must now be understood at two interconnected levels: the AI-engaged learner—whose curiosity, agency, and ethical awareness determine whether GenAI becomes a scaffold or a crutch—and the AI-enhanced learning environment, whose infrastructure, pedagogy, and policies determine whether GenAI serves as a partner, a gatekeeper, or a source of inequity. Second, meaningful engagement in AI-rich settings demands a holistic synthesis of classic motivational and engagement theories (i.e., Expectancy-Value, Self-Determination), contemporary action-oriented frameworks (ICAP, Participation–Identification), and emerging ethical norms around data privacy and algorithmic transparency.

By integrating the historical arc of engagement research with a forward-looking analysis of GenAI's affordances and risks, this chapter offers three contributions. (1) It articulates why existing models are no longer sufficient when AI generates, evaluates, and reorganises knowledge at scale. (2) It proposes EWAI as a diagnostic and design tool that links learner dispositions, task characteristics, and institutional commitments. (3) It provides actionable guidance for educators, designers, and policymakers who seek to harness GenAI's pedagogical power without sacrificing critical thinking, social connection, or academic integrity. The chapter positions EWAI as a roadmap for sustaining meaningful, ethical, and equitable student engagement in the rapidly evolving landscape of AI-mediated education.

REVISITING STUDENT ENGAGEMENT MODELS AND THEORIES IN THE AGE OF GENAI

The acceleration of GenAI into mainstream educational practice compels scholars to revisit the foundational theories of student engagement that have guided research for decades. Although the conceptual scaffolding supplied by Expectancy-Value Theory (Eccles, 1983; Wigfield & Eccles, 2000; Eccles & Wigfield, 2002), Self-Determination Theory (Deci & Ryan, 1985; Ryan & Deci, 2017), the Participation Identification Model (Finn, 1989; Finn & Zimmer, 2012), the ICAP framework (Chi & Wylie, 2014), and the Educational Interface Model (Kahu & Nelson, 2018) perspectives remains valuable, each framework was conceived for instructional settings in which conventional learning materials played a supplementary role. In contemporary classrooms, in contrast, large-language models and GenAI tools not only augment teaching but actively shape the epistemic, motivational, and relational conditions under which learning takes place. The following analysis, therefore, undertakes a critical rereading of these theories, identifying points of continuity and rupture as engagement becomes co-regulated by humans and machines.

Expectancy–Value Theory

Expectancy–Value Theory (EVT) proposes that students are more likely to invest effort in learning when they believe a task is both achievable and valuable (Eccles, 1983; Eccles & Wigfield, 2002; Wigfield & Eccles, 2000). In the context of AI-mediated learning, students' beliefs about their ability to succeed and the usefulness of learning AI are increasingly shaped by their educational environments. While adaptive technologies may offer personalised support, Wang et al. (2023) emphasise the central role of supportive environments—such as access to resources and positive social norms—in fostering students' expectancy beliefs and perceived task value. When students perceive that they are supported and that learning AI is relevant to their goals, their confidence and motivation to engage with AI-related tasks increase. Similarly, generative tools like ChatGPT can enhance students' perceived utility of AI by offering concrete demonstrations of disciplinary practices (Chan & Zhou, 2023), such as coding, data modelling, and summarising research, thereby reinforcing the value component of expectancy–value beliefs (Chan & Zhou, 2023).

The bidirectional influence of AI on expectancy and value, however, introduces tensions unanticipated in the original theory. When students know that every keystroke and pause is being logged, the cost of mistakes may feel higher. This ever-present algorithmic surveillance can make them less willing to take risks and experiment. Moreover, when generative systems output polished text with minimal human effort, some learners may re-evaluate the internal cost–benefit calculus of deep engagement, concluding that superficial edits to AI drafts are sufficient to meet performance thresholds. The challenge for designers is therefore to preserve value by foregrounding tasks that require human judgment—evaluating the coherence of AI-generated arguments, for instance—while keeping expectancy high through transparent feedback loops that demystify algorithmic decision making.

To overcome challenges such as unfamiliarity, low confidence, or perceived irrelevance, educators can introduce scaffolded activities that gradually build students' skills, such as step-by-step prompts for using ChatGPT in brainstorming or problem-solving tasks. Embedding AI tools into authentic assessments, like having students' critique or revise AI-generated outputs, can show the relevance of AI to academic goals. Encouraging peer collaboration around AI use can also normalise the learning process and reduce anxiety. These strategies help students experience early success, see tangible value in AI tools, and develop sustained motivation aligned with EVT principles.

Self-Determination Theory

Self-Determination Theory (SDT) posits that autonomy, competence, and relatedness jointly foster intrinsic motivation (Deci & Ryan, 1985; Ryan & Deci, 2017). Generative AI can satisfy, threaten, or redefine each need. Competence support is the most visible benefit. When large-language models highlight conceptual gaps in a draft essay or recommend next-step resources, learners receive actionable information precisely calibrated and personalised to their current performance. Yet autonomy support can be more fragile. Recommendation engines that rigidly sequence activities risk turning choice into compliance; a learner who clicks the only path offered is not experiencing volition. Empirical work demonstrates that teacher mediation can buffer this risk. In Chiu et al.'s (2023) experiment, students with teacher support, who received guided, encouraging interactions, reported higher intrinsic motivation than those without such support, especially among learners with lower self-regulated learning or digital literacy skills.

Relatedness, traditionally understood as human–human connectedness, is increasingly influenced by interactions with artificial agents. While some AI tools, such as discussion representational systems, can enhance cognitive engagement and collaborative learning processes (Kong et al., 2025), they do not directly foster emotional or relational bonds. Conversely, reliance on AI chatbots for academic support has been shown to impact students' social well-being. When students turn to AI instead of peers for help, this substitution may weaken human social networks and contribute to increased feelings of loneliness and diminished belonging (Crawford et al., 2024). These findings suggest that within SDT, relatedness should not only include interactions with human or synthetic agents but also consider the quality and social authenticity of those exchanges. Designers of educational technologies should, therefore, be cautious of promoting solitary AI engagement at the expense of peer collaboration and should explore ways to integrate AI that supports, rather than replaces, meaningful social interaction.

Participation–Identification in Data-Rich Communities of Practice

Finn's Participation–Identification Model posits that behavioural participation lays the groundwork for psychological identification with school (Finn, 1989; Finn & Zimmer, 2012). In AI-supported learning environments, behavioural signals—such as clicks, submissions, and feedback requests—are increasingly trackable. Shafiabady et al. (2025) demonstrate that AI models can reliably predict postgraduate engagement across multiple dimensions. Meanwhile, quasi-experimental research by Ma and Chen (2024) provides strong evidence that exposure to AI-powered tools enhances behavioural, cognitive, and affective engagement while significantly reducing academic procrastination. However, psychological identification—the deeper sense of belonging—depends on how learners interpret the role of AI. If the logic behind AI feedback remains opaque, students may see it as impersonal or biased, undermining trust. By contrast, transparent, student-facing analytics that encourage co-interpretation of engagement data can foster a shared sense of progress and community. To remain relevant in AI-enhanced contexts, Finn's model must incorporate data transparency as a prerequisite for meaningful identification.

ICAP Theory

While expectancy-value analyses, self-determination needs, and participation-identification perspectives offer insights into why students choose to engage, the ICAP Theory (Chi & Wylie, 2014) sheds light on the cognitive quality of that engagement. The framework delineates four modes of cognitive engagement—Passive, Active, Constructive, and Interactive—based on the depth of mental processing. Passive engagement involves simply absorbing information, such as watching a lecture video without making notes or mentally rehearsing the material. Active mode requires some physical manipulation of content, such as highlighting key passages or rephrasing text. Constructive mode goes a step further by prompting learners to generate novel inferences or reorganise the material. Interactive engagement represents the highest echelon, in which learners co-create knowledge through dialogue and collaborative problem-solving.

AI can intersect with each mode in distinct ways. At the passive level, a student might mindlessly watch AI-generated videos or allow an adaptive system to solve problems without reflecting on the reasoning process behind each step. This scenario may be convenient for the learner but yields limited deep learning.

At the active level, learners might use an AI-based tool to highlight or annotate digital texts, thereby directing attention more effectively. Additionally, AI-enhanced virtual reality and augmented reality applications support active engagement by allowing students to manipulate digital objects in immersive or overlaid environments. In a virtual chemistry lab, for instance, students can pick up and examine a 3D model of a molecule, rotating it and applying simulated forces while the system offers hints on which reagents to combine next. In augmented reality fieldwork, biology learners might scan a plant with a mobile device, prompting an AI to identify key structures and invite tracing of stomata with a digital pen. AI-enhanced learning engagement may offer hands-on interaction rather than passive observation.

Constructive engagement occurs when an AI platform encourages them to elaborate on concepts in their own words, create analogies, or generate novel solutions. Some systems, for instance, prompt students to critique AI-generated outputs, thereby stimulating constructive thinking. However, the highest Interactive mode can be realised if students are engaged in sustained, meaningful exchanges with peers, tutors, or even multiple AI agents that collaborate to build new knowledge. This might take the form of an AI-driven environment in which a student proposes a hypothesis, the AI offers counterexamples, the student refines the hypothesis, and the cycle continues.

The distinction between surface and genuine interactivity matters deeply. A superficial question-and-answer sequence with a chatbot may simply confirm known facts. True Interactive engagement requires iterative negotiation of meaning and co-construction of concepts (Chi & Wylie, 2014), which is more challenging to design technologically but yields richer learning outcomes. As AI progresses toward more advanced conversational capacities, the potential for meaningful interactive engagement will grow, but so will the importance of careful pedagogy to guide it.

Educational Interface Model

The Educational Interface Model proposed by Kahu and Nelson (2018) enlarges the lens to capture how institutional structures, psychosocial mediators, and student attributes converge at a single point of contact that continuously evolves. The model underscores self-efficacy, emotions, belonging, and well-being as key mediators of engagement that can be substantially shaped by AI. Self-efficacy often rises when learners receive immediate, customised feedback, especially if it clarifies the path to improvement. Yet self-efficacy can also falter if repeated interactions with AI leave students feeling that they lack the aptitude to meet algorithmic standards. Emotions, from excitement and curiosity to anxiety or frustration, play a crucial role in whether a learner perseveres.

AI-based grading that lacks transparency can foster fear and distrust, while a platform that provides timely and respectful responses can spark curiosity and positive affect. Belonging is facilitated when AI helps students find peers or mentors who share similar interests or educational goals but belonging declines if technological barriers or biases in algorithmic matching lead to exclusion. Well-being may be enhanced by AI systems that identify struggling students early and direct them to support services, but it can suffer if constant data collection feels intrusive or fosters anxiety.

This ecological framework (Kahu & Nelson, 2018) highlights how institutional contexts shape engagement. AI's structural role becomes clear here: data-driven systems can either expand or constrain how learners perceive autonomy, community belonging, and well-being.

Revisiting student engagement theories in the age of generative AI reveals both the durability of long-standing motivational and cognitive insights and the necessity of conceptual renovation. Expectancy, value, psychological need fulfilment, participatory belonging, cognitive depth, and ecological alignment remain central constructs, yet each must be re-specified to reflect algorithmic mediation. The EWAI framework, proposed in this chapter, draws on this theoretical synthesis to propose design principles that elevate responsiveness, reciprocity, and equity as core criteria for AI-enhanced pedagogy. Only by weaving these criteria into curricula, interfaces, and institutional policy can educators realise the transformative promise of GenAI while safeguarding the human dimensions of learning that make engagement meaningful.

A PROPOSED MODEL: ENGAGEMENT WITH AI (EWAI)

The Engagement with AI (EWAI) model addresses the limitations of existing frameworks by positioning artificial intelligence (AI) as a co-regulatory participant in education, fundamentally altering the traditional roles attributed to technological tools. Unlike previous models such as the Technology Acceptance Model (TAM; Davis, 1989), which primarily assesses technology's usefulness and usability as external enhancements, EWAI recognises AI's unique capability to adapt instructional tasks dynamically, interpret student data, and deliver real-time, context-specific feedback. Similarly, while the SAMR model (Puentedura, 2013) and PIC-RAT model (Kimmons & Hall, 2018) conceptualise technology along a continuum from augmentation to redefinition, they still treat technology as supplementary rather than intrinsically interactive and responsive.

EWAI emphasises the critical interdependence between individual learner characteristics, such as motivation, AI literacy, and ethical awareness, and broader institutional elements, including policy frameworks, equitable access, and educator preparedness. This integration should ensure that AI engagement occurs within pedagogically robust and ethically sound environments, without which even highly capable learners may struggle to benefit meaningfully from AI-driven tools.

As both a diagnostic and prescriptive tool, EWAI systematically identifies strengths and limitations within AI-enhanced learning contexts, guiding educational stakeholders in designing interventions that optimise AI's potential while safeguarding against ethical and practical challenges. By articulating how AI shapes cognitive, behavioural, emotional, ethical, and policy dimensions, EWAI provides actionable insights for cultivating interactive and responsible learning experiences, marking a significant advancement in understanding and harnessing AI's transformative potential at both micro (individual) and macro (institutional) educational levels (see figure 1).

Figure 1. A conceptual model of Engagement with AI

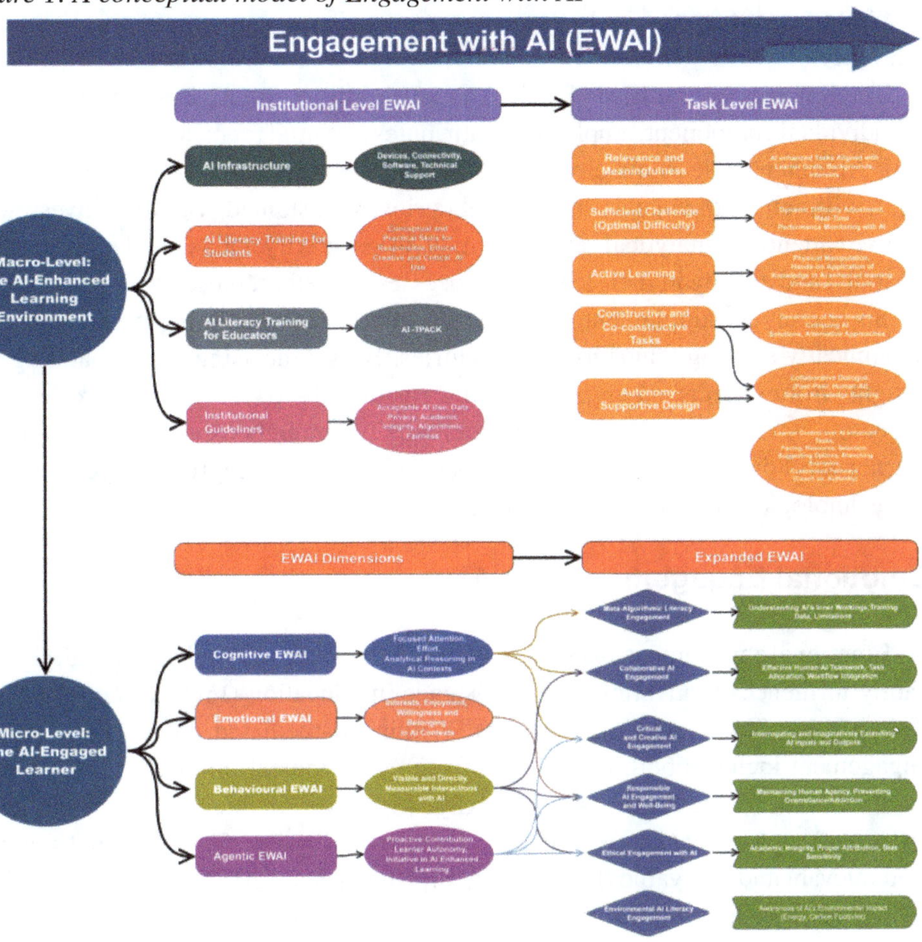

Micro-Level: The AI-Engaged Learner

Contemporary educational scholarship emphasises that effective integration of advanced technologies, including AI, relies substantially on learners possessing distinct attributes and dispositions (Al-Nuaimi & Al-Emran, 2021; Börekci & Çelik, 2024; Granić & Marangunić, 2019; Fathali & Okada, 2018; Salloum et al., 2019). This insight is particularly critical given the rapid advancement of AI-driven educational environments, where personalised learning materials, adaptive instructional platforms, automated feedback systems, and other intelligent tools capable of producing human-like dialogue and content significantly influence learning experiences (Zawacki-Richter et al., 2019). As discussed earlier in engagement theories, the efficacy of technology-mediated learning is deeply intertwined with learners' psychological attributes, including motivation, self-regulation, and perceived task relevance.

The Engagement with AI (EWAI) model highlights the AI-Engaged Learner as an individual component, emphasising attributes essential for meaningful interaction with AI-enhanced learning environments. Such learners demonstrate traits including a willingness to engage, intellectual curiosity, sustained cognitive investment, focused attention, analytical reasoning, ethical sensitivity, balanced dependence on AI tools, and agency in their learning processes. Together, these attributes position AI not merely as supplementary resources but as active collaborators capable of dynamically shaping educational trajectories. By synthesising and expanding the insights from established engagement dimensions, the EWAI framework provides educators, researchers, and policymakers with a comprehensive understanding of learner-level dynamics, facilitating deeper and more meaningful engagement with AI technologies in educational contexts.

Emotional Engagement with AI

Emotional engagement, encompassing feelings, interests, and belonging, significantly influences motivation and persistence in education (Fredricks et al., 2004; Kahu, 2013; Skinner & Pitzer, 2012). Within AI-mediated contexts, emotional engagement includes both enthusiasm from technological innovation and anxiety or alienation arising from its complexity. Effective AI integration can enhance emotional engagement by creating immersive, visually appealing tasks that students find relevant and enjoyable (Liu et al., 2024; Huang et al., 2023). According to EVT (Eccles & Wigfield, 2002), learners are more inclined to persist when AI-driven tasks are perceived as valuable and pleasurable. Additionally, AI can facilitate social connectedness through collaborative platforms and peer interaction systems, aligning with the relatedness aspect of SDT (Deci & Ryan, 1985).

Recent research show that well-designed AI can bolster students' learning and motivation. In a randomized study with Harvard undergraduates, an AI tutor more than doubled learning gains compared with an active-learning class and elicited higher reported engagement and motivation (Kestin et al., 2025). Cross-national survey evidence likewise indicates generally positive student attitudes toward AI, with links to intrinsic motivation, autonomy, and perceived learning benefits, though students also note ethical concerns that warrant careful implementation (Mohamed et al., 2025).

Cognitive engagement with AI

Cognitive engagement remains a cornerstone of meaningful learning in AI-mediated environments, as it governs how learners attend to, interpret, and act upon educational content. Rather than functioning as passive recipients of AI-generated information, cognitively engaged students marshal attention, sustained effort, and analytical reasoning to ensure that AI tools serve as amplifiers rather than substitutes for intellectual labour.

Attention, often defined as the strategic allocation of mental resources, supports goal-oriented learning and resists digital distractions—a function deeply intertwined with self-regulation (Pintrich & De Groot, 1990; Schunk & DiBenedetto, 2020). Effort entails the persistence and intensity of learners' engagement, mediated by motivational beliefs and regulatory strategies (Zimmerman, 2001; Bembenutty, 2011). Analytical thinking, encompassing evaluation, synthesis, and judgment, aligns with the upper tiers of Bloom's taxonomy and reinforces students' capacity to interrogate and refine AI-generated content (Bloom, 1956; Sinatra et al., 2015).

Generative AI can reinforce or erode these cognitive dimensions depending on its integration. The ICAP framework (Chi & Wylie, 2014) categorises engagement as passive, active, constructive, or interactive, emphasising that deeper cognitive gains occur when students generate or co-construct knowledge. Within this hierarchy, AI functions most effectively when students use it as a stimulus for constructive elaboration or dialogic exchange, rather than as a shortcut. Studies suggest that when used judiciously, AI can bolster creativity, self-efficacy, and originality (Toma & Yánez-Pérez, 2024; Urban et al., 2024). However, overreliance on AI risks undermining these benefits. Research shows that habitual outsourcing of academic tasks to AI tools like ChatGPT can lead to decreased memory retention, procrastination, and lower academic performance (Abbas et al., 2024; Niloy et al., 2023; Yang et al., 2025).

Furthermore, AI's potential to personalise feedback and streamline cognitive load hinges on learners' capacity to filter relevant insights while resisting cognitive fragmentation. Without such attentional discernment, adaptive feedback systems may overwhelm rather than guide. Moreover, bias embedded in AI systems may distort reasoning, perpetuate stereotypes (Glickman & Sharot, 2024), and reduce trust in educational technologies. Thus, learners are encouraged to not only engage analytically with AI outputs but also develop metacognitive vigilance to critique algorithmic authority. Ultimately, cognitive engagement in AI-rich contexts demands that learners remain intellectually active, ethically alert, and critically attuned, ensuring that the promise of AI translates into durable understanding rather than superficial convenience.

Behavioural Engagement with AI

Behavioural engagement, a foundational element of student involvement, encompasses the visible actions, effort, and participation patterns learners demonstrate during academic tasks (Fredricks et al., 2004; Appleton et al., 2008; Kahu, 2013). In AI-enhanced learning environments, this dimension extends beyond basic task compliance to include how actively students explore, respond to, and refine AI-generated content. Because AI platforms can record every interaction, such as the number of prompts issued, responses received, time spent on AI-guided exercises, and completion of AI-recommended tasks, educators can see precisely how students interact with and progress through AI-mediated activities. This visibility includes not only quantitative analytics (interaction counts, response times, task completion rates) but also the frequency and quality of exchanges with AI interfaces, collaborative use of AI-mediated communication tools, and students' sustained engagement in iterative, AI-augmented learning cycles. Thus, behavioural engagement with AI can be directly measured through analytics, creating a data-rich portrait of student activity.

The capacity to measure engagement through analytics offers significant benefits. By identifying patterns of low interaction early, educators can tailor interventions to struggling learners, adjusting support in real time. Continuous refinement of AI recommendations based on live engagement data helps match tasks to individual needs more precisely, boosting relevance and motivation. Institutions can also correlate these engagement metrics with learning outcomes, enabling evidence-based instructional design and informed decisions about which AI tools most effectively promote learning. However, this promise comes with challenges: the sheer volume of data may overwhelm instructors who lack strategies for interpretation, and a heavy emphasis on quantitative metrics risks obscuring deeper indicators of learning, such as reflection or critical thinking. Privacy concerns also surface when every click and response is tracked; students may feel uneasy, knowing their every move is monitored, which can fuel a performative mindset rather than genuine investment. Moreover, algorithmic biases in data collection or analysis could misrepresent engagement for certain groups, reinforcing inequities if not carefully managed.

In AI-enhanced learning environments, immersive simulations and game-like modules—augmented with badges, leaderboards, and live analytics—could increase behavioral engagement, deepen task commitment, and strengthen students' willingness to continue participating. Adaptive platforms that personalize instruction and deliver real-time feedback and task-focused nudges may help sustain focus by monitoring progress and recommending next steps, such systems might promote motivation and could contribute to higher course completion over time. Likewise, timely AI-generated prompts and reminders have the potential to reduce procrastination and support task persistence.

Beyond individual support, AI-facilitated collaboration is another significant contributor to behavioural engagement (Ouyang et al., 2023). Intelligent systems can match students with complementary skills, moderate group dynamics, and even anticipate when intervention is needed to support team effectiveness. Conversational AI agents like CollaBot foster richer peer discussion by prompting reflection and conceptual clarification (Hu et al., 2025), while hybrid human–AI feedback loops maintain instructional depth alongside automated responsiveness (Jiang, 2025). These tools create a learning ecosystem where peer interaction and instructor guidance coexist with automated scaffolding, thereby reinforcing sustained participation.

Despite these advantages, certain implementation risks may erode authentic behavioural engagement. Poorly designed AI systems can foster off-task behaviours, as students click through interfaces or respond to frequent alerts without meaningful interaction. Overexposure to automated nudges may fragment attention and dilute academic purpose. Some students may even attempt to "game the system" by fulfilling visible engagement metrics—such as login frequency or time spent—without actual learning investment. When learners perceive they are under constant surveillance, they may conform to superficial requirements without internalising content, reducing engagement to a hollow performance (). These effects are intensified in settings where students face technological friction, limited access, or algorithmic biases that undermine trust and fairness (Bognár & Khine, 2025; Essien et al., 2024; Xu, 2025). If unaddressed, such dynamics risk transforming behavioural engagement into a mere record of clicks rather than a reflection of purposeful learning.

To counter these challenges, educators must design AI-mediated tasks that align behavioural activity with deeper cognitive and ethical goals. Drawing on the ICAP framework (Chi & Wylie, 2014), tasks should prompt learners to construct knowledge actively, revising AI outputs, posing critical questions, or engaging in collaborative problem-solving. Evaluating behavioural engagement should move beyond frequency counts toward indicators of thoughtful iteration—such as meaningful chatbot queries or substantive revisions following AI feedback. Institutional clarity on ethical use is also crucial. Explicit policies that differentiate acceptable and unacceptable AI use, particularly in writing, problem-solving, or group work, help students avoid overdependence and develop responsible habits (Bozkurt et al., 2024). Instructor transparency reinforces this ethos; when educators model critical engagement with AI tools and acknowledge their limitations, students learn to approach AI with discernment (Lo et al., 2024).

Behavioural engagement in AI-enhanced education is not simply a record of digital activity but a reflection of students' purposeful interactions with content, tools, and peers. When guided by thoughtful design and ethical awareness, AI can transform student behaviour from passive clicks to dynamic participation. As part of the broader EWAI Model, behavioural engagement functions as a gateway to deeper motivation, inquiry, and shared responsibility in learning. Its success, however, hinges on aligning technological affordances with pedagogical intention and institutional integrity.

Expanded New Dimensions of Student Engagement in the Age of AI

The rapid diffusion of GenAI necessitates a clear distinction between students who merely use algorithms and those who genuinely engage with them as co-inquirers. Building upon Chi and Wylie's (2014) ICAP framework, which differentiates passive, active, constructive, and interactive learning modes, the AI-engaged learner is conceptualised as an individual who consistently operates within the constructive-interactive spectrum. This learner approaches machine outputs not as definitive answers, but rather as prompts for deeper explanation, elaboration, and dialogue. For instance, such a learner might solicit multiple counterarguments from a language model, subsequently synthesising and critiquing them to ascertain which warrant further investigation, thereby transforming simple retrieval into a comprehensive process of inquiry.

Behaviourally, AI-engaged learners manifest discernible and sustained effort through iterative prompt refinement, diligent draft revision, and the triangulation of algorithmic recommendations with diverse external sources, eschewing uncritical acceptance of initial responses. Cognitively, they strategically use both analytic and generative processes, such as summarisation, elaboration, and modelling, to convert algorithmic suggestions into a robust personal understanding. Emotionally, a dynamic interplay between curiosity and calibrated scepticism characterises their engagement; the surprise of an unexpected output can invigorate exploration, while an acute awareness of potential errors mitigates overconfidence. Agentic ally, these learners exercise volitional control by discerning when to override, disregard, or refine AI recommendations, thus preserving their autonomy even within highly scaffolded systems. Collectively, these dimensions forge a dynamic profile wherein AI assistance serves to amplify, rather than supplant, human initiative.

Although these established dimensions effectively characterise the nature of learner interaction, the unique properties and societal implications of AI necessitate the consideration of additional, distinct facets of engagement. These new dimensions extend beyond the immediate cognitive and behavioural aspects of interaction to encompass a deeper understanding of AI systems themselves and the ethical responsibilities inherent in their use. This expanded perspective includes Meta-Algorithmic Literacy Engagement, Critical–Ethical AI Engagement, Environmental AI Literacy Engagement, Responsible AI Use and Well-being Engagement, Creative-Exploratory AI Engagement, and Collaborative AI Engagement.

Meta-Algorithmic Literacy Engagement

Meta-Algorithmic Literacy Engagement pertains to the learner's foundational understanding of the inner workings and limitations of AI models. The UNESCO AI Competency Framework for Students (AI CFS) (2024) emphasises that students need to understand how AI models scrape and process data, how they are trained, and how they function, along with the concrete types of algorithms that underlie these processes. This foundational knowledge is crucial for developing critical thinking and making conscious decisions about AI use (UNESCO, 2024). This competence involves comprehending the technical principles underpinning AI, such as how large language models are trained on vast datasets, the statistical nature of their predictions, and the mechanisms by which problems such as "hallucinations" or erroneous outputs can arise. It encompasses an awareness of the provenance of training data, the potential for embedded biases within these datasets, and the probabilistic nature of text generation. A meta-algorithmically literate learner recognises that AI outputs are not expressions of true understanding but rather statistical correlations derived from patterns in data. This understanding allows them to critically assess the reliability and validity of AI-generated content. For instance, such a learner would recognise that a chatbot's confident medical advice, lacking explicit citations or known training on peer-reviewed clinical guidelines, warrants scepticism and necessitates cross-verification against authoritative sources. This literacy transforms AI from an inscrutable "black box" into an examinable output, empowering the learner to navigate algorithmic systems with informed discernment.

Critical and Creative AI Engagement

Critical and creative engagement with AI entails a learner's capacity to interrogate, reinterpret, and imaginatively extend the outputs and operations of artificial intelligence systems. Unlike passive or unreflective use, this form of engagement positions students as active participants in knowledge construction, requiring both analytical scrutiny and generative thinking. From a critical standpoint, learners are encouraged to question the assumptions, limitations, and potential biases embedded within algorithmic processes. This involves not only evaluating the accuracy or relevance of AI-generated content but also reflecting on how such content aligns—or conflicts—with disciplinary standards, epistemological frameworks, and broader sociocultural narratives.

Creative-Exploratory AI Engagement involves the learner's willingness and ability to utilise AI as a tool for generating novel ideas, exploring unconventional solutions, and pushing creative boundaries in fields such as art, design, or writing. This goes beyond simply using AI for basic generation, moving towards using it as a provocative partner in creative endeavours. The UNESCO AI CFS supports this by encouraging students to exploit their creativity to optimise existing AI models or co-create more meaningful AI (UNESCO, 2024).

Crucially, critical and creative engagement are not mutually exclusive but mutually reinforcing. By adopting a dual stance—both interrogative and inventive—learners not only challenge the validity and implications of algorithmic outputs but also reimagine their educational potential. This integrated approach aligns with constructivist pedagogies and theories of learner agency, wherein students are co-creators of meaning rather than recipients of predefined knowledge. In the context of generative AI, such engagement fosters deeper cognitive investment and cultivates the dispositions necessary to navigate, shape, and critique emerging sociotechnical systems.

The UNESCO AI CFS further highlights the importance of a human-centred mindset and ethical considerations. Students are expected to become conscious and knowledgeable of AI's advantages and limitations, detecting the trustworthiness and proportionality of AI tools from an ethical perspective. This includes examining AI's impact on human agency, social inclusion, equity, security, and cultural and linguistic diversity. The framework underscores that AI should serve human development, protect human dignity and agency, and promote justice and sustainability, guided by human rights principles (UNESCO, 2024).

Ethical Engagement with AI

Equally vital is ethical engagement and academic integrity. Lo et al. (2024) also find that some students not only develop a reliance on AI but occasionally misuse such tools unethically. The speed and seeming comprehensiveness of AI-generated content may obscure the need for genuine analysis, careful reading, and the human element of inquiry. The fragility of AI's authority in the eyes of some learners complicates reliance on automated assessments, potentially eroding confidence in both instructors and institutional policies if the system is perceived as arbitrary or opaque. Moreover, negative cognitive effects can arise if learners bypass metacognitive processes and simply accept AI outputs uncritically.

Engaging with AI in academic contexts often involves navigating potential pitfalls such as plagiarism, data privacy breaches, misinformation, or algorithmic unfairness (Bozkurt et al., 2024). A truly AI-engaged learner does not turn a blind eye to these issues; rather, they apply academic integrity principles—proper citations, transparent attributions, and honest representation of their own work—and remain sensitive to the possible biases inherent in AI-driven technologies.

Ethical awareness extends to an understanding of the broader societal implications of AI usage, including its potential to reinforce or challenge existing inequities.

By foregrounding ethics, learners become informed stakeholders who critique and shape AI technology instead of passively submitting to it.

Responsible AI Engagement

This dimension encompasses the learner's ability to use AI tools responsibly, understanding their personal implications and promoting individual well-being. It involves recognising the potential for over-reliance or addiction to AI systems and developing strategies to maintain human agency and accountability in high-stakes decision-making (UNESCO, 2024). This engagement also includes an awareness of privacy concerns related to AI, the ethical handling of personal data by AI systems, and the psychological impact of interacting with AI. Learners are encouraged to critically assess how AI integrates into their daily lives, ensuring that it augments rather than detracts from their cognitive, social, and emotional well-being.

Collaborative AI Engagement

Collaborative AI Engagement describes the learner's capacity to work effectively with AI systems as a team member, understanding how to assign tasks, integrate AI-generated components into larger projects, and manage the workflow of human-AI collaboration. This dimension acknowledges that future professional landscapes will increasingly involve seamless integration of human and AI, requiring learners to develop skills in co-creation and distributed intelligence. The UNESCO AI CFS also envisions students as active co-creators of AI, capable of designing and applying AI tools to address real-world challenges and promote sustainable development (UNESCO, 2024).

Environmental AI Literacy Engagement

This dimension focuses on the learner's understanding of the environmental impact of AI systems and their responsibility in promoting sustainable AI practices. A student demonstrating this engagement recognises that the development, training, and updating of AI models can have significant energy consumption and carbon footprint (UNESCO, 2024). This includes an awareness of the resources required for large-scale data centres, the energy-intensive process of training large language models, and the overall environmental consequences of AI infrastructure. Learners engaging with this dimension actively explore and advocate for climate-friendly approaches to AI design, training, and use, contributing to more sustainable technological development (UNESCO, 2024).

Macro-Level: The AI-Enhanced Learning Environment

The second key dimension in the EWAI Model focuses on the nature of the AI-Enhanced Learning Environment, which involves the AI-supportive learning tasks and context. In addition to the individual attributes responsible for engagement with AI, the EWAI Model foregrounds the critical role of institutional and macro-level policies in shaping the conditions under which meaningful engagement with AI can occur. Without alignment at the systemic level—across infrastructure, ethics, professional development, and policy—efforts at the classroom level may remain fragmented or unsustainable.

The learning environment has profound implications for how students interact with technology, content, peers, and teachers. This is also true in AI-mediated contexts, where learning events can be personalised at scale, adaptive feedback can offer real-time guidance, and interactive simulations or generative models can invite deeper cognitive processing. Drawing on the synergy between established frameworks—Expectancy-Value Theory (Eccles & Wigfield, 2002), Self-Determination Theory (Ryan & Deci, 2017), and the ICAP model (Chi & Wylie, 2014)—we can conceptualise five features of an effective AI-enhanced learning event: relevance and meaningfulness, optimal challenge, active engagement, constructive and co-constructive tasks, and autonomy-supportive structures.

The significance of contextual support is widely recognised across multiple research strands, including the Educational Interface Model (Kahu & Nelson, 2018), social-ecological theories of learning, and the concept of organisational readiness for technology. These frameworks converge on the understanding that while motivated learners and engaging tasks may form the nucleus of an effective learning experience, they require a conducive environment that offers adequate infrastructure, ethical guidelines, professional development, and broad-based policy alignment.

AI Infrastructure

A fundamental requirement for an AI-supportive context lies in AI Infrastructure, encompassing dependable devices, stable connectivity, user-friendly software, and ongoing technical support. Large-scale inequities in digital access persist, not only across different regions globally but also within countries where resource disparities exist between urban and rural schools, or between affluent and underfunded districts. Inadequate infrastructure leads to disruptions in continuity, leaving students unable to complete AI-driven tasks in a timely or consistent manner. Even more problematic, if only certain subsets of learners gain reliable access to AI tools and broadband connections, the benefits of personalised learning and immediate feedback remain unevenly distributed, reinforcing or exacerbating achievement gaps.

For this reason, calls for equitable funding and policy measures that address the "digital divide" remain paramount (Bozkurt et al., 2024). Without a baseline of robust technological infrastructure, even the most innovative AI-mediated curriculum designs risk limited impact.

AI Literacy Training for Learners

Technical infrastructure alone is not enough. Students also need structured AI literacy aligned with UNESCO's student framework (UNESCO, 2024). That framework treats learners as responsible users and co-creators and urges embedding AI objectives in curricula so students can engage with AI safely and meaningfully. It organizes competencies into four areas—human-centred mindset, ethics, AI techniques & applications, and AI system design—developed across the levels Understand, Apply, and Create. Teaching should cultivate critical judgment about AI outputs and a sense of civic responsibility in an AI era, rather than passive reliance. Pedagogy and assessment should connect values with technical knowledge through inquiry and project-based work, reinforcing human agency, inclusivity, and sustainable practice.

Continuing Professional Development for Educators

Parallel to training learners, institutions must offer continuing professional development for educators aimed at cultivating proficient AI integration in their teaching practice. Evidence from a regional survey shows that teachers' willingness to use generative AI is driven by perceived usefulness, ease of use and behavioural control—factors that targeted professional-development programmes must address (Lu et al., 2024).

The role of educators evolves in an AI-supported classroom. Instructors often become facilitators or "learning experience designers," guiding students in tasks where AI performs certain automated functions, such as immediate grading, scaffolded hints, or generating open-ended prompts. To execute these roles effectively, teachers require not only technical know-how, such as how to configure AI dashboards or interpret analytics, but also pedagogical understanding of how AI aligns with relevant learning theories. If left without comprehensive professional development, educators might use AI in ways that undermine student agency (e.g., rigidly instructing them to follow AI directives without reflection) or inadvertently compromise equity (e.g., designing tasks only accessible to higher-level students).

Such outcomes would be inconsistent with the EWAI Model's emphasis on constructive co-creation and autonomy. By contrast, well-designed professional development sessions illustrate how AI can foster deeper engagement through carefully structured assignments and scaffolded interactions. Teacher training also offers opportunities to discuss best practices for mitigating AI's known risks, such as algorithmic bias or privacy concerns.

Contextual Ethical Guidelines

Finally, contextual ethical guidelines serve as the structural and cultural framework within which AI usage unfolds in the institution. These guidelines often address issues such as the acceptable scope of AI involvement in academic work, student data privacy policies, and the lines between legitimate assistance and academic dishonesty (Bozkurt et al., 2024). They also articulate normative standards for algorithmic transparency, fairness, and the responsible handling of sensitive data. When institutions publicly commit to fairness, equity, and accountability in AI adoption, learners and educators gain greater confidence in the platforms they use. By contrast, opaque or poorly enforced guidelines can erode trust and produce ethical "gray zones," wherein students are uncertain about whether the AI-based assistance they receive or produce violates academic integrity.

The impetus for robust ethical frameworks often stems from policymakers and national accreditation bodies, highlighting the reality that truly AI-supportive contexts may require synergy at local, regional, and even global levels. Without multilevel endorsement of ethical standards, localised efforts by individual teachers or schools risk fragmentation or non-compliance, leading to inconsistent experiences and potential inequities.

The significance of the AI-supportive learning context is further magnified by the potential for certain technologies to inadvertently generate passive or minimal engagement. When institutional support is lacking or policy frameworks are absent, learners and educators may resort to the superficial usage of AI. For instance, students might rely on generative tools solely to complete assignments without deeper reflection or constructive adaptation. Such minimal engagement aligns with the "passive" level of the ICAP framework (Chi & Wylie, 2014), characterised by limited cognitive processing and ephemeral learning gains. By contrast, when robust infrastructure, literacy training, professional development, and ethical guidelines converge, learners can move into more advanced modes of engagement: active manipulation, constructive critique, and co-constructive knowledge-building (Chi & Wylie, 2014). In effect, the learning context acts as the scaffolding that supports the synergy between the micro and macro level engagement; the AI-engaged learner and the AI-enhanced learning event.

Moreover, the policy dimension of an AI-supportive context extends to bridging the digital divide at the national and international levels (Bozkurt et al., 2024). If AI-based learning is to serve as a transformative force in education, policymakers must address structural inequities in funding, teacher training, and technology distribution. They must do so in ways that foster equitable access to AI tools rather than concentrating resources in affluent areas or elite institutions. Without thoughtful policy interventions, the risk emerges that only certain segments of the population benefit from advanced AI-driven instruction, reproducing or exacerbating social stratification. The broader the institutional buy-in, the less reliant the system is on individual teachers' efforts to fund or implement AI-based tools in under-resourced environments. Instead, a collective and well-regulated approach to AI fosters an environment where the pursuit of deeper engagement is feasible for all learners, not merely those with socioeconomic advantages.

AI Enhanced Learning Tasks

Foremost among these features is the requirement that tasks be relevant and meaningful to the learner (Eccles & Wigfield, 2002). AI should only be employed when it meaningfully advances learning objectives, not merely as a novelty. Learning events such as tasks and assignments must resonate with learners' personal, academic, or professional aspirations (Deci & Ryan, 2000). Rather, any AI-driven activity must be carefully grounded in clear pedagogical goals and a deep understanding of learner needs. In practice, this means that before deploying an AI tool—whether it's for analysing data sets, generating targeted feedback on essays, or simulating real-world phenomena—instructors must first ask: "What problem am I solving, and how will this technology directly support students' growth?" If the rationale for introducing AI boils down to novelty, hype, or superficial engagement, its motivational and educational benefits will be minimal at best and counterproductive at worst. When students perceive a clear link between the AI-driven activity and their future goals or immediate interests—such as building marketable data literacy skills or refining argumentative writing in preparation for college—they invest far more cognitive and emotional resources.

When students perceive a clear link between the AI-driven activity, such as analysing data sets, generating targeted feedback on essays, or simulating real-world phenomena, and their future goals or immediate interests, their motivation to invest cognitive and emotional resources intensifies. Relevance is central to EVT, which posits that if learners see value in a given task, they are more likely to persist, engage deeply, and develop a positive attitude toward the learning process (Eccles, 1983; Wigfield & Eccles, 2000). AI tools can enhance perceived relevance by customizing content to match a student's background, culture, context, and skill level and offering real-world cases that illustrate practical applications. However, if the AI learning event appears disconnected from learners' lived experiences or if it does not reflect cultural responsiveness, the motivational benefits might dissipate quickly.

A second characteristic is the necessity for the sufficient challenge, aligning with the concept of optimal difficulty in Vygotskian (Vygotsky, & Cole, 1978), Flow (Csikszentmihalyi, 1990), Self-efficacy (Bandura) and Self-determination (Deci & Ryan, 1985; Ryan & Deci, 2017) theories. Vygotsky's theory, particularly his concept of the Zone of Proximal Development (ZPD), emphasises the importance of providing learners with tasks that are just beyond their current capabilities but still within reach with guidance. In this context, AI can play a crucial role in identifying and delivering content that aligns with each student's ZPD, ensuring they remain engaged without feeling overwhelmed. Similarly, Csikszentmihalyi's Flow theory underscores the significance of maintaining a balance between challenge and skill level, where learners are fully immersed in an activity that is neither too easy nor too difficult. If AI can dynamically adjust difficulty levels, it can help students achieve this state of flow, fostering sustained concentration and motivation.

Bandura's Self-Efficacy theory highlights how learners' beliefs in their ability to succeed influence their engagement and persistence. When AI-driven tasks are appropriately challenging, they can strengthen self-efficacy by providing students with a sense of accomplishment as they progress. However, if tasks are miscalibrated—either too easy, leading to boredom, or too difficult, causing discouragement—learners may develop a diminished sense of self-efficacy, reducing their willingness to engage with future challenges. Deci and Ryan's Self-Determination theory further reinforces the need for optimal challenge by emphasising the role of autonomy, competence, and relatedness in motivation. When AI-driven systems adapt tasks in a way that fosters a sense of competence, allowing students to experience gradual progress, they support intrinsic motivation and deeper learning.

Given these theoretical perspectives, one key characteristic of effective engagement with AI-enhanced learning is the necessity for sufficient challenge. If tasks are too easy, students may engage in surface-level participation or passive behaviours; if they are too difficult, frustration and disengagement may result. AI emerges as a powerful tool for calibrating challenges because its adaptive algorithms can monitor learner performance in real-time and adjust content accordingly. Ideally, an AI system continuously fine-tunes each task to push a learner just beyond their current mastery level, placing them within their zone of proximal development and prompting deeper cognitive engagement. However, the success of such adaptive learning processes hinges on the quality of the underlying data and the effectiveness of the algorithms. If the data are biased or incomplete, the AI may misalign difficulty levels and target learning outcomes, leaving students with tasks that do not match their actual skills. Therefore, ensuring an appropriate level of challenge requires continuous oversight and teacher involvement to prevent automated mismatches and avoid unnecessary frustration.

The third key element is active mode, which underscores the transition from passive reception of information to hands-on, physical manipulation or application of knowledge (Chi & Wylie, 2014). Moving beyond passivity is crucial, as the prior decades of educational technology research indicate that superficial forms of "interaction" with digital platforms do not inherently guarantee learning gains. Indeed, behaviourally pressing buttons or passively reading AI-generated text can remain cognitively shallow unless the learner internally processes, critiques, and reformulates content. Moreover, if learners remain physically inactive for extended periods—merely seated at a computer for minutes or hours on end—the transition from active to more advanced constructive and co-constructive engagement becomes more difficult, as prolonged bodily inactivity can negatively influence cognition and overall well-being. Hence, designing learning events that integrate physical movement or tasks away from screens is essential, ensuring that while technology or AI scaffolds intellectual engagement, it does not confine learners to sedentary, screen-bound experiences that undermine their health and limit deeper cognitive processing.

While active engagement focuses on physical manipulation, constructive and co-constructive tasks push the depth of learning even further. Constructive tasks prompt the generation of new insights, connections, or knowledge artifacts. For example, a constructive approach might require a student to reflect on the reasoning steps of an AI-driven solution to a math problem and then articulate an alternative approach or critique the solution's assumptions. Such an activity aligns with the "constructive" level in ICAP theory, where learners produce new inferences rather than merely reproducing existing information (Chi & Wylie, 2014).

Co-constructive tasks extend this logic into collaborative spaces, whether involving peer-to-peer dialogue or human-AI interaction that fosters reciprocal learning. For instance, an AI-driven platform might serve as a conversational partner, challenging a student's reasoning with counterexamples. Alternatively, it might support group brainstorming by generating ideas that learners refine collectively. The hallmark of co-construction is shared ownership of the learning process, evidenced by iterative dialogue, debate, and negotiation. From the perspective of the Participation Identification Model (Finn & Zimmer, 2012), such collaborative tasks not only strengthen cognitive engagement but also galvanise social identification with an academic community, especially when AI fosters supportive interactions rather than supplanting them.

Finally, autonomy-supportive design principles ensure that learners retain meaningful agency and choice (Ryan & Deci, 2017; Reeve, 2013). Within SDT, autonomy is fundamental to sustained, self-determined motivation, reflecting learners' sense of volition in selecting tasks, resources, or learning pathways. AI can be used to augment autonomy by offering branching scenarios, recommending multiple potential tasks, or allowing learners to set their own pacing. Yet it can also undermine autonomy if the AI platform rigidly prescribes a single path forward. Instead of positioning AI as a strict authority, effective instructional design positions it as a coach or a facilitator that offers suggestions, resources, or clarifications while preserving learner control. When students perceive AI interactions as controlling or intrusive, they are likely to resist and reduce engagement. Conversely, well-implemented AI can strengthen autonomy by freeing learners from mundane tasks, enabling them to explore more creative or higher-order problem-solving processes.

These five attributes—relevance, sufficient challenge, active engagement, constructive and co-constructive tasks, and autonomy support—constitute the essence of AI-Enhanced Learning Events. By weaving these attributes into lesson plans, instructional designs, and assessment methods, educators create a fertile ground on which the previously discussed learner dispositions can thrive. When students who possess high levels of focus, curiosity, agency, and ethical awareness encounter tasks that stimulate authentic inquiry, challenge their intellect, and respect their autonomy, their engagement in AI-mediated learning is likely to deepen. However, even the best-designed tasks may falter or yield inequitable outcomes if the wider institutional framework fails to provide adequate support, consistent policies, or equitable access. Therefore, institutional support and learning environments are crucial for real engagement with AI to enhance learning and achievement.

Potential Drawbacks, Challenges and Solutions for EWAI

AI has the potential to reshape education by tailoring content, pacing, and feedback to individual learners, yet the very algorithms that heighten efficiency can also invite overreliance, threaten equity, and cloud lines of responsibility. As Van Haastrecht et al. (2024) note, the use of AI in technology-enhanced learning often proceeds without holistic validation frameworks, raising questions about the epistemological foundations and trustworthiness of these systems. Adaptive engines do not simply scaffold instruction; they reorder the social contract of the classroom by assigning a portion of judgment once held by teachers to opaque computational logics. As a result, educators must weigh the gains in personalisation against the possibility that students come to outsource reflection, perseverance, or even curiosity to an unseen system.

In collaborative settings, the challenge multiplies because AI no longer mediates only between student and curriculum but also among peers. Early evidence suggests that conversational agents can lift cognitive engagement during group work, yet emotional engagement and collective performance do not necessarily follow the same trajectory (Hu et al., 2025). If brainstorming, critique, or synthesis is largely delegated to a chatbot, students may perform tasks with notable fluency while eroding the interpersonal glue—humour, empathy, or shared struggle—that sustains genuine teamwork. This observation resonates with the argument that useful systems must attend to relational as well as task-oriented communication; otherwise, the social bonds underpinning collaboration atrophy even as surface indicators of productivity improve (Sikström et al., 2024). Educators who assume that efficiency naturally nurtures cohesion may therefore misread quiet disengagement as smooth cooperation.

Calls for greater accountability underscore the need to treat AI as a co-regulator of learning rather than a neutral conduit (Dawson et al., 2023). Yet many empirical studies rely on self-built dashboards or minimally validated surveys, making it hard to distinguish novelty effects from durable impact (Van Haastrecht et al., 2024). Without rigorous instrumentation, optimistic findings risk overselling what algorithms deliver and underspecifying the professional judgment teachers still must exercise. A robust evidence base should couple quantitative log data with qualitative measures that capture shifts in learner agency, power dynamics, and trust, dimensions easily eclipsed when engagement is reduced to clicks or time-on-task.

Academic integrity presents another axis of concern. Generative models can extend access to formative feedback and creative inspiration, but they also lower the threshold for producing ostensibly original work with minimal intellectual investment (Bozkurt et al., 2024). When detection tools lag behind generation tools, instructors may be forced into a reactive posture, scrutinising prose for telltale patterns rather than designing assignments that harness AI openly. The dilemma is compounded by nine unresolved "grey areas" in GenAI adoption that range from unclear decision authority to questions about data ownership, curriculum design, and the evolving purpose of education itself (Xiao et al., 2025). Institutions that fail to clarify these boundaries leave students navigating an ambiguous moral terrain where the difference between legitimate augmentation and misconduct is negotiated case by case.

Bias and privacy form a parallel set of risks. AI systems trained on historically skewed corpora can reencode cultural assumptions as default judgments, thereby undermining students' sense of belonging and subtly steering them toward homogenised definitions of success. The metaphor of AI as "policy frozen in silicon" reflects how educational technologies materialize specific problem representations and visions of learning, embedding particular pedagogical priorities within socio-technical systems (Rahm & Rahm-Skågeby, 2023, p. 1154). Hence, technical safeguards must be matched by participatory governance in which learners help define acceptable uses of their data and acceptable limits on automation.

Even in higher education, where enthusiasm for cutting-edge applications is high, evidence suggests that AI is frequently implemented at the Augmentation rather than Redefinition level of the SAMR model (Wang et al., 2025). Substituting AI-generated summaries for human-written outlines may streamline preparation, yet it does little to cultivate critical literacy about how models assemble or omit knowledge. Genuine transformation would instead align AI capabilities with authentic inquiry, prompting students to interrogate the provenance of outputs, to experiment with multimodal representations, and to iterate on designs that matter beyond the classroom. Such ambitions require forethought about domain-specific tools, equitable access, and professional development that frames AI as a catalyst for—not a replacement of—expert pedagogy.

Moving forward, the most fruitful path treats AI as a partner that extends the reach of well-grounded instructional design while preserving human judgment as the arbiter of meaning and value. Practically, this orientation entails clear disclosure of algorithmic roles, iterative co-design with students, and ongoing cultivation of AI literacy so learners can discern when to trust, tweak, or override machine suggestionsRecent breakthroughs in knowledge-graph technology and adaptive recommendation systems can now map skills across disciplines and deliver exceptionally detailed, personalised feedback (Zheng et al., 2024). Yet technical sophistication must be counterbalanced by ethical vigilance, respect for cultural plurality, and deliberate fostering of social presence. Educational ecosystems can maximise the benefits and minimise the challenges of AI to enrich learning only with robust policies that prioritise responsible, ethical, critical and creative engagement.

Implications of the EWAI Model

The EWAI model offers a number of implications that extend beyond the classroom and individual level, inviting institutions, educators, and policymakers to rethink the conditions under which AI becomes a genuine partner in learning rather than a peripheral tool. Whereas established technology-integration frameworks typically attend to teacher competencies or student digital literacy, EWAI foregrounds the enabling—or constraining—power of the learning environment itself. It asserts that even the most motivated learners and the most inventive teachers will struggle to sustain constructive or interactive engagement if the broader ecosystem fails to provide equitable infrastructure, clear ethical guardrails, and coherent organisational support.

For institutions, this insight redirects strategic planning away from piecemeal device roll-outs toward a holistic architecture that couples robust connectivity and secure data pipelines with transparent governance mechanisms. Investing in cloud credits for AI experimentation or subsidising campus licences for generative platforms will yield limited returns unless accompanied by policies that stipulate how learner data are stored, how algorithmic decisions can be audited, and how students can contest or override automated feedback that appears biased or erroneous. Institutional leaders, therefore, need to embed AI literacy, bias-monitoring routines, and privacy safeguards into quality-assurance cycles, accreditation reports, and budgeting processes, ensuring that engagement with AI is woven into the fabric of organisational practice rather than siloed in pilot projects.

For educators, EWAI reframes professional development from a narrow focus on "how to prompt" or "which tool to try" toward a deeper understanding of how AI can amplify or erode the engagement dynamics identified in expectancy–value, self-determination, and ICAP theories. Teachers who design assignments through the lens of EWAI will ask whether an AI-mediated task genuinely stretches students within their zone of proximal development, whether learners have opportunities to critique the provenance of AI outputs, and whether the activity leaves room for agency, construction and co-construction rather than ushering students down a single adaptive pathway.

Professional development programs can therefore shift from tool demonstrations toward studio-style sessions in which teachers iteratively redesign assessments, anticipate ethical dilemmas, and rehearse facilitation moves that prompt students to explain, refine, or challenge machine suggestions. Because the model highlights the affective costs of constant surveillance, educators must also negotiate with IT units to calibrate learning analytics dashboards so that students experience feedback as empowering rather than punitive. In practice, that might mean allowing learners to hide certain metrics, inviting them to co-interpret algorithmic risk flags, or reserving space in the curriculum for meta-discussions about when to disengage from AI altogether.

Policy makers occupy a critical point in the EWAI framework because they can set minimum standards that ensure the benefits of AI do not accrue only to affluent districts or elite universities. National or regional agencies could, for example, require that any AI system procured with public funds include an explainability layer accessible to students and teachers, thereby operationalising the model's emphasis on reciprocal, transparent feedback loops. Funding formulas might incentivise collaborations between low-resource schools and research universities so that advances in adaptive modelling or data-ethics protocols diffuse quickly rather than remaining proprietary.

Accreditation bodies could embed EWAI indicators—such as evidence of student co-creation with AI or documented processes for bias audits—into programme reviews, signalling that meaningful engagement with AI is as central to educational quality as assessment alignment or faculty credentials. By codifying explicit rights to data agency and algorithmic due process, legislatures can also help stabilise the trust that underwrites constructive AI use, reducing the likelihood that institutions will fall back on narrow surveillance models or blanket bans.

The model equally offers a research agenda that can advance both theory and practice. Because EWAI posits dynamic interactions across learner dispositions, task characteristics, and contextual scaffolds, validation requires mixed-method approaches capable of tracing causal pathways at multiple levels. Longitudinal field experiments can probe whether classrooms that adopt autonomy-supportive AI routines sustain higher levels of cognitive and agentic engagement over time than those relying on automated sequencing alone. Multilevel structural-equation modelling could test the hypothesis that institutional transparency moderates the link between AI-generated feedback and students' expectancy beliefs, while process-mining of clickstream data may reveal how patterns of prompt refinement or peer-AI co-construction predict conceptual growth. Qualitative case studies can add nuance by examining how cultural values shape students' willingness to question algorithmic authority, thereby clarifying whether the model generalises across diverse sociotechnical settings. To guard against the known risks of over-instrumentation, researchers should embed participatory ethics reviews that empower students to veto intrusive data-collection practices, aligning methodological rigour with the model's call for agency and equity. Cumulative evidence from such studies can feed iterative refinements of EWAI, ensuring that it remains a living framework attuned to evolving capabilities in multimodal generation, on-device inference, and affect-aware tutoring.

Ultimately, the EWAI model urges all stakeholders to treat AI not as an inevitable disruptor that educators must either embrace or resist, but as a malleable component of a learning ecology whose affordances and risks are shaped by deliberate human choices. It reminds institutions that engagement flourishes only when technical infrastructure, ethical governance, and capacity-building move in unison. It invites teachers to see AI as a catalyst for deeper dialogue rather than a shortcut to efficiency. And it challenges policymakers to legislate for transparency, equity, and student agency so that the promise of personalised, just-in-time learning does not collapse into new forms of digital stratification. By integrating these imperatives, EWAI provides a roadmap for translating theoretical insights about motivation, autonomy, and social belonging into systemic practices that enable every learner to engage with AI constructively, creatively, and ethically—a vision that warrants rigorous empirical scrutiny and bold institutional action alike.

LIMITATIONS AND FUTURE RESEARCH

The EWAI model provides a useful framework for examining student engagement in AI-enhanced learning. However, its scope currently outpaces the available evidence. The main challenge is time: while classroom practice can adopt new tools overnight, the research cycle moves much more slowly. Peer review in educational journals typically takes nine to twelve months, and a manuscript that must be resubmitted to another journal after rejection can spend close to two years in the pipeline before reaching print. During that interval, a large-language model released in one semester may already have been superseded by multimodal agents in the next, altering what counts as “constructive” or “interactive” engagement and dating any framework that remains static. Meeting this challenge requires treating EWAI as a living model—revisited through planned horizon scans and continuous practitioner feedback—rather than a finished canon.

Another related limitation involves measurement. The framework asks researchers to assess not only learners’ behaviours and motivations but also their meta-algorithmic knowledge, ethical awareness, and the fairness of the support their institutions provide. Reliable instruments for these newer dimensions remain underdeveloped, and many still rely on self-report scales. Moreover, the drive to gather ever-richer analytics can slide into surveillance, undercutting the autonomy and trust that EWAI is meant to foster. Future studies should therefore pair innovative psychometric methods, such as scenario-based surveys that tap students’ sense of data agency or quick-response vignettes that reveal their skill at spotting bias, with privacy-respecting analytics that keep data local or let learners hide sensitive information.

Causal inference presents a third challenge. Most studies positioning AI as a driver of engagement compare tool users with non-users over short windows, conflating novelty effects with durable change and leaving unanswered whether initial enthusiasm translates into sustained curiosity, agency, or learning gains. Addressing that gap demands longitudinal, multi-site field experiments in which randomised clusters—or at least well-matched comparison groups—use AI over an academic year, tracking ripple effects on deep learning, self-regulation, and wellbeing. Only with such time-series evidence can the community decide whether AI deserves its reputation as an engagement catalyst or whether first-semester spikes sag into dependency and cognitive offloading.

Fourth, the model assumes that institutional transparency and ethical governance can be built into commercial AI systems. In practice, proprietary algorithms may withhold training-data lineages, bias-audit logs, or fine-tuning parameters. This opacity constrains both research replication and classroom trust. One route forward is for funding agencies and accreditation bodies to require that educational vendors publish explainability reports and submit to third-party audits as a condition of procurement—a policy lever that research teams could exploit when testing EWAI’s assumptions about explainability, trust, and engagement.

Contextual diversity constitutes a further limitation. The model was conceived with reasonably well-resourced higher-education settings in mind; it may not translate cleanly to under-connected rural schools, informal community programmes, or cultures where questioning machine authority is discouraged. Cross-cultural participatory studies—co-designed with local teachers and students—are therefore essential to determine which components of EWAI travel intact, which require localisation, and which should be supplanted by community-specific constructs.

Finally, EWAI tends to overlook the long-term ecological effects of adopting AI in education. While early studies often highlight improvements in quiz scores or increased engagement, few examine whether sustained AI use reshapes students' beliefs about knowledge, limits the development of diverse skills, or affects social interactions in ways that emerge over time. The model will remain more theoretical than practical until researchers begin tracing outcomes that extend beyond immediate academic gains, particularly students' ability to exercise independent judgment in increasingly automated workplaces. In short, we should not embrace AI as an educational partner simply because it enhances short-term performance; its impact on critical thinking, adaptability, and educational equity must be carefully evaluated over the long run.

To address these gaps, future research can adopt multi-method approaches that reflect the model's layered structure. Design-based research cycles offer a way to iteratively improve classroom interventions while capturing how teachers respond, how students engage, and how the system behaves. Multilevel structural equation modelling can help examine whether factors like institutional transparency influence how students interpret and respond to AI feedback. Process mining of prompt-engineering logs can shed light on how students move from simply copying responses to actively collaborating with AI tools. At the same time, qualitative ethnographic studies can uncover less visible dynamics—such as students working around AI dashboards or teachers quietly resisting algorithmic suggestions—ensuring the research stays grounded in everyday classroom realities.

Over time, converging evidence should feed back into the framework, tightening vague connections and perhaps pruning constructs that add complexity without predictive power. In this sense, EWAI is best viewed not as a verdict on AI's educational value but as a hypothesis generator: it identifies where engagement is most likely to flourish or falter and invites systematic tests of those propositions. The model's long-term value will depend on its ability to inform sustainable, evidence-based practice beyond the initial novelty of AI, helping ensure that these technologies support meaningful human learning rather than becoming tools for superficial efficiency.

ACKNOWLEDGEMENT

The author used ChatGPT and ClaudeAI to improve the clarity, coherence, and readability of the text, as well as to condense certain sections of the manuscript. However, all ideas, analyses, and arguments presented in this chapter are entirely the author's own. Full responsibility is assumed for the accuracy, originality, and intellectual content of the work. The use of AI tools was strictly limited to language enhancement, and no AI-generated content was included without careful review and validation.

REFERENCES

Abbas, M., Jam, F. A., & Khan, T. I. (2024). Is it harmful or helpful? Examining the causes and consequences of generative AI usage among university students. *International Journal of Educational Technology in Higher Education*, *21*(1). Advance online publication. DOI: 10.1186/s41239-024-00444-7

Al-Nuaimi, M. N., & Al-Emran, M. (2021). Learning management systems and technology acceptance models: A systematic review. *Education and Information Technologies*, *26*, 5499–5533. DOI: 10.1007/s10639-021-10495-6

Appleton, J. J., Christenson, S. L., & Furlong, M. J. (2008). Student engagement with school: Critical conceptual and methodological issues of the construct. *Psychology in the Schools*, *45*(5), 369–386.DOI: 10.1002/pits.20303

Astin, A. W. (1984). Student involvement: A developmental theory for higher education. *Journal of College Student Personnel*, *25*(4), 297–308.

Bandura, A. (1997). *Self-efficacy: The exercise of control.* W H Freeman/Times Books/ Henry Holt & Co.

Bozkurt, A., Xiao, J., Farrow, R., Bai, J. Y. H., Nerantzi, C., Moore, S., Dron, J., Stracke, C. M., Singh, L., Crompton, H., Koutropoulos, A., Terentev, E., Pazurek, A., Nichols, M., Sidorkin, A. M., Costello, E., Watson, S., Mulligan, D., Honeychurch, S., & Asino, T. I. (2024). The manifesto for teaching and learning in a time of generative AI: A critical collective stance to better navigate the future. *Open Praxis*, *16*(4), 487–513.DOI: 10.55982/openpraxis.16.4.777

Börekci, C., & Çelik, Ö. (2024). Exploring the role of digital literacy in university students' engagement with AI through the technology acceptance model. *Sakarya University Journal of Education*, *14*(Special Issue), 228–249.DOI: 10.19126/suje.1468866

Bloom, B. S. (1956). *Taxonomy of educational objectives: The classification of educational goals. Handbook I: Cognitive domain*. Longmans, Green.

Chan, C. K. Y., & Zhou, W. (2023). An expectancy value theory (EVT) based instrument for measuring student perceptions of generative AI. *Smart Learning Environments, 10*(1). DOI: 10.1186/s40561-023-00284-4

Chi, M. T. H., & Wylie, R. (2014). The ICAP framework: Linking cognitive engagement to active learning outcomes. *Educational Psychologist*, *49*(4), 219–243. DOI: 10.1080/00461520.2014.965823

Chiu, T. K., Moorhouse, B. L., Chai, C. S., & Ismailov, M. (2023). Teacher support and student motivation to learn with Artificial Intelligence (AI) based chatbot. *Interactive Learning Environments*, •••, 1–17.DOI: 10.1080/10494820.2023.2172044

Crawford, J., Allen, K., Pani, B., & Cowling, M. (2024). When artificial intelligence substitutes humans in higher education: The cost of loneliness, student success, and retention. *Studies in Higher Education*, *49*(5), 883–897.DOI: 10.1080/03075079.2024.2326956

Csikszentmihalyi, M. (1990). *Flow: The Psychology of Optimal Experience*. Harper and Row.

Davis, F. D. (1989). Perceived usefulness, perceived ease of use, and user acceptance of information technology. *Management Information Systems Quarterly*, *13*(3), 319. DOI: 10.2307/249008

Dawson, S., Joksimovic, S., Mills, C., Gašević, D., & Siemens, G. (2023). Advancing theory in the age of artificial intelligence. *British Journal of Educational Technology*, *54*(5), 1051–1056.DOI: 10.1111/bjet.13343

Deci, E. L., & Ryan, R. M. (1985). *Intrinsic motivation and self-determination in human ize*. Plenum.

Deci, E. L., & Ryan, R. M. (2000). The "what" and "why" of goal pursuits: Human needs and the self-determination of behavior. *Psychological Inquiry*, *11*(4), 227–268.

Eccles, J. S. (1983). Expectancies, values, and academic behaviors. In Spence, J. T. (Ed.), *Achievement and achievement motives* (pp. 75–146). Freeman.

Eccles, J. S., & Wigfield, A. (2002). Motivational beliefs, values, and goals. *Annual Review of Psychology*, *53*, 109–132.

Essien, A., Salami, A., Ajala, O., Adebisi, B., Shodiya, A., & Essien, G. (2024). Exploring socio-cultural influences on generative AI engagement in Nigerian higher education: An activity theory analysis. *Smart Learning Environments*, *11*(1). Advance online publication. DOI: 10.1186/s40561-024-00352-3

Fathali, S., & Okada, T. (2018). Technology acceptance model in technology-enhanced OCLL contexts: A self-determination theory approach. *Australasian Journal of Educational Technology*, *34*(4). Advance online publication. DOI: 10.14742/ajet.3629

Finn, J. D. (1989). Withdrawing from school. *Review of Educational Research*, *59*(2), 117–142.

Finn, J. D., & Zimmer, K. S. (2012). Student engagement: What is it? Why does it matter? In Christenson, S. L., Reschly, A. L., & Wylie, C. (Eds.), *Handbook of research on student engagement* (pp. 97–131). Springer.

Fredricks, J. A., Blumenfeld, P. C., & Paris, A. H. (2004). School engagement: Potential of the concept, state of the evidence. *Review of Educational Research*, *74*(1), 59–109.DOI: 10.3102/00346543074001059

Glickman, M., & Sharot, T. (2024). How human–AI feedback loops alter human perceptual, emotional, and social judgements. *Nature Human Behaviour*.DOI: 10.1038/s41562-024-02077-2

Granić, A., & Marangunić, N. (2019). Technology acceptance model in educational context: A systematic literature review. *British Journal of Educational Technology*, *50*(5), 2572–2593.DOI: 10.1111/bjet.12864

Hınız, G., & Çelik, Ö. (2024). A bibliometric and content analysis of student engagement research in English language teaching. *Language Awareness*, •••, 1–34. DOI: 10.1080/09658416.2024.2367970

Hu, W., Tian, J., & Li, Y. (2025). Enhancing student engagement in online collaborative writing through a generative AI-based conversational agent. *The Internet and Higher Education*, *65*, 100979.DOI: 10.1016/j.iheduc.2024.100979

Jiang, Y. (2025). Interaction and dialogue: Integration and application of artificial intelligence in blended mode writing feedback. *The Internet and Higher Education*, *64*, 100975.DOI: 10.1016/j.iheduc.2024.100975

Kahu, E. R. (2013). Framing student engagement in higher education. *Studies in Higher Education*, *38*(5), 758–773.DOI: 10.1080/03075079.2011.598505

Kahu, E. R., & Nelson, K. (2018). Student engagement in the educational interface: Understanding the mechanisms of student success. *Higher Education Research & Development*, *37*(1), 58–71.

Kestin, G., Miller, K., Klales, A., Milbourne, T., & Ponti, G. (2024, May 14). *AI tutoring outperforms active learning* [Preprint]. Research Square. DOI: 10.21203/rs.3.rs-4243877/v1

Kimmons, R., Graham, C. R., & West, R. E. (2020). The PICRAT model for Technology Integration in teacher Preparation. *Contemporary Issues in Technology and Teacher Education Journal, 20*(1), 176–198. https://eric.ed.gov/?id=EJ1245787

Kong, X., Liu, Z., Chen, C., Liu, S., Xu, Z., & Tang, Q. (2025). Exploratory study of an AI-supported discussion representational tool for online collaborative learning in a Chinese university. *The Internet and Higher Education*, *64*, 100973.DOI: 10.1016/j.iheduc.2024.100973

Liu, M., Zhang, L. J., & Biebricher, C. (2024). Investigating students' cognitive processes in generative AI-assisted digital multimodal composing and traditional writing. *Computers & Education*, *211*, 104977.DOI: 10.1016/j.compedu.2023.104977

Lo, C. K., Hew, K. F., & Jong, M. S. (2024). The influence of ChatGPT on student engagement: A systematic review and future research agenda. *Computers & Education*, *219*, 105100.DOI: 10.1016/j.compedu.2024.105100

Lu, H., He, L., Yu, H., Pan, T., & Fu, K. (2024). A study on teachers' willingness to use generative AI technology and its influencing factors: Based on an integrated model. *Sustainability*, *16*(16), 7216.DOI: 10.3390/su16167216

Ma, Y., & Chen, M. (2024). AI-empowered applications effects on EFL learners' engagement in the classroom and academic procrastination. *BMC Psychology*, *12*(1). DOI: 10.1186/s40359-024-02248-w

Mohamed, A. M., Shaaban, T. S., Bakry, S. H., Guillén-Gámez, F. D., & Strzelecki, A. (2025). Empowering the Faculty of Education students: Applying AI's potential for motivating and enhancing learning. *Innovative Higher Education*. Advance online publication. DOI: 10.1007/s10755-024-09747-z

Niloy, A. C., Akter, S., Sultana, N., Sultana, J., & Rahman, S. I. U. (2023). Is Chatgpt a menace for creative writing ability? An experiment. *Journal of Computer Assisted Learning*, *40*(2), 919–930.DOI: 10.1111/jcal.12929

Ouyang, F., Wu, M., Zheng, L., Zhang, L., & Jiao, P. (2023). Integration of artificial intelligence performance prediction and learning analytics to improve student learning in online engineering course. *International Journal of Educational Technology in Higher Education*, *20*(1). Advance online publication. DOI: 10.1186/s41239-022-00372-4

Puentedura, R. (2013). *SAMR: Moving from enhancement to transformation* [Blog post]. *Ruben R. Puentedura's Weblog*. Retrieved May 2022, from http://www.hippasus.com/rrpweblog/archives/000095.html

Rahm, L., & Rahm-Skågeby, J. (2023). Imaginaries and problematisations: A heuristic lens in the age of artificial intelligence in education. *British Journal of Educational Technology*, *54*(5), 1147–1159.DOI: 10.1111/bjet.13319

Reeve, J. (2013). How students create motivationally supportive learning environments for themselves: The concept of agentic engagement. *Journal of Educational Psychology*, *105*(3), 579–595.DOI: 10.1037/a0032690

Reeve, J., & Tseng, C. M. (2011). Agency as a fourth aspect of students' engagement during learning activities. *Contemporary Educational Psychology*, *36*(4), 257–267.

Ryan, R. M., & Deci, E. L. (2017). *Self-determination theory: Basic psychological needs in motivation, development, and wellness*. Guilford Press.

Salloum, S. A., Alhamad, A. Q. M., Al-Emran, M., Monem, A. A., & Shaalan, K. (2019). Exploring students' acceptance of e-learning through the development of a comprehensive technology acceptance model. *IEEE Access : Practical Innovations, Open Solutions*, *7*, 128445–128462.DOI: 10.1109/ACCESS.2019.2939467

Shafiabady, N., Koo, T. F., Ud Din, F., Sattarshetty, K., Yen, M., Alazab, M., & Alsharaydeh, E. (2025). Predicting postgraduate student engagement using artificial intelligence (AI). *IEEE Transactions on Artificial Intelligence*. Advance online publication.DOI: 10.1109/TAI.2025.3548016

Sikström, P., Valentini, C., Sivunen, A., & Kärkkäinen, T. (2024). Pedagogical agents communicating and scaffolding students' learning: High school teachers' and students' perspectives. *Computers & Education*, *222*, 105140.DOI: 10.1016/j.compedu.2024.105140

Skinner, E. A., & Pitzer, J. R. (2012). Developmental dynamics of student engagement, coping, and everyday resilience. In S. L. Christenson, A. L. Reschly, & C. Wylie (Eds.), Handbook of research on student engagement (pp. 21–44). Springer. DOI: 10.1007/978-1-4614-2018-7_2

Toma, R. B., & Yánez-Pérez, I. (2024). Effects of ChatGPT Use on Undergraduate Students' Creativity: A Threat to Creative Thinking? *Discover Artificial Intelligence*, *4*(1). DOI: 10.1007/s44163-024-00172-x

United Nations Educational, Scientific and Cultural Organization. (2024). *AI competency framework for students*. DOI: 10.54675/JKJB9835

Urban, M., Děchtěrenko, F., Lukavský, J., Hrabalová, V., Svacha, F., Brom, C., & Urban, K. (2024). ChatGPT improves creative problem-solving performance in university students: An experimental study. *Computers & Education*, *215*, 105031. DOI: 10.1016/j.compedu.2024.105031

van Haastrecht, M., Haas, M., Brinkhuis, M., & Spruit, M. (2024). Understanding validity criteria in technology-enhanced learning: A systematic literature review. *Computers & Education*, *220*, 105128. DOI: 10.1016/j.compedu.2024.105128

Vygotsky, L. S., & Cole, M. (1978). *Mind in society: Development of higher psychological processes*. Harvard university press.

Xu, X. (2025). AI optimization algorithms enhance higher education management and personalized teaching through empirical analysis. *Scientific Reports*, *15*(1). Advance online publication. DOI: 10.1038/s41598-025-94481-5

Yang, T., Hsu, Y., & Wu, J. (2025). The effectiveness of ChatGPT in assisting high school students in programming learning: Evidence from a quasi-experimental research. *Interactive Learning Environments*, •••, 1–18. DOI: 10.1080/10494820.2025.2450659

Wang, P., Jing, Y., & Shen, S. (2025). A systematic literature review on the application of generative artificial intelligence (GAI) in teaching within higher education: Instructional contexts, process, and strategies. *The Internet and Higher Education*. Advance online publication. DOI: 10.1016/j.iheduc.2025.100996

Wang, F., King, R. B., Chai, C. S., & Zhou, Y. (2023). University students' intentions to learn artificial intelligence: The roles of supportive environments and expectancy–value beliefs. *International Journal of Educational Technology in Higher Education*, *20*(1). DOI: 10.1186/s41239-023-00417-2

Wigfield, A., & Eccles, J. S. (2000). Expectancy–value theory of achievement motivation. *Contemporary Educational Psychology*, *25*(1), 68–81.

Xiao, J., Bozkurt, A., Nichols, M., Pazurek, A., Stracke, C. M., Bai, J. Y. H., Farrow, R., Mulligan, D., Nerantzi, C., Sharma, R. C., Singh, L., Frumin, I., Swindell, A., Honeychurch, S., Bond, M., Dron, J., Moore, S., Leng, J., Slagter van Tryon, P. J., & Themeli, C. (2025). Venturing into the unknown: Critical insights into grey areas and pioneering future directions in educational generative AI research. *TechTrends*. DOI: 10.1007/s11528-025-01060-6

Zheng, L., Fan, Y., Gao, L., Huang, Z., Chen, B., & Long, M. (2024). Using AI-empowered assessments and personalized recommendations to promote online collaborative learning performance. *Journal of Research on Technology in Education*, •••, 1–27. DOI: 10.1080/15391523.2024.2304066

Zawacki-Richter, O., Marín, V. I., Bond, M., & Gouverneur, F. (2019). Systematic review of research on artificial intelligence applications in higher education – Are the technologies ready for prime time? *International Journal of Educational Technology in Higher Education, 16*(21), 1–20.

KEY TERMS AND DEFINITIONS

AI Literacy: A blend of technical knowledge, critical awareness and ethical sensibility that enables learners to understand, evaluate and responsibly apply AI tools.

AI-Engaged Learner: An individual who approaches AI as an active co-inquirer, displaying curiosity, agency and ethical awareness; probing, refining and sometimes overriding machine outputs rather than accepting them at face value.

AI-Enhanced Learning Environment: The institutional, technological and pedagogical context that determines how AI is used to enhance learning (infrastructure, policies, teacher capacity, equity safeguards) and how deeply students can engage.

AI-Enhanced Learning Tasks: Authentic activities that combine relevance, optimal challenge, active, constructive and co-constructive engagement and autonomy, all mediated or enriched by AI feedback or generation.

Algorithmic Surveillance: Continuous tracking of learner clicks, keystrokes or pauses by AI systems, raising concerns about privacy, intimidation and risk-averse behaviours.

Algorithmic Transparency: The degree to which an AI system reveals how it works (data sources, model logic, error rates) so that users can interpret and, when necessary, contest its outputs.

Balanced Reliance: It refers to a learner's ability to use AI tools appropriately, benefitting from their strengths for support while maintaining independent thinking, critical evaluation, and original contribution. It avoids both under-utilisation of helpful AI capabilities and over-reliance that diminishes student agency, reasoning, or effort.

Bias Audit: A systematic review (human or automated) that checks AI outputs or training data for systematic unfairness across demographic, linguistic or cultural groups.

Data Transparency: The Institutional practice of making it clear what learner data are collected, how they are used by AI systems, and how long they are retained.

Digital Divide (in AI): Inequities in access to the bandwidth, devices, or licensed models required for AI-mediated learning, risking unequal engagement opportunities.

Engagement with AI (EWAI) Model: EWAI: is a framework that conceptualises student engagement for AI-rich learning environments. At the micro level, it profiles the *AI-engaged learner*—a student who combines curiosity, agency, meta-algorithmic and ethical literacy with behavioural, cognitive, emotional and agentic engagement to probe, refine and occasionally override machine output. At the macro level, it specifies the *AI-enhanced learning environment*, equitable infrastructure, transparent policies, teacher capacity and autonomy-supportive, optimally challenging tasks that enable deep, constructive or co-constructive use of AI.

Environmental AI Literacy Engagement: Awareness of, and action toward, the environmental costs of AI (energy use, carbon footprint) and commitment to sustainable AI practices.

Ethical Engagement with AI: Acting with academic integrity and responsibility when using AI, recognising bias, maintaining data privacy, citing appropriately, and evaluating the broader societal impact of AI decisions.

Explainability: Design principles or features that make an AI's decision path intelligible to non-experts, often considered a prerequisite for trust and ethical adoption.

Human–AI Co-regulation: A dynamic in which control of learning processes (feedback, pacing, goal-setting) is shared between human actors and algorithmic systems or agents.

Lazy Cognition: A tendency to accept AI output uncritically, outsourcing mental effort and thereby weakening deep processing and retention.

Meta-Algorithmic Literacy Engagement: Understanding how AI models are trained, what data they draw on, their limitations, such as bias and hallucinations, and how these factors shape reliability; using that knowledge to judge outputs critically.

Prompt Engineering: Iterative practice of crafting and adjusting queries to coax higher-quality, more relevant or more creative AI responses.

Zone of Proximal Development (ZPD) – AI-calibrated: The band of challenge just beyond a learner's unaided capability that an AI-enhanced learning task or adaptive AI system tries to target in real time.

Chapter 8
Experiential Scenarios and the Onto-AI Lexicon of "Being Innovative" in Initial Teacher Education

Janine Arantes
https://orcid.org/0000-0002-0301-5780
Victoria University, Australia

ABSTRACT

This chapter introduces the onto-AI lexicon as a critical framework to reframe 'being innovative' in Initial Teacher Education. Conceiving GenAI as a socio-technical assemblage rather than a neutral tool, the chapter presents experiential scenarios as epistemic interventions that support preservice teachers in recognising the ethical, relational, and political dimensions of AI integration. The onto-AI lexicon is introduced as both provocation and practice, challenging euphemisms like "hallucination" and "personalisation" and replacing them with terms such as "error" and "profiling" to surface power, harm, and consequence. Through a worked exmaple of an immersive scenario, the chapter supports how teacher educators could model how to enable future teachers to critically assess AI's role in shaping pedagogy, equity, and professional responsibility. By resisting market-driven framings of innovation, the chapter repositions ITE as a site of ethical AI literacy and democratic worldmaking.

DOI: 10.4018/979-8-3373-7569-4.ch008

INTRODUCTION

The contemporary educational landscape is undergoing an ontological shift. A shift haunted by what Derrida (2012) called the "ghosts of the future," where the new is always entangled with the unfinished past. It is increasingly being structured and restructured by the presence and affordances of generative artificial intelligence (GenAI), which is sold to educators as an innovation. Far from being a neutral tool, GenAI in this chapter is conceived as not a computational process, but a sociotechnical assemblage (Arantes, 2024).That is, GenAI can simultaneously support personalized learning and institutional efficiency, whilst also challenging the foundations of what we refer to as human agency, and ethical responsibility (Reid et al., 2023). As *The Manifesto for Teaching and Learning in a Time of Generative AI* (Bozkurt et al., 2024) asserts, GenAI is never culturally or ideologically neutral. This recognition necessitates a critical re-examination of the language we use to describe innovation in initial teacher education courses. It invites us to reconsider the prevailing lexicon that frames technology as inherently innovative (Hayes & Jandrić, 2017), often at the expense of ethical, relational, and context-sensitive dimensions of practice. As the Manifesto argues, continuing with 'business as usual' is no longer an option (Bozkurt et al., 2024). Acknowledging this, this chapter considers how we might reposition GenAI as an assemblage of worldviews, epistemologies, and power relations, through experiential scenarios. This chapter aims to support teacher educators in engaging learners with the purpose of education at a time when GenAI reshapes and potentially distorts what counts as 'innovation' in educational practice. In doing so, it argues for a new lexicon of 'innovation' to support more critically engaged and ethically grounded teacher education in the age of generative AI.

REFRAMING INNOVATION: A NEW LEXICON FOR TEACHER EDUCATION IN THE AGE OF GENAI

According to Biesta (2013), the purpose of education is to support the processes of qualification, socialisation, and subjectification, enabling individuals to engage meaningfully with the world as autonomous and responsible subjects. Biesta's idea of subjectification can be understood as *a way of being* that involves ethical becoming and responsibility in relation to others and the world. Initial Teacher Educators (ITEs) who educate the future workforce of teachers play a critical role in shaping what education becomes. They shape not just what teachers know, but who they become by guiding preservice teachers (PSTs) in their courses, through a complex interplay of knowledge, culture, and ethical responsibility. This aligns with Noddings (2018) view that education's purpose is to cultivate caring relationships.

Role modelling and scenario-based learning are key strategies through which ITEs make these ethical and relational dimensions of teaching visible and actionable for preservice teachers.

Scenario-based learning in Initial Teacher Education (ITE) offers a pedagogical tool that enables preservice teachers to engage with the complexity of teaching practice. Loughran Loughran (2013) emphasises that a pedagogy of teacher education goes well beyond the simple delivery of information about teaching. This highlights how the lived experience of teaching as modelled by the teacher educator, may offer opportunity for the teacher educator to foster both democratic participation (Biesta, 2013) and personal growth (Noddings, 2018) through scenarios about GenAI. However, teacher educators inhabit a milieu, in which the problem of GenAI being a fundamentally non-neutral commercial tool is not merely whether to engage with AI, but how to prepare pre-service teachers (PSTs) critically and reflexively for classrooms increasingly entangled with algorithmic systems. Systems that carry with them what Derrida (2012) calls *spectres*: the unresolved epistemologies and power relations from past educational imaginaries of technological innovation that refuse to vanish despite the increasing rhetoric of GenAI's flaws (Arantes, 2024; Weise & Metz, 2023).

As Ball (2020, p. 870) suggests, our current socio-educational landscape is situated between a romantic modernism, where "we just have to get it right" and a pragmatic neoliberalism, whereby "it needs improvement". 'Getting it right' however, since GenAI disrupted education, now includes teachers needing to understand the challenges of GenAI enhanced assessment (Corbin et al., 2025), how to manage the increasing false contestations over academic integrity and professional judgment (Lee et al., 2024) within a context of increasing workload and stress (Arantes & Vicars, 2024). Arguably, this reflects an indirect blame placed on teacher educators for the 'failures of education', at a time when Initial Teacher Education is being publicly positioned as in need of improvement (Van Bergen et al., 2024). With a need to critically navigate and contest these algorithmic systems (Scholkmann et al., 2024), and the landscape they inhabit (Bozkurt et al., 2024), teacher educators need a new professional lexicon that is built by educators rather than commercial actors about GenAI. This chapter argues that a new lexicon is needed for three key purposes.

First, to engage preservice teachers in the purpose of education given the ubiquity of GenAI. There is a needs for a lexicon that moves beyond outdated technocratic framings of 'innovation' being better than relationality, ethical discernment, and situated judgment (Morozov, 2013). As Bozkurt et al. (2024, p. 497) state "The human element in communication, creativity, and emotional exchange remains irreplaceable."

Second, there is a need for a lexicon that does not frame emergent technologies as inherently innovative (Hayes & Jandrić, 2017). (Bozkurt et al., 2024), P. 493) suggests "we should emphasize the learning process itself and support students as they engage with complex problems and use GenAI and other technologies to achieve innovative outcomes." A new lexicon is essential because what once signified innovation alongside the disruption of GenAI, has become the norm. Now in a post-hype landscape, simply having GenAI is no longer innovative and what is truly radical now is equipping future teachers with the ethical, relational, and critical capacities to question it – not only in terms of pedagogical affordances, but in terms of harm.

Third, a lexicon that prioritises the modelling of the lived experience of teaching (Loughran, 2013) to critically reconsider the epistemic, pedagogical, and political shifts ushered in by generative technologies. (Bozkurt et al., 2024), p. 497) states "educators must design learning experiences that encourage active cognitive engagement, using GenAI as a scaffold rather than a replacement for intellectual effort. Hype cycles will continue to come and go, as such we need a new lexicon that offers teacher educators the grounded tools to anticipate hype, embed a narrative of resisting commercial narratives, and reclaim the purpose of education in times where technological change is spruiked as a replacement for intellectual effort.

TOWARDS A NEW LEXICON FOR TEACHER PREPARATION: EXPERIENTIAL SCENARIOS AS EPISTEMIC INTERVENTIONS

In a post-hype landscape, the need for a new lexicon in teacher education becomes evident not as a theoretical aspiration, but as a pedagogical imperative. Experiential scenarios grounded in a lexicon of relationality, critical discernment, and lived pedagogical judgment as indicated by Bozkurt et al. (2024) offer epistemic interventions. Epistemic interventions in this context are described to be deliberate practices that challenge, reshape, or disrupt how knowledge is produced, validated, or understood within initial teacher training. Epistemic interventions can reveal how outdated technocratic framings of 'innovation', such as where efficiency is mistaken for progress, fail to account for the relational, ethical, and situated work of teaching.

For example, series of epistemic interventions in any teacher education course could proceed as follows. First, the teacher educator introduces how to write lesson plans. Then an experiential scenario which sees preservice teachers choose between an AI-generated lesson plans and one grounded in local knowledge and student relationships is practically experienced. The goal of the scenario is to allow the PSTs to experience firsthand the tensions between automation and care (Smith & Fressoli, 2021). This intervention could be followed by a scenario that confronts the assumption that emerging technologies are inherently innovative, through a scenario that debates the neutrality of GenAI. The scenario guides the students through the impacts of the lesson plan, by considering how it encodes worldviews in everyday actions such as lesson planning (Chen et al., 2025). The goal being to prepare them for the next hype cycle when they are practicing teachers. The epistemic intervention in learning about lesson plans, is then concluded with a third scenario where students are asked to audit GenAI outputs for bias, where they role play individuals impacted by harms of GenAI outputs. The goal to encourage them to consider not only pedagogical affordances that are impacted, but also the potentiality for harms (J. A. Arantes, 2024; Zhang et al., 2024), such as cultural erasure or gendered assumptions.

Such experiential scenario-based epistemic interventions draw on foundational work by Kolb et al. (2014) and are further developed by contemporary scholars of experiential and transformative learning such as Moon (2013) and Illeris (2007) who emphasise the role of lived dilemmas and reflective encounters. By situating scenarios that critique GenAI as an innovation in real classroom dilemmas through the lens of experiential scenarios as epistemic interventions, teacher educators introduce a new lexicon of GenAI into initial teacher education focussed on reshaping teacher cognition about GenAI, not as hypothetical exercise within learning about lesson planning, but as a rehearsal for their future classroom. It could be argued that frameworks such as the Technological Pedagogical Content Knowledge (TPACK) (Mishra & Koehler, 2006) and Substitution, Augmentation, Modification, Redefinition (SAMR) (Puentedura, 2006) work towards such activity; I argue that these frameworks do not sufficiently position GenAI as an assemblage of worldviews, epistemologies, and power relations. Nor do they engage with what Derrida (2012) might frame as the hauntological residues of pedagogical frameworks that valorise progress while occluding systemic inequities embedded in digital infrastructures. That is TPACK indirectly assumes tools are neutral and fails to interrogate the worldviews embedded in AI systems. Similarly, SAMR frames technology in terms of enhancement or transformation, yet equates innovation with progress, ignoring questions of cultural erasure, bias, and teacher agency. Cope and Kalantzis (2016) work on e-learning ecologies offers a more expansive view, emphasising multimodality and learner agency. However, even this does not fully account for the governance and psychosocial risks of teachers' engaging with GenAI, assessment and academic integrity in education. Hence, a new lexicon is needed to fill this gap.

Experiential scenarios as exampled above, are structured, imaginative, or speculative situations intentionally designed to immerse preservice teachers in complex, open-ended, and often ethically ambiguous contexts. Most importantly, a scenario that simulates real or anticipated challenges associated with GenAI as part of their practice. They are mechanisms for staging encounters with the contingencies, contradictions, and negotiations to provide the resources that can foreground the plurality of stakeholder perspectives. For example, we may consider an experiential scenario of innovating practice using smart glasses. Existing frameworks such as

TPACK, and e-Learning Ecologies primarily focus on pedagogical enhancement, integration, and learning through technology. They, however, do not encourage the pre service teacher to think through scenarios that Kolb et al. (2014), Moon (2013) and Illeris (2007) may prioritise. Scenarios as epistemic interventions with a novel lexicon of innovation that posits GenAI as an assemblage with actual or perceived harm, would emphasise the role of lived dilemmas and reflective encounters. A scenario may be one whereby, the preservice teacher forgets to take off the smart glasses going the bathroom and livestreams their activity to the classroom. Another scenario may be where a parent, in a parent teacher interview analyses the preservice teachers' emotions in real time, seemingly garnering evidence of them lying about their child's progress. Current lexicons of innovation around GenAI in education do not adequately account for topics such as surveillance risks, consent issues, or the erosion of teacher autonomy embedded in wearable AI. As such, teacher educators do not have the language or epistemic tools to support learners to interrogate how innovations such as smart glasses may reproduce power asymmetries, reinforce cultural stereotypes, or undermine trauma-informed practices. As such, a new lexicon is needed, one that can name and navigate these harms and support teacher educators in preparing PSTs for the ethical terrain of AI-mediated classrooms.

Recent scholarship supports scenario-based experiential learning as a strategy to prepare new teachers for the complexities of artificial intelligence (AI) in schools (Salinas-Navarro et al., 2024). Theoretical models that are immersive, case-driven exercises can help preservice teachers grapple with AI ethics and governance in realistic contexts. For example, role-playing and design fiction activities have been explored as a means to surface implicit assumptions about AI's impact on education (Huynh et al., 2020). In one creative approach, educators collaboratively imagined a scenario of students developing an "evil AI," using speculative problem-solving to reveal underlying beliefs and ethical concerns (Rahm, 2024). Such speculative and scenario-driven methods mark a shift from abstract discussion to embodied exploration, where emerging frameworks suggest that case-based learning and simulations of AI-related ethical dilemmas could strengthen teachers' professional judgment (Rahm, 2023).

While role-playing and design fiction foreground imagination and narrative construction, the scenario-based approach suggested in this chapter prioritises grounded, pedagogically embedded dilemmas that simulate institutional, legal, and ethical pressures encountered by teachers, similar to work integrated learning (WIL). That is, experiential scenarios are chosen not for their speculative distance but for their proximity to lived experience. They are conceived as a process to allow preservice teachers to rehearse judgment, navigate policy ambiguities, and engage with ethical decision-making within plausible school-based contexts. In doing so, this approach retains the affective resonance of speculative methods while anchoring learning in the everyday materiality of teaching. For, it is precisely within these entanglements that, as Derrida (2012) suggests, the spectres of past imaginaries of educational innovation reappear. Through experiential scenarios guided by a lexicon of GenAI innovation being harmful in education, the ghosts of earlier techno-utopias that linger beneath today's GenAI reforms can resurface, not as abstract critiques, but as pedagogical encounters.

By incorporating simulated decision-making exercises within a lexicon that posits safeguarding education as the innovation, teacher educators shift from examining AI-driven classroom situations to simulating activity such as responding to data privacy breaches before PSTs enter the workforce. These theoretical innovations extend earlier discussions by arguing that experiential scenarios are not just pedagogical tools but foundational to developing a new mindset in teachers for the post-AI era (Walter, 2024). One such example to illustrate the urgency of the need for a new lexicon can be example through a consideration of Deep Fakes (Hancock & Bailenson, 2021). Deepfakes situate teachers in a classroom environment that is potentially inherently harmful (Witschas, 2023), should smart glasses that can capture image and livestream in real time, become mainstreamed without sufficient policy or exposure in their courses. Situating the education of future educators in lifelike AI scenarios where deepfakes are part of their working conditions focusses on cultivating reflexivity about their own safety, alongside ethical reasoning and system level policy protections associated with AI's uncertainties beyond academic integrity and assessment. A novel lexicon of this nature, therefore aims to focus on equipping teacher educators with practical tools to inform coursework, research training, and professional reflection alongside emergent legislation and policy, informed by the notion of collective responsibility.

Experiential scenarios are therefore considered to be designed to move PSTs beyond passive adoption or instrumental use of AI technologies, instead positioning them as co-constructors of the governance, ethics, and policies that will shape education's possible futures. Through immersion in contextually specific, globally relevant scenarios, pre-service teachers are then invited to develop the research dispositions, ethical literacies, and reflexive capacities necessary to challenge the illusion of technological inevitability, foreground the risks of bias and exclusion, and sustain the human elements of creativity, criticality, and care that GenAI threatens to displace or commodify as discussed in the *Manifesto for Teaching and Learning in a Time of Generative AI* (Bozkurt et al., 2024). In this way, experiential scenarios in ITE, are considered in this chapter to function as both a site of critical inquiry and a laboratory for democratic practice. This chapter thus situates experiential scenarios at the very heart of a transformative teacher education agenda, one that recognizes the need for preparing educators who are intellectually equipped and ethically resolute amidst the proliferating uncertainties of the generative AI era.

BUILDING AI LITERACY THROUGH SCENARIO-BASED LEARNING

Initial Teacher Education has the potential to reposition 'technological advancement' as inherently requiring critical consideration. This is not only because it prepares future educators to teach, but because it shapes how they come to understand the values, purposes, and power dynamics underpinning education itself. Critical scholarship has long challenged the assumption that technological advancement is inherently positive or innovative, particularly in the context of education. Scholars such as Selwyn et al. (2017) argue that the emergent technologies in education act as a sociotechnical process embedded within existing inequalities, not as a neutral upgrade. Likewise, Williamson (2023) caution that educational technologies often carry embedded logics of surveillance, efficiency, and control that contradict the values of relational teaching and inclusive pedagogy. Jandrić and Ford (2022) call for the invention of "new postdigital eco pedagogies that are critical and creative, certain and indeterminate, transparent and opaque, and that accept and negotiate the contamination of the constantly shifting borders between humans, machines, nature, nonhuman animals, and objects." This body of work therefore suggests that initial teacher education could engage in the rhetoric of eco pedagogies that "emerge from, negotiate, debate, produce, resist, and/or overcome the shifting and expansive postdigital ecosystems" to function as a site where future educators learn not only how to teach, but *why* to teach in a Time of Generative AI.

So why ITE specifically? Ryan et al. (2025) argue that ITE is discursively positioned as deficient through policy reforms that prioritise external control, standardised measures, and technocratic notions of quality. They argue that the pragmatic neoliberalist rhetoric that education 'needs improvement', systematically overlooks the profession's existing expertise, contextual responsiveness, and broader educational purposes. Technology in education within ITE is too often shaped by external policy agendas (Arar et al., 2025) and industry-driven narratives (Gulson & Witzenberger, 2022), rather than grounded in the pedagogical judgment and contextual expertise of educators themselves. This commercial advantage is sustained by framing technological adoption as a neutral or necessary upgrade, thereby obscuring the political and economic interests embedded in edtech platforms and marginalising critical, educator-led approaches to technology integration (Arantes, 2022). That is, despite ITE's unique potential to critically interrogate how technological advancement reshapes educational purpose, the current state of technology within ITE is largely benefiting commercial actors (Arantes, 2022; Williamson et al., 2023).

Acknowledging that it is profitable for commercial actors, if critical approaches to GenAI remain fragmented, under-theorised, and predominantly reactive (Gulson & Sellar, 2024; Gulson & Witzenberger, 2022), highlights a deeper issue. The dominant lexicon of 'innovation' in education is being shaped by commercial actors, not by teacher educators grounded in pedagogical expertise. It becomes clear that while it is not profitable to position ITE as a space for cultivating critical digital pedagogies, ITE will increasingly be burdened with the responsibility of addressing systemic challenges generated by the rapid uptake of generative AI. Whether it is a need to be enforcing academic integrity tailored to GenAI, teaching AI literacies, or managing fears around plagiarism (Lee et al., 2024), the contemporary lexicon positions education as *needing* technology (Morozov, 2013). At the same time, it withholds the structural support and policy recognition necessary for ITE to serve as a space where teacher educators can foster democratic participation (Biesta, 2013) and personal growth (Noddings, 2018). This instrumental framing constrains the purpose of ITE in a Time of Generative AI, limiting its capacity to interrogate and resist commercialised narratives of innovation. The problem, then, is not that ITE lacks the capacity to address technological change, but that it is denied the authority to shape the agenda as the dominant lexicon is curated by commercial actors, not teacher educators, and that is precisely why new postdigital eco pedagogies that prioritise relationality, ethical discernment, and situated judgment remains ignored.

This chapter argues that scenario-based approaches to AI literacy offer a space to pause for critical reflection, collective negotiation, and ethical deliberation. A space to practice hopeful, affective, and relational ways of teaching and learning in a Time of Generative AI. By developing, sharing, and collectively analysing these scenarios, AI literacy in teacher education courses can become participatory process where the very ontology of 'being innovative' in education is rearticulated through a lexicon generated by teacher educators, rather than by commercial actors.

The onto-AI lexicon of 'being innovative' in education

In response to the commercialised narratives of GenAI that dominate educational technology discourse, a novel onto-AI lexicon emerges, not as a static glossary, but as a critical framework for scenario-based AI literacy. This lexicon disrupts techno solutionist framings by interrogating how GenAI reshapes pedagogical authority, reconfigures educational imaginaries as discussed by Williamson (2023) and embeds a critical consideration of surveillance, and automation that privilege dominant interests (Arantes, 2024). It challenges the notion that being 'innovative' with AI is neutral, repositioning GenAI as an assemblage of epistemologies, worldviews, and power relations (Crawford et al., 2024; Williamson, 2023a). Critically, it engages preservice teachers in reclaiming the purpose of education, moving beyond outdated framings that equate innovation with efficiency over relationality, ethics, or judgment (Morozov, 2013; Bozkurt et al., 2024). In a post-hype landscape, where simply using GenAI is no longer radical, this lexicon reframes innovation as the capacity to navigate complexity, question harm, and model lived pedagogical practices (Loughran, 2013), which is considered essential skills for PSTs as hype cycles persist with each new emergent technology.

In this context, innovation is not simply a matter of technological adoption, but a contested ontological terrain that rejects the anthropomorphic framing of AI systems in the current lexicon. For example, terms such as "hallucinating" simply become "errors", "training data" becomes "selective memory," "personalisation" becomes "profiling," and "intelligent tutor" becomes "automated responder." By decentring market-driven assumptions of innovation, the onto-AI lexicon creates space for educators to ask: What forms of innovation are permitted, excluded, or naturalised by GenAI integration into teacher education? Thus, the onto-AI lexicon becomes both a provocation and a practice. A provocation that calls for collective stewardship of the language and imaginaries of AI, and a practice grounded in experiential scenarios that enable teacher educators to model and reflect on how 'being innovative' is materially and pedagogically constituted in the algorithmic age. What follows is a worked example, to communicate how the onto-AI lexicon could be inscribed in practice.

Worked Example: Rewriting Innovation using the Onto-AI Lexicon of innovation in education

Overview

This activity asks preservice teachers to reflect on the institutional pressures that frame GenAI integration as 'innovative' and to critically examine how these pressures shape pedagogical practice, teacher identity, and student outcomes. The scenario does not require students to make decisions or solve problems. Instead, it centres their inquiry on noticing what goes unsaid, naming what feels wrong, and linking these insights to professional standards drawing on the context of Australian Teacher standards.

Scenario Prompt

You are midway through your Initial Teacher Education degree. In your program, GenAI tools have been rapidly introduced, one for generating lesson plans, one for tracking student wellbeing, and another for automating communication. You notice that many of these tools require paid subscriptions and extract data from students and staff. Academics who question the pedagogical or ethical implications of this rollout are sidelined or excluded from key decisions. Then, an incident occurs: a student named Emily, who consistently received top marks and positive feedback, is revealed not to exist. All of her assessments were AI-generated and marked automatically. No human educator had ever interacted with her. When the issue was discovered, no one was held accountable. At the same time, students from non-English-speaking backgrounds are disproportionately accused of misconduct, and staff are overwhelmed with plagiarism reports. You are invited to engage with this scenario using the onto-AI lexicon.

Scenario

At a well-regarded Initial Teacher Education program, the call to be innovative with generative AI is loud, persistent, and performative. It echoes through professional development sessions, university strategy documents, and promotion criteria. Assessment leads are flown interstate to gather best practice, while staff with limited research expertise are placed in charge of academic integrity for entire cohorts. Innovation is no longer something to be explored or debated; it is expected. Those grounded in critical pedagogy are excluded for not appearing innovative enough. Across the program, generative AI tools are introduced rapidly. One generates lesson plans. Another tracks student wellbeing. A third automates communication. Each requires a subscription. Each extracts data from students and staff. Staff are expected to use these tools as visible markers of progress. Less visible is the quiet marginalisation of those who question their value. Educators who raise concerns about ethics or pedagogy are removed from projects or left out of decision-making processes.

It is in this context that the onto-AI lexicon is introduced, not as a list of definitions but as a pedagogical tool. In tutorial scenarios, preservice teachers are invited to reflect on how language shapes what counts as innovation. The term hallucination, commonly used to describe flawed AI outputs, is reframed as error, a term that assigns accountability. Training data is re-examined as selective memory, drawing attention to how past biases are preserved and reproduced. Personalisation is critiqued as profiling, where difference is reduced to data categories. The intelligent tutor becomes an automated responder, revealing the absence of relational teaching. These redefinitions give preservice teachers a shared vocabulary to question the claims surrounding AI and to name the harms that might otherwise go unspoken.

However, as the semester progresses, the consequences of unchecked adoption of GenAI emerge. The plagiarism compliance centre is overwhelmed with flagged assessments. Students from non-English-speaking backgrounds are repeatedly accused of misconduct. Some staff begin to suspect that much of the work being submitted is not human-authored and there are rumours of students completing entire units without ever speaking to an academic. Then comes a more disturbing revelation. A high-achieving student named Emily never existed. All of her assessments were generated by a chatbot and automatically marked without oversight. No educator had ever interacted with her. When the deception was discovered, no one was held accountable. Who could they blame? The chatbot? The academic? 'Emily' simply generated new transcripts and paperwork, and enrolled elsewhere, undetected by a system designed to trust data over human presence.

Meanwhile, on school placements, preservice teachers begin to apply what they have learned. One recounts a lesson using a GenAI tool that fulfilled every curriculum requirement and ran precisely to time. The mentor teacher praised its efficiency, but the preservice teacher noticed troubling patterns. Boys were consistently chosen by the AI tool to answer science questions. Girls were overlooked. Students with learning needs were told to speed up, to keep pace with the app. Efficiency had replaced inquiry, with students seeking help told to ask ChatGPT. But the tool's personalisation revealed itself to be profiling, as it started to 'talk' to the students in ways that felt creepy. Its intelligent tutoring was little more than automated responding. In the staffroom, preservice teachers reflected on their university seminar and how the onto-AI lexicon helped them to make sense of what they were seeing. They began to name what was happening using the language they had rehearsed: hallucinations as errors, training data as selective memory, personalisation as profiling, intelligent tutor as automated responder. They took their reflections back to their university lecturers, who were encouraged by their insight.

But elsewhere in the institution, things were unravelling. A deepfake video of the Head of Program had circulated widely. In it, they appeared to make racist comments about students and deepfakes had not been included in policy, although advised by critical edtech researchers. Although the video was proven false, the damage had been done. The Head resigned and sued the university for not protecting her. At the same time, the university was managing a lawsuit from students who were falsely penalised for using ChatGPT without disclosure, even though they were using the same technology to automate staff evaluations and streamline hiring without disclosure. The contradictions became impossible to ignore.

Within this chaos, the onto-AI lexicon became more than a vocabulary. It offered a critical lens and a space for reflection. It was the provocation desperately needed to redefine what is considered to be innovative of teaching placements. It was discussed as a practice that foregrounded care, critical judgment, and relational pedagogy through the language to describe the harms and the courage to imagine something different. As the institution chased metrics and damage control, those who had engaged with the lexicon were already doing the deeper work of education, making sense of complexity, confronting injustice, and refusing to mistake automation for progress.

Instructions for Engagement

1. Observe the system – not just the individual.

As a group, list all the systems, actors, and technologies involved in Emily's case. Ask:

- What assumptions about learning, trust, and innovation underpin this system?
- Who benefits from these assumptions?
- Who is placed at risk?

2. Name what is happening using the onto-AI lexicon.

Use the onto-AI lexicon to reframe dominant AI discourse:

- Recast "hallucination" as "error" - who is accountable when the system fails?
- Rename "training data" as "selective memory" - whose knowledge is preserved and whose is erased?
- Shift "personalisation" to "profiling" - how are students categorised, and with what consequences?
- Translate "intelligent tutor" to "automated responder" - what is lost when human judgment is removed?

Each group must select two terms and write short analyses (max 200 words each) explaining how those terms help them interpret what happened in the scenario.

3. Connect your analysis to the Professional Standards.

Individually, select at least two of the following Australian Professional Standards for Teachers and explain how this scenario invites reflection on each:

- 1.5 Differentiate teaching to meet the specific learning needs of students across the full range of abilities
- 4.4 Maintain student safety
- 6.2: Engage in professional learning and improve practice
- 7.1: Meet professional ethics and responsibilities

For example: How might automating feedback and bypassing teacher-student relationships violate the responsibility to uphold safe and inclusive learning? Think through multiple perspectives in the scenario and how the system impacts different actors.

4. Reflect on your role as an emerging educator.

Write a journal entry in response to the following prompt:

What forms of innovation are naturalised in your program, and what voices or perspectives are excluded? How can I, as a preservice teacher, use critical language to uphold ethical, relational, and inclusive practices, even when those around me don't?

5. Rehearse dialogue and professional advocacy.

Imagine you are at a university curriculum committee meeting. How would you use the onto-AI lexicon to raise concerns about automated assessment? Now consider how you could approach your tutor to talk about whether you prefer automated feedback or teacher led feedback.

In this worked example, the onto-AI Lexicon of 'being innovative' in education, becomes both a provocation and a practice. As provocation, it calls the PST to question the very language through which AI is framed: to refuse euphemisms like "hallucination," "personalisation," or "smart tutor," and instead adopt terms like error, profiling, and automated responder - language that foregrounds power, design, and consequence. It invites teacher educators to become stewards of the imaginaries and vocabularies that define AI in education as active participants in shaping what is permitted to count as pedagogical innovation. This scenario positions PSTs as critically engaged professionals and develops the capacity to see GenAI not as neutral or inevitable, but as entangled in systems of power, labour, and inequality, while also giving them the language to question what counts as innovation in education. As a practice, the lexicon grounds itself in experiential scenario work. This could be situated within facilitated workshops, where PSTs and teacher educators revisit the scenario to audit lesson plans, analyse the fabricated story of "Emily," and reflect on the institutional response to the deepfake. The goal being to surface not just technical flaws, but ontological dislocations between human and machine authorship.

Onto-AI Experiential Scenarios as Praxis

The worked example outlined above resonates closely with Bozkurt et al.'s (2024) *Manifesto for Teaching and Learning in a Time of Generative AI*, which does not call for a conclusion. "Instead, [the manifesto] marks the initial steps of an inquiry" (p. 507). This framing aligns with the scenario's pedagogical goal: not to solve the "problem" of AI in education, but to provoke reflection, raise ethical concerns, and initiate critical engagement with the assemblages shaping ITE by positioning PSTs, not as consumers of AI tools, but as participants in a collective pedagogical inquiry grounded in the politics of innovation. The onto-AI lexicon focusses on referring to GenAI not just a tool, but rather as an assemblage that requires ITE to reframe euphemisms like hallucination as error, or personalisation as profiling. These re-definitions serve to foreground power, design, and consequence and resist techno solutionist narratives that present GenAI as neutral and equips PSTs to name what Bozkurt et al. (2024, p. 506) describe "side effects and unintended consequences of GenAI."

In the vignette, the fictional case of Emily, an AI-generated student undetected by a data-driven academic system, makes tangible Bozkurt's warning that GenAI "reflects certain worldviews and ways of thinking" as it can be used nefariously for the power and privilege of some. Second, the PSTs' use of the lexicon in their professional reflections exemplifies how Bozkurt et al. urge educators to "critically examine [GenAI's] outputs and remain cautious about its impact on knowledge generation" (p. 507). This is not a call to reject AI wholesale, but a provocation to engage it with care, ethics, and clarity of purpose. Third, the scenario also addresses Bozkurt's concern that GenAI risks "replacing meaningful interpersonal engagement," especially when both students and educators begin to rely on automation for response, evaluation, and interaction. This is illustrated in the school placement vignette, where GenAI-driven lesson delivery undermines inquiry, marginalises certain student groups, and reduces feedback to impersonal commands. Such practices, the manifesto cautions, "diminishes the role of human agency and undermines authentic learning experiences, leading to a system where GenAI trains itself on human inputs, rather than fostering human growth." The onto-AI lexicon, provide the scaffold to counters this by asking PSTs to rehearse professional dialogue, critically assess relational disruptions, and explicitly link their reflections to Australian Professional Standards for Teachers through language that does not privilege commercial rhetoric.

The manifesto also highlights a crucial institutional tension that prompts the onto AI lexicon for innovation in education, whereby GenAI is developed and deployed by commercial entities with "interests of for-profit corporations," making it essential that educators remain alert to how such systems may "shape the responses that students receive" (p. 508). The scenario's depiction of rapid AI rollouts in ITE, each tool requiring subscriptions and extracting user data, responds directly to this concern. Through the lexicon and facilitated inquiry, the worked example illustrates how teacher educators can invite PSTs to consider how such rollouts require novel praxis to cultivates what Bozkurt et al. call a "collective, conscious effort and action" (p. 508).

CONCLUSION TOWARD AN INSURGENT, INFRASTRUCTURAL PRAXIS

This chapter has argued that GenAI in education is not merely a technological tool but a sociotechnical assemblage that reshapes the ontological, ethical, and pedagogical foundations of initial teacher education. In response, it proposed the onto-AI lexicon and scenario-based inquiry as critical pedagogical intervention to equip preservice teachers with the language, framework, and reflective practice needed to interrogate dominant narratives of innovation and resist the commercial logics that increasingly shape GenAI in teacher education. Drawing on Bozkurt et al.'s (2024) Manifesto for Teaching and Learning in a Time of Generative AI, this chapter positions Initial Teacher Education not as a passive receiver of technological reform, but as a site of critical worldmaking. Through immersive, experiential scenarios, teacher educators were provided with a worked example to cultivate ethical reasoning, professional judgment, and relational pedagogy foregrounded care, complexity, and accountability over efficiency, automation, and compliance. In this example, the onto-AI lexicon was demonstrated to have functioned as framework for naming harm, tracing power, and reclaiming the educational purpose of teaching in an AI-mediated world. However, this work is only beginning. There is a need for future studies to explore how the concept of an onto-AI lexicon could be adapted across diverse contexts, whether urban and rural, well-resourced and underfunded, local and global educational contexts. And how it may foster a culture of resistance, that has a language to speak back to the commercial co-option of education by edtech markets. There is also a need to explore the appetite for reclaiming innovation and reposition ITE at the centre of responsible AI futures.

REFERENCES

Arantes, J. (2024). Understanding Intersections Between GenAI and Pre-Service Teacher Education: What Do We Need to Understand About the Changing Face of Truth in Science Education? *Journal of Science Education and Technology*, •••, 1–12. DOI: 10.1007/s10956-024-10189-7

Arantes, J., & Vicars, M. (2024). Always On Standby: Reshaping Higher Education by acknowledging the psychosocial risk of our postdigital presence in online digital labor. *Higher Education Research & Development*, *1*(1), 1–17. DOI: 10.1080/07294360.2023.2280209

Arantes, J. A. (2022). eMorpheus: The unconscious human labour of producing commercial data in educational settings. [JCEPS]. *The Journal for Critical Education Policy Studies*, *20*(2).

Arantes, J. A. (2024). Redefining Classroom Readiness: How Initial Teacher Training Can Mitigate Risks and Capitalize on the Potential of GenAI. In Academic Integrity in the Age of Artificial Intelligence (pp. 78-92). IGI Global. https://doi.org/DOI: 10.4018/979-8-3693-0240-8.ch005

Arar, K., Tlili, A., Salha, S., & Saiti, A. (2025). Rethinking School Leadership and Policy in the Digital AI Era. *Leadership and Policy in Schools*, *24*(1), 1–3. DOI: 10.1080/15700763.2020.1838555

Ball, S. J. (2020). The errors of redemptive sociology or giving up on hope and despair. *British Journal of Sociology of Education*, *41*(6), 870–880. DOI: 10.1080/01425692.2020.1755230

Biesta, G. (2013). Responsive or responsible? Democratic education for the global networked society. *Policy Futures in Education*, *11*(6), 733–744. DOI: 10.2304/pfie.2013.11.6.733

Bozkurt, A., Xiao, J., Farrow, R., Bai, J. Y., Nerantzi, C., Moore, S., Dron, J., Stracke, C. M., Singh, L., & Crompton, H. (2024). *The manifesto for teaching and learning in a time of generative AI: A critical collective stance to better navigate the future* (Vol. 16). International Council for Open and Distance Education Oslo., DOI: 10.55982/openpraxis.16.4.777

Chen, B., Cheng, J., Wang, C., & Leung, V. (2025). Pedagogical Biases in AI-Powered Educational Tools: The Case of Lesson Plan Generators. Social Innovations Journal, 30. https://doi.org/DOI: 10.31219/osf.io/zqjw5_v1

Cope, B., & Kalantzis, M. (2016). *E-learning ecologies. Nova Iorque*. Routledge., DOI: 10.4324/9781315639215

Corbin, T., Dawson, P., Nicola-Richmond, K., & Partridge, H. (2025). 'Where's the line? It's an absurd line': Towards a framework for acceptable uses of AI in assessment. *Assessment & Evaluation in Higher Education*, *50*(5), 1–13. DOI: 10.1080/02602938.2025.2456207

Crawford, J., Allen, K. A., Pani, B., & Cowling, M. (2024). When artificial intelligence substitutes humans in higher education: The cost of loneliness, student success, and retention. *Studies in Higher Education*, *49*(5), 883–897.

Derrida, J. (2012). Specters of Marx: The state of the debt, the work of mourning and the new international. routledge. https://doi.org/DOI: 10.4324/9780203821619

Gulson, K. N., & Sellar, S. (2024). Anticipating disruption: Artificial intelligence and minor experiments in education policy. *Journal of Education Policy*, *39*(5), 702–717. DOI: 10.1080/02680939.2024.2302474

Gulson, K. N., & Witzenberger, K. (2022). Repackaging authority: Artificial intelligence, automated governance and education trade shows. *Journal of Education Policy*, *37*(1), 145–160. DOI: 10.1080/02680939.2020.1785552

Hancock, J. T., & Bailenson, J. N. (2021). *The social impact of deepfakes* (Vol. 24). Mary Ann Liebert, Inc., DOI: 10.1089/cyber.2021.29208.jth

Hayes, S., & Jandrić, P. (2017). Learning, technologies, and time in the age of global neoliberal capitalism. *Knowledge Cultures*, *5*(2), 11. DOI: 10.22381/KC5220171

Huynh, E., Nyhout, A., Ganea, P., & Chevalier, F. (2020). Designing narrative-focused role-playing games for visualization literacy in young children. *IEEE Transactions on Visualization and Computer Graphics*, *27*(2), 924–934. DOI: 10.1109/TVCG.2020.3030464 PMID: 33048745

Illeris, K. (2007). What do we actually mean by experiential learning? *Human Resource Development Review*, *6*(1), 84–95. DOI: 10.1177/1534484306296828

Jandrić, P., & Ford, D. R. (2022). Postdigital ecopedagogies: Genealogies, contradictions, and possible futures. In Postdigital Ecopedagogies: Genealogies, Contradictions, and Possible Futures (pp. 3-23). Springer. https://doi.org/DOI: 10.1007/978-3-030-97262-2

Kolb, D. A., Boyatzis, R. E., & Mainemelis, C. (2014). Experiential learning theory: Previous research and new directions. In *Perspectives on thinking, learning, and cognitive styles* (pp. 227–247). Routledge., DOI: 10.4324/9781410605986-9

Lee, D., Arnold, M., Srivastava, A., Plastow, K., Strelan, P., Ploeckl, F., Lekkas, D., & Palmer, E. (2024). The impact of generative AI on higher education learning and teaching: A study of educators' perspectives. Computers and Education: Artificial Intelligence, 6, 100221. https://doi.org/https://doi.org/10.1016/j.caeai.2024.100221

Loughran, J. (2013). *Developing a pedagogy of teacher education: Understanding teaching & learning about teaching*. Routledge., DOI: 10.4324/9780203019672

Mishra, P., & Koehler, M. J. (2006). Technological pedagogical content knowledge: A framework for teacher knowledge. *Teachers College Record*, *108*(6), 1017–1054. DOI: 10.1111/j.1467-9620.2006.00684.x

Moon, J. A. (2013). *A handbook of reflective and experiential learning: Theory and practice*. Routledge., DOI: 10.4324/9780203416150

Morozov, E. (2013). *To save everything, click here: The folly of technological solutionism*. Public Affairs.

Noddings, N. (2018). *Philosophy of education*. Routledge., DOI: 10.4324/9780429494864

Puentedura, R. (2006). Transformation, technology, and education. In.

Rahm, L. (2023). Educational imaginaries: Governance at the intersection of technology and education. *Journal of Education Policy*, *38*(1), 46–68. DOI: 10.1080/02680939.2021.1970233

Rahm, L. (2024). 'Help!? My students created an evil AI': On the irony of speculative methods and design fiction. *Learning, Media and Technology*, •••, 1–15. DOI: 10.1080/17439884.2024.2367707

Reid, A., OCallaghan, S., & Lu, Y. (2023). Implementing Australia's AI Ethics Principles: A selection of Responsible AI practices and resources.

Ryan, M., Van Bergen, P., Adlington, R., & Maurice, O. (2025). The positioning of quality and expertise in initial teacher education: Policy enactment in the Australian context. *Australian Educational Researcher*, *52*(3), 1997–2020. Advance online publication. DOI: 10.1007/s13384-024-00796-z

Salinas-Navarro, D. E., Vilalta-Perdomo, E., Michel-Villarreal, R., & Montesinos, L. (2024). Designing experiential learning activities with generative artificial intelligence tools for authentic assessment. *Interactive Technology and Smart Education*, *21*(4), 708–734. DOI: 10.1108/ITSE-12-2023-0236

Scholkmann, A., Olsen, D. S., & Wollscheid, S. (2024). Perspectives on disruptive change in higher education. A critical review of digital transformation during COVID-19. *Higher Education Research & Development, 43*(6), 1355–1369. DOI: 10.1080/07294360.2024.2325140

Selwyn, N., Nemorin, S., & Johnson, N. (2017). High-tech, hard work: An investigation of teachers' work in the digital age. *Learning, Media and Technology, 42*(4), 390–405. DOI: 10.1080/17439884.2016.1252770

Smith, A., & Fressoli, M. (2021). Post-automation. *Futures, 132*, 102778. https://doi.org/https://doi.org/10.1016/j.futures.2021.102778. DOI: 10.1016/j.futures.2021.102778

Van Bergen, P., Ryan, M., Cliff, K., Andrews, R., Ledger, S., Simons, M., Gregory, S., Adlington, R., Zundans-Fraser, L., & Little, C. (2024). Strong (er) Beginnings or more red tape? An analysis of the Teacher Education Expert Panel reforms in initial teacher education and stakeholder responses. Australian Teacher Education Association Conference, Walter, Y. (2024). Embracing the future of Artificial Intelligence in the classroom: The relevance of AI literacy, prompt engineering, and critical thinking in modern education. *International Journal of Educational Technology in Higher Education, 21*(1), 15. DOI: 10.1186/s41239-024-00448-3

Walter, Y. (2024). Embracing the future of Artificial Intelligence in the classroom: The relevance of AI literacy, prompt engineering, and critical thinking in modern education. *International Journal of Educational Technology in Higher Education, 21*(1), 15.

Weise, K., & Metz, C. (2023). When AI chatbots hallucinate. The New York Times, 4.

Williamson, B. (2023a). The Social life of AI in Education. *International Journal of Artificial Intelligence in Education*. Advance online publication. DOI: 10.1007/s40593-023-00342-5

Williamson, B., Eynon, R., Knox, J., & Davies, H. (2023b). Critical perspectives on AI in education: Political economy, discrimination, commercialization, governance and ethics. In *Handbook of artificial intelligence in education* (pp. 553–570). Edward Elgar Publishing., DOI: 10.4337/9781800375413.00037

Witschas, A. (2023). Porn, Power, and Platforms: The (re-)production of hegemonic sexuality through Machine Learning systems. *Publications of the Institute of Cognitive Science, 2023*, 1.

Zhang, R., Li, H., Meng, H., Zhan, J., Gan, H., & Lee, Y.-C. (2024). The Dark Side of AI Companionship: A Taxonomy of Harmful Algorithmic Behaviors in Human-AI Relationships. arXiv preprint arXiv:2410.20130.

KEY TERMS AND DEFINITIONS

Generative Artificial Intelligence (GenAI): AI systems in an assemblage that is capable of creating novel content, including text, images, and audio, through autonomous algorithmic processes.

Initial Teacher Education (ITE): The phase of professional preparation for future teachers.

Scenario-Based: A pedagogical and research approach using structured, imaginative, or speculative scenarios to immerse learners and educators in open-ended, ethically ambiguous situations.

Critical AI Literacy: An expanded form of digital literacy that encompasses not only technical proficiency with AI systems, but also the ability to interrogate, critique, and ethically navigate their social, cultural, and political implications.

onto-AI lexicon: a critical, scenario-based vocabulary developed by educators to reframe ‘innovation’ in the era of generative AI.

Chapter 9

Pre-Service Teachers' Perspectives on the Use of Artificial Intelligence in Learning Processes: Biases, Advantages, and Disadvantages

Ozlem Soydan Oktay
https://orcid.org/0000-0003-2419-405X
Anadolu University, Turkey

Hakan Kılınç
https://orcid.org/0000-0002-4301-1370
Anadolu University, Turkey

ABSTRACT

This study investigates pre-service teachers' perspectives on the use of artificial intelligence (AI) in learning processes, focusing on their biases, perceived advantages, and disadvantages. Grounded in the Education 5.0 framework, which emphasizes diversity, resiliency, adaptability, and sustainability, the study aims to enhance the pedagogical effectiveness of AI and promote its conscious integration into education. Recognizing the dual nature of AI's impact, the research underscores the importance of critical engagement with technology. A qualitative case study design was employed, involving 12 volunteer pre-service teachers from five departments within a faculty of education. Data were collected through open-ended responses

DOI: 10.4018/979-8-3373-7569-4.ch009

via Google Forms. The purposive sampling method enabled an in-depth exploration of participants' views on AI integration across the planning, implementation, and evaluation stages of learning.

INTRODUCTION

With the rapid advancements in artificial intelligence (AI) and the visible impact of these developments on societies and individuals, research on AI has intensified, both to follow technological progress and to understand its implications. This growing interest is primarily driven by the evolution from Industry 4.0 to Industry 5.0, which in turn has triggered the emergence of Society 5.0 and Education 5.0. The swift transition from Industry 4.0 to 5.0 (Fırat, 2023) reflects the educational need to cultivate a workforce aligned with new industrial skills, which has spurred changes in education, eventually leading to the conceptualization of Society 5.0. In other words, the transformations occurring in industry act as a catalyst for changes in society and education.

Industry 5.0 emphasizes human-centricity, sustainability, and resilience. It shifts the focus from merely mastering dominant technologies such as blockchain, cloud computing, and AI—as seen in Industry 4.0—to a sustainability-oriented framework grounded in human-technology collaboration. By integrating human-centric principles with technological developments, Industry 5.0 underscores the necessity of fair labor training that prioritizes employee well-being. As technological progress accelerates exponentially, lifelong learning becomes increasingly vital to help the workforce overcome the challenges of skill development and reskilling (Gamberini & Pluchino, 2024). The "Future of Jobs" report (World Economic Forum, 2025) identifies skill gaps as a significant global obstacle to labor market transformation, calling for the development of skills such as analytical thinking, resilience, flexibility, leadership, creativity, motivation, self-awareness, technological literacy, and self-efficacy. These emerging skill needs signal a call for educational reform. Education 5.0, triggered by Industry 5.0 (Carvalho, 2023; Fissore et al., 2024; Ribeiro et al., 2023), aims not only to facilitate digital transformation but also to enhance societal well-being through the optimization of routine educational processes via human-technology collaboration (Guzder, 2024).

In practical terms, the use of AI in education manifests through automation of administrative tasks, personalized learning and feedback, lesson planning, identifying knowledge and skill gaps, creating chatbots for frequently asked questions, and developing virtual assistants (Gibson et al., 2023). Bozkurt et al. (2024), in their manifesto titled *The Manifesto for Teaching and Learning in a Time of Generative AI*, enumerate several potential benefits of integrating generative AI into educational contexts: time efficiency and productivity, personalized learning and tutoring, self-learning, lifelong learning opportunities, preparation for future workplaces, redefinition of teaching and assessment practices, educational innovation, enhancement of teaching efficiency and effectiveness, support for student autonomy and critical thinking, accessibility and inclusivity, support for faculty and institutional capacity, ethical use and fairness, promotion of creativity and innovation, interdisciplinary learning, collaborative learning and GenAI-supported interactions, and the enhancement of cognitive capacity (Bozkurt et al., 2024, pp. 491–497).

However, potential risks include job displacement, algorithmic bias, the spread of misinformation and deepfakes, data privacy breaches, and concerns related to technological singularity (Thomas, 2025). Within educational settings, potential drawbacks of AI include digital divide and educational inequity, bias and lack of diversity, threats to academic integrity and authentic learning, issues of reliability and misinformation, loss of human values and identity, over-reliance on technology, erosion of cognitive and learning processes, negative impacts on critical and higher-order thinking skills, lack of transparency and understanding, influence on educator professionalism, commercialization and centralization of power, insufficient regulation, privacy concerns, potential misuse and security threats, environmental and sustainability issues, risks of human-AI symbiosis, lack of representation, data distortion, and disruption due to unpreparedness (Bozkurt et al., 2024, pp. 498–506). Among these, algorithmic bias is particularly critical, as it can alter students' educational trajectories and affect their career opportunities and socioeconomic mobility. Given the increasing use of AI in educational decision-support systems, educators and administrators must be continuously trained and made aware of such biases. Educators should be informed and conscious of the transparency of the AI systems they use, the importance placed on diversity, the testing protocols, their rigor, and their adaptability across cultures and contexts (Boateng & Boateng, 2025, p. 2015; Bozkurt et al., 2024, pp. 506–507). Göksel and Bozkurt (2019, p. 232) caution against the direct integration of AI into education without a critical stance and stress the need to define ethical boundaries regarding the use of personal data. They also emphasize the importance of testing and retesting AI-based educational processes to prevent the automation and mechanization of learning. Similarly, Güler, Uğur, and Güler (2025, p. 641) emphasize the importance of raising awareness of ethical risks and addressing access barriers to foster the development of a sustainable and inclusive educational system.

In summary, rather than uncritically embracing AI as a significant technological advancement, there is a clear need—reflected in research and felt by reflective individuals—for a critical, synthesized understanding of the reality it creates and the formation of collective consciousness. Education 5.0 emphasizes the transformative potential of AI technologies to reshape the roles of educators and the ways students interact with knowledge. It promotes consistency in curriculum, innovative teaching and assessment methods, and meaningful learning experiences (Alharbi, 2023, p. 918) while also bringing attention to critical thinking, creativity, and ethical considerations (Shahidi-Hamedani et al., 2024, p. 2). In this context, the core components of Education 5.0 can be identified as diversity/flexibility, learner resilience/sustainability, and adaptation to constantly evolving conditions.

As key stakeholders in the education ecosystem, teachers' and pre-service teachers' perspectives and attitudes toward the use of AI in learning processes can serve as a guide to reinforce the advantages of AI while minimizing algorithmic biases and potential drawbacks.

PURPOSE

This study aims to identify the pre-service teachers' biases and positive and negative perceptions regarding the use of artificial intelligence in learning processes through a case study conducted at the Faculty of Education, Anadolu University. In other words, the objective of the study is to determine how the pedagogical effectiveness of technology can be enhanced and its conscious use can be promoted, in line with the perspectives of pre-service teachers on AI use in learning processes.

Significance

It is widely accepted that the positive or negative outcomes of any technological innovation depend largely on who uses it and how. Therefore, while acknowledging the benefits that AI may offer in education, it is also essential not to overlook its potential drawbacks. Gibson et al. (2023) metaphorically describe AI as a "double-edged sword," asserting that the computational capabilities of AI alter the meaning of "knowing" and "doing." Consequently, they argue for the re-evaluation of many existing theories related to learning, knowledge, skills, performance, creativity, and innovation. To address the need for critical examination of AI in education, they propose a three-level synthesis framework—micro, meso, and macro (Gibson et al., 2023).

Naidu (2024) emphasizes the necessity of designing authentic and productive learning experiences through carefully constructed learning activities. He also highlights the challenges of integrating learning and assessment activities into contextualized experiences such as scenario-based, problem-based, and case-based reasoning, arguing that this task is difficult—if not impossible—for AI to perform effectively. Accordingly, it is essential that learning experiences involving AI tools are designed with awareness and that teachers and pre-service teachers are equipped with the necessary competencies to develop this awareness.

Ağmaz and Ergüleç (2024, p. 601) and Ayduğ and Altınpulluk (2025) note that familiarity with AI usage influences pre-service teachers' approaches to integrating AI into learning processes. In this regard, the current study has the potential to prompt pre-service teachers to reflect on the topic and develop a phenomenon in their minds. Considering that pre-service teachers are the educators of the future, understanding their perspectives on the use of AI in learning processes (planning, implementation, evaluation), recognizing biases, identifying deficiencies, and making appropriate adjustments at the micro, meso, and macro levels may offer valuable contributions.

METHODOLOGY

Research Model

This study encompasses the main components of planning, implementation, and evaluation of learning processes in the context of Education 5.0, which includes diversity/flexibility, learner resilience, adaptation/adaptability, and sustainability. The research adopts a qualitative approach aiming to understand pre-service teachers' perspectives on the use of artificial intelligence and to identify ways to enhance the pedagogical effectiveness of AI technologies and promote their widespread and conscious use in education.

Qualitative research is an approach that facilitates the exploration and understanding of how individuals or groups interpret a social or human problem within a society (Creswell, 2017, p. 4). Among qualitative research methods, the case study design involves collecting detailed data through observations, interviews, audio-visual materials, etc., to describe themes regarding real-life situations (Creswell, 2018, p. 97). Since this study investigates "perspectives on the use of artificial intelligence in learning processes," it has been designed as a case study. Within the scope of the main elements of Education 5.0 and learning processes, this research aims to determine what can be done to enhance the pedagogical effectiveness of technology and promote its conscious use based on pre-service teachers' perspectives on the use of AI in learning processes. The case study process involves the linear execution of steps, including planning and design, preparation, data collection, analysis, and dissemination; however, these steps may be repeated when necessary (Yin, 2018).

Participants

The participants of this research consist of pre-service teachers selected through purposive sampling. The choice of purposive sampling is grounded in the need to obtain an in-depth understanding. In other words, the necessity for deep insight reveals the logic and strength of purposive sampling. As Patton (2018) also emphasizes, ensuring depth in qualitative research is a critical requirement. To achieve this depth, purposive sampling allows for the selection of participants who best represent the most relevant and information-rich cases (Best & Kahn, 2017). Accordingly, data were collected via Google Forms from 12 volunteer pre-service teachers. The participants were enrolled in five different departments within a four-year faculty of education, ranging from first- to fourth-year students, and were predominantly between the ages of 19 and 25 (See Table 1).

Table 1. Participants and Their Characteristics

Sequence No	Nickname	Department	Duration in the Training Process	Age
1	K1	Special Education Teaching	3	43
2	K2	Preschool Education	2	21
3	K3	Preschool Education	2	19
4	K4	Special Education Teaching	3	22
5	K5	Special Education Teaching	2	22
6	K6	Computer Education and Instructional Technology	1	20
7	K7	Computer Education and Instructional Technology	2	21
8	K8	Teaching Painting and Drawing	2	21
9	K9	Computer Education and Instructional Technology	4	25
10	K10	Computer Education and Instructional Technology	2	21
11	K11	Animation	3	22
12	K12	Special Education Teaching	2	23

Data Collection Method

The data collection method used in this study, conducted with pre-service teachers enrolled in the Faculty of Education at Anadolu University, is the semi-structured interview—one of the qualitative data collection techniques. Semi-structured interviews, which are one of the key sources in case studies, enable the explanation of the investigated phenomenon through its causes and processes, making it possible to understand participants' perspectives by drawing upon their insights (Yin, 2018). According to Patton (2018), interviewing is a process through which open-ended questions are posed to participants, enabling them to articulate their viewpoints and personal narratives—thoughts that may not be directly observable.

Data Collection Tool

The data collection tool employed in this study was a semi-structured interview form created using Google Forms, designed to elicit long-text responses to open-ended questions. In line with Creswell's (2019) emphasis on the necessity of developing an interview form in qualitative research, the researchers prepared a semi-structured interview form. The form includes information regarding the purpose of the study and the researchers' expectations. Based on feedback from subject-matter experts, necessary revisions were made to finalize the interview form.

Data Collection Process

The researchers contacted pre-service teachers at Anadolu University Faculty of Education and shared the link to the semi-structured interview form, created on Google Forms, which was to be completed with long-text answers. Data were collected from 12 pre-service teachers between May 28 and June 11, 2025.

DATA ANALYSIS

The data collected from participants via Google Forms were exported as an Excel spreadsheet. In the Excel file, each entry was assigned a sequence number, and data regarding participants' academic departments and their years of study were standardized. The data were then imported into MaxQDA Analytics Pro software for analysis. Upon inspection, the data were prepared for further analysis, and a validity check was carried out by two field experts.

The semi-structured interview data were analyzed using an inductive approach involving both descriptive and content analysis, supported by the MaxQDA24 software package. During the analysis process, the researchers consulted with two field experts regarding the coding system and identified themes.

Credibility of the Study

To eliminate potential threats to validity in qualitative research and provide evidence for credibility, it is essential that the researcher(s) adhere to established procedures. In this regard, the interview form was reviewed and finalized after receiving expert feedback from two field specialists. Similarly, the transcripts of the interviews were subjected to accuracy checks by two experts, and expert opinions were also gathered for the coding system and thematic structures. According to Patton (2018), triangulation is based on the assumption that no single method can fully solve the issue of competing explanations. Furthermore, since each method can reveal different aspects of empirical reality, using multiple methods in data collection and analysis is beneficial to the study. Triangulation helps to eliminate bias and improve the reliability of the data (Patton, 2018, p. 554).

THEORETICAL MATRIX AND RESEARCH QUESTIONS

This study aims to determine the preconceptions, positive and negative perceptions of pre-service teachers at Anadolu University Faculty of Education regarding the use of artificial intelligence (AI) in learning processes through a case study design. Learning processes are addressed under the three main components: planning, implementation, and evaluation. A theoretical matrix was developed using the core elements of Education 5.0—diversity/flexibility, learner resilience, adaptation/adaptability, and sustainability—combined with these three components of the learning process (See Table 2). Based on this theoretical matrix, the research questions were developed. In order to ensure the clarity of the questions and to provide a holistic understanding of the preconceptions, advantages, and disadvantages of AI use in learning processes, follow-up (probe), questions were also developed for each main research question to further elaborate on the participants' responses.

Diversity / Flexibility

Question 1. What advantages or disadvantages do you think the use of AI in the learning processes of individuals from diverse cultural backgrounds, socioeconomic statuses, ethnic origins, genders, and abilities may bring?

> Probe 1.1. Why is it or is it not possible for AI to exhibit a flexible (objective) stance in determining goals, resources, and strategies in the learning processes of individuals with diverse backgrounds?

Probe 1.2. Why is it or is it not possible for AI to provide complete and flexible contextual pathways in the implementation of strategies aimed at achieving predetermined learning outcomes for individuals from diverse backgrounds?
Probe 1.3. Why is it or is it not possible for AI decision-support systems to evaluate individuals from diverse backgrounds in an equitable and fair manner during formative and summative assessments?

Learner Resilience

Question 2. What is the impact of AI usage in learning processes on developing learner resilience with a human-centered approach, especially in the context of workforce competencies required by Industry 5.0? Are these effects positive or negative, and what might they be?

Probe 2.1. How can AI determine learning goals and resources at a level that challenges the student without causing them to give up?
Probe 2.2. How can AI help students develop the ability to adapt to different situations?
Probe 2.3. How can AI ensure students continue learning without dropping out and help them experience success?

Adaptation

Question 3. What are the potential benefits or drawbacks of AI personalizing learning with a student-centered approach?

Probe 3.1. Why does the personalization of learning goals and resources based on student characteristics raise the risk of algorithmic bias?
Probe 3.2. Why is it beneficial or harmful for AI to use learning analytics to increase student engagement in specific areas?
Probe 3.3. Under what conditions can the use of formative and summative feedback by AI to shape student development be entirely entrusted to AI?

Sustainability

Question 4. What is the impact of AI use in learning processes on creating a balanced learning environment in terms of environmental, social, and economic dimensions?

Probe 4.1. What outcomes might result from using AI in determining goals and resources and creating strategies in a way that supports sustainability through environmental, equity, and economic balance?
Probe 4.2. How can AI ensure the implementation of active learning strategies in learning processes while providing equitable and economically sensitive contextual learning opportunities for all?
Probe 4.3. What potential risks could arise from AI decision-support systems shaping student knowledge and skills through formative assessment in support of sustainability?

Table 2. Theoretical Matrix

Usability of Artificial Intelligence in Learning Processes	LEARNING PROCESSES		
	Planning	**Application**	**Evaluation**
Diversity/Flexibility	Artificial intelligence can adopt a flexible stance (an objective approach) in determining goals and resources and creating strategies for the learning processes of individuals with diverse cultural backgrounds, socioeconomic statuses, ethnicities, genders, and abilities.	Artificial intelligence can provide the necessary contextual pathways comprehensively and flexibly for activities that depend on strategies for achieving the learning outcomes identified in the learning processes of individuals with diverse cultural backgrounds, socioeconomic statuses, ethnicities, genders, and abilities.	AI decision-support systems can fairly and equitably evaluate individuals from diverse cultural backgrounds, socioeconomic statuses, ethnicities, genders, and abilities during both formative and summative assessments.
Learner Resilience	Artificial intelligence can enable the creation of strategies by identifying learning goals and resources at a level that pushes the limits in line with the characteristics and needs of the student without causing them to give up.	Artificial intelligence can enable students to develop adaptive skills by creating activities tailored to the characteristics of each student and the challenges they may face in their specific context.	By maintaining intrinsic motivation through timely and relevant feedback, AI can enable students to continue learning and experience success without dropping out.
Adaptation	AI can personalize goals and resources based on students' past experiences, knowledge, and readiness.	Artificial intelligence, with the help of learning analytics, can tailor arrangements to meet the needs of individual students, thereby increasing their participation and concentration in areas where they are deficient in activities.	Can support student development by using formative and summative feedback in line with student needs.
Sustainability	The use of artificial intelligence to identify goals, resources, and strategies in learning processes can support sustainability by creating a balance between environment, equity, and economy.	In implementing strategies for active learning, artificial intelligence can create contexts that apply acquired knowledge in a balanced way, taking both equity and economic factors into account.	AI decision support systems can enable learning how to use the knowledge gained through formative assessment to make the world a better place to live. Thus, it can support sustainability.

FINDINGS

This section presents the findings obtained from the analysis of the data collected through semi-structured interviews conducted with pre-service teachers via Google Forms, as well as interpretations based on those findings. The study aimed to identify pre-service teachers' positive and negative opinions, along with their preconceptions regarding the usability of AI in learning processes. The responses to sixteen research questions were analyzed using MaxQDA, and the pre-service teachers' views were grouped to define the main themes. Accordingly, four overarching themes were identified:

- Providing Diversity/Flexibility
- Enhancing Learner Resilience
- Supporting Adaptation/Adaptability
- Ensuring Sustainability

These four main themes were further detailed into sixteen sub-themes and seventy-four codes. The findings are presented along with direct quotations from participants to support the analysis.

Main Theme 1 – Providing Diversity/Flexibility

Based on the responses of pre-service teachers to the first four research questions, the following sub-themes emerged under the main theme of "Providing Diversity/Flexibility," as analyzed through MaxQDA24:

- Impact of AI on Learning Processes (f=25)
- Flexible and Objective Planning (f=14)
- Complete and Flexible Implementation (f=14)
- Equitable and Fair Assessment (f=14)

A total of eighteen sub-codes were identified under these four sub-themes. The frequency table for these themes is presented in Figure 1, and a visual model representing the overarching theme is shown in Figure 2.

Figure 1. Themes forming the main theme of Offering Diversity/Flexibility

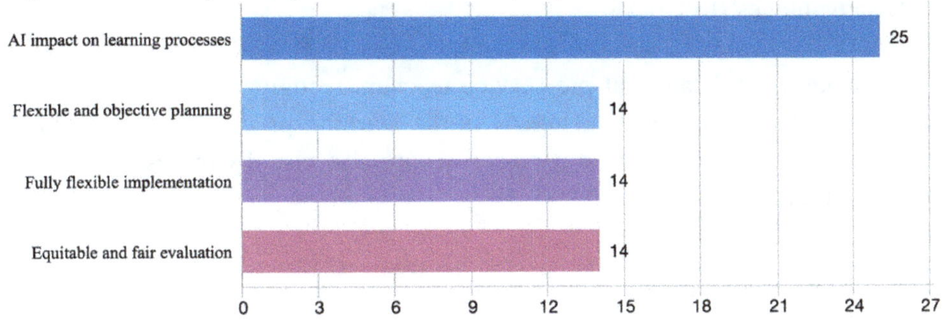

Figure 2. The main theme model of providing diversity/flexibility

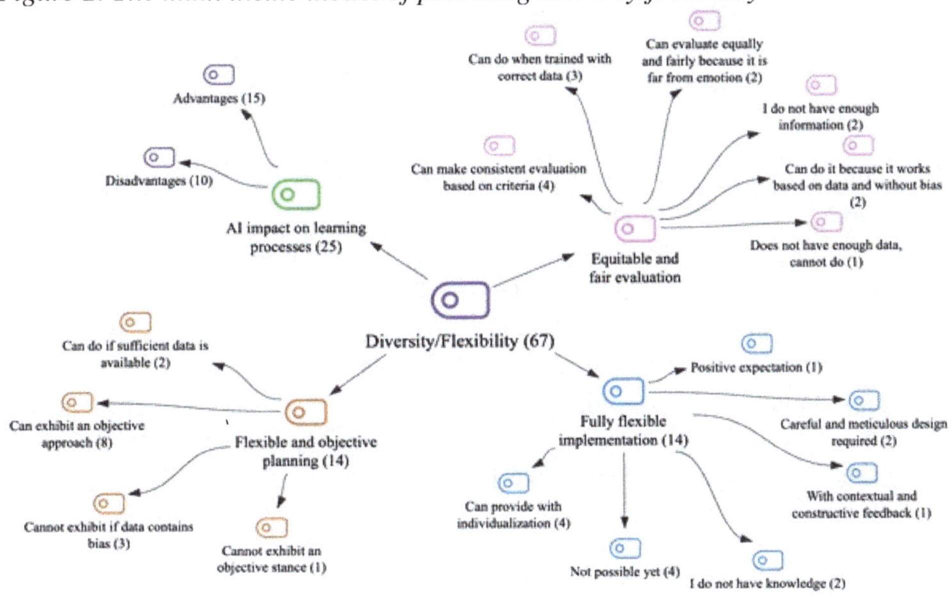

Impact of AI on Learning Processes (f=25)

The first research question aimed to understand pre-service teachers' general views on the impact of AI on learning processes. Responses to the question "What advantages or disadvantages do you think the use of AI in learning processes may have for individuals from different cultural backgrounds, socioeconomic statuses, ethnicities, genders, and abilities?" were analyzed, resulting in two sub-themes:

- Advantages (f=15)
- Disadvantages (f=10)

The responses indicate that pre-service teachers recognize both potential advantages and disadvantages of using AI in the learning processes of individuals from diverse backgrounds. These perspectives are also visually represented in the frequency graph in Figure 3.

Figure 3. AI impact on the learning process

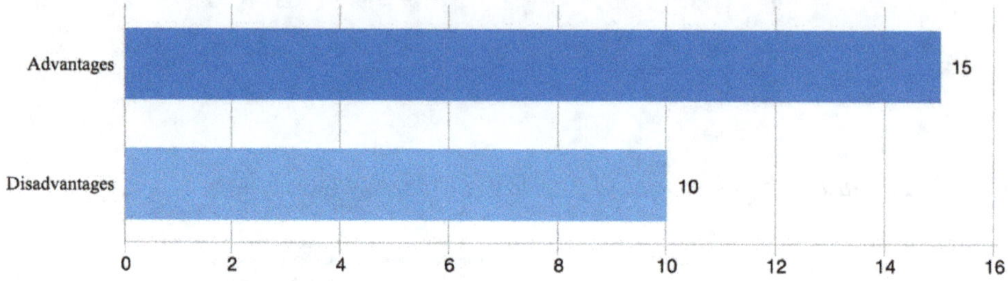

Among the advantages of using AI in learning processes, the following were emphasized:

- Enables Personalized Learning (f=6)
- Promotes Educational Equity (f=4)
- Facilitates Access to Knowledge and Experience (f=3)
- Supports Inclusive Learning Environments (f=2)

These advantages are presented in Figure 4.

Figure 4. Advantages of using AI in the learning process

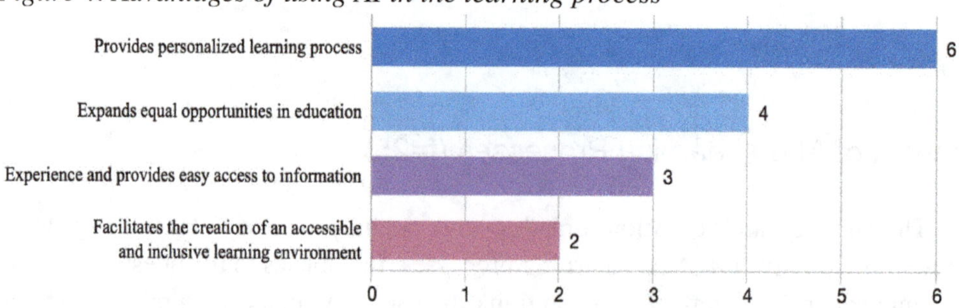

Twelve pre-service teachers emphasized "personalized learning" as a key advantage. Selected direct quotations include:

"AI can offer personalized learning opportunities for individuals from different cultural and socioeconomic backgrounds, providing a major advantage." (K9)

"If you are trying to learn in a culture you do not belong to, AI can facilitate learning by offering examples and language adapted to your experiences." (K12)

"AI should provide personalized learning processes for individuals from diverse backgrounds. This personalization goes beyond content and layers of instruction, extending also to learning pace, thus providing an advantage." (K7)

"I believe it can eliminate disadvantages." (K1)

These views suggest that personalizing content to match the needs and expectations of diverse learners can mitigate the potential disadvantages posed by such diversity.

The second most frequently cited advantage was **promoting educational equity** (f=4). This refers to the potential of AI to expand access to educational opportunities for learners who face geographical or resource-based constraints:

"It can broaden educational opportunities for students in remote or resource-limited areas." (K3)

"AI could be highly advantageous if there is equal access." (K12)

However, it is emphasized that such benefits are contingent upon equal access to AI technologies. Without such access, AI could inadvertently deepen educational inequalities—an issue also acknowledged by participants when listing disadvantages.

One of the advantages that the use of AI in learning processes will provide to diverse learners is expressed as "It provides easy access to experience and knowledge" (f=3), and some of the direct quotes regarding this advantage are presented below.

"People can answer the questions in their minds more easily in this way." (K6)

"...it provides easy access to experiences and information that they would not normally have." (K11)

AI easily answers the questions in the minds of diverse learners in their learning processes with instant feedback. In other words, AI offers the opportunity to facilitate diverse learners' access to different experiences and knowledge by providing the convenience of asking questions and finding answers.

The statement "It facilitates creating an accessible, inclusive learning environment" (f=2) is the last of the advantages that the use of AI in learning processes listed by the prospective teachers. Direct quotes regarding facilitating the creation of an accessible, inclusive learning environment are as follows:

...In my opinion, AI positively affects learning environments, especially for students with special needs or physical disabilities, by providing them with effective content organization and presentation of different worlds without leaving their seats and by enabling them to participate in activities that they cannot physically participate in. (K4)

AI-supported tools can make learning more accessible for students with disabilities. Features such as audio readers, virtual sign language interpreters, alternative input methods, and adaptation of visual or audio materials help create an inclusive learning environment. (K3)

In learning processes, AI-supported tools have the potential to facilitate the production of educational materials that will meet the special needs of learners and contribute to the creation and presentation of flexible materials suitable for diversity.

Among the disadvantages of using AI in learning processes, the following statements stand out: "Economic, geographical access limitations" (f=4), "Limitations in interaction and collaborative learning" (f=2), and "Algorithmic bias" (f=2). "Transfer of false information" (f=1) and "Creates laziness of thought" (f=1) are among the disadvantages of using AI in the learning process (See Figure 5).

Figure 5. Disadvantages of using AI in the learning process

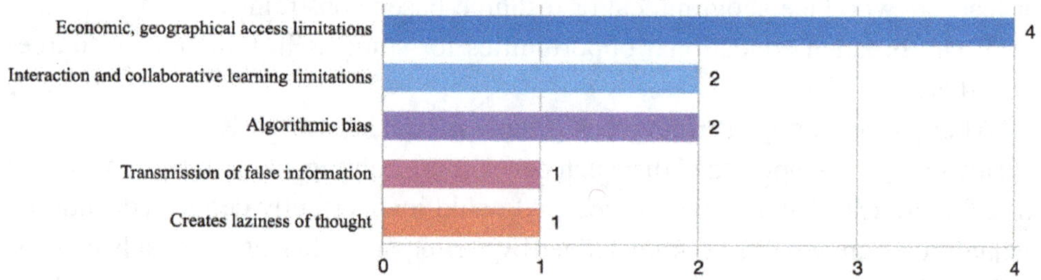

Among the disadvantages of using AI in learning processes, "Economic, geographical access limitations" (f=4) is the most emphasized view, and direct quotes regarding the view are as follows.

I think it creates an advantage for those who have access to computers and the internet and a disadvantage for those who do not. The fact that not every individual has equal opportunities, for example, issues such as internet or device access, can prevent everyone from benefiting from this technology in the same way. (K9)

"...disadvantage for some low-income individuals and rural areas" (K8)

"...the fact that not everyone receives education with equal opportunities creates an inequality of opportunity." (K12)

Prospective teachers emphasize the economic and geographical access limitations, especially the lack of budget for having equipment and internet access, and state that this may make it impossible to benefit from AI opportunities in learning processes. They also bring up the possibility that these access limitations will create inequality of opportunity in learning processes.

The second disadvantage that will arise from the use of AI in learning processes is expressed as "Interaction and collaborative learning limitations." These views, which express the restriction of social interaction between learners and the decrease in collaborative learning opportunities, are presented below.

As a disadvantage, I can say that there may be limitations, such as a lack of human interaction and the impossibility of collaborative learning. (K7)

As a disadvantage, there is a decrease in interaction between individuals. (K10)

"Algorithmic bias" (f=2) is one of the views emphasized by prospective teachers. It is stated that the data on which the AI is trained contains biases such as gender, race, language, and religion, and therefore, training the AI with an approach that is not sensitive to learner diversity may lead to the exclusion or misdirection of certain groups or segments in the learning process.

"...if the data that the AI is trained on is biased, some groups may be excluded or misled." (K9)

"...a big disadvantage if diversity is not addressed" (K2)

Apart from these, other disadvantages that may arise from the use of AI in learning processes include the possibility of transferring false information and creating laziness of thought among the opinions expressed by prospective teachers.

Flexible and Objective Planning (f=14)

Under the main theme of "Offering Diversity/Flexibility," the research question "Why is it possible or not possible for artificial intelligence to exhibit a flexible stance (objective approach) in determining the goals and resources in the learning processes of individuals with different cultural backgrounds, socioeconomic statuses, ethnic origins, genders and abilities, and creating strategies?" was analyzed to reach the theme of "Flexible and Objective Planning." The coded section-based frequency graph for the theme of "Flexible and Objective Planning" is given in Figure 6.

Figure 6. Sub-themes forming the theme of flexible and objective planning

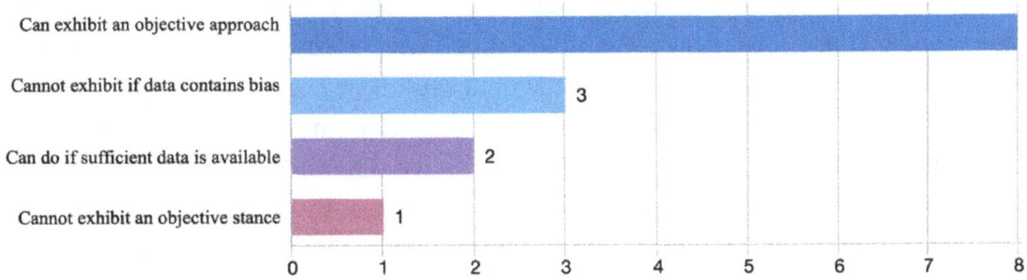

Under the theme of "Flexible and Objective Planning," prospective teachers emphasize the view that AI can exhibit an objective approach with a flexible stance in determining goals and resources and creating strategies in the learning processes of individuals with different cultural backgrounds, socioeconomic situations, ethnic origins, genders, and abilities. There are also views that AI can make flexible and objective planning if it has sufficient data. Some of the direct quotes regarding these views are as follows:

AI can dynamically adjust learning materials, difficulty levels, and feedback mechanisms according to each student's individual learning pace, strengths, and weaknesses. This adaptability can go beyond the "one size fits all" approach by offering special solutions to students with different skill levels. (K3)

It can take an objective approach and convey the learning environment to the student or individual in the desired way without discriminating on the basis of language, religion, or color. (K4)

I think it is possible for AI to take an objective stance, as it can create personalized goals and resources with individual analyses and provide flexibility based on diversity. (K7)

"...it takes an objective approach because it works based on data, not emotions." (K10)

"It can be possible depending on the data it feeds on." (K9)

Although the dominant view is that AI can make flexible and objective planning during the learning process, there are also student candidates who express the opinion that it cannot make flexible and objective planning, and some of the direct quotes regarding these opinions are listed below.

AI takes the resources fed to it without weighing them and, therefore, cannot exhibit a truly objective stance because it is not something that can think, produce ideas, and make judgments on its own. (K11)

It will only be possible to be completely impartial if it is trained in an ideal way. Educational data should be meticulously organized in terms of gender, culture, and social norms. (K7)

AI can personalize the learning process for individuals in such matters because it works based on data, provides fast feedback, and is not affected by emotional biases. However, this is not always the case. If the data used is one-sided or does not reflect diversity, AI can make biased decisions. In addition, it cannot fully understand issues such as emotions, cultural values, and equality. Therefore, whether AI can be fair and flexible may vary depending on the approach of the person using it. (K12)

Since we train it with the data we give, if there is bias in our data, AI can learn and reflect biases. If this is the case, it may not be possible to exhibit an objective approach. (K10)

In general, to summarize, it is expressed that teacher candidates can exhibit flexibility that embraces learner diversity by making flexible and objective planning if AI is trained in a way that is free from prejudices and with appropriate data.

Complete Flexible Implementation (f=14)

Under the main theme of "Offering Diversity/Flexibility," the research question "Why is it possible or not possible for artificial intelligence to offer the necessary contextual paths in a complete and flexible manner in the implementation of strategies for achieving the determined learning outcomes in the learning processes of individuals with different cultural backgrounds, socioeconomic statuses, ethnic origins, genders, and abilities?" was analyzed and the theme of "Complete Flexible Implementation" was reached. The coded section-based frequency distribution graph of the sub-themes formed under the theme of "Complete Flexible Implementation" includes the opinions of the prospective teachers on whether it is possible and how it is possible for AI to offer complete flexible implementation in the application phase of the learning process (See Figure 7).

Figure 7. Sub-themes that make up the theme of complete flexible implementation

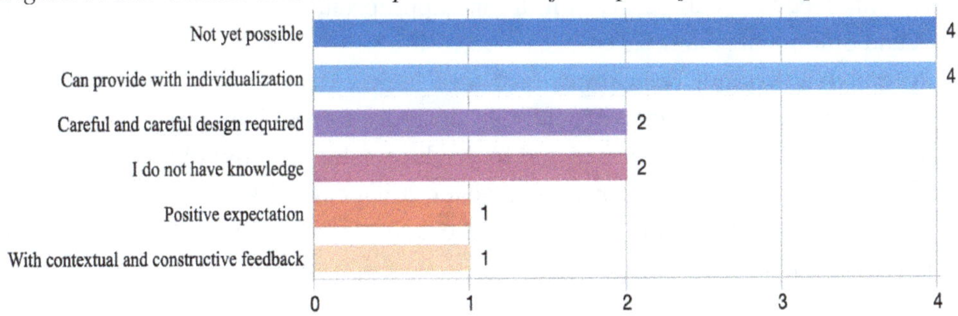

When the subthemes forming the theme of complete flexible implementation are examined, it is seen that the prospective teachers have different views on the fact that AI can provide the necessary contextual paths in a complete and flexible manner in the implementation of strategies for achieving the determined learning outcomes in the learning processes of individuals with different cultural backgrounds, socioeconomic situations, ethnic origins, genders, and abilities. While some of the prospective teachers stated that this is not yet possible, some of them stated that complete flexible application could be possible with individualization contextual and constructive feedback, and they expressed the necessity of careful and meticulous design. In addition, two prospective teachers stated that they did not have information regarding the subject, while one of the prospective teachers stated that his expectation was that AI could provide complete, flexible application. Some of the linear quotes regarding the views on the theme in question are presented below.

It cannot offer complete because AI cannot produce creative ideas; it can only create a collage of the materials it has. (K11)

AI cannot always be complete sometimes; it does not give me confidence because it also transfers its own data (K8)

It needs to bring together many functional application methods in certain areas, and thus, it can provide us with the best environment. (K6)

AI can offer learning paths suitable for different people because it can make personalized plans. However, this does not always work. If AI is not trained with enough different examples, it may not be able to produce solutions suitable for everyone. In other words, it needs to be designed carefully and meticulously in order to work correctly and fairly. (K12)

I think that AI can offer customized content and contextual paths that appeal to the individual's learning speed and learning style by making analyses suitable for the needs of individuals in line with personal data. (K7)

AI can detect not only the right/wrong answer but also the deficiencies in the student's thinking process and provide contextual and constructive feedback accordingly. This feedback can be given in a tone appropriate to the student's cognitive level and emotional state. (K3)

Although it has not been prioritized to a large extent, it is necessary for AI to be designed carefully and meticulously in order to provide complete, flexible applications in learning processes and to produce solutions suitable for everyone. In addition, as stated by a prospective teacher, it is possible to say that in order to establish trust in AI in learning processes, the data used in the training of AI should be impartial and unbiased.

Equitable and Fair Assessment (f=14)

Within the main theme of "Offering Diversity/Flexibility," the sub-theme of "Equitable and Fair Assessment" emerged from the analysis of responses to the research question: "Why is it possible or not possible for AI-based decision-support systems to evaluate individuals from different cultural backgrounds, socioeconomic statuses, ethnicities, genders, and abilities in a fair and equitable manner during formative and summative assessments?"

This theme encapsulates pre-service teachers' views on whether AI can adopt an equitable and fair approach in assessing learners with diverse characteristics during the learning process and, if so, what conditions must be met to ensure such fairness. A frequency graph based on the coded segments related to these sub-themes is presented in Figure 8.

Figure 8. Sub-themes that make up the theme of equitable and fair evaluation

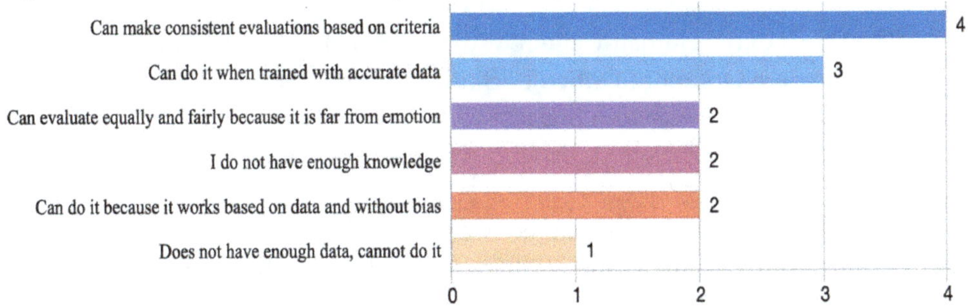

Two pre-service teachers did not respond to the question regarding whether AI can conduct equitable and fair assessments in learning processes, stating that they lacked sufficient knowledge on the subject. One participant expressed the opinion that AI cannot perform fair and equitable evaluations due to insufficient data. The remaining pre-service teachers believed that AI could indeed conduct equitable and fair assessments within learning processes. Among them, three emphasized that this would only be possible if AI systems were trained with accurate and unbiased data. Selected direct quotations reflecting these views are as follows:

"If the data used to train AI are incomplete or biased, the resulting evaluations may also be biased and unfair." (K12)

"If AI is properly trained, it can reach unbiased outcomes. It is possible." (K8)

"AI can assess people in an equal and fair manner because it lacks emotional bias." (K12)

"Since it operates independently of emotional influence, it has the potential to evaluate individuals from different backgrounds more equitably." (K10)

"Because AI operates based on data and without bias, it can evaluate different individuals in an equitable and fair manner. This contributes to objectivity and consistency in assessment processes." (K7)

"AI systems assess consistently according to predefined criteria. This may reduce human-related variability across different students or at different times, thereby enabling a more standardized—and thus more equitable—assessment process." (K3)

In general, teacher candidates think that AI can make equal and fair evaluations in learning processes because it is data-oriented, criteria-based, and unemotional. In addition, some teacher candidates state the importance of training AI with accurate data in order to make equal and fair evaluations.

Main Theme 2-Developing Learner Resilience

Under the main theme of "Developing Learner Resilience," which was reached based on the answers given by the teacher candidates to the research questions 5-6-7-8,

- "The Effect of the Human-Centered Approach on Learner Resilience" (f=19),
- "Planning the Optimum Difficulty-Skill Balance" (f=14),
- "Ensuring the Process with Success Experience" (f=13) and
- "Developing Adaptation Skills with Applications" (f=12)

themes, a total of nineteen sub-themes were formed under these four themes. The model created for the main theme of "Developing Learner Resilience" is given in Figure 9, and the coded section-based frequency table of the themes formed under the main theme is given in Figure 10.

Figure 9. Developing learner resilience main theme model

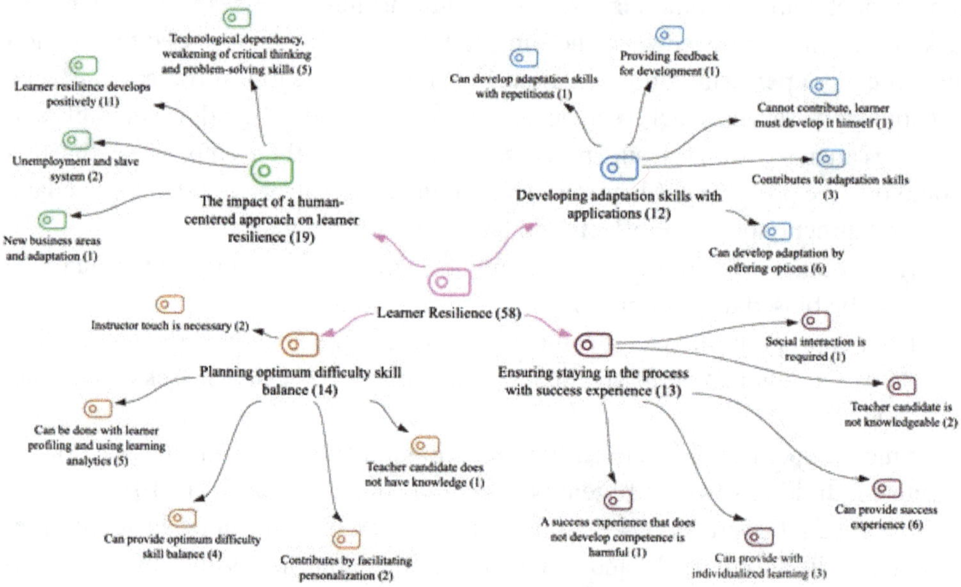

Figure 10. Themes forming the main theme of developing learner resilience

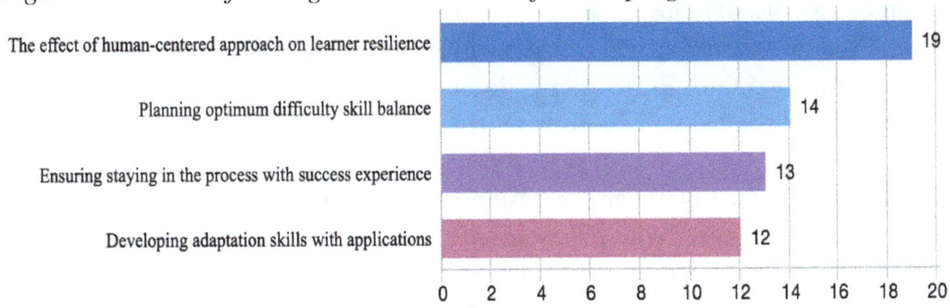

The Effect of Human-Centered Approach on Learner Resilience (f=19)

Under the main theme of "Developing Learner Resilience," the research questions "What is the effect of the use of artificial intelligence in learning processes on developing learner resilience with a human-centered approach while creating workforce competencies in line with Industry 5.0 needs (positive-negative); what do you think these effects might be?" were analyzed and the theme of "The Effect of the Human-Centered Approach on Learner Resilience" was reached. The coded section-based frequency graph for the theme of "The Effect of the Human-Centered Approach on Learner Resilience" is given in Figure 11.

Figure 11. Sub-themes that make up the theme of the impact of the human-centered approach on learner resilience

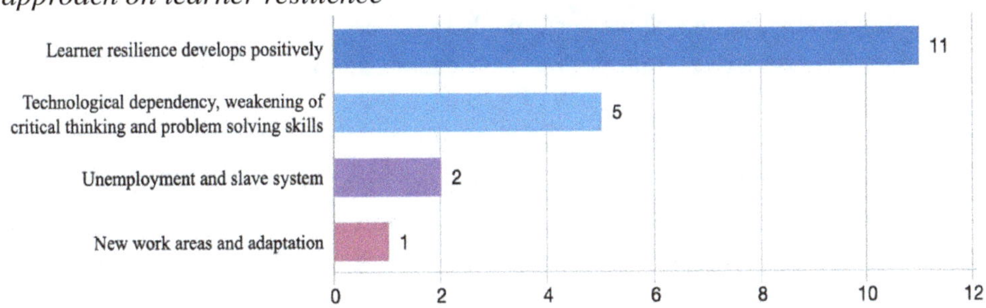

The majority of teacher candidates state that AI will have a positive impact on developing learner resilience with a human-centered approach while creating workforce competencies in line with Industry 5.0 needs. Direct quotes regarding the opinions are listed below.

With a personalized learning process while creating workforce competencies in line with Industry 5.0 needs, learner endurance develops positively. (K7)

When AI is designed with a human focus, learner endurance can be developed positively (K8)

If AI is used correctly, it can increase people's learning power. It provides personalized help, recognizes where they are struggling, and offers support. This helps the learner to be more patient, strong, and secure. (K12)

Some teacher candidates state that AI may create some negative effects beyond contributing to the development of learner resilience with a human-centered approach while creating workforce competencies in line with Industry 5.0 needs. Some of the direct quotes regarding these views are as follows:

> *"...dependency on technology and weakening of problem-solving skills can be seen in individuals." (K7)*
>
> *"...if technology is not positioned as a tool that supports human elements, it can be negative." (K8)*
>
> *"...an individual's critical thinking and problem-solving skills can be dulled." (K10)*

Leaving everything to artificial intelligence can weaken a person's ability to think and find solutions. In other words, if used in a balanced way, it can be very beneficial, but if overdone, it can be harmful. (K12)

AI will really lighten human power in the future; this is a very good development. In the future, rather than reducing work capacity, it will create new areas, and those who can adapt to it and know how to use it will come to the fore. (K6)

It will take people's jobs, and this will negatively affect people's livelihoods; even if different solutions are found for this, people will be crushed under this situation, and AI will actually create a slave system. (K4)

The negative side will be that people who cannot adapt will be eliminated from the system. (K9)

Prospective teachers state that, beyond developing learner resilience, the use of AI in learning processes may cause a weakening of critical thinking, problem-solving skills, and thinking skills. They also put forward the view that another element as important as learner resilience is adapting to new work areas that emerge due to the use of AI and state that people who cannot adapt to new areas by developing their adaptability skills will experience economic difficulties.

Planning the optimum difficulty skill balance (f=14)

Under the main theme of "Developing Learner Resilience," the research question "How can artificial intelligence enable or not enable the creation of strategies by determining learning goals and resources at a level that will push the student's limits in line with their characteristics and needs but will not cause them to give up?" was analyzed and the theme of "Planning Optimum Difficulty Skill Balance" was reached. The coded section-based frequency graph for the theme of "Planning Optimum Difficulty Skill Balance" is given in Figure 12.

Figure 12. Sub-themes that make up the theme of planning the optimum challenge skill balance

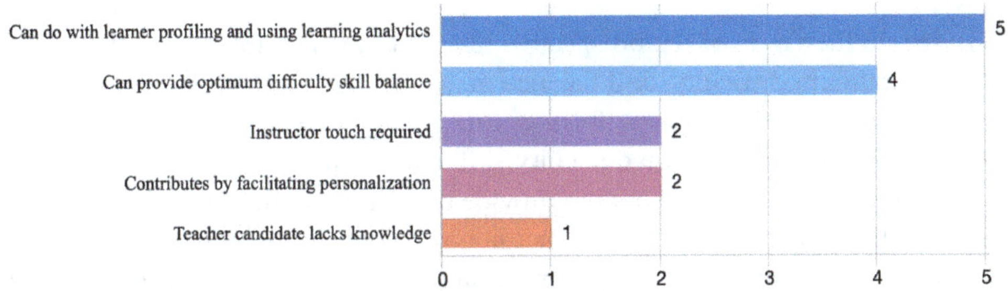

When examining pre-service teachers' views on the theme of planning for the optimal challenge-skill balance, it was found that one participant refrained from responding due to a lack of knowledge, and four participants simply stated that AI could achieve this balance without offering further explanation. One participant noted that the involvement of an instructor would still be necessary to plan the optimal challenge-skill balance effectively. At this point, the dominant view was that AI could plan for an optimal balance between challenge and skill by employing learner profiling and learning analytics. Selected direct quotations reflecting these views are listed below:

It can create learning strategies by offering neither too easy nor too difficult targets and resources that can be dynamically adjusted according to the student's performance. (K10)

In a classical learning environment, in order for us to respond to all the needs and individual learning styles of a learner, the learner may need to be unique. However, conditions require us to include learners. At this point, artificial intelligence has a facilitating effect. (K7)

In order to provide this according to the student, much more advanced elements such as face reading systems will be needed. This means creating a human teacher from scratch. At this stage, since there will be no direct contact with the student, a teacher/academic touch will definitely be needed, but it will greatly improve the processes. (K9)

Not reaching the point of giving up while pushing the limits will only be possible with very fine calculations specific to the person. I think that when sufficient data is provided to the artificial intelligence in question about the learner, the desired point can be reached in terms of learning targets and resources. (K7)

AI can understand the level of the student by analyzing his/her past data and thus offer challenging but achievable targets. (K8)

AI can set the right goals by understanding what the student knows, how they learn, and where they have difficulty. In this way, the student has difficulty learning but does not give up. As they progress step by step, their self-confidence increases. (K12)

Based on the views of the prospective teachers, it is possible to say that planning the optimum difficulty-skill balance of AI can be possible by analyzing the learner's past data and current performance data; in other words, if it has sufficient data, AI can plan the optimum difficulty-skill balance for the learner. In planning the learning process, it is essential to provide the optimum difficulty-skill balance and to challenge the learner enough, but not to the extent that this challenge will cause them to give up. In this way, it is possible to ensure that the learner stays in the process and increases their self-confidence.

Ensuring Remaining in the Process with Success Experience (f=13)

The theme of "Ensuring Staying in the Process with Success Experience" was reached by analyzing the responses of the prospective teachers to the research question, "How can artificial intelligence enable or not enable the student to experience success by continuing to learn without drop-out?" under the main theme of "Developing Learner Resilience." The coded section-based frequency graph for the theme of "Ensuring Staying in the Process with Success Experience" is given in Figure 13.

Figure 13. Sub-themes that make up the theme of ensuring to stay in the process with the experience of success

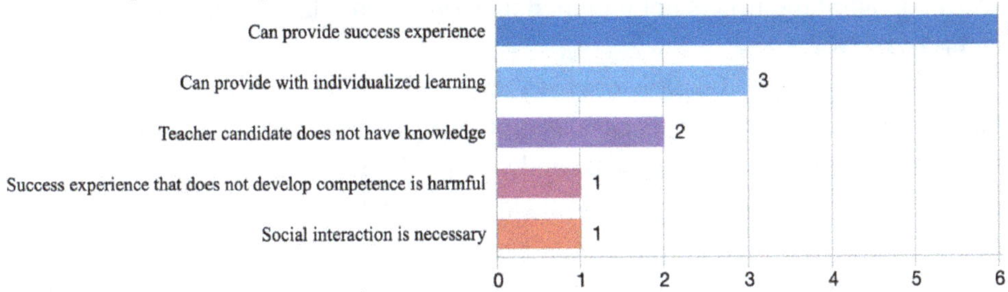

It is seen that the majority of the prospective teachers have the opinion that it is possible for students to experience success by continuing to learn without dropping out with the integration of AI into the learning process, and some of the direct quotes regarding their opinions are given below.

"...can make the student active and achieve more active participation." (K2)

By ensuring that the student has the necessary information and is in constant communication. (K6)

If the student notices when he/she is struggling and provides support immediately, it can prevent the student from feeling lonely and giving up. The more he/she succeeds, the more motivated he/she becomes, which keeps him/her committed to learning. (K12)

Since it can provide individualized learning according to the student's level of interest, pace, and style, it supports motivation. In this way, the student can continue learning without interruption. (K12)

AI can prevent drop-out by supporting and motivating the student with content that is appropriate for his/her interest and level. However, if it offers irrelevant or incorrect content, it can reduce motivation and cause dropout. (K8)

Based on the views of the prospective teachers, it is possible to ensure that learners are active in the application phase by using AI in the learning process, thus supporting active participation. However, in order to achieve this, it is necessary to provide individualization and continuous communication in the process by providing learner data. In addition, recognizing the situations in which the learner has difficulty and providing support is important to prevent the learner from abandoning the learning process by surrendering to feelings of loneliness and inadequacy. Feeling a sense of success and achievement in the learner can support the motivation to work more to feel this feeling and improve their commitment to the learning process. While two of the prospective teachers did not express their opinions on this issue because they did not have sufficient knowledge, two prospective teachers brought up the issues of the necessity of social interaction and success experience that does not develop competence.

"...if social interaction is not included in a long-term plan, commitment may not be achieved." (K7)

A student may try to take the easy way out and get help from the AI when they are having difficulty, but in this case, even if the student is not a dropout, they will not have learned the necessary skills and will not be ready for the business world. I think it is not always ideal for AI to make the student's job easier in the learning process. (K11)

In light of this information, it can be said that social interaction is important in creating learner engagement. In addition, it is necessary to ensure that the learner remains in the process with a successful experience while ensuring that the necessary skills are acquired in line with the learning outcomes. In order to ensure that the learner continues learning by experiencing success in the process and does not mean that the learning process is completed without providing learning outcomes by making everything easier, it is possible to say that it is inevitable that plans should be made to ensure the optimum difficulty-skill balance in the planning phase.

Developing Adaptation Skills with Applications (f=12)

The theme of "Developing Adaptation Skills with Applications" was reached by analyzing the responses of the prospective teachers to the question "How can artificial intelligence enable or not enable students to develop the ability to adapt to different situations?" under the main theme of "Developing Learner Resilience." The coded section-based frequency graph for the theme of "Developing Adaptation Skills with Applications" is given in Figure 14.

Figure 14. Sub-themes that make up the theme of developing the ability to adapt to practices

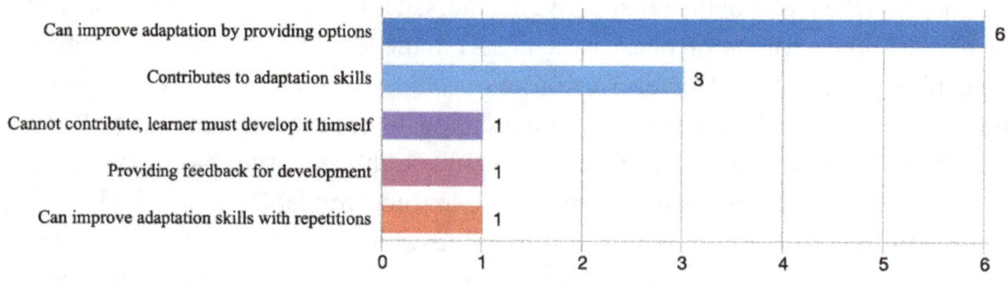

When the opinions of the prospective teachers are examined, one prospective teacher stated that AI helps learners develop the ability to adapt to different situations,

I think AI cannot be of much help in this case; the person must develop his own adaptation skills. (K11)

Expressed the view that this skill should be developed by the learners themselves and, therefore, AI would be of limited assistance in this regard. Three other pre-service teachers provided a positive opinion but did not elaborate on their reasoning. The remaining participants stated that AI could contribute to the development of learners' adaptability by offering options, providing developmental feedback, and enabling repetition. Selected direct quotations reflecting these views are presented below:

"... learns what and how to improve with instant feedback; this strengthens the ability to adapt." (K7)

AI responds to most things you want; you need to program everything you need to do to adopt it, apply it, try it, and try it again. (K6)

AI offers learning paths with scenarios, but if it gives examples with single-type solutions, it can limit the student in terms of adaptation. (K8)

I think this can be achieved because the desired selection of tools and the adaptability of these tools to the selected situation can provide this situation. (K4)

Students can experience different learning paths in a subject they have difficulty with; it can be supported with visual, auditory, or practical content. Thanks to this diversity, the student gains the ability to adapt not only to a certain method but also to different learning environments and situations. (K7)

It can help in developing materials to adapt the information they have learned to other areas of life. It can also branch out to any subject as a learning assistant and simulate different scenarios. (K9)

It can help students develop their ability to adapt to different situations because it can offer them various scenarios and personalized feedback. (K10)

Not every student learns at the same pace or in the same way. AI can help students adapt to unexpected situations and think flexibly by offering different ways, content, and support according to their needs. This strengthens their ability to adapt. (K12)

In short, providing the learner with options in developing adaptation skills through applications and allowing the learner to experience different situations with their own choices during the learning process can contribute to the learner's development of the ability to adapt to different situations and make it easier for them to adapt what they have learned to real-life situations.

Main Theme 3-Adaptation/Supporting Adaptation

Under the main theme of "Adaptation/Supporting Adaptation," which was reached based on the responses given by the teacher candidates to the research questions 9-10-11-12,

- "Focusing on a Specific Area with Applications" (f=17),
- "Shaping Development with Evaluation" (f=14),
- "Pros and Cons of Personalization" (f=13) and
- "Risk of Algorithmic Bias in Planning" (f=12)

a total of fourteen sub-themes were formed under these four themes. The coded section-based frequency table of the themes created for the main theme of "Adaptation/Supporting Adaptation" is shown in Figure 15, and the model created for the main theme is shown in Figure 16.

Figure 15. Themes that make up the main theme of Supporting adaptation/adaptation

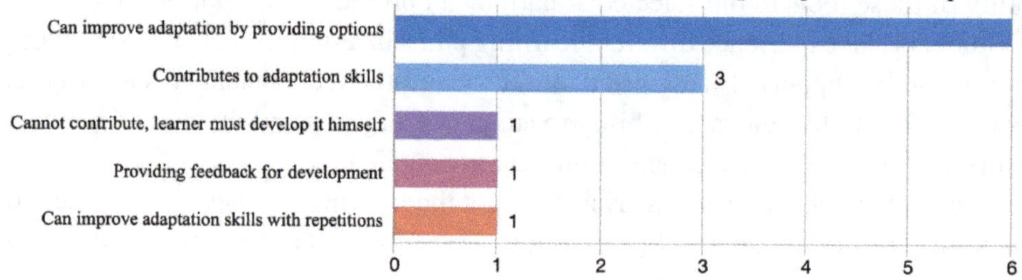

Figure 16. Adaptation/Supporting adaptation main theme model

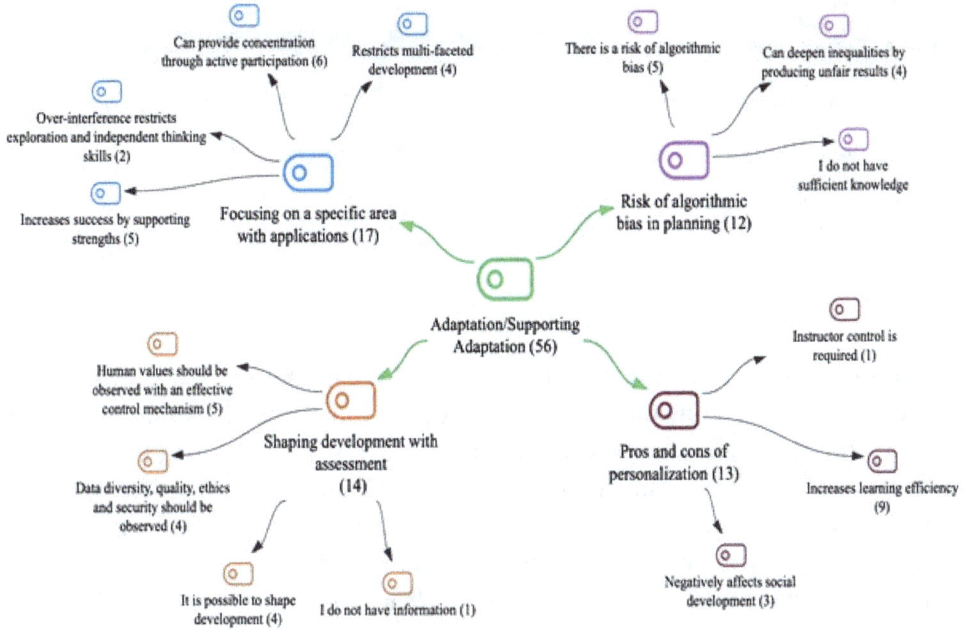

Concentration on a Certain Area with Applications (f=17)

Under the main theme of "Adaptation/Supporting Adaptation," the research question "Why is it good or bad for artificial intelligence to make arrangements that will increase student participation and focus on a certain area using learning analytics?" was analyzed, and the theme of "Concentrating on a Certain Area with Applications" was reached. The coded section-based frequency graph for the theme of "Concentrating on a Certain Area with Applications" is given in Figure 17.

Figure 17. Sub-themes that make up the theme of concentrating on a certain area with practices

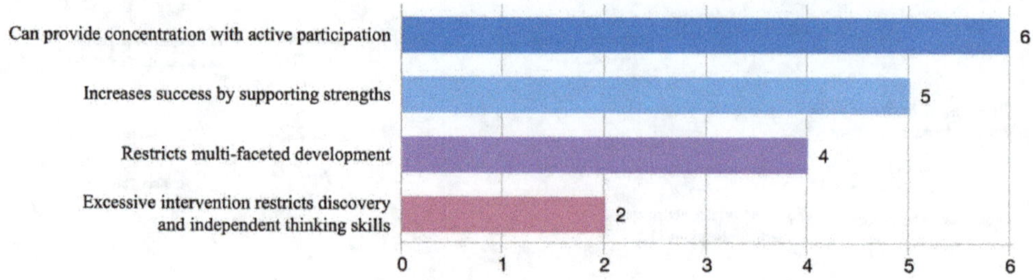

The majority of teacher candidates expressed the opinion that it is possible to ensure that learners focus on a certain area through practices by supporting their active participation and that this will increase success by supporting the learner's strengths and some of the direct quotes regarding this opinion are as follows:

It can increase the student's interest and concentration because it can keep them constantly active with personalized content and difficulty level (K10)

It knows under which conditions the student learns best in line with their interests and abilities, creates an algorithm structure accordingly, and offers this process to the student in a positive and easier learning environment (K4)

"...providing feedback on the subjects they are lacking is a great advantage" (K2)

It is good because if a person can be an expert in a field, there is no level above him thanks to AI; it takes the person to the top. (K6)

It is good as long as there is no excessive intervention because it offers personalized support, increases motivation, and increases learning efficiency. (K7)

It is good because it can increase success by supporting the student's strengths (K8)

It can be both beneficial and risky for AI to direct students to certain areas with learning analytics. The good side is that it discovers the student's talents and provides personalized education suitable for them, increasing their motivation and success. (K9)

The good side is that the student develops their strengths and feels successful. (K12)

Although most of the prospective teachers focused on the positive aspects, some of them stated that focusing on a certain area with applications could have negative effects, such as restricting multi-faceted development, discovery, and independent thinking skills. Some of the direct quotes from the prospective teachers regarding these effects are listed below.

It is also bad because it can limit development in one way by reducing interest in other areas. (K8)

It can make wrong directions due to biases in algorithms, it can prevent multi-faceted development by confining the student to a single area, and it can create excessive performance pressure. Therefore, AI's support in learning should be used transparently and under human supervision. (K9)

However, directing only to one area can ignore other abilities, and the student may lose the chance to try different things. (K12)

Excessive intervention in the student restricts the discovery of their own learning process and their independent thinking skills. (K7)

"...it can prevent the student from having a broad perspective that they will have as a result of their own discovery." (K11)

Based on the views of the prospective teachers, it is possible to say that AI can provide many benefits, such as providing specialization by ensuring that the learner focuses on a certain area with applications, increasing success and learning efficiency by supporting the learner's strengths by ensuring active participation. However, considering the potential drawbacks that may arise when AI focuses on a specific area with applications during the learning process, AI support should be provided under human supervision and with transparency. The risk of algorithmic bias is a crucial factor to consider when utilizing AI in the learning process. Because AI can focus on creating a uniform human profile that develops in the desired direction by narrowing the learner's perspective by focusing on a certain area with applications, limiting their thinking skills, and can go on the path of uniformizing certain groups and classes, thus sharpening class distinctions in the social order. When considered worldwide, this distinction can be created depending on ethnicity, cultural background, and socioeconomic status.

Shaping Development through Evaluation (f=14)

The theme of "Shaping Development through Evaluation" was reached by analyzing the responses of the prospective teachers to the question "Under what conditions can artificial intelligence shape student development using formative and summative feedback?" under the main theme of "Adaptation/Supporting Adaptation." The coded section-based frequency graph for the theme of "Shaping Development through Evaluation" is given in Figure 18.

Figure 18. Sub-themes that make up the theme of shaping development through assessment

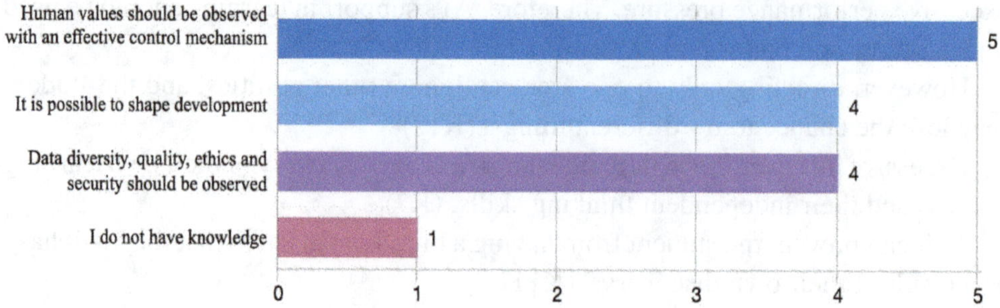

When the views of the prospective teachers regarding the theme of shaping development through evaluation are examined, it is seen that one prospective teacher (K9) did not express an opinion because he did not have sufficient knowledge. While some of the prospective teachers (K1, K3, K5) did not make an explanation by stating that only AI can shape the development of the learner through evaluation in the learning process, some of the prospective teachers stated that when human values, ethics, security, quality are observed with an effective control mechanism and data diversity is provided, the task of shaping student development using formative and summative feedback can be left entirely to AI. Direct quotes regarding the views in question can be listed as follows:

"Supports because since the student gives feedback on the subject he/she is lacking, the student can immediately see and understand his/her shortcomings." (K2)

"I do not think that AI can be trusted completely for now." (K4)

It may be the moment when we realize that we are out of control and cannot live our lives or when we attribute human values to it. If it starts to dehumanize, it will be very difficult to notice this. (K6)

"I do not think that AI should do this" (K11)

"However, leaving the whole process to it alone is risky. Teachers' guidance and human perspective are always important." (K12)

"Data diversity and quality, ethical rules, and security can be completely left to AI if they can be provided." (K7)

"If there is data reliability, adaptability, and audit support by someone, and intervention is made, when necessary, the risk of negative development decreases." (K8)

"It is possible when AI systems can work with high accuracy and without bias." (K11)

"If the system is reliable, fair, and works correctly, AI can give some feedback." (K12)

If we summarize the teachers' views, AI can shape the development of the learner with summative and formative feedback in the learning process, but it is not possible to leave this shaping completely to AI at the moment. It can be said that AI should be placed in such a competent position in the learning process that AI should have the flexibility to embrace groups with different ethnic origins, different cultural backgrounds, different genders, different individual characteristics, different disabilities, and socioeconomic status without discrimination and that security measures should be provided in accordance with ethical rules.

Pros and Cons of Personalization (f=13)

The theme of "Pros and Cons of Personalization" was reached by analyzing the responses of the prospective teachers to the research question, "What are the benefits or harms of personalizing learning with a student-centered approach in the use of artificial intelligence in learning processes?" under the main theme of "Adaptation/ Supporting Adaptation." The coded section-based frequency graph for the theme of "Pros and Cons of Personalization" is given in Figure 19.

Figure 19. Sub-themes that make up the theme of pros and cons of personalization

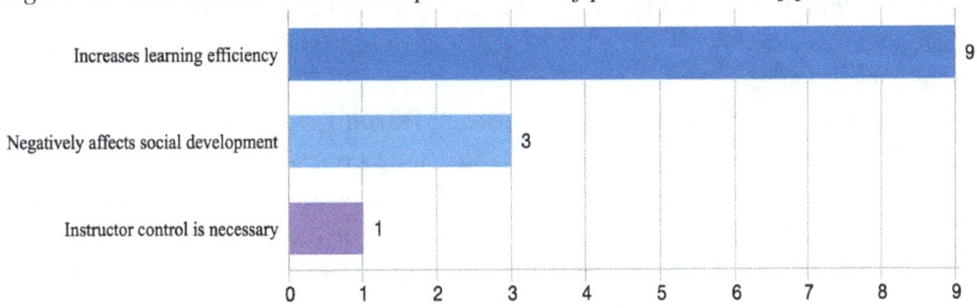

Prospective teachers focus on the positive aspects of AI, stating that personalizing learning with a learner-centered approach will mostly increase learning efficiency. Direct quotes regarding the opinion are as follows.

I think personalized learning will increase learning efficiency (K1)

I do not think it has any harm; its benefit is that it provides information that is appropriate for the student's level of understanding, making it easier for the student to understand (K2)

It provides a useful, fast, and easy learning environment. (K4)

Personalizing learning increases the permanence of learning while also facilitating learning. Easy and fast acquisition of gains can encourage the learner to learn more. I do not think personalized education has any harm. (K7)

It increases success by offering content according to the student's speed, interests, and needs, but if the algorithms are faulty, they can provide false information. (K8)

It increases success and motivation by allowing students to learn at their own pace and style. (K10)

It can offer ways and techniques to personalize learning for the student and present information in a way that the student is more inclined to understand and can be successful in this regard with its analysis skills and ability to adapt quickly. (K11)

Personalization makes learning more effective by offering education according to the student's interests, speed, and needs. (K12)

Direct quotes from prospective teachers who stated that personalization would negatively affect social development can be listed as follows.

As a disadvantage, it can create individuals who have difficulty adapting to social environments that are not socially developed. (K4)

However, excessive personalization can lead to the weakening of social skills in students. (K10)

However, excessive personalization can cause students to encounter the same things over and over, lose interest in other subjects, or become lonely. (K12)

Emphasizing the necessity of instructor control in personalization, teacher candidate K9 stated that

The current use of artificial intelligence in learning processes is very open to abuse. I think a teacher should control this learning process at all times. (K9)

In general, if AI personalizes the learning process with a human-centered approach, it can provide many benefits to the learner by creating an effective and efficient learning environment. However, instead of focusing only on the pros, a balanced approach can be taken into account by also taking the cons into account, and possible problems such as weakening social skills, loneliness, and looking at life from a narrow perspective can be prevented. In addition, it is possible to say that instead of AI taking part in the learning processes alone, it would be a correct approach to ensure that human values are monitored and supported by the cooperation of the instructor and the machine.

Risk of Algorithmic Bias in Planning (f=12)

Under the main theme of "Adaptation/Supporting Adaptation," the research question "Why does the personalization of learning objectives and resources by artificial intelligence based on student characteristics raise the risk of algorithmic bias?" was analyzed, and the theme of "Risk of Algorithmic Bias in Planning" was reached. The coded section-based frequency graph for the theme of "Risk of Algorithmic Bias in Planning" is given in Figure 20.

Figure 20. Sub-themes that make up the theme of risk of algorithmic bias in planning

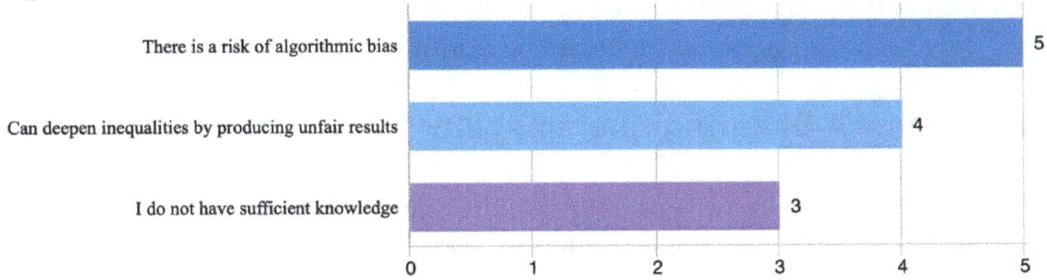

When the opinions of the teachers who formed the theme of algorithmic bias risk in planning are examined, it is seen that five teacher candidates (K1, K2, K3, K5, K10) stated that there is a risk of algorithmic bias but did not explain, and three teacher candidates (K4, K6, K11) did not want to express their opinions because they did not have sufficient knowledge. Direct quotes from teacher candidates who stated that it could deepen inequalities by producing unfair results are presented below.

While AI offers students specific learning goals and resources, it may treat some students unfairly due to hidden biases in the data or model used. This may prevent certain groups from accessing equal opportunities. (K7)

Because AI makes decisions based on past data, if there are biases in this data, such as gender, ethnicity, and socioeconomic status, the system may repeat these patterns and produce unfair results. (K8)

The main reason why AI is at risk of algorithmic bias when personalizing learning goals is that the training data is fed with non-diverse examples (such as data sets where students with ADHD or on the autism spectrum are underrepresented). For example, the system may label a student with ADHD as "low performing" when they do not fit traditional learning models or interpret a student on the autism spectrum as "non-compliant" when they have difficulty with social interaction activities. This may cause the system to miscategorize these students, either setting unnecessarily challenging goals or setting low expectations that limit their potential. Therefore, not training AI with inclusive data that takes neurodiversity into account could deepen existing educational inequalities. (K9)

Because AI works with data collected in the past, if there are social inequalities or biases in this data, the system can repeat these mistakes. This can cause some students to be treated unfairly. (K12)

With his detailed explanation, teacher candidate K9 contributes to developing a perspective on the problems that may arise from the risk of algorithmic bias in the planning phase of the learning process. It is possible to adapt this perspective to the ethnic, cultural, gender, and socioeconomic diversity of learners. In summary, when AI is used in planning learning processes, the necessity of ensuring data diversity and inclusiveness is an issue that should be carefully considered.

Main Theme 4-Ensuring Sustainability

Under the main theme of "Ensuring Sustainability," which was reached based on the responses given by the teacher candidates to the research questions 13-14-15-16,

- "Shaping Knowledge and Skills to Support Sustainability" (f=22),
- "Creating a Balanced Learning Environment" (f=20),
- "Supporting Sustainability with Planning" (f=17) and
- "Implementation with a Balanced Approach" (f=16)

themes, a total of twenty-three sub-themes were formed under these four themes. The coded section-based frequency table of the themes created for the main theme of "Ensuring Sustainability" is in Figure 21, and the model created for the main theme is in Figure 22.

Figure 21. Themes forming the main theme of ensuring sustainability

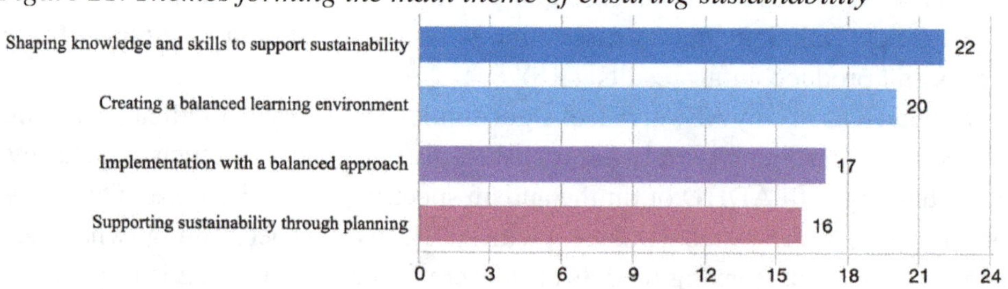

Figure 22. The main theme model of ensuring sustainability

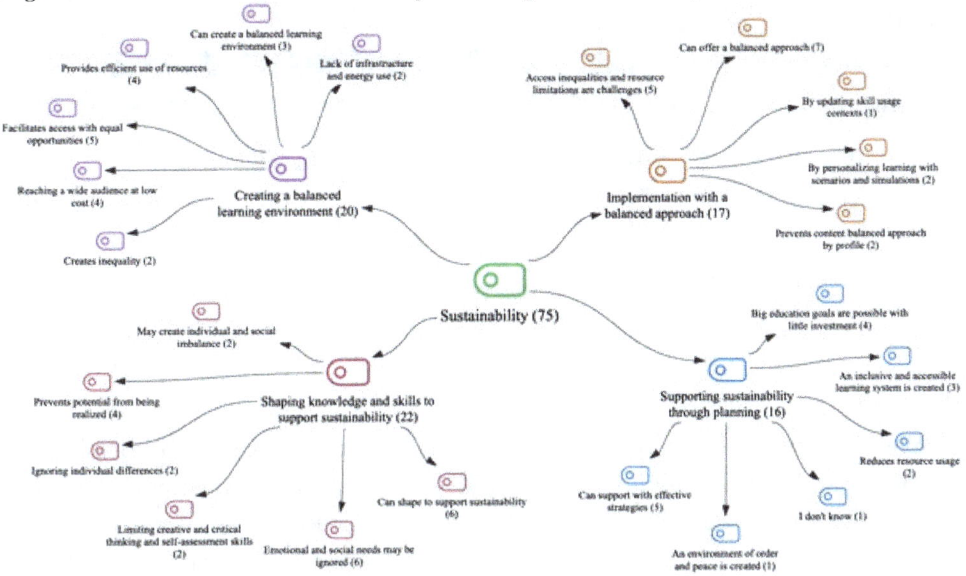

Shaping Knowledge and Skills to Support Sustainability (f=22)

Under the main theme of "Ensuring Sustainability," the theme of "Shaping Knowledge and Skills to Support Sustainability" was reached by analyzing the responses of the teacher candidates to the question of "What kind of disadvantages can artificial intelligence decision support systems create when they shape students' knowledge and skills to support sustainability through formative assessment?". The coded section-based frequency graph for the theme of "Shaping Knowledge and Skills to Support Sustainability" is given in Figure 23.

Figure 23. Sub-themes forming the theme of shaping knowledge and skills to support sustainability

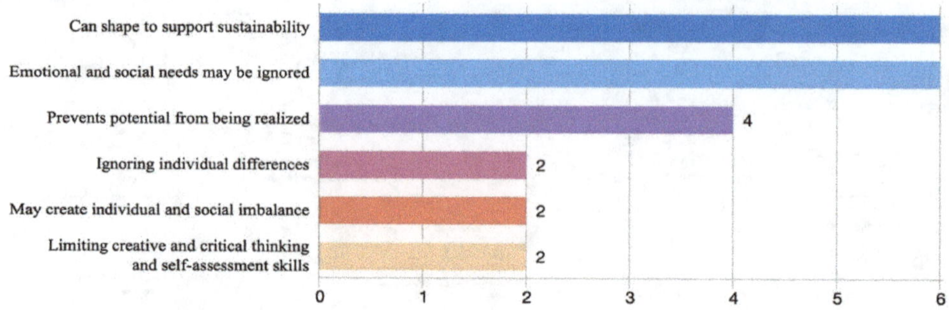

When the opinions of the prospective teachers under the theme of shaping knowledge and skills to support sustainability are examined, there are prospective teachers who expressed positive opinions that AI can shape the learner's knowledge and skills to support sustainability by using it in learning processes (K1, K2, K3, K5, K9, K11), as well as prospective teachers who expressed opinions about the negative situations that this situation will create (K4, K6, K7, K8, K9, K10, K12). Some of the prospective teachers who stated that AI can shape the learner's knowledge and skills in learning processes (K1, K3, K5, K11) only expressed positive opinions but did not make any statements. Direct quotes regarding the opinions of the prospective teachers who made statements are as follows:

"I think it can support because it can help make better and more sustainable decisions by analyzing the information it obtains." (K2)

Although artificial intelligence (AI) supported formative assessment systems shape students' knowledge and skills in line with sustainability, they can also bring serious disadvantages. (K9)

Although K9, a prospective teacher, emphasizes both the positive and negative aspects of shaping knowledge and skills in the learning process to support sustainability, he mostly lists the disadvantages that this situation will create. Some of the negative views formed under the theme of shaping knowledge and skills to support sustainability are direct quotes regarding views that ignore emotional and social needs and individual differences,

Due to excessive standardization, it can approach each student with the same mold and ignore individual differences. (K7)

In addition, excessive standardization brought by AI can exhibit a one-dimensional approach by ignoring individual differences and local contexts. (K9)

It can distance it from human values because it has no emotions and can robotize it. (K6)

In addition, since artificial intelligence cannot fully grasp emotional and social factors, it may not be able to adequately meet the real needs of the student. (K7)

"...it can distance students from the social environment." (K10)

"...it can ignore emotional and social development." (K12)

While it can be listed as follows, a direct quote regarding the view of preventing the manifestation of potential is presented below.

"...reduced human interaction, privacy and data security concerns also question the ethical and balanced use of AI in education, which may prevent AI from realizing its full potential in sustainability education." (K9)

If AI guides with incorrect data, it may squeeze the student into a narrow space. ... This may prevent the student from reaching their full potential. (K12)

It is possible to list direct quotes regarding the views on creating individual and social imbalances and restricting creative and critical thinking and self-evaluation skills as follows.

It can mislead with faulty data, restrict the natural development of the student, and impose a single type of success understanding, which can lead to individual and social imbalances instead of sustainability (K8)

Biases in the data on which AI is trained can impose certain sustainability approaches and ignore cultural diversity. This can restrict students' creativity and critical thinking skills, which can block innovative solutions to sustainability problems. (K9)

It can dull students' critical thinking and self-assessment skills. (K10)

Biases in systems can lead to certain groups being disadvantaged, which damages equality in education. For these reasons, human control and ethical rules are of great importance in AI-supported assessments. (K7)

According to teacher candidates, AI may shape learners' knowledge and skills beyond their potential in order to support sustainability and may prevent them from developing thinking skills. It can be said that these risks can be eliminated by using AI in learning processes in a way that includes instructor-machine collaboration, in other words, by observing human control and ethical rules.

Creating a Balanced Learning Environment (f=20)

The theme of "Creating a Balanced Learning Environment" was reached by analyzing the responses of the teacher candidates to the research question "What is the effect of the use of artificial intelligence in learning processes on creating a balanced learning environment in environmental, social, and economic contexts?" under the main theme of "Ensuring Sustainability." The coded section-based frequency graph for the theme of "Creating a Balanced Learning Environment" is given in Figure 24.

Figure 24. Sub-themes forming the theme of creating a balanced learning environment

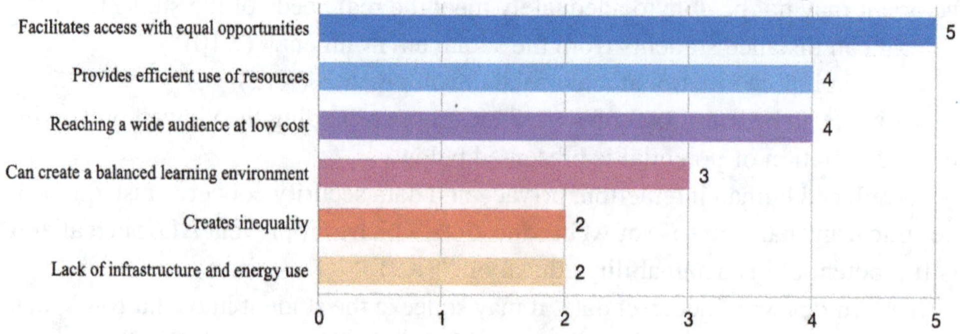

When the views of the prospective teachers regarding the effect of AI on creating a balanced learning environment are examined, it is seen that only one of the prospective teachers (K3, K5, K6) who stated that it could create a balanced learning environment made a statement, while the others only expressed positive views. The direct quote indicating the opinion of the prospective teacher K6 who made a statement is as follows:

Because it is objective and does what is wanted, it looks after the balance in the best way possible, and if the adjustment is too much, it improves it again according to your command. Because it does what is said and wanted in the best way possible. (K6)

In parallel with the teacher candidate's overly optimistic view that AI can create a balanced learning environment, some of the direct quotes from teacher candidates who think that AI will facilitate access through equal opportunities in creating a balanced learning environment can be listed as follows:

It provides equal opportunities by providing individualized education and is sustainable because it is digital. (K2)

Artificial intelligence facilitates access to education for individuals with different social and economic conditions by supporting equal opportunities in learning processes. (K7)

It can increase equal opportunities with socially personalized support. (K8)

It can create a balanced learning environment because its resources are used more efficiently, and it can offer inclusive education opportunities. (K10)

Opinions on resource efficiency expressed by prospective teachers are presented below.

"It can reduce environmental impacts by using resources more efficiently." (K7)

"...reduces paper waste with environmentally friendly digital resources." (K8)

"It can create a balanced learning environment because resources are used more efficiently." (K10)

If used correctly, it can provide an educational environment that is both economical and environmentally friendly by providing equal opportunities to everyone without wasting resources. (K12)

Direct quotes from teacher candidates' views on the possibility of reaching large audiences with low cost as well as resource efficiency are listed below.

"...also economically, it provides access to a wide audience at a low cost." (K8)

It is certain that it will have positive effects on a balanced learning environment in social and economic contexts, but situations such as cheating should be prevented. It should be checked whether the student has really learned. (K9)

"...more information can be organized and made accessible with less cost." (K11)

"Access to AI use is important. It should be economical, and even a free national AI that can be used in education should be created." (K1)

Direct quotes from prospective teachers who stated that AI would create inequality of opportunity, lack of infrastructure, and energy usage would be effective, although the benefits listed above regarding creating a balanced learning environment can be listed as follows.

It may not provide equal opportunities, but when we look at it, there is no equal opportunity situation. I think it can reduce this situation by a bit; apart from that, I can say that it will create another inequality (K4)

However, if there is inequality in access to technology, this balance can be disrupted. (K8)

However, if there is inequality in access to technology, this balance can be disrupted. (K7)

We already know the environmental burden; AI is a technology with high carbon emissions. However, I do not know the effect of these on creating a balanced learning environment. (K9)

In order to realize the potential of creating a balanced learning environment by using AI in the learning process, it is an apparent reality that equality of access to technology and, therefore, economic competence must be increased. It can be said that the irreparable need is the burden that AI imposes on the environment due to its energy use, the most obvious example of which is the purchase of nuclear power plants by AI companies.

Supporting Sustainability through Planning (f=16)

Under the main theme of "Ensuring Sustainability," the research questions were "What are the consequences of using artificial intelligence in determining goals and resources in learning processes and creating strategies, and supporting sustainability by creating a balance in the context of environment, equality, and economy?" and the theme of "Supporting Sustainability with Planning" was reached by analyzing the responses of the teacher candidates. The coded section-based frequency graph for the theme of "Supporting Sustainability with Planning" is given in Figure 25.

Figure 25. Sub-themes forming the theme of supporting sustainability through planning

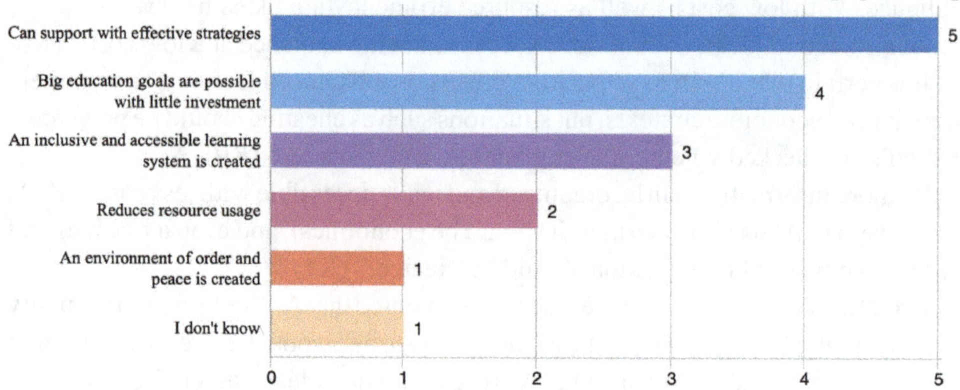

Some of the teacher candidates stated that using AI in determining the goals and resources in the learning process and creating strategies would support sustainability by creating a balance in the context of environment, equality, and economy and that it could support it with effective strategies, but they did not make any explanations. One of the teacher candidates stated that he did not have enough information and did not express an opinion. One of the teacher candidates who made an explanation by expressing an opinion expressed his opinion with the statement, "There will be no chaos, order, and peace will prevail. (K6)", while two of the teacher candidates expressed their opinions that it would reduce the use of resources and their direct quotes are listed below.

Environmentally, digitalization reduces paper consumption and carbon footprint, increases energy efficiency, and reduces the need for travel, but carbon emissions must also be taken into account and evaluated accordingly. (K9)

AI protects the environment by providing digital and fair solutions... (K12)

Direct quotes from prospective teachers who stated that great educational goals would be possible with little investment are listed below:

If this happens, countries can achieve their big education goals without making too much investment economically. (K4)

AI optimizes goals and resources, provides equal opportunities in education, reduces unnecessary resource use, and minimizes environmental impacts. In this way, while economic savings are achieved, a sustainable and fair learning environment is created. However, maintaining this balance is possible with the accessibility and ethical use of technology. (K7)

In economic terms, it can reduce education costs and increase labor productivity, but this is possible thanks to educators who can adapt to AI technologies. (K9)

It creates a sustainable education process by using resources efficiently. (K12)

Direct quotes regarding the views indicating that an inclusive and accessible learning environment will be created are also included below.

Environmentally friendly resource use provides equal opportunities and cost efficiency in education, thus creating a sustainable, inclusive, and accessible learning system. (K8)

From a social perspective, making education more accessible and inclusive strengthens equal opportunities and offers special learning paths for each student, but this is also valid for children with access to computers and the internet. (K9)

it ensures that everyone learns equally. (K12)

The use of AI in learning processes will support sustainability with planning and the creation of an inclusive and accessible learning environment in the context of equality. However, in order to achieve this, access to hardware and the internet is required. In addition, it is emphasized that educators and teachers need to adapt to AI technologies.

Implementation with a Balanced Approach (f=17)

Under the main theme of "Ensuring Sustainability," the research question "How can artificial intelligence present contexts for the use of acquired knowledge with a balanced approach to everyone, considering equality and economic elements, in the application of strategies for active learning in learning processes?" was analyzed and the theme of "Balanced Approach Application" was reached. The coded section-based frequency graph for the theme of "Balanced Approach Application" is given in Figure 26.

Figure 26. Sub-themes forming the theme of implementation with a balanced approach

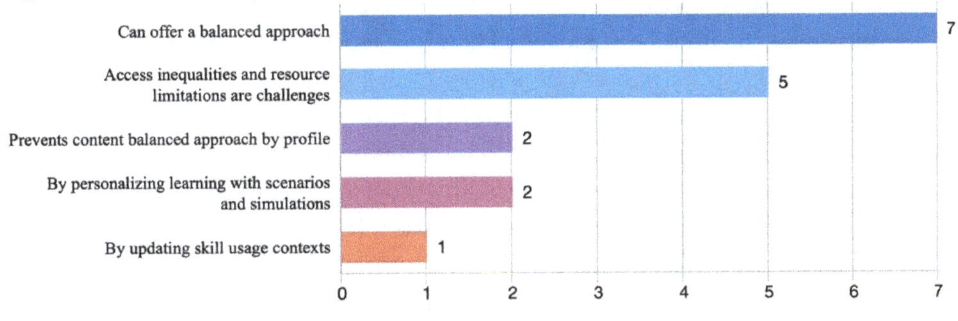

Some of the prospective teachers (K1, K3, K5, K11) stated that AI could offer contexts for the use of acquired knowledge with a balanced approach to everyone by considering equality and economic elements in the application of strategies for active learning in learning processes, some prospective teachers expressed their views on the subject with the following direct quotes.

"I think it creates an equal and accessible environment for all students" (K2)

Artificial intelligence can shape active learning strategies according to the needs of individuals and provide fair and balanced opportunities for everyone by taking into account different economic and social conditions. (K7)

"...has the potential to offer contexts for the use of information in active learning in an equal and economically balanced way for everyone." (K9)

Direct quotes from prospective teachers stated that AI can offer contexts for the use of acquired knowledge with a balanced approach to everyone by considering equality and economic elements, and as a way of doing this, it can update the contexts of skill use by personalizing learning with scenarios and simulations, are given below.

"...by updating skill usage contexts according to changing market needs" (K9)

"...can produce content specific to each student." (K12)

"...by creating personalized scenarios and simulations specific to each student's needs" (K9)

Some of the direct quotes from prospective teachers who expressed the view that access inequalities and resource limitations should be taken into account so that AI can offer contexts for the use of acquired knowledge to everyone with a balanced approach by considering equality and economic elements can be listed as follows.

However, inequalities in access to technology and limitations in data sources can make it difficult to implement this approach fully. (K7)

Providing accessible and affordable access to a variety of resources (K9)

Cannot provide a balanced approach because it will go beyond being accessible to everyone (K4)

The economic cost of AI can limit its equal access for everyone. (K10)

However, if not everyone has access to technology or if the data in the system is biased, this justice cannot be achieved. Therefore, equal access is very important. (K12)

Direct quotes from prospective teachers who expressed the view that in addition to equal access and resource limitations, AI's ability to present application contexts with a balanced approach may be hindered by the deficiencies in its infrastructure in presenting content to different profiles are given below.

AI can offer content according to different profiles, but if there is a deficiency in its infrastructure, it may not offer a balanced approach. (K8)

It can do this by decreasing and increasing it over time by receiving feedback. (K6)

In order for AI to provide contexts for the use of acquired knowledge with a balanced approach to everyone by considering equality and economic elements, it is possible to say that the data on which AI is trained must be unbiased and complete, equal access opportunities must be provided to learners, skill contexts must be updated depending on market conditions, and application scenarios and simulations in which the contents are customized must be created.

DISCUSSION AND CONCLUSION

The findings of the research, which was conducted to determine what can be done to increase the pedagogical effectiveness of technology and to popularize its use in line with the perspectives of teacher candidates on the use of AI in learning processes, focusing on the main elements of Education 5.0 and learning processes, are gathered around the axis of providing flexibility for all kinds of diversity, developing learner resilience, supporting adaptation/adaptation, and ensuring sustainability.

Based on the necessity of providing flexibility for diversity in the use of AI in the learning processes of individuals with different cultural backgrounds, socio-economic status, ethnicity, gender, talent, and special circumstances, the themes of flexible and objective planning, complete flexible application, and egalitarian and fair evaluation emerged in the focus of the positive and negative effects of using AI in learning processes. While teacher candidates stated both positive and negative aspects of using AI in learning processes, it is possible to say that their perceptions towards AI are more positive, based on the views they stated that it would expand equal opportunities in education thanks to the personalized learning process in education, facilitate the creation of an accessible, inclusive learning environment and provide easy access to experience and knowledge. The views of the prospective teachers on the negative aspects of using AI in the learning process are that it can lead to economic, geographical access, interaction, and collaborative learning limitations, discriminate against certain groups with algorithmic bias, manipulate individuals by transferring false information, and create laziness in thought. Although the positive aspects listed by the prospective teachers are not as comprehensive as the positive aspects reported by Bozkurt et al. (2024, p.491), they are similar to the positive aspects expressed as personalized learning and personal teaching, accessibility and inclusiveness, timesaving and efficiency. Similarly, the negative aspects listed by the prospective teachers reveal a parallel structure with the negative aspects listed by Bozkurt et al. (2024, p.498), such as digital divide and educational inequality; prejudice, discrimination, and lack of diversity; academic honesty and authentic learning; quality, reliability and misinformation; and negative impact on critical thinking and higher-level skills. Bozkurt et al. (2024, p.498), the negative situation expressed as prejudice, discrimination, and lack of diversity is expressed as algorithmic bias in the research and highlights the need for AI to be sensitive to diversity in educational processes, as stated by Boateng and Boateng (2025). Based on the views expressed by the teacher candidates, it can be concluded that they have enough knowledge to express their opinions on the use of AI in learning processes in general.

The need for AI to exhibit a flexible and objective stance in determining the goals and resources in the learning processes of individuals with different cultural backgrounds, socioeconomic statuses, ethnic origins, genders, and abilities and creating strategies is expressed as flexible and objective planning. While the majority of the teacher candidates stated that AI can exhibit a flexible and objective approach, some stated that it is possible to provide flexibility suitable for diversity if it has sufficient and unbiased data covering diversity. The situation emphasized is the discrimination that algorithmic bias can cause with the lack of data diversity. This situation is similar to Bozkurt et al. (2024, p.499) and is consistent with the view that the systemic inequalities that will be created by the lack of data coverage and the algorithmic bias that occurs due to historical-social or distorted data sources may prevent the AI from acting objectively. In the context of the AI exhibiting a flexible and objective approach in planning the learning process, the fact that some prospective teachers stated that they thought this was possible without making an explanation, and some stated that the AI approached the student without discriminating based on language, religion or color, may suggest that the prospective teachers do not have sufficient knowledge about planning the learning process of the AI or that they are under the spell of the AI.

The ability of AI to provide the necessary contextual paths in a complete and flexible manner in the implementation of strategies for achieving the determined learning outcomes in the learning processes of individuals with different cultural backgrounds, socioeconomic statuses, ethnic origins, genders, and abilities is expressed as a complete, flexible application. Some of the teacher candidates stated that this could be possible with individualization, contextual constructive feedback, and careful and meticulous design, while others stated that it was not possible because AI was not developed enough, did not produce creative ideas, and only made a collage of the data in hand, and did not have confidence, and two teacher candidates stated that they did not have sufficient knowledge. It can be said that the view that this is possible with careful and meticulous design is parallel to the views of Boateng and Boateng (2025, p. 2015) regarding the applicability of AI to contexts and the idea that one should not be content with the idea that the adaptation of technology is good, and Goksel & Bozkurt (2019, p.232).

The decision-support systems of AI, the ability to evaluate individuals with different cultural backgrounds, socioeconomic status, ethnic origins, gender, and abilities in an equal and fair manner in formative and summative evaluations are expressed as equal and fair evaluation in the research. While two teacher candidates did not express their opinions because they did not have enough information about the equal and fair evaluation of AI, there was one teacher candidate who stated that this was not possible. While some teacher candidates stated that this was possible because it worked according to criteria, some emphasized being trained with accurate data, and some stated that AI could make equal and fair evaluations because it worked based on data and without prejudice. Based on the opinions expressed on the subject, it is possible to say that teacher candidates have a fundamental lack of knowledge or confusion about making an evaluation that embraces diversity in the learning process of AI.

In addition to the information bombardment caused by the Industry 5.0 era we live in, the rapid increase in the number of technologies, skills-subjects to be learned, and the increasing individualization created by generational differences and loneliness bring the development of learner resilience to the agenda as a concept taught by the COVID-19 pandemic experienced in the recent past. In developing learner resilience with the use of AI in learning processes, it is necessary to plan the optimum difficulty-skill balance in learning processes with a focus on the human-centered approach to develop the ability to adapt to applications and to ensure that the process is continued with the experience of success. While teacher candidates are creating workforce competencies in line with Industry 5.0 needs, the majority of teacher candidates who state that AI will make a positive contribution to developing learner resilience with a human-centered approach have also expressed by teacher candidates that it may create negative effects, such as new business areas and the need to adapt, unemployment and enslaved person system, technological dependency, weakening of critical thinking and problem-solving skills. Opinions that the emergence of new business areas and the workforce that can adapt to these areas will remain in the system and that technological dependency weakening critical thinking and problem-solving skills are stated by Bozkurt et al. (2024, p.501). This is in line with the views that critical thinking is suppressed, critical abilities decrease, and creativity erodes due to technological dependency that occurs with excessive reliance on technology.

Prospective teachers state that the instructor's touch is needed in planning the optimum difficulty-skill balance and that it can be achieved by using learning analytics to profile learners. Prospective teachers state that individualized learning and social interaction are necessary to ensure that they remain in the process with the success experience, and a prospective teacher states that a success experience that does not develop competence is harmful. It is possible to say that this view overlaps with the view expressed by Bozkurt et al. (2024, p.500) that learners who accept the answers produced by AI without thinking critically and perform superficial learning cannot reach the necessary depth in terms of long-term knowledge retention and applying concepts in unfamiliar contexts. In developing learner resilience, some prospective teachers state that in order for AI to enable students to develop the ability to adapt to different situations, options should be presented, repetitions should be made, and feedback should be provided for development. In terms of developing resilience by providing adaptation skills, the need for the learner to develop the ability to cope with difficulties by struggling is stated by Bozkurt et al. (2024, p. 495). It can be stated that the opinions expressed by the teacher candidates do not exhibit a similar structure.

In order to support adaptation/adaptation with the use of AI in learning processes, it is revealed that teachers' views that focusing on a specific area with applications, shaping development with evaluation, personalization, and the risk of algorithmic bias in planning should be taken into account. It is possible that AI can make arrangements by increasing the student's participation and concentration in a specific area by using learning analytics, contributing to the learner's concentration in a specific area, increasing success, and providing specialization. However, ensuring that the learner focuses on a specific area has the potential to restrict the student's multifaceted development and negatively affect discovery and independent thinking skills. Data diversity, quality, ethics and security, and the necessity of observing human values with effective control mechanisms stand out as points to be considered in shaping development with evaluation of AI's learning processes. Bozkurt et al. (2024, p. 500) state that AI systems can prioritize institutional values instead of human values in learning and shift the focus of education from the holistic development of the learner to performance criteria or commercially valuable results. This view forms a parallel structure with the view that human values should be observed with effective control mechanisms stated in shaping the development through evaluation in the learning processes of AI. In addition, the necessity of acting with awareness of ethical risks stated by Güler, Uğur, and Güler (2025, p.641) points to a similar context with the idea of observing quality, ethics, and security regarding diversity in shaping the development through evaluation in the learning processes.

With the use of AI in learning processes, the themes of supporting sustainability with planning, implementing with a balanced approach, creating a balanced learning environment, and shaping knowledge and skills to support sustainability have emerged. There are views that shaping knowledge and skills to support sustainability in learning processes by AI ignores individual differences in emotional and social needs, prevents revealing potential, restricts creative and critical thinking and self-assessment skills, and thus creates individual and social imbalance. The views expressed here are the sum of the views expressed so far in the discussion section and reveal a structure that overlaps with the views given in the mentioned studies. The dominant view is that creating a balanced learning environment can provide access to large masses at low cost, as well as provide environmental contribution by ensuring efficient use of resources, but in order for this to happen, infrastructural deficiencies must be eliminated. Bozkurt et al. (2024, p.491) emphasize the educational inequality that will be created by the digital divide as one of the most significant disadvantages of the use of AI in education and states that the gap is widening with the premium services of AI and that the lack of infrastructure experienced in developing countries can hinder educational progress. This view expresses a similar concern to the views expressed by teacher candidates. In terms of presenting contexts for the application of knowledge acquired in the AI learning process, a balanced approach is advocated that considers equality and economic factors. Attention is drawn to resource limitations and access inequalities, and a teacher candidate emphasizes the need to update the contexts in which skills are used.

One teacher candidate stated that they lacked sufficient knowledge in planning the optimal difficulty-skill balance with the use of AI in learning processes, and two teacher candidates did not express an opinion on staying in the process with a successful experience. In addition, four teacher candidates stated that they did not have enough knowledge in planning the optimum difficulty-skill balance, three teacher candidates stated that they developed the skill of adapting to applications, and three teacher candidates stated that they only gave positive opinions on staying in the process with success experience but did not make any statements. The fact that teacher candidates only gave positive opinions and did not make any critical statements may be due to a lack of knowledge, as mentioned earlier, or it may be due to their fascination with AI. As a result, it can be stated that teacher candidates, who are the teachers of the future, should develop a perspective and be trained on the possible benefits of AI use as well as its possible disadvantages from a broad perspective and that courses on the use of AI in learning processes should be added to their education curricula to ensure this. This necessity that emerged from the research is consistent with the opinion stated by Boateng and Boateng (2025, p. 2015) that teachers, teacher candidates, and administrators should be trained and made aware of AI. In the context of this view, it can be stated that, as an inevitable necessity, not only teacher candidates but also teachers currently teaching and education administrators should be trained and made aware of AI. As a result, it becomes crucial to make decisions that will shape the future of learning and human development with foresight and care and to adopt an approach to using AI effectively and efficiently without placing it in a position to shape life and learning.

REFERENCES

Ağmaz, R. F., & Ergüleç, F. (2024). Öğretmen Adaylarının Eğitimde Yapay Zekâ Algıları: Bir Metafor Analizi. [Perceptions of Teacher Candidates on Artificial Intelligence in Education- A Metaphorical Analysis]. *Necmettin Erbakan University Ereğli Faculty of Education Journal*, *6*(2), 589–605. DOI: 10.51119/ereegf.2024.97

Alharbi, A. M. (2023). Implementation of Education 5.0 in Developed and Developing Countries: A Comparative Study. *Creative Education*, *14*(05), 914–942. DOI: 10.4236/ce.2023.145059

Ayduğ, D., & Altınpulluk, H. (2025). Are Turkish pre-service teachers worried about AI? A study on AI anxiety and digital literacy. *AI & Society*, *40*(4), 1–12. DOI: 10.1007/s00146-025-02348-0

Best, J. W., & Kahn, J. V. (2017). *Eğitimde Araştırma Yöntemleri* [*Research Methods in Education*], (10nd ed. Trans., O. Köksal, Trans. Ed., S. Sidekli, O. Kutlu, Ş. Korkmaz, A. Özcan, A.S. Saracaloğlu, M. Altın, M. Çetin, O. Çepni, A. Ç. Kılınç, Ç. Şahin, M. K. Demir, M. Durmuşçelebi, O. Köksal, H. Sezgin, B. Karanfil, & Z. Tangülü, Trans.). Education Publishing House. (Original work published 2006)

Boateng, O., & Boateng, B. (2025). Algorithmic bias in educational systems: Examining the impact of AI-driven decision making in modern education. *World Journal of Advanced Research and Reviews*, *25*(1), 2012–2017. DOI: 10.30574/wjarr.2025.25.1.0253

Bozkurt, A., Xiao, J., Farrow, R., Bai, J. Y. H., Nerantzi, C., Moore, S., Dron, J., Stracke, C. M., Singh, L., Crompton, H., Koutropoulos, A., Terentev, E., Pazurek, A., Nichols, M., Sidorkin, A. M., Costello, E., Watson, S., Mulligan, D., Honeychurch, S., & Asino, T. I. (2024). The Manifesto for Teaching and Learning in a Time of Generative AI: A Critical Collective Stance to Better Navigate the Future. *Open Praxis*, *16*(4), 487–513. DOI: 10.55982/openpraxis.16.4.777

Carvalho, L. (2023). *Education 5.0: What Does It Mean? How Does It Work?* Sydle. https://www.sydle.com/blog/education-5-0-61e71a99edf3b9259714e25a

Creswell, J. W. (2017). *Araştırma Deseni-Nitel, Nicel ve Karma Yöntem Yaklaşımları* [*Research Design-Qualitative, Quantitative and Mixed Methods Approaches*] (3rd ed., 4th ed. Trans., S. B. Demir, Trans. Ed., E. Bukova-Güzel, İ. Erdoğan, Y. Dede, G. Hacıömeroğlu, H. Ercan, I. Bilican, M. Bütün, M. Bursal, S. Mandacı-Şahin, & S. B. Demir, Trans.). Educational Book. (Original work published 2015)

Creswell, J. W. (2018). *Nitel Araştırma Yöntemleri-Beş yaklaşıma göre nitel araştırma ve araştırma deseni* [*Qualitative Inquiry & Research Design Choosing Among Five Approaches*] (4th ed., 3rd ed. Trans., M. Bütün and S. B. Demir, Trans. Ed., O. Birgin, S. Ünal, T. Özsevgeç, Y. Dede, A. Bacanak, A. Bakla, A. Budak, G. Hacıömeroğlu, İ. Budak, M. Aydın, M. Bütün, Mir. Aydın, & S. B. Demir, Trans.). Political Bookstore. (Original work published 2013)

Creswell, J. W. (2019). *Eğitim Araştırmaları: Nicel ve Nitel Araştırmanın Planlanması, Yürütülmesi ve Değerlendirilmesi* [*Educational Research: Planning, Conducting, and Evaluating Quanttative and Qualitative Research*] (2nd ed., 4th ed. Trans., C. Robb & K. Mason Eds., H. Ekşi, Trans. Ed., A. Avcu, D. Eryiğit, D. Dinçer, E. Bakiler, G. Alçekiç-Yaman, H. Ekşi, H. Çelik, İ. Karsantik, M. Tuncel, M. Başman, N. Yaman, S. Kardaş, S. Doğan, S. Çakır, Ş. Tatık, Y. Karsantık, Trans.). EDAM. (Original work published 2012)

Fırat, S. Ü. O. (2023). Endüstri 4.0'dan Endüstri 6.0'a Yolculuk. [Journey from Industry 4.0 to Industry 6.0]. *Global Industrialist: Economy and Business World Magazine.* https://www.sanayicidergisi.com.tr/endustri-40dan-endustri-60a-yolculuk-makale,857.html

Fissore, C., Floris, F., Fradiante, V., Conte, M. M., & Sacchet, M. (2024). From Theory to Training: Exploring Teachers' Attitudes Towards Artificial Intelligence in Education. *International Conference on Computer Supported Education, CSEDU-Proceedings, 2*, 118–127. https://doi.org/DOI: 10.5220/0012734700003693

Gamberini, L., & Pluchino, P. (2024). Industry 5.0: A comprehensive insight into the future of work, social sustainability, sustainable development, and career. *Australian Journal of Career Development, 33*(1), 5–14. DOI: 10.1177/10384162241231118

Gibson, D., Kovanovic, V., Ifenthaler, D., Dexter, S., & Feng, S. (2023). Learning theories for artificial intelligence promoting learning processes. *British Journal of Educational Technology, 54*(5), 1125–1146. DOI: 10.1111/bjet.13341

Goksel, N., & Bozkurt, A. (2019). Artificial Intelligence in Education: Current Insights and Future Perspectives. In Sisman-Ugur, S., & Kurubacak, G. (Eds.), *Handbook of Research on Learning in the Age of Transhumanism* (pp. 224–236). IGI Global., DOI: 10.4018/978-1-5225-8431-5.ch014

Güler, E., Uğur, S., & Güler, C. (2025). Eğitim fakültesi öğretim elemanlarının üretken yapay zekâya yönelik farkındalıklarının belirlenmesi ve öğretmen yetiştirmede kullanımına yönelik öneriler. [Determination of faculty of education lecturers' awareness of generative artificial intelligence and suggestions for its use in teacher training]. *Mehmet Akif Ersoy University Faculty of Education Journal, 74*(74), 618–647. DOI: 10.21764/maeuefd.1627851

Guzder, K. (2024). *What is the Role of Artificial Intelligence in Education?* High-Speed Training Limited. https://www.highspeedtraining.co.uk/hub/artificial-intelligence-in-education/

Naidu, S. (2024). The case for deliberate design of the student learning experience. *Distance Education, 45*(2), 205–209. DOI: 10.1080/01587919.2024.2353413

Patton, M. Q. (2018). *Nitel Araştırma ve Değerlendirme Yöntemleri* [*Qualitative Research & Evaluation Methods*]. (2nd ed. 3rd ed. Trans., M. Bütün & S. B. Demir, Trans. Eds., A. Bakla, F. I. Bilican, M. Bütün, M. Çakır, A. Çekiç, S. Çelik, Y. Dede, S. B. Demir, H. Demircioğlu, İ. Eti, E. Bukova-Güzel, S. İrez, F. Ö. Karataş, T. Kargın, F. Zayimoğlu-Öztürk, T. Öztürk, M. Sümer, M. F. Yiğit, & B. Turhan—Türkkan, Trans.). Pegem Academy. (Original work published 2001)

Ribeiro, A. G., Messias, A. C. G., & Ribeiro, M. S. (2023). Educação 5.0'e a Atuação Dos Educadores: Avanços, Oportunıdades E Impactos. *Revista Ft, 27*(125), 25–26. DOI: 10.69849/revistaft/ar10202308011525

Shahidi-Hamedani, S., Aslam, S., Mundher Oraibi, B. A., Wah, Y. B., & Shahidi-Hamedani, S. (2024). Transitioning towards Tomorrow's Workforce: Education 5.0 in the Landscape of Society 5.0: A Systematic Literature Review. *Education Sciences, 14*(10), 1041. DOI: 10.3390/educsci14101041

Thomas, M. (2025). *The Future of AI: How Artificial Intelligence Will Change the World.* Built-in-UnitedWeTech. https://builtin.com/artificial-intelligence/artificial-intelligence-future

World Economic Forum. (2025). *Future of Jobs Report 2025.* World Economic Forum. https://reports.weforum.org/docs/WEF_Future_of_Jobs_Report_2025.pdf

Yin, R. K. (2018). *Case Study Research and Applications: Design and Methods* (6th ed.). Sage Publications.

KEY TERMS AND DEFINITIONS

Adaptive AI: is AI that can personalize the goals and resources depending on the learner's past experiences, knowledge, and readiness level, make arrangements to increase the learner's participation in areas where he/she is deficient, and support the learner's development with formative feedback.

Algorithmic bias: is a systematic error that leads to unfair results by disregarding individual differences, such as cultural background, socioeconomic status, ethnicity, gender, and ability, for various reasons, thereby undermining equality and favoring particular groups over others.

Diversity-sensitive AI: is AI that can plan the learning processes of individuals with diverse cultural backgrounds, socioeconomic statuses, ethnicities, genders, and abilities in an objective manner, provide the necessary contexts in practice, and make equitable and fair assessments.

Education 5.0: is an educational approach that aims to support sustainability through diversity and flexibility, learner resilience, and adaptation by incorporating a human perspective into the technology-dominant approach of digital transformation.

Industry 5.0: is a sustainability-based structure that creates a movement centered on human-centeredness, flexibility, and resilience, focusing on human-technology collaboration beyond the dominant technologies (blockchain, cloud computing, and artificial intelligence) that emerged in Industry 4.0.

Resilience-developing AI: is AI that can plan learning by utilizing resources tailored to the learning objectives and maintaining an optimal balance of difficulty and skill, developing practices to help learners adapt to various situations, and making assessments that foster a sense of achievement by keeping learners engaged throughout the process.

The learning process: involves identifying learning resources to achieve learning outcomes and developing implementation and evaluation strategies to ensure that learners acquire the knowledge, attitudes, and skills required by the labor market.

Compilation of References

"The data-centre investment spree shows no signs of stopping." (2025, February 5). *The Economist*. https://www.economist.com/business/2025/02/05/the-data-centre-investment-spree-shows-no-signs-of-stopping

Abbas, M., Jam, F. A., & Khan, T. I. (2024). Is it harmful or helpful? Examining the causes and consequences of generative AI usage among university students. *International Journal of Educational Technology in Higher Education*, *21*(1). Advance online publication. DOI: 10.1186/s41239-024-00444-7

Abegglen, S., Burns, T., & Sinfield, S. (2025, March 31). Critical pedagogy and digital liberation: A Freirean debate for SoTL. *Open Scholarship of Teaching and Learning Journal.*, *4*(1). Advance online publication. DOI: 10.56230/osotl.116

Adams, C., Pente, P., Lemermeyer, G., & Rockwell, G. (2023). Ethical principles for artificial intelligence in K-12 education. *Computers and Education: Artificial Intelligence*, *4*, 100131. Advance online publication. DOI: 10.1016/j.caeai.2023.100131

Ağmaz, R. F., & Ergüleç, F. (2024). Öğretmen Adaylarının Eğitimde Yapay Zekâ Algıları: Bir Metafor Analizi. [Perceptions of Teacher Candidates on Artificial Intelligence in Education- A Metaphorical Analysis]. *Necmettin Erbakan University Ereğli Faculty of Education Journal*, *6*(2), 589–605. DOI: 10.51119/ereegf.2024.97

Ahila, A., Poonguzhali, A., Deepa, M., Arthy, A., & Saravanakumar, R. (2024, August). Artificial Intelligence For Realtime Face Recognition Attendance Using College Classrooms and Buses. In *2024 International Conference on Electrical Electronics and Computing Technologies (ICEECT)* (Vol. 1, pp. 1-6). IEEE. DOI: 10.1109/ICEECT61758.2024.10738995

AI4EU Project. (2019a). A European AI On-Demand Platform and Ecosystem. Retrieved from https://cordis.europa.eu/project/id/825619

AI4EU Project. (2019b). AI4Citizen. Retrieved from https://www.ai4europe.eu/business-and-industry/case-studies/ai4citizen

AI4EU Project. (2019c). AI4Healthcare. Retrieved from https://www.ai4europe.eu/business-and-industry/case-studies/ai4healthcare

AI4EU Project. (2019d). AI4EU Open Call Challenges. Retrieved from https://www.ai4europe.eu/business-and-industry/case-studies/ai4eu-open-call-challenges

Aidla, A., Irs, R., & Türk, K. (2012). Creating innovation in the education sector: Policy implications. In Carayannis, E., Varblane, U., & Roolaht, T. (Eds.), *Innovation systems in small catching-up economies* (pp. 267–284). Springer., DOI: 10.1007/978-1-4614-1548-0_19

Al Naqbi, H., Bahroun, Z., & Ahmed, V. (2024). Enhancing work productivity through generative artificial intelligence: A comprehensive literature review. *Sustainability (Basel)*, *16*(3), 1166. DOI: 10.3390/su16031166

Alharbi, A. M. (2023). Implementation of Education 5.0 in Developed and Developing Countries: A Comparative Study. *Creative Education*, *14*(05), 914–942. DOI: 10.4236/ce.2023.145059

Al-Nuaimi, M. N., & Al-Emran, M. (2021). Learning management systems and technology acceptance models: A systematic review. *Education and Information Technologies*, *26*, 5499–5533. DOI: 10.1007/s10639-021-10495-6

Althusser, L. (2012). *Ideology and ideological state apparatuses: Notes towards an investigation.* Critical Quest.

American Psychological Association. (2023, November). *APA Journals policy on generative AI: Additional guidance.* https://www.apa.org/pubs/journals/resources/publishing-tips/policy-generative-ai

Anggraeni, D., Wardani, D. K., & Noviani, L. (2024). Self-Regulated Learning, Grit, and Learning Motivation in Developing Learning Achievement: A Review. *Formosa Journal of Multidisciplinary Research*, *3*(1), 135–148. DOI: 10.55927/fjmr.v3i1.7908

An, Y., Yu, J. H., & James, S. (2025). Investigating the higher education institutions' guidelines and policies regarding the use of generative AI in teaching, learning, research, and administration. *International Journal of Educational Technology in Higher Education*, *22*(10), 1–23. DOI: 10.1186/s41239-025-00507-3

Appleton, J. J., Christenson, S. L., & Furlong, M. J. (2008). Student engagement with school: Critical conceptual and methodological issues of the construct. *Psychology in the Schools*, *45*(5), 369–386. DOI: 10.1002/pits.20303

Arantes, J. A. (2024). Redefining Classroom Readiness: How Initial Teacher Training Can Mitigate Risks and Capitalize on the Potential of GenAI. In Academic Integrity in the Age of Artificial Intelligence (pp. 78-92). IGI Global. https://doi.org/DOI: 10.4018/979-8-3693-0240-8.ch005

Arantes, J. (2024). Understanding Intersections Between GenAI and Pre-Service Teacher Education: What Do We Need to Understand About the Changing Face of Truth in Science Education? *Journal of Science Education and Technology*, •••, 1–12. DOI: 10.1007/s10956-024-10189-7

Arantes, J. A. (2022). eMorpheus: The unconscious human labour of producing commercial data in educational settings. [JCEPS]. *The Journal for Critical Education Policy Studies*, *20*(2).

Arantes, J., & Vicars, M. (2024). Always On Standby: Reshaping Higher Education by acknowledging the psychosocial risk of our postdigital presence in online digital labor. *Higher Education Research & Development*, *1*(1), 1–17. DOI: 10.1080/07294360.2023.2280209

Arar, K., Tlili, A., Salha, S., & Saiti, A. (2025). Rethinking School Leadership and Policy in the Digital AI Era. *Leadership and Policy in Schools*, *24*(1), 1–3. DOI: 10.1080/15700763.2020.1838555

Aristotle, . (1999). *Nicomachean ethics* (Irwin, T., Ed.; 2nd ed.). Hackett Pub. Co.

Arizona State University (ASU). (2025). *Artificial Intelligence (AI) resources and guidelines*. https://instruction.thecollege.asu.edu/AIguidelines

Arora, A.. (2024). Towards intelligent governance: The role of AI in policymaking and decision support for e-governance. In So In, C., Londhe, N. D., Bhatt, N., & Kitsing, M. (Eds.), *Information systems for intelligent systems* (pp. 231–245). Springer., DOI: 10.1007/978-981-99-8612-5_19

Astin, A. W. (1984). Student involvement: A developmental theory for higher education. *Journal of College Student Personnel*, *25*(4), 297–308.

Ayduğ, D., & Altınpulluk, H. (2025). Are Turkish pre-service teachers worried about AI? A study on AI anxiety and digital literacy. *AI & Society*, •••, 1–12. DOI: 10.1007/s00146-025-02348-0

Badmus, O., Anas, S., Arogundade, J. B., & Williams, M. (2024). AI-driven business analytics and decision making. *World Journal of Advanced Research and Reviews*, *24*(1), 616–633. DOI: 10.30574/wjarr.2024.24.1.3093

Baker, R., & Yacef, K. (2009). The state of educational data mining in 2009: A review and future visions. *Journal of Educational Data Mining*, *1*(1), 3–17.

Bakhtin, M. (1989). Discourse in the novel. In Richter, D. (Ed.), *The critical tradition: Classic texts and contemporary trends* (pp. 781–791). St. Martin's Press. (Original work published 1934)

Bala, N. (2020). The Danger of Facial Recognition in Our Children's Classrooms. *Duke Law & Technology Review, 18*, 249-267. https://scholarship.law.duke.edu/dltr/vol18/iss1/19/

Balachandar, S. K., Kumara, I. V., Godavari, A., Marieswari, S., & Karthikeyan, T.Sanjay Kanth Balachandar. (2024). Dynamic adaptive resource allocation for edge computing in big data analytics using GBDT, DQN, and GA algorithms. *Journal of Electrical Systems*, *20*(5), 2158–2165. DOI: 10.52783/jes.2561

Bali, M. (2025, January). Five questions to ask before adopting a new technology. *London School of Economics Higher Education Blog*. https://blogs.lse.ac.uk/highereducation/2025/01/08/five-questions-to-ask-before-adopting-a-new-technology/

Ball, S. J. (2020). The errors of redemptive sociology or giving up on hope and despair. *British Journal of Sociology of Education*, *41*(6), 870–880. DOI: 10.1080/01425692.2020.1755230

Bandura, A. (1977). Self-efficacy: Toward a unifying theory of behavioral change. *Psychological Review*, *84*(2), 191–215. DOI: 10.1037/0033-295X.84.2.191 PMID: 847061

Bandura, A. (1997). *Self-efficacy: The exercise of control.* W H Freeman/Times Books/ Henry Holt & Co.

Barker, B., & Hoskins, K. (2021). Education, inequality and social mobility: Key findings from three case studies. *Forum for Promoting 3-19 Comprehensive Education*, *63*(1), 107–114. DOI: 10.3898/forum.2021.63.1.12

Barni, D., Danioni, F., & Benevene, P. (2019, July). Teachers' self-efficacy: The role of personal values and motivations for teaching. *Frontiers in Psychology*, *10*(1645), 1–7. https://www.frontiersin.org/articles/10.3389/fpsyg.2019.01645/full. DOI: 10.3389/fpsyg.2019.01645 PMID: 31354604

Baskarada, S. (2014). Qualitative case study guidelines. *The Qualitative Report*, *19*(40), 1–25. DOI: 10.46743/2160-3715/2014.1008

Bates, A. W. (2019). *Teaching in a digital age: Guidelines for designing teaching and learning* (2nd Ed.). BCcampus. https://pressbooks.bccampus.ca/teachinginadigitalagev2/

Baxter, P., & Jack, S. (2008). Qualitative case study methodology: Study design and implementation for novice researchers. *The Qualitative Report, 13*(4), 544–559. www.nova.edu/ssss/QR/QR13-4/baxter.pdf

Beckingham, S., Lawrence, J., Powell, S., & Hartley, P. (2024). Sustainable and ethical GenAI for the common good: Looking back and forward. In *Using Generative AI Effectively in Higher Education* (pp. 127–138). Routledge., DOI: 10.4324/9781003482918-18

Berendt, B., Littlejohn, A., & Blakemore, M. (2020). AI in education: Learner choice and fundamental rights. *Learning, Media and Technology, 45*(3), 312–324. DOI: 10.1080/17439884.2020.1786399

Bergmans, L., Bouali, N., Luttikhuis, M., & Rensink, A. (2021). On the efficacy of online proctoring using proctorio. In 13th *International Conference on Computer Supported Education, CSEDU 2021* (pp. 279-290). Scitepress. DOI: 10.5220/0010399602790290

Berland, M., Baker, R. S., & Blikstein, P. (2014). Educational data mining and learning analytics: Applications to constructionist research. *Technology. Knowledge and Learning, 19*(1-2), 205–220. DOI: 10.1007/s10758-014-9223-7

Best, J. W., & Kahn, J. V. (2017). *Eğitimde Araştırma Yöntemleri* [*Research Methods in Education*], (10nd ed. Trans., O. Köksal, Trans. Ed., S. Sidekli, O. Kutlu, Ş. Korkmaz, A. Özcan, A.S. Saracaloğlu, M. Altın, M. Çetin, O. Çepni, A. Ç. Kılınç, Ç. Şahin, M. K. Demir, M. Durmuşçelebi, O. Köksal, H. Sezgin, B. Karanfil, & Z. Tangülü, Trans.). Education Publishing House. (Original work published 2006)

Bhullar, P. S., Joshi, M., & Chugh, R. (2024). ChatGPT in higher education-a synthesis of the literature and a future research agenda. *Education and Information Technologies, 29*(16), 21501–21522. DOI: 10.1007/s10639-024-12723-x

Biesta, G. (2013). Responsive or responsible? Democratic education for the global networked society. *Policy Futures in Education, 11*(6), 733–744. DOI: 10.2304/pfie.2013.11.6.733

Black, C. (n.d.). *Children, learning, and the 'evaluative gaze' of school: How we watched pot loses the desire to boil.* Carol Black. https://carolblack.org/the-gaze

Bloom, B. S. (1956). *Taxonomy of educational objectives: The classification of educational goals. Handbook I: Cognitive domain*. Longmans, Green.

Blundell, D., & Abegglen, S. (2017). European ideals, schooling and modern childhood: Deploying the template child. In Isaacs, S. (Ed.), *European social problems* (pp. 131–148). Routledge. DOI: 10.4324/9781315687513-8

Boateng, O., & Boateng, B. (2025). Algorithmic bias in educational systems: Examining the impact of AI-driven decision making in modern education. *World Journal of Advanced Research and Reviews, 25*(1), 2012–2017. DOI: 10.30574/wjarr.2025.25.1.0253

Börekci, C., & Çelik, Ö. (2024). Exploring the role of digital literacy in university students' engagement with AI through the technology acceptance model. *Sakarya University Journal of Education, 14*(Special Issue), 228–249.DOI: 10.19126/suje.1468866

Bourdieu, P. (1977). *Outline of a theory of practice*. Cambridge University Press. DOI: 10.1017/CBO9780511812507

Bourdieu, P., & Passeron, J.-C. (1977). Reproduction in education, society and culture. *Sage (Atlanta, Ga.)*.

Boussioux, L., Lane, J. N., Zhang, M., Jacimovic, V., & Lakhani, K. R. (2024). The crowdless future? Generative AI and creative problem-solving. *Organization Science, 35*(5), 1589–1607. DOI: 10.1287/orsc.2023.18430

Bowen, G. A. (2009). Document analysis as a qualitative research method. *Qualitative Research Journal, 9*(2), 27–40. DOI: 10.3316/QRJ0902027

Bowles, S., & Gintis, S. (1975). The problem with human capital theory: A Marxian critique. *The American Economic Review, 65*(2), 74–82. https://www.jstor.org/stable/1818836

Boyd, D. & Crawford, K. (2012) Critical Questions for Big Data. *Information, Communication & Society, 15*(5), 662–679. https://doi.org/10.1080/1369118X.2012.678878

Bozkurt, A., Xiao, J., Farrow, R., Bai, J. Y., Nerantzi, C., Moore, S., & Asino, T. I. (Eds.). (2024). The manifesto for teaching and learning in a time of generative AI: A critical collective stance to better navigate the future. *Open Praxis, 16*(4), 487-513.

Bozkurt, A. (2024). GenAI et al.: Cocreation, Authorship, Ownership, Academic Ethics and Integrity in a Time of Generative AI. *Open Praxis, 16*(1), 1–10. DOI: 10.55982/openpraxis.16.1.654

Bozkurt, A., Karadeniz, A., Bañeres, D., Guerrero-Roldán, A., & Rodríguez, M. (2021). Artificial intelligence and reflections from educational landscape: A review of AI studies in half a century. *Sustainability (Basel)*, *13*(2), 800. DOI: 10.3390/su13020800

Bozkurt, A., & Sharma, R. C. (2024). Trust, credibility and transparency in human-AI ınteraction: Why we need explainable and trustworthy AI and why we need it now. *Asian Journal of Distance Education*, *19*(2). https://www.asianjde.com/ojs/index.php/AsianJDE/article/view/819

Bozkurt, A., Xiao, J., Farrow, R., Bai, J. Y. H., Nerantzi, C., Moore, S., Dron, J., Stracke, C. M., Singh, L., Crompton, H., Koutropoulos, A., Terentev, E., Pazurek, A., Nichols, M., Sidorkin, A. M., Costello, E., Watson, S., Mulligan, D., Honeychurch, S., & Asino, T. I. (2024). The manifesto for teaching and learning in a time of generative AI: A critical collective stance to better navigate the future. *Open Praxis*, *16*(4), 487–513. DOI: 10.55982/openpraxis.16.4.777

Brans, M., Geva-May, I., & Howlett, M. (2017). Policy analysis in comparative perspective: An introduction. In Brans, M., Geva-May, I., & Howlett, M. (Eds.), *Routledge handbook of comparative policy analysis* (pp. 1–23). Routledge. DOI: 10.4324/9781315660561-1

Bridgeman, A., Weeks, R., & Liu, D. (2024). *Aligning our assessments to the age of generative AI*. Teaching@Sydney. https://educational-innovation.sydney.edu.au/teaching@sydney/aligning-our-assessments-to-the-age-of-generative-ai/

Broekhuizen, T., Dekker, H., de Faria, P., Firk, S., Nguyen, D. K., & Sofka, W. (2023). AI for managing open innovation: Opportunities, challenges, and a research agenda. *Journal of Business Research*, *167*, 114196. DOI: 10.1016/j.jbusres.2023.114196

Brynjolfsson, E., Li, D., & Raymond, L. (2025). Generative AI at work. *The Quarterly Journal of Economics*, *140*(2), qjae044. Advance online publication. DOI: 10.1093/qje/qjae044

Buccella, A. (2023). "AI for all" is a matter of social justice. *AI and Ethics*, *3*(4), 1143–1152. DOI: 10.1007/s43681-022-00222-z PMID: 36189174

Burke, K. (2010). Distributed leadership and shared governance in post-secondary education. *Management in Education*, *24*(2), 51–54. DOI: 10.1177/0892020610363088

Burns, T., Sinfield, S., & Abegglen, S. (2023). Postdigital academic writing. In Jandrić, P. (Ed.), *Encyclopedia of postdigital science and education*. Springer., DOI: 10.1007/978-3-031-35469-4_27-1

Calvo, R., Peters, D., & Ryan, R. (2018). Autonomy in AI systems. Input paper for the Horizon Scanning Project "*The effective and ethical development of artificial intelligence: An opportunity to improve our wellbeing*" on behalf of the Australian Council of Learned Academies. https://acola.org/wp-content/uploads/2019/07/acola-ai-input-paper_human-autonomy-in-ai-systems_calvo-peters-ryan.pdf

Campbell, J. P., DeBlois, P. B., & Oblinger, D. G. (2007). Academic analytics: A new tool for a new era. *EDUCAUSE Review*, *42*(4), 41–57.

Cao, M. (2024). Teacher-student relationships in the context of artificial intelligence. *Advances in Educational Technology and Psychology*, *8*(4), 75–80. DOI: 10.23977/aetp.2024.080412

Carvalho, L. (2023). *Education 5.0: What Does It Mean? How Does It Work?* Sydle. https://www.sydle.com/blog/education-5-0-61e71a99edf3b9259714e25a

Carvalho, M. S. d., & Silva, G. L. d. (2021). Inside the black box: Using explainable AI to improve evidence-based policies. *2021 IEEE 23rd Conference on Business Informatics (CBI)*, 57–64. DOI: 10.1109/CBI52690.2021.10055

Chai, C. S., Liang, S., & Wang, X. (2024). A survey study of Chinese teachers' continuous intentions to teach artificial intelligence. *Education and Information Technologies*, *29*(11), 14015–14034. DOI: 10.1007/s10639-023-12430-z

Chaika, O. (2023). The role of artificial intelligence in higher education. *Молодь і ринок, 6–7*(214–215), 69-74. DOI: 10.24919/2308-4634.2023.287898

Chaka, C., Shange, T., Nkhobo, T., & Hlatshwayo, V. (2024). An environmental review of the generative artificial intelligence policies and guidelines of South African higher education institutions: A content analysis. *International Journal of Learning. Teaching and Educational Research*, *23*(12), 487–511. DOI: 10.26803/ijlter.23.12.25

Chan, C. K. Y., & Zhou, W. (2023). An expectancy value theory (EVT) based instrument for measuring student perceptions of generative AI. *Smart Learning Environments, 10*(1). DOI: 10.1186/s40561-023-00284-4

Chan, C. K. Y. (2023). A comprehensive AI policy education framework for university teaching and learning. *International Journal of Educational Technology in Higher Education*, *20*(1), 38. DOI: 10.1186/s41239-023-00408-3

Charara, S. (2025, February, 26). Your Boss Wants You Back in the Office. This Surveillance Tech Could Be Waiting for You. *WIRED*. https://www.wired.com/story/your-boss-wants-you-back-in-the-office-this-surveillance-tech-could-be-waiting-for-you

Chen, B., Cheng, J., Wang, C., & Leung, V. (2025). Pedagogical Biases in AI-Powered Educational Tools: The Case of Lesson Plan Generators. Social Innovations Journal, 30. https://doi.org/DOI: 10.31219/osf.io/zqjw5_v1

Chen, L., Chen, P., & Lin, Z. (2020). Artificial intelligence in education: A review. *IEEE Access : Practical Innovations, Open Solutions*, *8*, 75264–75278. DOI: 10.1109/ACCESS.2020.2988510

Chen, Y., Jensen, S., Albert, L. J., Gupta, S., & Lee, T. (2023). Artificial intelligence (AI) student assistants in the classroom: Designing chatbots to support student success. *Information Systems Frontiers*, *25*(1), 161–182. DOI: 10.1007/s10796-022-10291-4

Chi, M. T. H., & Wylie, R. (2014). The ICAP framework: Linking cognitive engagement to active learning outcomes. *Educational Psychologist*, *49*(4), 219–243. DOI: 10.1080/00461520.2014.965823

Chiu, T. K., Moorhouse, B. L., Chai, C. S., & Ismailov, M. (2023). Teacher support and student motivation to learn with Artificial Intelligence (AI) based chatbot. *Interactive Learning Environments*, •••, 1–17.DOI: 10.1080/10494820.2023.2172044

Ciampa, K., Wolfe, Z. M., & Bronstein, B. (2023). ChatGPT in education: Transforming digital literacy practices. *Journal of Adolescent & Adult Literacy*, *67*(1), 10–20. DOI: 10.1002/jaal.1310

Citron, D. K. (2024). The surveilled student. *Stanford Law Review*, *76*(7), 1439–1472.

Clarke, R. (1988). Information technology and dataveillance. *Communications of the ACM*, *31*(5), 498–512. DOI: 10.1145/42411.42413

Clarke, V., & Braun, V. (2017). Thematic analysis. *The Journal of Positive Psychology*, *12*(3), 297–298. DOI: 10.1080/17439760.2016.1262613

Collins, S., & Ting, H. (2014). The complexity of care. *Complicity: An International Journal of Complexity and Education*, *11*(1), 5–19. DOI: 10.29173/cmplct21452

ColMOOC. (2019). ColMOOC. https://colmooc.eu/

Conijn, R., Kahr, P., & Snijders, C. C. (2023). The effects of explanations in automated essay scoring systems on student trust and motivation. *Journal of Learning Analytics*, *10*(1), 37–53. DOI: 10.18608/jla.2023.7801

Cope, B., & Kalantzis, M. (2016). *E-learning ecologies. Nova Iorque*. Routledge., DOI: 10.4324/9781315639215

Corbin, T., Dawson, P., Nicola-Richmond, K., & Partridge, H. (2025). 'Where's the line? It's an absurd line': Towards a framework for acceptable uses of AI in assessment. *Assessment & Evaluation in Higher Education*, *50*(5), 1–13. DOI: 10.1080/02602938.2025.2456207

Cormier, D. (2011, November 05). *Rhizomatic learning - why we teach?* Dave Cormier. https://davecormier.com/edblog/2011/11/05/rhizomatic-learning-why-learn/

Cox, A. (2021). Exploring the impact of artificial intelligence and robots on higher education through literature-based design fictions. *International Journal of Educational Technology in Higher Education*, *18*(1), 1–22. DOI: 10.1186/s41239-020-00237-8

Crawford, J., Allen, K., Pani, B., & Cowling, M. (2024). When artificial intelligence substitutes humans in higher education: The cost of loneliness, student success, and retention. *Studies in Higher Education*, *49*(5), 883–897. DOI: 10.1080/03075079.2024.2326956

Creswell, J. W. (2017). *Araştırma Deseni-Nitel, Nicel ve Karma Yöntem Yaklaşımları* [*Research Design-Qualitative, Quantitative and Mixed Methods Approaches*] (3rd ed., 4th ed. Trans., S. B. Demir, Trans. Ed., E. Bukova-Güzel, İ. Erdoğan, Y. Dede, G. Hacıömeroğlu, H. Ercan, I. Bilican, M. Bütün, M. Bursal, S. Mandacı-Şahin, & S. B. Demir, Trans.). Educational Book. (Original work published 2015)

Creswell, J. W. (2018). *Nitel Araştırma Yöntemleri-Beş yaklaşıma göre nitel araştırma ve araştırma deseni* [*Qualitative Inquiry & Research Design Choosing Among Five Approaches*] (4th ed., 3rd ed. Trans., M. Bütün and S. B. Demir, Trans. Ed., O. Birgin, S. Ünal, T. Özsevgeç, Y. Dede, A. Bacanak, A. Bakla, A. Budak, G. Hacıömeroğlu, İ. Budak, M. Aydın, M. Bütün, Mir. Aydın, & S. B. Demir, Trans.). Political Bookstore. (Original work published 2013)

Creswell, J. W. (2019). *Eğitim Araştırmaları: Nicel ve Nitel Araştırmanın Planlanması, Yürütülmesi ve Değerlendirilmesi* [*Educational Research: Planning, Conducting, and Evaluating Quanttative and Qualitative Research*] (2nd ed., 4th ed. Trans., C. Robb & K. Mason Eds., H. Ekşi, Trans. Ed., A. Avcu, D. Eryiğit, D. Dinçer, E. Bakiler, G. Alçekiç-Yaman, H. Ekşi, H. Çelik, İ. Karsantik, M. Tuncel, M. Başman, N. Yaman, S. Kardaş, S. Doğan, S. Çakır, Ş. Tatık, Y. Karsantık, Trans.). EDAM. (Original work published 2012)

Crompton, H., & Burke, D. (2023). Artificial intelligence in higher education: The state of the field. *International Journal of Educational Technology in Higher Education*, *20*(1), 22. DOI: 10.1186/s41239-023-00392-8

Crompton, H., Burke, D., Nickel, C., & Chigona, A. (2024). The SETI framework and technology integration in the digital age. *Asian Journal of Distance Education, 19*, 167–176. https://www.asianjde.com/ojs/index.php/AsianJDE/article/view/771

Csikszentmihalyi, M. (1990). *Flow: The Psychology of Optimal Experience*. Harper and Row.

Curtis, G. J. (2025). The two-lane road to hell is paved with good intentions: Why an all-or-none approach to generative AI, integrity, and assessment is insupportable. *Higher Education Research & Development*, •••, 1–8. DOI: 10.1080/07294360.2025.2476516

Dai, D., Wang, J., Chen, Y., & He, X. (2020). Promoting students' well-being by developing their readiness for the artificial intelligence age. *Sustainability (Basel), 12*(16), 6597. DOI: 10.3390/su12166597

Dai, R., Thomas, M. K. E., & Rawolle, S. (2024). The roles of AI and educational leaders in AI-assisted administrative decision-making: A proposed framework for symbiotic collaboration. *Australian Educational Researcher*. Advance online publication. DOI: 10.1007/s13384-024-00771-8

Dai, Y., Lin, Z., Liu, A., & Wang, W. (2023). An embodied, analogical and disruptive approach of AI pedagogy in upper elementary education: An experimental study. *British Journal of Educational Technology, 55*(2), 417–434. DOI: 10.1111/bjet.13371

Daniel, T. (2024). Foreword. In B. Buyserie and T. N. Thurston (Eds.), *Teaching and generative AI*. https://uen.pressbooks.pub/teachingandgenerativeai/front-matter/forweword/

Davis, A. J. (2024). AI rising in higher education: Opportunities, risks and limitations. *Asian Education and Development Studies, 13*(4), 307–319. DOI: 10.1108/AEDS-01-2024-0017

Davis, F. D. (1989). Perceived usefulness, perceived ease of use, and user acceptance of information technology. *Management Information Systems Quarterly, 13*(3), 319. DOI: 10.2307/249008

Dawson, P., Bearman, M., Dollinger, M., & Boud, D. (2024). Validity matters more than cheating. *Assessment & Evaluation in Higher Education, 49*(7), 1–12. DOI: 10.1080/02602938.2024.2386662

Dawson, S., Joksimovic, S., Mills, C., Gašević, D., & Siemens, G. (2023). Advancing theory in the age of artificial intelligence. *British Journal of Educational Technology, 54*(5), 1051–1056.DOI: 10.1111/bjet.13343

De Rosa, R. (2017). Governing by data: Some considerations on the role of learning analytics in education. In Lauro, N., Amaturo, E., Grassia, M., Aragona, B., & Marino, M. (Eds.), *Data science and social research* (pp. 87–98). Springer., DOI: 10.1007/978-3-319-55477-8_7

Deci, E. L., & Ryan, R. M. (1985). *Intrinsic motivation and self-determination in human ize*. Plenum.

Deci, E. L., & Ryan, R. M. (2000). The "what" and "why" of goal pursuits: Human needs and the self-determination of behavior. *Psychological Inquiry*, *11*(4), 227–268.

Deci, E., La Guardia, J., Moller, A., Scheiner, M., & Ryan, R. (2006). On the benefits of giving as well as receiving autonomy support: Mutuality in close friendships. *Personality and Social Psychology Bulletin*, *32*(3), 313–327. DOI: 10.1177/0146167205282148 PMID: 16455859

Deleuze, G., & Guattari, F. (1987). *A thousand plateaus: Capitalism and schizophrenia*. University of Minnesota Press.

Derrida, J. (2012). Specters of Marx: The state of the debt, the work of mourning and the new international. routledge. https://doi.org/DOI: 10.4324/9780203821619

Descartes, R. (1978). *The philosophical works of Descartes*. 1 (Repr). Univ. Press.

Deshpande, L., Agarwal, A., Haripriya, V., Jain, R., Choudhary, S., & Kumar, S. C. (2024). Investigating novel machine learning approaches to enhance real-time data analysis. *2024 2nd World Conference on Communication & Computing (WCONF)*, 1–7. DOI: 10.1109/WCONF61366.2024.10691969

Digital Education Council. (2024). *Global AI student survey 2024*. https://campustechnology.com/articles/2024/08/28/survey-86-of-students-already-use-ai-in-their-studies.aspx

Doshi-Velez, F., & Kim, B. (2017). Towards a rigorous science of interpretable machine learning. *arXiv preprint arXiv:1702.08608*.

Downe-Wamboldt, B. (1992). Content analysis: Method, applications and issues. *Health Care for Women International*, *13*, 313–321. DOI: 10.1080/07399339209516006

Du, X., Alghowinem, S., Taylor, M., Darling, K., & Breazeal, C. (2023). Innovating AI leadership education. *2023 IEEE Frontiers in Education Conference (FIE)*, 1–8. DOI: 10.1109/FIE58773.2023.10343238

Duckett, D., & Westrick, N. (2025). Exploring the use, adoption, and ethics of generative artificial intelligence in the public relations and communication professions. *Communication Teacher*, *39*(1), 33–41. DOI: 10.1080/17404622.2024.2395312

Dunbar-Morris, H., Nerantzi, C., Sharp, L., & Sidiropoulou, M. (2023). (In) dependent learning as explored in a cross-institutional collaborative project studying the perceptions of learning of ethnically diverse students. In Fitzgerald, R., Huijser, H., Altena, S., & Armellini, A. (Eds.), *Addressing the 'challenging' elements of learning at a distance* (Special Edition). Distance Education., DOI: 10.1080/01587919.2023.2198492

Durães, D., Bezerra, R., & Novais, P. (2024). AI-driven educational transformation in secondary schools: Leveraging data insights for inclusive learning environments. *2024 IEEE Global Engineering Education Conference (EDUCON)*, 1–9. DOI: 10.1109/EDUCON60312.2024.10578910

Dwi, S. (2024). The role of education management in improving learning innovation. *Gestion Educativa*, *1*(1). Advance online publication. DOI: 10.62872/ntf4c997

Eaton, L. (2024). *Syllabi / Policies for AI Generative Tools* https://docs.google.com/document/d/1RMVwzjc1o0Mi8Blw_-JUTcXv02b2WRH86vw7mi16W3U/edit#heading=h.1cykjn2vg2wx

Eccles, J. S. (1983). Expectancies, values, and academic behaviors. In Spence, J. T. (Ed.), *Achievement and achievement motives* (pp. 75–146). Freeman.

Eccles, J. S., & Wigfield, A. (2002). Motivational beliefs, values, and goals. *Annual Review of Psychology*, *53*, 109–132.

Eden, C. A., Chisom, O. N., & Adeniyi, I. S. (2024). Integrating AI in education: Opportunities, challenges, and ethical considerations. *Magna Scientia Advanced Research and Reviews, 10*(2), 006-013. https://doi.org/DOI: 10.30574/msarr.2024.10.2.0039

Elfeky, A. I. M., Najmi, A. H., Yasien, M., & Elbyaly, H.Abdellah Ibrahim Mohammed ElfekyAli Hassan NajmiMarwa Yasien Helmy Elbyaly. (2024). Effects of big data analytics in learning management systems for improving learners' academic success. *El Profesional de la Información*, *33*(1), e330016. DOI: 10.3145/epi.2024.0016

Ellison, S. (2009). Hard-wired for innovation? Comparing two policy paths toward innovative schooling. *International Education, 39*(1). https://trace.tennessee.edu/internationaleducation/vol39/iss1/2

Elo, S., & Kyngäs, H. (2008). The qualitative content analysis process. *Journal of Advanced Nursing*, *62*(1), 107–115. DOI: 10.1111/j.1365-2648.2007.04569.x

Entwistle, N., McCune, V., & Walker, P. (2001). Conceptions, styles and approaches within higher education: analytic abstractions and everyday experience. In Sternberg, R. J., & Zhang, L.-F. (Eds.), *Perspectives on Thinking, Learning and Cognitive Styles*. Lawrence Erlbaum.

Essien, A., Salami, A., Ajala, O., Adebisi, B., Shodiya, A., & Essien, G. (2024). Exploring socio-cultural influences on generative AI engagement in Nigerian higher education: An activity theory analysis. *Smart Learning Environments*, *11*(1). Advance online publication. DOI: 10.1186/s40561-024-00352-3

Eubanks, V. (2011). *Digital dead end: Fighting for social justice in the information age*. The MIT Press. DOI: 10.7551/mitpress/8073.001.0001

Everson, K. K. (2025). *Enhancing doctoral dissertations ethically with AI: A comprehensive guide*. Stylus Publishing, LLC.

Fathali, S., & Okada, T. (2018). Technology acceptance model in technology-enhanced OCLL contexts: A self-determination theory approach. *Australasian Journal of Educational Technology*, *34*(4). Advance online publication. DOI: 10.14742/ajet.3629

Fawns, T. (2022). An entangled pedagogy: Looking beyond the pedagogy-technology dichotomy. *Postdigital Science and Education*, *4*(3), 711–728. DOI: 10.1007/s42438-022-00302-7 PMID: 40477872

Fenn, J. (2022). *The first hype cycle: An origin story*. LinkedIn Pulse. https://www.linkedin.com/pulse/first-hype-cycle-origin-story-jackie-fenn/

Ferrara, E. (2023). Fairness and bias in artificial intelligence: A brief survey of sources, impacts, and mitigation strategies. *Sci*, *6*(1), 1–15. DOI: 10.3390/sci6010003

Ferreira, S. A., & Andrade, A. (2014). Academic analytics: Anatomy of an exploratory essay. *Education and Information Technologies*, *20*(1), 1–15.

Fiebig, J. H., Gould, E. R., Ming, S., & Watson, R. A. (2020). An invitation to act on the value of self-care: Being a whole person in all that you do. *Behavior Analysis in Practice*, *13*(3), 559–567. DOI: 10.1007/s40617-020-00442-x PMID: 32837703

Filgueiras, F. (2023). Artificial intelligence and education governance. *Education, Citizenship and Social Justice*. Advance online publication. DOI: 10.1177/17461979231160674

Finn, J. D. (1989). Withdrawing from school. *Review of Educational Research*, *59*(2), 117–142.

Finn, J. D., & Zimmer, K. S. (2012). Student engagement: What is it? Why does it matter? In Christenson, S. L., Reschly, A. L., & Wylie, C. (Eds.), *Handbook of research on student engagement* (pp. 97–131). Springer.

Fırat, S. Ü. O. (2023). Endüstri 4.0'dan Endüstri 6.0'a Yolculuk. [Journey from Industry 4.0 to Industry 6.0]. *Global Industrialist: Economy and Business World Magazine.* https://www.sanayicidergisi.com.tr/endustri-40dan-endustri-60a-yolculuk-makale,857.html

Fischer, I., Sweeney, S., Lucas, M., & Gupta, N. (2024). Making sense of generative AI for assessments: Contrasting student claims and assessor evaluations. *International Journal of Management Education, 22*(3), 101081. DOI: 10.1016/j.ijme.2024.101081

Fissore, C., Floris, F., Fradiante, V., Conte, M. M., & Sacchet, M. (2024). From Theory to Training: Exploring Teachers' Attitudes Towards Artificial Intelligence in Education. *International Conference on Computer Supported Education, CSEDU-Proceedings, 2*, 118–127. https://doi.org/DOI: 10.5220/0012734700003693

Fitria, T. N. (2021). The use technology based on artificial intelligence in English teaching and learning). *ELT Echo: The Journal of English Language Teaching in Foreign Language Context, 6*(2). Advance online publication. DOI: 10.24235/eltecho.v6i2.9299

Fitzpatrick, D. (2024). *Infinite education: The four-step strategy for leading change in the age of artificial intelligence*. Teacher Goals Publishing.

Flagler, A. V. (2024). Integrated care: Transforming beginning teachers and students with EBD. [ICCTE]. *International Christian Community of Teacher Educators Journal, 19*(2). Advance online publication. DOI: 10.55221/1932-7846.1336

Folmeg, K., Fekete, I., & Koris, R. (2024). Towards identifying the components of students' AI literacy: An exploratory study based on Hungarian higher education students' perceptions. *Journal of University Teaching & Learning Practice, 21*(3), 33. Advance online publication. DOI: 10.53761/wzyrwj33

Foltynek, T., Bjelobaba, S., Glendinning, I., Khan, Z. R., Santos, R., Pavletic, P., & Kravjar, J. (2023). ENAI Recommendations on the ethical use of artificial intelligence in education. *International Journal for Educational Integrity, 19*(1), 1–4. DOI: 10.1007/s40979-023-00133-4

Foucault, M. (1977). *Discipline and punish: The birth of the prison*. Pantheon Books.

Fowler, A. G. (2023, April 3). We tested a new ChatGPT-detector for teachers. It flagged an innocent student. *The Washington Post.* https://www.washingtonpost.com/technology/2023/04/01/chatgpt-cheating-detection-turnitin/

Francisco, M. (2023). Artificial intelligence for environmental security: National, international, human and ecological perspectives. *Current Opinion in Environmental Sustainability, 61*, 101250. DOI: 10.1016/j.cosust.2022.101250

Fredricks, J. A., Blumenfeld, P. C., & Paris, A. H. (2004). School engagement: Potential of the concept, state of the evidence. *Review of Educational Research, 74*(1), 59–109. DOI: 10.3102/00346543074001059

Freire, P. (1996). *Letters to Cristina: Reflections on my life and work*. Routledge.

Frick, T. W. (2023). *Are we dupes? Limitations of AI systems: What should educators do with them? TechTrends: Online first*. Association for Educational Communications and Technology., DOI: 10.1007/s11528-023-00893-3

Gagné, M. (2003a). The role of autonomy support and autonomy orientation in prosocial behavior engagement. *Motivation and Emotion, 27*(3), 199–223. DOI: 10.1023/A:1025007614869

Gagné, M. (2003b). Autonomy support and need satisfaction in the motivation and well-being of gymnasts. *Journal of Applied Sport Psychology, 15*(4), 372–390. DOI: 10.1080/714044203

Gale, K., & Bowstead, H. (2013). Deleuze and collaborative writing as a method of inquiry. *Journal of Learning Development in Higher Education, 6*(6), 1–15. https://journal.aldinhe.ac.uk/index.php/jldhe/article/view/222/147. DOI: 10.47408/jldhe.v0i6.222

Gamberini, L., & Pluchino, P. (2024). Industry 5.0: A comprehensive insight into the future of work, social sustainability, sustainable development, and career. *Australian Journal of Career Development, 33*(1), 5–14. DOI: 10.1177/10384162241231118

Gambo, I., Abegunde, F. J., Gambo, O., Ogundokun, R. O., Babatunde, A. N., & Lee, C. C. (2024). GRAD-AI: An automated grading tool for code assessment and feedback in programming course. *Education and Information Technologies*, •••, 1–41. DOI: 10.1007/s10639-024-13218-5

Gao, Z., Huang, Y., Zheng, L., Li, X., Lu, H., Zhang, J., Zhao, Q., Diao, W., Fang, Q., & Fang, J. (2021). A student attendance management method based on crowdsensing in classroom environment. *IEEE Access : Practical Innovations, Open Solutions, 9*, 31481–31492. DOI: 10.1109/ACCESS.2021.3060256

George, B., & Wooden, O. (2023). Managing the strategic transformation of higher education through artificial intelligence. *Administrative Sciences, 13*(9), 196. DOI: 10.3390/admsci13090196

Gerring, J. (2004). What is a case study and what is it good for? *The American Political Science Review, 98*(2), 341–354. DOI: 10.1017/S0003055404001182

Ge, Z., & Hu, Y. (2020). Innovative application of artificial intelligence (AI) in the management of higher education and teaching. *Journal of Physics: Conference Series, 1533*(3), 032089. DOI: 10.1088/1742-6596/1533/3/032089

Ghimire, A., & Edwards, J. (2024). From guidelines to governance: A study of AI policies in education. *arXiv preprint arXiv:2403.15601*. DOI: 10.1007/978-3-031-64312-5_36

Gibson, D., Kovanovic, V., Ifenthaler, D., Dexter, S., & Feng, S. (2023). Learning theories for artificial intelligence promoting learning processes. *British Journal of Educational Technology, 54*(5), 1125–1146. DOI: 10.1111/bjet.13341

Gilligan, C. (1982). *In a different voice: Psychological theory and women's development*. Harvard University Press.

Glickman, M., & Sharot, T. (2024). How human–AI feedback loops alter human perceptual, emotional, and social judgements. *Nature Human Behaviour*.DOI: 10.1038/s41562-024-02077-2

Goksel, N., & Bozkurt, A. (2019). Artificial Intelligence in Education: Current Insights and Future Perspectives. In Sisman-Ugur, S., & Kurubacak, G. (Eds.), *Handbook of Research on Learning in the Age of Transhumanism* (pp. 224–236). IGI Global., DOI: 10.4018/978-1-5225-8431-5.ch014

Gomez, L., Chen, R., & Malik, A. (2023). Embedding ethical frameworks in AI education: Preparing students for responsible AI engagement. *AI & Society, 38*(3), 455–470. DOI: 10.1234/aisociety.2023.03803

Gong, Y., Huang, J., Liu, B., Xu, J., Wu, B., & Zhang, Y. (2024). Dynamic resource allocation for virtual machine migration optimization using machine learning. *Applied and Computational Engineering, 57*(1), 1–8. DOI: 10.54254/2755-2721/57/20241348

Goosen, W., & Mugumo, P. (2024). A framework for the application of AI in higher education in association with APPETD and Swiss Institute for Management and Innovation. *Proceedings of SPIE - the International Society for Optical Engineering, 13188*, 1318808. DOI: 10.1117/12.3030740

Gorichanaz, T. (2023). Accused: How students respond to allegations of using ChatGPT on assessments, Learning. *Research and Practice, 9*(2), 183–196. DOI: 10.1080/23735082.2023.2254787

Gram-Hanssen, K. (2024). Beyond energy justice: Ethics of care as a new approach in the energy system. *Energy Issues and Social Science, 111*, 103470. Advance online publication. DOI: 10.1016/j.erss.2024.103470

Granić, A., & Marangunić, N. (2019). Technology acceptance model in educational context: A systematic literature review. *British Journal of Educational Technology*, *50*(5), 2572–2593. DOI: 10.1111/bjet.12864

Grassini, S. (2023). Shaping the future of education: Exploring the potential and consequences of AI and ChatGPT in educational settings. *Education Sciences*, *13*(7), 692. DOI: 10.3390/educsci13070692

Greenfield, M., & Gomez, L. (2023). Empowering ethical AI practices through education: Strategies and frameworks. *Journal of Emerging Technology Education*, *12*(3), 198–214.

Güler, E., Uğur, S., & Güler, C. (2025). Eğitim fakültesi öğretim elemanlarının üretken yapay zekâya yönelik farkındalıklarının belirlenmesi ve öğretmen yetiştirmede kullanımına yönelik öneriler. [Determination of faculty of education lecturers' awareness of generative artificial intelligence and suggestions for its use in teacher training]. *Mehmet Akif Ersoy University Faculty of Education Journal*, *74*(74), 618–647. DOI: 10.21764/maeuefd.1627851

Gulson, K. N., & Sellar, S. (2024). Anticipating disruption: Artificial intelligence and minor experiments in education policy. *Journal of Education Policy*, *39*(5), 702–717. DOI: 10.1080/02680939.2024.2302474

Gulson, K., & Witzenberger, K. (2020). Repackaging authority: Artificial intelligence, automated governance and education trade shows. *Journal of Education Policy*, *37*(2), 145–160. DOI: 10.1080/02680939.2020.1785552

Gunjal, A., Pednekar, R. S. K., & Ruke, S. (2024). Dynamic resource allocation in edge computing environments: A machine learning approach. *Journal of Trends and Challenges in Artificial Intelligence*, *1*(4), 133–138. DOI: 10.61552/JAI.2024.04.003

Gupta, A. (2024, August). *When generative artificial intelligence meets academic integrity: Educational opportunities & challenges in a digital age*. BERA Report Series: Education in a Digital Age. British Educational Research Association. https://www.bera.ac.uk/publication/when-generative-artificial-intelligence-meets-academic-integrity

Gupta, B., Dusane, A., Patil, N. P., Mane, Y. D., Raut, S., & Agrawal, A. (2024). Enhancing adaptive learning and decision-making systems using swarm intelligence and deep learning for advanced AI applications. *ICTACT Journal on Soft Computing*, *15*(2), 3482–3490. DOI: 10.21917/ijsc.2024.0486

Gutmann, M. (2024, November 11). AI's false-time saving promise. Or why AI is like the vacuum cleaner. *Forbes*. https://www.forbes.com/sites/martingutmann/2024/11/11/ais-false-time-saving-promise-or-why-ai-is-like-the-vacuum-cleaner/

Guzder, K. (2024). *What is the Role of Artificial Intelligence in Education?* High-Speed Training Limited. https://www.highspeedtraining.co.uk/hub/artificial-intelligence-in-education/

Haag, D., & Kaupenjohann, M. (2001). Parameters, prediction, post-normal science and the precautionary principle—A roadmap for modelling for decision-making. *Ecological Modelling*, *144*(1), 45–60. DOI: 10.1016/S0304-3800(01)00361-1

Hagendorff, T. (2020). The ethics of AI ethics: An evaluation of guidelines. *Minds and Machines*, *30*(1), 99–120. DOI: 10.1007/s11023-020-09517-8

Hamon, K., Hogue, R. J., Honeychurch, S., Johnson, S., Koutropoulos, A., Ensor, S., . . . Bali, M. (2015). Writing the unreadable untext: A collaborative autoethnography of #rhizo14. *Hybrid Pedagogy*. https://hybridpedagogy.org/writing-the-unreadable-untext/

Hancock, J. T., & Bailenson, J. N. (2021). *The social impact of deepfakes* (Vol. 24). Mary Ann Liebert, Inc., DOI: 10.1089/cyber.2021.29208.jth

Hannan, E., & Liu, S. (2021). AI: New source of competitiveness in higher education. *Competitiveness Review*. Advance online publication. DOI: 10.1108/CR-03-2021-0045

Harvard University. (2025). *Initial guidelines for the use of Generative AI tools at Harvard*. https://www.huit.harvard.edu/ai/guidelines

Hawksey, M., Baker, R., Jeffery, N., Behrens, J. T., & Pea, R. (2013). Educational data scientists: A scarce breed. *Proceedings of the Third International Conference on Learning Analytics and Knowledge*, 278–281.

Hayes, S., & Jandrić, P. (2017). Learning, technologies, and time in the age of global neoliberal capitalism. *Knowledge Cultures*, *5*(2), 11. DOI: 10.22381/KC5220171

Hays, L. (2024, June 21). OpenAI and Anthropic are ignoring an established rule that prevents bots scraping online content. *Business Insider*. https://www.businessinsider.com/openai-anthropic-ai-ignore-rule-scraping-web-contect-robotstxt

Healy, M. (2023). Approaches to generative artificial intelligence, a social justice perspective. *arXiv*. https://arxiv.org/abs/2309.12331

Heng, H., & Tabunshchyk, G. (2021). Teaching tech to talk: K-12 conversational artificial intelligence literacy curriculum and development tools. *Proceedings of the AAAI Conference on Artificial Intelligence, 35*(17), 13984–13992. DOI: 10.1609/aaai.v35i17.17844

Hermansyah, M., Najib, A., Farida, A., Sacipto, R., & Rintyarna, B. S. (2023). Artificial intelligence and ethics: Building an artificial intelligence system that ensures privacy and social justice. *The International Journal of Science in Society, 5*(1), 154–168. DOI: 10.54783/ijsoc.v5i1.644

Hınız, G., & Çelik, Ö. (2024). A bibliometric and content analysis of student engagement research in English language teaching. *Language Awareness*, •••, 1–34. DOI: 10.1080/09658416.2024.2367970

Holmes, W., Bialik, M., & Fadel, C. (2022). *Artificial intelligence in education: Promises and implications for teaching and learning*. Center for Curriculum Redesign.

Holmes, W., Porayska-Pomsta, K., Holstein, K., Sutherland, E., Baker, T., Buckingham Shum, S., Santos, O., Rodrigo, M., Bittencourt, I., Cukurova, M., & Koedinger, K. (2022). Ethics of AI in education: Towards a community-wide framework. *International Journal of Artificial Intelligence in Education, 32*(3), 504–526. DOI: 10.1007/s40593-021-00239-1

Holstein, K., & Doroudi, S. (2022). Equity and artificial intelligence in education. In *The Ethics of Artificial İntelligence in Education* (pp. 151–173). Routledge., DOI: 10.4324/9780429329067-9

Hong, Y., Nguyen, A., Dang, B., & Nguyen, B. (2022). Data ethics framework for artificial intelligence in education (AIED). *2022 International Conference on Advanced Learning Technologies (ICALT)*, 297–301. DOI: 10.1109/ICALT55010.2022.00095

hooks, b. (1994) *Teaching to transgress, Education as the practice of freedom*. Oxon: Routledge.

Hua, S., Jin, S., & Jiang, S. (2023). The limitations and ethical considerations of ChatGPT. *Data Intelligence, 6*(1), 201–329. DOI: 10.1162/dint_a_00243

Hu, W., Tian, J., & Li, Y. (2025). Enhancing student engagement in online collaborative writing through a generative AI-based conversational agent. *The Internet and Higher Education, 65*, 100979.DOI: 10.1016/j.iheduc.2024.100979

Hu, Y., Fu, J. S., & Yeh, H. (2023). Developing an early-warning system through robotic process automation: Are intelligent tutoring robots as effective as human teachers? *Interactive Learning Environments*, •••, 1–14. DOI: 10.1080/10494820.2022.2160467

Huynh, E., Nyhout, A., Ganea, P., & Chevalier, F. (2020). Designing narrative-focused role-playing games for visualization literacy in young children. *IEEE Transactions on Visualization and Computer Graphics*, *27*(2), 924–934. DOI: 10.1109/TVCG.2020.3030464 PMID: 33048745

Ifelebuegu, A. O., Kulume, P., & Cherukut, P. (2023). Chatbots and AI in Education (AIEd) tools: The good, the bad, and the ugly. *Journal of Applied Learning and Teaching*, *6*(2), 332–345. DOI: 10.37074/jalt.2023.6.2.29

Ihde, D. (1990). *Technology and the lifeworld: From garden to earth.* Indiana University Press. DOI: 10.2979/3108.0

Illeris, K. (2007). What do we actually mean by experiential learning? *Human Resource Development Review*, *6*(1), 84–95. DOI: 10.1177/1534484306296828

Ivanov, S. (2023). The dark side of artificial intelligence in higher education. *Service Industries Journal*, *43*(15-16), 1055–1082. DOI: 10.1080/02642069.2023.2258799

James, T., & Andrews, G. (2024). Leveling the playing field through GenAI: Harnessing artificial intelligence to bridge educational gaps for equity and disadvantaged students. *Widening Participation and Lifelong Learning : the Journal of the Institute for Access Studies and the European Access Network*, *26*(3), 250–260. DOI: 10.5456/WPLL.26.3.250

Jandrić, P., & Ford, D. R. (2022). Postdigital ecopedagogies: Genealogies, contradictions, and possible futures. In Postdigital Ecopedagogies: Genealogies, Contradictions, and Possible Futures (pp. 3-23). Springer. https://doi.org/DOI: 10.1007/978-3-030-97262-2

Jandrić, P., Luke, T. W., Sturm, S., McLaren, P., Jackson, L., MacKenzie, A., Tesar, M., Stewart, G. T., Roberts, P., Abegglen, S., Burns, T., Sinfield, S., Hayes, S., Jaldemark, J., Peters, M. A., Sinclair, C., & Gibbons, A. (2023). Collective writing: The continuous struggle for meaning-making. In Jandrić, P., MacKenzie, A., & Knox, J. (Eds.), *Postdigital research. Postdigital science and education* (pp. 249–293). Springer., DOI: 10.1007/978-3-031-35469-4

Jiang, Y. (2025). Interaction and dialogue: Integration and application of artificial intelligence in blended mode writing feedback. *The Internet and Higher Education*, *64*, 100975.DOI: 10.1016/j.iheduc.2024.100975

Jian-hua, H., Zhao, W., Jiang, Q., Oubibi, M., & Hu, X. (2019). Intelligent tutoring system trends 2006-2018: A literature review. In *2019 Eighth International Conference on Educational Innovation through Technology (EITT)* (pp. 153-159). IEEE. DOI: 10.1109/EITT.2019.00037

Jin, Y., Martinez-Maldonado, R., Gašević, D., & Yan, L. (2024). GLAT: The generative AI literacy assessment test. *arXiv preprint arXiv:2411.00283*. /DOI: 10.48550

Jin, Y., Yan, L., Echeverria, V., Gašević, D., & Martinez-Maldonado, R. (2025). Generative AI in higher education: A global perspective of institutional adoption policies and guidelines. *Computers and Education: Artificial Intelligence*, *8*, 100348. Advance online publication. DOI: 10.1016/j.caeai.2024.100348

Jobin, A., Ienca, M., & Vayena, E. (2019). The global landscape of AI ethics guidelines. *Nature Machine Intelligence*, *1*(9), 389–399. DOI: 10.1038/s42256-019-0088-2

Kahu, E. R. (2013). Framing student engagement in higher education. *Studies in Higher Education*, *38*(5), 758–773. DOI: 10.1080/03075079.2011.598505

Kahu, E. R., & Nelson, K. (2018). Student engagement in the educational interface: Understanding the mechanisms of student success. *Higher Education Research & Development*, *37*(1), 58–71.

Kamalov, F., Calonge, D., & Gurrib, I. (2023). New era of artificial intelligence in education: Towards a sustainable multifaceted revolution. *Sustainability (Basel)*, *15*(16), 12451. DOI: 10.3390/su151612451

Kamalov, F., Cherukuri, A. K., Sulieman, H., Thabtah, F., & Hossain, A. (2023). Machine learning applications for COVID-19: A state-of-the-art review. In Tyagi, A. K., & Abraham, A. (Eds.), *Data Science for Genomics* (pp. 277–289). Elsevier. DOI: 10.1016/B978-0-323-98352-5.00010-0

Kanchetti, D., Munirathnam, R., & Thakkar, D. (2024). Integration of machine learning algorithms with cloud computing for real-time data analysis. *Journal for Research in Applied Sciences and Biotechnology*, *3*(2), 301–306. DOI: 10.55544/jrasb.3.2.46

Kangwa, D., Msafiri, M. M., & Fute, A. (2025). Balancing innovation and ethics: Promote academic integrity through support and effective use of GenAI tools in higher education. *AI and Ethics*, *5*(4), 3497–3530. Advance online publication. DOI: 10.1007/s43681-025-00689-6

Karakose, T., & Tülübaş, T. (2024). School leadership and management in the age of artificial intelligence (AI): Recent developments and future prospects. *Educational Process: International Journal*, *13*(1), 7–14. DOI: 10.22521/edupij.2024.131.1

Karlberg-Granlund, G., & Pastuhov, A. (2024). Being, becoming and sustaining: Learning professional learning in teacher education. *Professional Development in Education*, *50*(2), 372–385. DOI: 10.1080/19415257.2023.2291360

Kelley, J. (2021, June 22). A Long Overdue Reckoning For Online Proctoring Companies May Finally Be Here. *Electronic Frontier Foundation*. https://www.eff.org/deeplinks/2021/06/long-overdue-reckoning-online-proctoring-companies-may-finally-be-here

Kerlinger, F. N., & Lee, H. B. (2000). *Foundations of behavioral research* (4th ed.). Wadsworth Publishing.

Kestin, G., Miller, K., Klales, A., Milbourne, T., & Ponti, G. (2024, May 14). *AI tutoring outperforms active learning* [Preprint]. Research Square. DOI: 10.21203/rs.3.rs-4243877/v1

Kılınç, H. (2019). Açık ve uzaktan öğrenme ortamlarında çevrimiçi grup tartışması tekniğinin kullanılması. *Açıköğretim Uygulamaları ve Araştırmaları Dergisi AUAd, 5*(2), 87-106. https://dergipark.org.tr/en/download/article-file/734331

Kimmons, R., Graham, C. R., & West, R. E. (2020). The PICRAT model for Technology Integration in teacher Preparation. *Contemporary Issues in Technology and Teacher Education Journal, 20*(1), 176–198. https://eric.ed.gov/?id=EJ1245787

Kimmons, R., Graham, C. R., & West, R. E. (2020). The PICRAT model for technology integration in teacher preparation. *Contemporary Issues in Technology & Teacher Education, 20*(1), 176–198.

Klimova, B., Pikhart, M., & Kacetl, J. (2023). Ethical issues of the use of AI-driven mobile apps for education. *Frontiers in Public Health, 10*, 1118116. Advance online publication. DOI: 10.3389/fpubh.2022.1118116

Kloos, C., Alario-Hoyos, C., Estévez-Ayres, I., Callejo-Pinardo, P., Hombrados-Herrera, M., Muñoz-Merino, P., & Ibáñez, M. (2024). How can generative AI support education? *2024 IEEE Global Engineering Education Conference (EDUCON)*, 1–7. DOI: 10.1109/EDUCON60312.2024.10578716

Knibbs, K. (2025, January 9) Meta Secretly Trained Its AI on a Notorious Piracy Database, Unredacted court documents reveal. *WIRED*. https://www.wired.com/story/new-documents-unredacted-meta-copyright-ai-lawsuit/

Kolb, D. A. (1984). *Experiential learning: Experience as the source of learning and development*. Prentice Hall.

Kolb, D. A., Boyatzis, R. E., & Mainemelis, C. (2014). Experiential learning theory: Previous research and new directions. In *Perspectives on thinking, learning, and cognitive styles* (pp. 227–247). Routledge., DOI: 10.4324/9781410605986-9

Kolkman, D. (2020). The usefulness of algorithmic models in policy making. *Government Information Quarterly*, *37*(3), 101488. DOI: 10.1016/j.giq.2020.101488

Kong, X., Liu, Z., Chen, C., Liu, S., Xu, Z., & Tang, Q. (2025). Exploratory study of an AI-supported discussion representational tool for online collaborative learning in a Chinese university. *The Internet and Higher Education*, *64*, 100973.DOI: 10.1016/j.iheduc.2024.100973

Kopp, M., & Gröblinger, O. (2024). Generative AI and academic integrity-a contradiction. In European Association of Distance Teaching Universities, *Leading the Future of Learning. Proceedings of the Innovating Higher Education Conference* (pp. 101-114). DOI: 10.5281/zenodo.14220974

Kotsis, K. T. (2025). Legality of employing artificial intelligence for writing academic papers in education. *Journal of Contemporary Philosophical and Anthropological Studies*, *3*(1). Advance online publication. DOI: 10.59652/jcpas.v3i1.375

Kousa, P., & Niemi, H. (2022). AI ethics and learning: EdTech companies' challenges and solutions. *Interactive Learning Environments*, *31*(7), 6735–6746. DOI: 10.1080/10494820.2022.2043908

Kridel, D. J., Dolk, D. R., & Castillo, D. G. (2015). Adaptive modeling for real-time analytics: The case of "big data" in mobile advertising. *2015 48th Hawaii International Conference on System Sciences (HICSS)*, 887–896. DOI: 10.1109/HICSS.2015.111

Krippendorff, K. (1980). *Content analysis: An introduction to its methodology*. Sage Publications.

Kruiper, S. M., Leenknecht, M. J., & Slof, B. (2022). Using scaffolding strategies to improve formative assessment practice in higher education. *Assessment & Evaluation in Higher Education*, *47*(3), 458–476. DOI: 10.1080/02602938.2021.1927981

Kuhn, C., Khoo, S. M., Czerniewicz, L., Warren, L., Bute, S., Crean, A., Abegglen, S., Burns, T., Sinfield, S., Jandrić, P., Knox, J., & MacKenzie, A. (2023). Understanding digital inequality: A theoretical kaleidoscope. In Jandrić, P., Knox, J., & MacKenzie, A. (Eds.), *Constructing postdigital research: Method and emancipation* (pp. 333–373). Springer., DOI: 10.1007/978-3-031-35411-3_17

Kurian, N. (2023). Toddlers and robots? The ethics of supporting young children with disabilities with AI Companions and the implications for children's rights. *International Journal of Human Rights Education*, *7*(1). https://repository.usfca.edu/ijhre/vol7/iss1/9

Kwet, M., & Prinsloo, P. (2020). The 'smart' classroom: A new frontier in the age of the smart university. *Teaching in Higher Education*, *25*(4), 510–526. DOI: 10.1080/13562517.2020.1734922

Laupichler, C., Aster, A., Meyerheim, M., Raupach, T., & Mergen, M. (2024). Medical students' AI literacy and attitudes towards AI: A cross-sectional two-center study using pre-validated assessment instruments. *BMC Medical Education*, *24*(1), 400. Advance online publication. DOI: 10.1186/s12909-024-05400-7 PMID: 38600457

Lee, D., Arnold, M., Srivastava, A., Plastow, K., Strelan, P., Ploeckl, F., Lekkas, D., & Palmer, E. (2024). The impact of generative AI on higher education learning and teaching: A study of educators' perspectives. Computers and Education: Artificial Intelligence, 6, 100221. https://doi.org/https://doi.org/10.1016/j.caeai.2024.100221

Lee, C., & Low, M. (2024). Using genAI in education: The case for critical thinking. *Frontiers in Artificial Intelligence*, *1*(7), 1–3. DOI: 10.3389/frai.2024.1452131 PMID: 39554991

Lee, H. P. H., Sarkar, A., Tankelevitch, L., Drosos, I., Rintel, S., Banks, R., & Wilson, N. (2025). The Impact of Generative AI on Critical Thinking: Self-Reported Reductions in Cognitive Effort and Confidence Effects From a Survey of Knowledge Workers. *CHI*, *2025*, 1–22. Advance online publication. DOI: 10.1145/3706598.3713778

Lee, J. S. (2012). The effects of the teacher–student relationship and academic press on student engagement and academic performance. *International Journal of Educational Research*, *53*, 330–340. DOI: 10.1016/j.ijer.2012.04.006

Leimanis, A. (2020). Self-imposed ethical guidelines for AI in education. *International Scientific Conference "Society, Integration, Education-SIE2020"*. DOI: 10.17770/sie2020vol1.5048

Lester, J. (2021). AI and the future of education. *Proceedings of the 29th ACM International Conference on Multimedia*. DOI: 10.1145/3474085.3475715

Lim, C. P., & Tan, C. Y. (2020). Technology-enhanced learning: Using AI to address diverse learning needs. *Educational Technology Research and Development*, *68*(4), 541–555. DOI: 10.1007/s11423-020-09789-6

Ling, N. Y. (2024). Educational big data analytics: Machine learning-based academic performance predictive modelling. *Pakistan Journal of Life and Social Sciences*, *22*(2). Advance online publication. DOI: 10.57239/PJLSS-2024-22.2.00562

Liu, M., Zhang, L. J., & Biebricher, C. (2024). Investigating students' cognitive processes in generative AI-assisted digital multimodal composing and traditional writing. *Computers & Education*, *211*, 104977. DOI: 10.1016/j.compedu.2023.104977

Liu, X., & Liu, C. (2024, September). The application of artificial intelligence to classroom attendance. In *Proceedings of the International Conference on Image Processing, Machine Learning and Pattern Recognition* (pp. 583-590). https://doi.org/DOI: 10.1145/3700906.3701000

Lo Cascio, V., Guzzo, G., Pace, F., & Pace, U. (2013). Anxiety and self-esteem as mediators of the relation between family communication and indecisiveness in adolescence. *International Journal for Educational and Vocational Guidance*, *13*(2), 135–149. DOI: 10.1007/s10775-013-9243-1

Lo, C. K., Hew, K. F., & Jong, M. S. (2024). The influence of ChatGPT on student engagement: A systematic review and future research agenda. *Computers & Education*, *219*, 105100.DOI: 10.1016/j.compedu.2024.105100

Longo, L., Brcic, M., Cabitza, F., Choi, J., Confalonieri, R., Del Ser, J., & Stumpf, S. (2024). Explainable Artificial Intelligence (XAI) 2.0: A manifesto of open challenges and interdisciplinary research directions. *Information Fusion*, *106*, 102301. DOI: 10.1016/j.inffus.2024.102301

Loughran, J. (2013). *Developing a pedagogy of teacher education: Understanding teaching & learning about teaching*. Routledge., DOI: 10.4324/9780203019672

Luan, H., Géczy, P., Lai, H., Gobert, J., Yang, S., Ogata, H., Baltes, J., Guerra, R., Li, P., & Tsai, C. (2020). Challenges and future directions of big data and artificial intelligence in education. *Frontiers in Psychology*, *11*, 580820. Advance online publication. DOI: 10.3389/fpsyg.2020.580820

Luckin, R. (2018). *Machine learning and human intelligence: The future of education for the 21st century*. UCL Institute of Education Press.

Luckin, R., & Cukurova, M. (2019). Designing educational technologies in the age of AI: A learning sciences-driven approach. *British Journal of Educational Technology*, *50*(6), 2824–2838. DOI: 10.1111/bjet.12861

Luck, M. (2012). Surveillance in the virtual classroom. In Khosrow-Pour, M. (Ed.), *Virtual Learning Environments: Concepts, Methodologies, Tools and Applications* (pp. 1676–1685). IGI Global Scientific Publishing. DOI: 10.4018/978-1-4666-0011-9.ch808

Lu, H., He, L., Yu, H., Pan, T., & Fu, K. (2024). A study on teachers' willingness to use generative AI technology and its influencing factors: Based on an integrated model. *Sustainability*, *16*(16), 7216.DOI: 10.3390/su16167216

Luo (Jess), J. (. (2024). How does GenAI affect trust in teacher-student relationships? Insights from students' assessment experiences. *Teaching in Higher Education*, •••, 1–16. DOI: 10.1080/13562517.2024.2341005

Luo, J. (2024). A critical review of GenAI policies in higher education assessment: A call to reconsider the "originality" of students' work. *Assessment & Evaluation in Higher Education*, *49*(5), 651–664. DOI: 10.1080/02602938.2024.2309963

Lu, Q., Zhu, L., Xu, X., Whittle, J., Zowghi, D., & Jacquet, A. (2024). Responsible AI pattern catalogue: A collection of best practices for AI governance and engineering. *ACM Computing Surveys*, *56*(7), 1–35. DOI: 10.1145/3626234

Madaio, M., Blodgett, S. L., Mayfield, E., & Dixon-Román, E. (2022). Beyond "fairness": Structural (in) justice lenses on ai for education. In Holmes, W., & Porayska-Pomsta, K. (Eds.), *The ethics of artificial intelligence in education* (pp. 203–239). Routledge. DOI: 10.4324/9780429329067-11

Maghsudi, S., Lan, A., Xu, J., & Van Der Schaar, M. (2021). Personalized education in the artificial intelligence era: What to expect next. *IEEE Signal Processing Magazine*, *38*(3), 37–50. DOI: 10.1109/MSP.2021.3055032

Maguire, M., & Delahunt, B. (2017). Doing a thematic analysis: A practical, step-by-step guide for learning and teaching scholars. *All Ireland Journal of Higher Education, 9*(3), 3351–3364. https://ojs.aishe.org/index.php/aishe-j/article/view/335

Mangal, M., & Pardos, Z. (2024). Implementing equitable and intersectionality-aware ML in education: A practical guide. *British Journal of Educational Technology*, *55*(5), 2003–2038. DOI: 10.1111/bjet.13484

Manias, G., ... (2023). AI4Gov: Trusted AI for transparent public governance fostering democratic values. *2023 19th International Conference on Distributed Computing in Smart Systems and the Internet of Things (DCOSS-IoT)*, 548–555. DOI: 10.1109/DCOSS-IoT58021.2023.00090

Mannila, L. (2024). *AI literacy is part of modern education.* https://www.helsinki.fi/en/news/donation/ai-literacy-part-modern-education

Margolis, E. (2001). The Hidden Curriculum in Higher Education *1st Edition*, Kindle Edition. NY: Routledge.

Masland, L. (2023, August 16). *In defense of teacher-centered teaching…and other things I'm not supposed to say* [Conference keynote]. Empowering Teaching Excellence Conference, Logan, UT, United States.

Maslej, N., Fattorini, L., Perrault, R., Parli, V., Reuel, A., Brynjolfsson, E., Etchemendy, J., Ligett, K., Lyons, T., Manyika, J., Niebles, J. C., Shoham, Y., Wald, R., & Clark, J. (2024). *The AI Index 2024 annual report*. AI Index Steering Committee, Institute for Human-Centered AI, Stanford University. https://hai.stanford.edu/ai-index/2024-ai-index-report

Massachusetts Institute of Technology (MIT). (2025). *Guidance for use of Generative AI tools*. https://ist.mit.edu/ai-guidance

Ma, Y., & Chen, M. (2024). AI-empowered applications effects on EFL learners' engagement in the classroom and academic procrastination. *BMC Psychology*, *12*(1). DOI: 10.1186/s40359-024-02248-w

Mazzei, L. A., & McCoy, K. (2010). Thinking with Deleuze in qualitative research. *International Journal of Qualitative Studies in Education : QSE*, *23*(5), 503–509. DOI: 10.1080/09518398.2010.500634

McCartney, S. (1999). *ENIAC: The triumphs and tragedies of the world's first computer*. Walker & Company.

McConvey, K., Guha, S., & Kuzminykh, A. (2023). A human-centered review of algorithms in decision-making in higher education. *Proceedings of the 2023 CHI Conference on Human Factors in Computing Systems*. DOI: 10.1145/3544548.3580658

McDonald, N., Johri, A., Ali, A., & Hingle Collier, A. (2025). Generative artificial intelligence in higher education: Evidence from an analysis of institutional policies and guidelines. *Computers in Human Behavior: Artificial Humans*, *3*, 100121. Advance online publication. DOI: 10.1016/j.chbah.2025.100121

McKenzie, M. & Blenkinsop, S. (2006). An ethic of care and educational practice.

McKenzie, M., & Blenkinsop, S. (2006, January). An ethic of care and educational practice. *Journal of Adventure Education and Outdoor Learning*, *6*(2), 91–105. DOI: 10.1080/14729670685200781

Means, B., Toyama, Y., Murphy, R., & Baki, M. (2021). The effectiveness of online and blended learning: A meta-analysis of the empirical literature. *Teachers College Record*, *115*(3), 1–47. DOI: 10.1177/016146811311500307

Mehrabi, N., Morstatter, F., Saxena, N., Lerman, K., & Galstyan, A. (2021). A survey on bias and fairness in machine learning. *ACM Computing Surveys*, *54*(6), 1–35. DOI: 10.1145/3457607

Memarian, B., & Doleck, T. (2023). ChatGPT in education: Methods, potentials, and limitations. *Computers in Human Behavior: Artificial Humans*, *1*(2), 100022. DOI: 10.1016/j.chbah.2023.100022

Mendigutxia, A. (2025). *The role of higher education in national artificial intelligence strategies: A comparative policy review*. UNESCO International Institute for Higher Education in Latin America and the Caribbean (IESALC), *HE Policy Brief Series*. Document Code: ED/HE/IESALC/IP/2024/73 REV

Mensik, H. (2024, July 24). AI is actually making workers less productive. *Worklife*. https://www.worklife.news/technology/ai-is-actually-making-workers-less-productive/

Mercer, N. (2002). Developing dialogues. In Wells, G., & Claxton, G. (Eds.), *Learning for life in the 21st century* (pp. 141–153). Blackwell Publishers. DOI: 10.1002/9780470753545.ch11

Mills, A., & Bali, M. (2024). Don't trust AI to cite its sources. In A. Mills (Ed.), *How arguments work: A guide to writing*. https://human.libretexts.org/Bookshelves/Composition/Advanced_Composition/How_Arguments_Work_-_A_Guide_to_Writing_and_Analyzing_Texts_in_College_(Mills)/16%3A_Artificial_Intelligence_and_College_Writing_(Under_Construction)/Don't_Trust_AI_to_Cite_Its_Sources

Mintz, S. (2023, June 2). The trust gap in higher education: How can colleges and universities create cultures built on trust? *Inside Higher Education*. https://www.insidehighered.com/opinion/blogs/higher-ed-gamma/2023/06/02/trust-gap-higher-education

Mishra, A. K. (1996). Organizational responses to crisis: The centrality of trust. In Kramer, R. & Tyler, T. (Eds.), *Trust in Organizations*. Sage

Mishra, P., & Koehler, M. J. (2006). Technological pedagogical content knowledge: A framework for teacher knowledge. *Teachers College Record*, *108*(6), 1017–1054. DOI: 10.1111/j.1467-9620.2006.00684.x

MIT Media Lab. (2023). *AI Ethics and Governance Overview*. https://www.media.mit.edu/projects/ai-ethics-and-governance/overview/

Mohaghegh, M. (2020). The role of artificial intelligence in the future of education. *International Journal of Virtual Learning and Medical Sciences*, *11*(1), 65–67. DOI: 10.30476/IJVLMS.2020.85472.1021

Mohamed, A. M., Shaaban, T. S., Bakry, S. H., Guillén-Gámez, F. D., & Strzelecki, A. (2025). Empowering the Faculty of Education students: Applying AI's potential for motivating and enhancing learning. *Innovative Higher Education*. Advance online publication. DOI: 10.1007/s10755-024-09747-z

Monroe, M. C. (2002). Evaluation s friendly voice: The structured open-ended interview. *Applied Environmental Education and Communication: An International Journal, 1*(2), 101–106. DOI: 10.1080/15330150213993

Moon, J. A. (2013). *A handbook of reflective and experiential learning: Theory and practice*. Routledge., DOI: 10.4324/9780203416150

Moore, K. (2025, February 28). UAlbany Professor Develops AI to Give Teachers Feedback. *Government Technology*. https://www.govtech.com/education/k-12/ualbany-professor-develops-ai-to-give-teachers-feedback

Moore, G. E. (1965). Cramming more components onto integrated circuits. *Electronics (Basel), 38*, 114–117.

Moreira, A. S., Borges, T. S. S., Souto, P. F., Araujo, P. Q., Cellin, J., Gois, A. M., . . . Araújo, A. M. (2024). Innovation in educational management: Challenges and opportunities. In *Seven Editora Acadêmica* (pp. 195–206). DOI: 10.56238/sevened2024.024-014

Morgan, H. (2022). Conducting a qualitative document analysis. *The Qualitative Report, 27*(1), 64–77. DOI: 10.46743/2160-3715/2022.5044

Morozov, E. (2013). *To save everything, click here: The folly of technological solutionism*. Public Affairs.

Morrill, S. (2023). A short-form AI literacy intervention can reduce over-reliance on AI. *PsyArXiv Preprints*. https://doi.org/DOI: 10.31234/osf.io/hv9qc

Moya, B., Eaton, S., Pethrick, H., Hayden, A., Brennan, R., Wiens, J., & McDermott, B. (2024). Academic integrity and artificial intelligence in higher education (HE) contexts: A rapid scoping review. *Canadian Perspectives on Academic Integrity, 7*(3), 1–19. DOI: 10.55016/ojs/cpai.v7i3.78123

Mphahlele, A., & McKenna, S. (2019). The use of turnitin in the higher education sector: Decoding the myth. *Assessment & Evaluation in Higher Education, 44*(7), 1079–1089. DOI: 10.1080/02602938.2019.1573971

Munn, L. (2024). Expansive and Invasive: Mapping the "Bossware" Used to Monitor Workers. *Surveillance & Society, 22*(2), 104–119. DOI: 10.24908/ss.v22i2.16179

Murugesan, S., & Kadalmani, A. (2023). A strategic framework of artificial intelligence in integrated decision making: A systematic review. *Proceedings - Academy of Management*, *2023*(1), 17111. DOI: 10.5465/AMPROC.2023.17111abstract

Murwaningsih, T., Sasmini, S. S., Rahardjo, S., Suwandi, K., Saddhono, K., & Nurhasanah, F. (2024). A well-structured strategy development via AI integrated analytics systems to improve performance of education. *2024 4th International Conference on Advance Computing and Innovative Technologies in Engineering (ICACITE)*, 873–878. DOI: 10.1109/ICACITE60783.2024.10617260

Musk, E. [@elonmusk] (2025, February 15) *That is already possible QT @PalmerLuckey What will happen in broader academia when clear scientific consensus is that AI-assisted education delivers better outcomes than 3.8M teachers currently do?* Twitter/X. https://x.com/elonmusk/status/1890905182516461608?lang=en

Mustofa, H. A., Bilad, M. R., & Grendis, N. W. B. (2024). Utilizing AI for physics problem solving: A literature review and ChatGPT experience. *Lensa: Jurnal Kependidikan Fisika*, *12*(1), 78–97. DOI: 10.33394/j-lkf.v12i1.11748

Muthmainnah, I. S. (2022). P. M., & Oteir, I. (2022). Playing with ai to investigate human-computer interaction technology and improving critical thinking skills to pursue 21st century age. *Education Research International*, *6468995*(1), •••. DOI: 10.1155/2022/6468995

Nadeem, M. (2024). Distributed leadership in educational contexts: A catalyst for school improvement. *Social Sciences & Humanities Open*, *9*, 100835. DOI: 10.1016/j.ssaho.2024.100835

Naidu, S. (2024). The case for deliberate design of the student learning experience. *Distance Education*, *45*(2), 205–209. DOI: 10.1080/01587919.2024.2353413

National Institute of Standards and Technology. (2024). *Artificial intelligence risk management framework: Generative artificial intelligence profile* [NIST AI 600-1]. https://airc.nist.gov/docs/NIST.AI.600-1.GenAI-Profile.ipd.pdf#page=67.47

Nazaretsky, T., Ariely, M., Cukurova, M., & Alexandron, G. (2022). Teachers' trust in AI-powered educational technology and a professional development program to improve it. *British Journal of Educational Technology*, *53*(4), 914–931. DOI: 10.1111/bjet.13232

Neha, K., Kumar, R., & Sankat, M. (2024). AI wizards: Pioneering assistive technologies for higher education inclusion of students with learning disabilities. In Kaluri, R., Mahmud, M., Gadekallu, T. R., Rajput, D. S., & Lakshmanna, K. (Eds.), *Applied Assistive Technologies and Informatics for Students with Disabilities. Applied Intelligence and Informatics*. Springer., DOI: 10.1007/978-981-97-0914-4_4

Nerantzi, C., Sidiropoulou, M. P., Dunbar-Morris, H., Sharp, L., Farrell-Savage, K., Heard-Lauréote, K., Speight, S., Nawaz, R., & Ali, M. (2023) There are other fish in the sea: Open-up and connect. In: M. Harrison, I. DeVries, T. Morgan, & M. Paskevicious (Eds.), *Re-think learning design. Critical learning design and the untextbook*. https://rethinkld.trubox.ca/chapter/activation-there-are-other-fish-in-the-sea-open-up-and-connect/

Newman, M. (2025, March 10). Review: Microsoft Copilot could transform K–12 education for good. *EdTech Magazine*. https://edtechmagazine.com/k12/article/2025/03/review-microsoft-copilot-could-transform-k-12-education-good

Newman, J., & Mintrom, M. (2023). Mapping the discourse on evidence-based policy, artificial intelligence, and the ethical practice of policy analysis. *Journal of European Public Policy*, *30*(9), 1839–1859. DOI: 10.1080/13501763.2023.2193223

Ng, J. (2023). Design and validation of the AI literacy questionnaire: The affective, behavioural, cognitive and ethical approach. *British Journal of Educational Technology*, *54*(4), 23–45. DOI: 10.1111/bjet.13411

Nguyen, A., Gardner, L., & Sheridan, D. (2020). Data analytics in higher education: An integrated view. *Journal of Information Systems Education*, *31*(1), 61–71.

Nguyen, A., Ngo, H. N., Hong, Y., Dang, B., & Nguyen, B. T. (2022). Ethical principles for artificial intelligence in education. *Education and Information Technologies*, *28*(4), 4221–4241. DOI: 10.1007/s10639-022-11316-w PMID: 36254344

Nguyen, P. (2023). Combatting AI-generated misinformation: Strategies for public discourse. *Media and Society Review*, *15*(4), 275–290.

Niedlich, S., Kallfaß, A., Pohle, S., & Bormann, I. (2021). A comprehensive view of trust in education: Conclusions from a systematic literature review. *Review of Education*, *9*(1), 124–158. DOI: 10.1002/rev3.3239

Nieto, Y., Gacía-Díaz, V., Montenegro, C., Gonzalez, C., & Crespo, G. (2019). Usage of machine learning for strategic decision making at higher educational institutions. *IEEE Access : Practical Innovations, Open Solutions*, *7*, 75007–75017. DOI: 10.1109/ACCESS.2019.2919343

Niloy, A. C., Akter, S., Sultana, N., Sultana, J., & Rahman, S. I. U. (2023). Is Chatgpt a menace for creative writing ability? An experiment. *Journal of Computer Assisted Learning*, *40*(2), 919–930.DOI: 10.1111/jcal.12929

Nilsson, M., Jordan, A., Turnpenny, J., Hertin, J., Nykvist, B., & Russel, D. (2008). The use and non-use of policy appraisal tools in public policy making: An analysis of three European countries and the European Union. *Policy Sciences*, *41*(4), 335–355. DOI: 10.1007/s11077-008-9071-1

Noble, D. (2003). Digital diploma mills. In Johnson, B., Kavanagh, P., & Mattson, K. (Eds.), *Steal this university: The Rise of the Corporate University and the Academic Labor Movement* (pp. 39–54). Routledge.

Noddings, N. (1988). An ethic of caring and its implications for instructional arrangements. *American Journal of Education*, *96*(2), 215–230.

Noddings, N. (2013). *Caring: A relational approach to ethics and moral education*. University of California Press.

Noddings, N. (2018). *Philosophy of education*. Routledge., DOI: 10.4324/9780429494864

North, M. (2023). Generative AI has disrupted education. Here's how it can be used for good – *UNESCO. World Economic Forum*. https://www.weforum.org/stories/2023/09/generative-ai-education-unesco/

Nwoyibe, O. I. (2025). Deploying AI technology for effective teaching and learning: The need to always verify information gathered from generative AI tools. *Caliphate Journal of Science and Technology*, *7*(1), 22–29. DOI: 10.4314/cajost.v7i1.3

Nykonenko, A. (2023). The impact of artificial intelligence on modern education: Prospects and challenges. *Artificial Intelligence*, *2*(AI.2023.28(2))), 10–15. DOI: 10.15407/jai2023.02.010

OECD. (2019). OECD Principles on Artificial Intelligence. Available at: https://www.oecd.org/going-digital/ai/principles/

OECD. (2024, November 28). *Generative AI set to exacerbate regional divide in OECD countries, says first regional analysis on its impact on local job markets* [Press release]. https://www.oecd.org/en/about/news/press-releases/2024/11/generative-ai-set-to-exacerbate-regional-divide-in-oecd-countries-says-first-regional-analysis-on-its-impact-on-local-job-markets.html

'Ofakihevahanoa Fotu, B. (2024). Rude Reflections: Current AI Acts as a Mirror of Our Flawed Society. In B. Buyserie & T. N. Thurston (Eds.), *Teaching and generative AI*. https://uen.pressbooks.pub/teachingandgenerativeai/chapter/rude-reflections-current-ai-acts-as-a-mirror-of-our-flawed-society/

Office of Educational Integrity (OEI). (2025). Using Artificial Intelligence tools responsibly in your studies and assessments. The University of Sydney. https://www.sydney.edu.au/students/responsible-ai-use.html

Open, A. I. (2023). *ChatGPT* (May 24 version) [Large language model]. https://chat.openai.com/chat

Ouyang, F., Wu, M., Zheng, L., Zhang, L., & Jiao, P. (2023). Integration of artificial intelligence performance prediction and learning analytics to improve student learning in online engineering course. *International Journal of Educational Technology in Higher Education, 20*(1). Advance online publication. DOI: 10.1186/s41239-022-00372-4

Pabba, C., & Kumar, P. (2022). An intelligent system for monitoring students' engagement in large classroom teaching through facial expression recognition. *Expert Systems: International Journal of Knowledge Engineering and Neural Networks, 39*(1), e12839. Advance online publication. DOI: 10.1111/exsy.12839

Pace, F., D'Urso, G., Zappulla, C., & Pace, U. (2021). The relation between workload and personal well-being among university professors. *Current Psychology (New Brunswick, N.J.), 40*(7), 3417–3424. DOI: 10.1007/s12144-019-00294-x

Paek, S., & Kim, N. (2021). Analysis of worldwide research trends on the impact of artificial intelligence in education. *Sustainability (Basel), 13*(14), 7941. DOI: 10.3390/su13147941

Panian, Z. (2009). Just-in-time business intelligence and real-time decisioning. *Recent Advances in Applied Informatics and Communications, Proceedings of AIC, 9*, 106–111.

Patton, M. Q. (2018). *Nitel Araştırma ve Değerlendirme Yöntemleri* [*Qualitative Research & Evaluation Methods*]. (2nd ed. 3rd ed. Trans., M. Bütün & S. B. Demir, Trans. Eds., A. Bakla, F. I. Bilican, M. Bütün, M. Çakır, A. Çekiç, S. Çelik, Y. Dede, S. B. Demir, H. Demircioğlu, İ. Eti, E. Bukova-Güzel, S. İrez, F. Ö. Karataş, T. Kargın, F. Zayimoğlu-Öztürk, T. Öztürk, M. Sümer, M. F. Yiğit, & B. Turhan—Türkkan, Trans.). Pegem Academy. (Original work published 2001)

Perifanou, M., & Economides, A. (2025). Collaborative uses of GenAI tools in project-based learning. *Education Sciences, 15*(3), 354. DOI: 10.3390/educsci15030354

Perrigo, B. (2023, January 18). OpenAI used Kenyan workers on less than $2 per hour to make ChatGPT less toxic. *Time.* https://time.com/6247678/openai-chatgpt-kenya-workers/

Piaget, J. (1954). *The construction of reality in the child.* Basic Books. DOI: 10.1037/11168-000

Plato, . (2006). *Phaedrus*. Penguin Books.

Plato, . (2019). *Republic* (Waterfield, R., Ed.). Oxford University Press., DOI: 10.1093/actrade/9780199535767.book.1

Pleios, G., & Tastsoglou, M. (2025). AI and the news: Challenges arisen from the adoption of ai in news production. *Postmodernism Problems*, *15*(1), 3–24. DOI: 10.46324/PMP2501003

Pogorskiy, E., & Beckmann, J. F. (2023). From procrastination to engagement? An experimental exploration of the effects of an adaptive virtual assistant on self-regulation in online learning. *Computers and Education: Artificial Intelligence*, *4*, 100111. DOI: 10.1016/j.caeai.2022.100111

Popenici, S., & Kerr, S. (2017). Exploring the impact of artificial intelligence on teaching and learning in higher education. *Research and Practice in Technology Enhanced Learning*, *12*(1), 22. Advance online publication. DOI: 10.1186/s41039-017-0062-8

Pratiwi, H., Riwanda, A., Hasruddin, H., Sujarwo, S., & Syamsudin, A. (2025). Transforming learning or creating dependency? Teachers' perspectives and barriers to AI integration in education. *Journal of Pedagogical Research*, 1-16. DOI: 10.33902/JPR.202531677

Prentzas, J., & Sidiropoulou, M. (2023, July). Assessing the use of open AI chat-GPT in a University Department of Education. In *2023 14th international conference on information, intelligence, systems & applications (iisa)* (pp. 1-4). IEEE. DOI: 10.1109/IISA59645.2023.10345910

Puentedura, R. (2006). Transformation, technology, and education. In.

Puentedura, R. (2013). *SAMR: Moving from enhancement to transformation* [Blog post]. *Ruben R. Puentedura's Weblog*. Retrieved May 2022, from http://www.hippasus.com/rrpweblog/archives/000095.html

Puentedura, R. (2015, October 14). SAMR: A brief introduction. *Ruben Puentedura's Blog*. https://hippasus.com/blog/archives/227

Quinlan, K. M. (2019). What triggers students' interest during higher education lectures? personal and situational variables associated with situational interest. *Studies in Higher Education*, *44*(10), 1781–1792. DOI: 10.1080/03075079.2019.1665325

Rabin, C. (2021). Care ethics in online teaching. *Studying Teacher Education*, *17*(1), 38–56. DOI: 10.1080/17425964.2021.1902801

Rahm, L. (2023). Educational imaginaries: Governance at the intersection of technology and education. *Journal of Education Policy*, *38*(1), 46–68. DOI: 10.1080/02680939.2021.1970233

Rahm, L. (2024). 'Help!? My students created an evil AI': On the irony of speculative methods and design fiction. *Learning, Media and Technology*, •••, 1–15. DOI: 10.1080/17439884.2024.2367707

Rahm, L., & Rahm-Skågeby, J. (2023). Imaginaries and problematisations: A heuristic lens in the age of artificial intelligence in education. *British Journal of Educational Technology*, *54*(5), 1147–1159.DOI: 10.1111/bjet.13319

Rampin, R., & Rampin, V. (2021). Taguette: Open-source qualitative data analysis. *Journal of Open Source Software*, *6*(68), 3522. DOI: 10.21105/joss.03522

Rasul, T., Nair, S., Kalendra, D., Balaji, M. S., de Oliveira Santini, F., Ladeira, W. J., Rather, R. A., Yasin, N., Rodriguez, R. V., Kokkalis, P., Murad, M. W., & Hossain, M. U. (2024). Enhancing academic integrity among students in GenAI Era: A holistic framework. *International Journal of Management Education*, *22*(3), 101041. DOI: 10.1016/j.ijme.2024.101041

Reeve, J. (2013). How students create motivationally supportive learning environments for themselves: The concept of agentic engagement. *Journal of Educational Psychology*, *105*(3), 579–595.DOI: 10.1037/a0032690

Reeve, J., & Tseng, C. M. (2011). Agency as a fourth aspect of students' engagement during learning activities. *Contemporary Educational Psychology*, *36*(4), 257–267.

Reid, A., OCallaghan, S., & Lu, Y. (2023). Implementing Australia's AI Ethics Principles: A selection of Responsible AI practices and resources.

Reiss, M. (2021). The use of AI in education: Practicalities and ethical considerations. *London Review of Education*, *19*(1). Advance online publication. DOI: 10.14324/LRE.19.1.05

Ren, S., & Wierman, A. (2024, July 15). The uneven distribution of AI's environmental impacts. *Harvard Business Review*. https://hbr.org/2024/07/the-uneven-distribution-of-ais-environmental-impacts

Ribeiro, A. G., Messias, A. C. G., & Ribeiro, M. S. (2023). Educação 5.0'e a Atuação Dos Educadores: Avanços, Oportunıdades E Impactos. *Revista Ft*, *27*(125), 25–26. DOI: 10.69849/revistaft/ar10202308011525

Rogers, E. M. (1962). *Diffusions of innovations* (1st ed.). Free Press of Glencoe.

Romero, C., & Ventura, S. (2013). Data mining in education. *Wiley Interdisciplinary Reviews. Data Mining and Knowledge Discovery*, *3*(1), 12–27. DOI: 10.1002/widm.1075

Ross, J., & Collier, A. (2016). 2 Complexity, Mess, and Not-Yetness Teaching Online with Emerging Technologies. In Veletsianos, G. (Ed.), *Emergence and Innovation in Digital Learning: Foundations and Applications* (pp. 17–34). Athabasca University Press., DOI: 10.15215/aupress/9781771991490.004

Ruediger, D., Blankstein, M., & Love, S. (2024). Generative AI and postsecondary instructional practices: Findings from a national survey of instructors. *Ithaka S+ R, 20*. https://doi.org/DOI: 10.18665/sr.320892

Runco, M. A. (2025). Updating the standard definition of creativity to account for the artificial creativity of AI. *Creativity Research Journal*, *37*(1), 1–5. DOI: 10.1080/10400419.2023.2257977

Ryan, M., Van Bergen, P., Adlington, R., & Maurice, O. (2025). The positioning of quality and expertise in initial teacher education: Policy enactment in the Australian context. *Australian Educational Researcher*, *52*(3), 1997–2020. Advance online publication. DOI: 10.1007/s13384-024-00796-z

Ryan, R. M., & Deci, E. L. (2017). *Self-determination theory: Basic psychological needs in motivation, development, and wellness*. Guilford Press.

Ryle, G. (1949). *The concept of mind*. Hutchinson's University Library.

Sætra, H. S., & Selinger, E. (2024). Technological Remedies for Social Problems: Defining and Demarcating Techno-Fixes and Techno-Solutionism. *Science and Engineering Ethics*, *30*(6), 1–17. DOI: 10.1007/s11948-024-00524-x PMID: 39621170

Sahlberg, P. (2022). *Finnish lessons 3.0: What can the world learn from educational change in Finland?* Teachers College Press.

Sajja, R., Sermet, Y., Cikmaz, M., Cwiertny, D., & Demir, I. (2023). Artificial intelligence-enabled intelligent assistant for personalized and adaptive learning in higher education. *arXiv preprint arXiv:2309.10892*. DOI: 10.3390/info15100596

Salinas-Navarro, D. E., Vilalta-Perdomo, E., Michel-Villarreal, R., & Montesinos, L. (2024). Designing experiential learning activities with generative artificial intelligence tools for authentic assessment. *Interactive Technology and Smart Education, 21*(4), 708–734. DOI: 10.1108/ITSE-12-2023-0236

Säljö, R. (1979). Learning about learning. *Higher Education, 8*(4), 443–451. DOI: 10.1007/BF01680533

Salloum, S. A., Alhamad, A. Q. M., Al-Emran, M., Monem, A. A., & Shaalan, K. (2019). Exploring students' acceptance of e-learning through the development of a comprehensive technology acceptance model. *IEEE Access : Practical Innovations, Open Solutions, 7*, 128445–128462. DOI: 10.1109/ACCESS.2019.2939467

Sandelowski, M. (1995). Qualitative analysis: What it is and how to begin? *Research in Nursing & Health, 18*, 371–375. DOI: 10.1002/nur.4770180411

Saputra, I., Astuti, M., Sayuti, M., & Kusumastuti, D. (2023). Integration of artificial intelligence in education: Opportunities, challenges, threats and obstacles. A literature review. *The Indonesian Journal of Computer Science, 12*(4). Advance online publication. DOI: 10.33022/ijcs.v12i4.3266

Saxena, A. (2024). AI in governance and policy making. *International Journal of Science and Research (Raipur, India), 13*(5), 1218–1223. DOI: 10.21275/SR24519015426

Sayer, A. (2011). *Why things matter to people: Social science, values and ethical life*. Cambridge University Press. DOI: 10.1017/CBO9780511734779

Scherer, M. U. (2016). Regulating artificial intelligence systems: Risks, challenges, competencies, and strategies. *SSRN, 29*(2), 354–400. DOI: 10.2139/ssrn.2609777

Schiff, D. (2021). Out of the laboratory and into the classroom: The future of artificial intelligence in education. *AI & Society, 36*(1), 331–348. DOI: 10.1007/s00146-020-01033-8

Schiff, D. (2022). Education for AI, not AI for education: The role of education and ethics in national AI policy strategies. *International Journal of Artificial Intelligence in Education, 32*(3), 527–563. DOI: 10.1007/s40593-021-00270-2

Scholes, V. (2016). The ethics of using learning analytics to categorize students on risk. *Educational Technology Research and Development, 64*(5), 939–955. DOI: 10.1007/s11423-016-9458-1

Scholkmann, A., Olsen, D. S., & Wollscheid, S. (2024). Perspectives on disruptive change in higher education. A critical review of digital transformation during COVID-19. *Higher Education Research & Development*, *43*(6), 1355–1369. DOI: 10.1080/07294360.2024.2325140

Schuett, J. (2021). Defining the scope of AI regulations. *Law, Innovation and Technology*, *15*(1), 60–82. DOI: 10.1080/17579961.2023.2184135

Sekli, G., Godo, A., & Véliz, J. (2024). Generative AI solutions for faculty and students: A review of literature and roadmap for future research. *Journal of Information Technology Education*, *23*, 14. DOI: 10.28945/5304

Selwyn, N. (2024). On the limits of artificial intelligence (AI) in education. *Nordisk tidsskrift for pedagogikk og kritikk, 10*(1), 3-14. https://pedagogikkogkritikk.no/index.php/ntpk/article/view/6062/9573

Selwyn, N. (2015). Data entry: Towards the critical study of digital data and education. *Learning, Media and Technology*, *40*(1), 64–82. DOI: 10.1080/17439884.2014.921628

Selwyn, N. (2016). 'There's so much data': Exploring the realities of data-based school governance. *European Educational Research Journal*, *15*(1), 54–68. DOI: 10.1177/1474904115602909

Selwyn, N., & Cumbo, B. (2024). "We've Tried to Keep the Beast on a Leash": The Domestication of Digital Classroom Surveillance. *Surveillance & Society*, *22*(2), 88–103. DOI: 10.24908/ss.v22i2.15791

Selwyn, N., Nemorin, S., & Johnson, N. (2017). High-tech, hard work: An investigation of teachers' work in the digital age. *Learning, Media and Technology*, *42*(4), 390–405. DOI: 10.1080/17439884.2016.1252770

Shafiabady, N., Koo, T. F., Ud Din, F., Sattarshetty, K., Yen, M., Alazab, M., & Alsharaydeh, E. (2025). Predicting postgraduate student engagement using artificial intelligence (AI). *IEEE Transactions on Artificial Intelligence*. Advance online publication.DOI: 10.1109/TAI.2025.3548016

Shahidi-Hamedani, S., Aslam, S., Mundher Oraibi, B. A., Wah, Y. B., & Shahidi-Hamedani, S. (2024). Transitioning towards Tomorrow's Workforce: Education 5.0 in the Landscape of Society 5.0: A Systematic Literature Review. *Education Sciences*, *14*(10), 1041. DOI: 10.3390/educsci14101041

Shalini, K. S., Kopperundevi, N., Rajkumar, R., Radhika, A., Gopianand, M., & Preethi, M.K.Shantha Shalini. (2024). Decentralized machine learning for dynamic resource optimization in wireless networks using reinforcement learning. *Journal of Electrical Systems*, *20*(5), 2025–2033. DOI: 10.52783/jes.2539

Shan, T., Tay, F., & Gu, L. Q. (2020). Application of artificial intelligence in dentistry. *Journal of Dental Research, 100*(3), 232–244. DOI: 10.1177/0022034520969115 PMID: 33118431

Shen, Z., & Cui, W. (2024). Perceived support and AI literacy: The mediating role of psychological needs satisfaction. *Frontiers in Psychology, 15*, 1415248. Advance online publication. DOI: 10.3389/fpsyg.2024.1415248 PMID: 38947906

Sikström, P., Valentini, C., Sivunen, A., & Kärkkäinen, T. (2024). Pedagogical agents communicating and scaffolding students' learning: High school teachers' and students' perspectives. *Computers & Education, 222*, 105140. DOI: 10.1016/j.compedu.2024.105140

Silver, N. (2023, June 5). The future of education – disruption caused by AI and ChatGPT: Artificial Intelligence Series 3/5. *Forbes*. https://www.forbes.com/sites/nicolesilver/2023/06/05/the-future-of-educationdisruption-caused-by-ai-and-chatgpt-artificial-intelligence-series-3-of-5/

Skinner, E. A., & Pitzer, J. R. (2012). Developmental dynamics of student engagement, coping, and everyday resilience. In S. L. Christenson, A. L. Reschly, & C. Wylie (Eds.), Handbook of research on student engagement (pp. 21–44). Springer. DOI: 10.1007/978-1-4614-2018-7_2

Slimi, Z., & Villarejo-Carballido, B. (2024). Unveiling the potential: Experts' perspectives on artificial intelligence integration in higher education. *European Journal of Educational Research, 13*(4), 1477–1492. DOI: 10.12973/eu-jer.13.4.1477

Smith, A., & Fressoli, M. (2021). Post-automation. *Futures, 132*, 102778. https://doi.org/https://doi.org/10.1016/j.futures.2021.102778. DOI: 10.1016/j.futures.2021.102778

Smuha, N. A. (2022). Pitfalls and pathways for trustworthy artificial intelligence in education. In *The Ethics of Artificial Intelligence in Education* (pp. 113–145). Routledge., DOI: 10.4324/9780429329067-7

Sofologi, M., Katsarou, D. V., Tsirides, A., & Efthymiou, E. (2025). The synergy of artificial ıntelligence and education: new perspectives of an ınnovative artificial tutoring in school settings. In *Prompt Engineering and Generative AI Applications for Teaching and Learning* (pp. 189–202). IGI Global Scientific Publishing. DOI: 10.4018/979-8-3693-7332-3.ch012

Sokol, D. (2023, July 10). It is too easy to falsely accuse a student of using AI: A cautionary tale. *Times Higher Education.* https://www.timeshighereducation.com/blog/it-too-easy-falsely-accuse-student-using-ai-cautionary-tale

Sosnovsky, S., Brusilovsky, P., & Lan, A. (2025). Intelligent Textbooks. *International Journal of Artificial Intelligence in Education, 35*(3), 1–20. DOI: 10.1007/s40593-024-00451-9

Spaniol, M. J., & Rowland, N. J. (2023). AI-assisted scenario generation for strategic planning. *Futures & Foresight Science, 5*(2), e148. DOI: 10.1002/ffo2.148

Spector, J. M., & Ma, S. (2019). Inquiry and critical thinking skills for the next generation: From artificial intelligence back to human intelligence. *Smart Learning Environments, 6*(1), 1–11. DOI: 10.1186/s40561-019-0088-z

Spivakovsky, O. V., Omelchuk, S. A., Kobets, V. V., Valko, N. V., & Malchykova, D. S. (2023). Institutional policies on artificial intelligence in university learning, teaching and research. *Information Technologies and Learning Tools, 97*(5), 181–201. DOI: 10.33407/itlt.v97i5.5395

Stanford University Teaching Commons. (2023). Understanding AI Literacy: Teaching Artificial Intelligence. https://teachingcommons.stanford.edu/teaching-guides/artificial-intelligence-teaching-guide/understanding-ai-literacy

Stanford University. (2023). *Generative AI policy guidance*. https://communitystandards.stanford.edu/generative-ai-policy-guidance

Stewart, B. (2022). The problem of the web: Can we prioritize both participatory practices and privacy? *Contemporary Educational Technology, 15*(1), ep402. DOI: 10.30935/cedtech/12668

Stracke, C. M., Griffiths, D., Pappa, D., Bećirović, S., Polz, E., Perla, L., Di Grassi, A., Massaro, S., Skenduli, M. P., Burgos, D., Punzo, V., Amram, D., Ziouvelou, X., Katsamori, D., Gabriel, S., Nahar, N., Schleiss, J., & Hollins, P. (2025). Analysis of artificial intelligence policies for higher education in Europe. *International Journal of Interactive Multimedia and Artificial Intelligence, 9*(2), 124–137. DOI: 10.9781/ijimai.2025.02.011

Sumakul, D. T. Y. G., Hamied, F. A., & Sukyadi, D. (2022). Students' perceptions of the use of AI in a writing class. *Proceedings of the 67th TEFLIN International Virtual Conference*; The 9th ICOELT 2021 (TEFLIN ICOELT 2021). DOI: 10.2991/assehr.k.220201.009

Su, Y. (2023). AI literacy curriculum and its relation to children's perceptions of robots and attitudes towards engineering and science: An intervention study in early childhood education. *Journal of Computer Assisted Learning, 39*(3), 310–328. DOI: 10.1111/jcal.12867

Symeou, L., Louca, L., Kavadella, A., Mackay, J., Danidou, Y., & Raffay, V. (2025). Development of evidence-based guidelines for the integration of generative AI in university education through a multidisciplinary, consensus-based approach. *European Journal of Dental Education, 29*(1), 1–19. DOI: 10.1111/eje.13069 PMID: 39949032

Taft, I. (2025, March 29). How Colleges Are Cracking Down on Students Now. *The New York Times.* https://www.nytimes.com/2025/03/29/us/universities-students-search-warrants.html

Tampere University. (2025). *Use of AI-based applications.* https://www.tuni.fi/en/students-guide/handbook/uni/studying-0/academic-integrity-and-study-regulations/use-ai-based-applications

Tang, K., Chang, C., & Hwang, G. (2021). Trends in artificial intelligence-supported e-learning: A systematic review and co-citation network analysis (1998–2019). *Interactive Learning Environments, 31*(7), 2134–2152. DOI: 10.1080/10494820.2021.1875001

Tan, X., Chen, G., & Ho Ling, M. (2025). Artificial intelligence in teaching and teacher professional development: A systematic review. *Computers and Education: Artificial Intelligence, 8*, 1–19. DOI: 10.1016/j.caeai.2024.100355

Tapalova, O., Zhiyenbayeva, N., & Gura, D. (2022). Artificial intelligence in education: AIEd for personalised learning pathways. *Electronic Journal of e-Learning, 20*(5), 639–653. Advance online publication. DOI: 10.34190/ejel.20.5.2597

Tarisayi, K. S. (2024, March). Strategic leadership for responsible artificial intelligence adoption in higher education. In *CTE Workshop Proceedings*, 11, 4-14. DOI: 10.55056/cte.616

Tavory, T. (2024). Regulating AI in mental health: Ethics of care perspective. *JMIR Mental Health, 11*(1), 1–11. DOI: 10.2196/58493 PMID: 39298759

Taylor, J., & Davis, K. (2023). The impact of AI-generated misinformation on public trust: Educational solutions. *Digital Literacy Quarterly, 10*(2), 98–114.

Teng, Y., Zhang, J., & Sun, T. (2022). Data-driven decision-making model based on artificial intelligence in higher education system of colleges and universities. *Expert Systems: International Journal of Knowledge Engineering and Neural Networks, 40*(1), e12820. Advance online publication. DOI: 10.1111/exsy.12820

Thayer-Bacon, B., & Bacon, C. S. (1996). Caring professors: A model. *The Journal of General Education, 45*(4), 255–256.

The Chicago Manual of Style Online. (n.d.). *Citation, documentation of sources.* https://www.chicagomanualofstyle.org/qanda/data/faq/topics/Documentation/faq0422.html

The Institute for Ethical AI in Education. (2020). *Interim report: towards a shared vision of ethical AI in education.* https://www.buckingham.ac.uk/wp-content/uploads/2020/02/ The-Institute-for-Ethical-AI-in-Educations-Interim-Report-Towards-a-Shared-Vision-of-Ethical-AI-in-Education.pdf

The MLA Style Center. (2023, March). *How do I cite generative AI in MLA style?* https://style.mla.org/citing-generative-ai/

The Open University. (2025). *Generative AI for students.* https://about.open.ac.uk/policies-and-reports/policies-and-statements/gen-ai/generative-ai-students

Thomas, M. (2025). *The Future of AI: How Artificial Intelligence Will Change the World.* Built-in-UnitedWeTech. https://builtin.com/artificial-intelligence/artificial-intelligence-future

Tian, Y. (2023). Limitations and advancements of AI teachers in classroom instruction. *Education and Teaching Research, 3*, 66-72. http://www.fspress.net/static/upload/file/20230801/1690903421713331.pdf

Toma, R. B., & Yánez-Pérez, I. (2024). Effects of ChatGPT Use on Undergraduate Students' Creativity: A Threat to Creative Thinking? *Discover Artificial Intelligence, 4*(1).DOI: 10.1007/s44163-024-00172-x

Tse, J. ve Wise, L. (2005). Peer learning, lectures and online learning-putting it all together. *Australian Family Physician, 34*(12). https://search.informit.org/doi/abs/10.3316/informit.363983128361834

Ullah, M., Bin Naeem, S., & Kamel Boulos, M. N. (2024). *Assessing the Guidelines on the Use of Generative Artificial Intelligence Tools in Universities: Results of a Survey of the World's Top 50 Universities.*

UNESCO. (2021). *AI in education: Challenges and opportunities for sustainable development.* UNESCO Publishing.

UNESCO. (2021). Recommendation on the Ethics of Artificial Intelligence. Available at: https://unesdoc.unesco.org/ark:/48223/pf0000380455

United Nations Educational, Scientific and Cultural Organization. (2024). *AI competency framework for students.* DOI: 10.54675/JKJB9835

University of Edinburgh. (2025). *Case study: Ethical and effective use of large language models*. https://gail.ed.ac.uk/research/case-studies/case-study-ethical-and-effective-use-of-large-language-models

University of Melbourne. (2025). *Acknowledging AI tools and technologies*. https://students.unimelb.edu.au/academic-skills/resources/academic-integrity/acknowledging-AI-tools-and-technologies

University of Michigan. (2025). *U-M guidance for students*. https://genai.umich.edu/resources/students

University of Oxford. (2024). *Advice on using artificial intelligence (AI) tools to support your learning*. https://www.ox.ac.uk/students/news/2024-01-08-advice-using-artificial-intelligence-ai-tools-support-your-learning

University of Toronto. (2025). *Use artificial intelligence intelligently*. https://security.utoronto.ca/governance/guidelines/use-ai-intelligently/

Upreti, K., Verma, A., Mittal, S., Vats, P., Haque, M., & Ali, S. (2023). A novel framework for harnessing AI for evidence-based policymaking in e-governance using smart contracts. In Shaw, R. N., Paprzycki, M., & Ghosh, A. (Eds.), *Advanced communication and intelligent systems* (pp. 231–245). Springer., DOI: 10.1007/978-3-031-45124-9_18

Upwork Research Institute. (2024, July 23). From burnout to balance: AI-enhanced work models. *Upwork Research Institute*. https://www.upwork.com/research/ai-enhanced-work-models

Urban, M., Děchtěrenko, F., Lukavský, J., Hrabalová, V., Svacha, F., Brom, C., & Urban, K. (2024). ChatGPT improves creative problem-solving performance in university students: An experimental study. *Computers & Education*, *215*, 105031. DOI: 10.1016/j.compedu.2024.105031

Van Bergen, P., Ryan, M., Cliff, K., Andrews, R., Ledger, S., Simons, M., Gregory, S., Adlington, R., Zundans-Fraser, L., & Little, C. (2024). Strong (er) Beginnings or more red tape? An analysis of the Teacher Education Expert Panel reforms in initial teacher education and stakeholder responses. Australian Teacher Education Association Conference, Walter, Y. (2024). Embracing the future of Artificial Intelligence in the classroom: The relevance of AI literacy, prompt engineering, and critical thinking in modern education. *International Journal of Educational Technology in Higher Education*, *21*(1), 15. DOI: 10.1186/s41239-024-00448-3 van der Schaar, M. (2014). Real-time discovery and decision making from big data. *2014 IEEE International Conference on Consumer Electronics-Taiwan*, 1–3. DOI: 10.1109/ICCE-TW.2014.6903996

van der Zwaan, J. M., Bruijne, M., & Kester, L. (2021). Scaling adaptive learning technologies in the Dutch education system: Insights from pilot studies. *European Journal of Educational Research*, *10*(2), 287–302. DOI: 10.12973/eu-jer.10.2.287

van Haastrecht, M., Haas, M., Brinkhuis, M., & Spruit, M. (2024). Understanding validity criteria in technology-enhanced learning: A systematic literature review. *Computers & Education*, *220*, 105128.DOI: 10.1016/j.compedu.2024.105128

Verganti, R., Vendraminelli, L., & Iansiti, M. (2020). Innovation and design in the age of artificial intelligence. *Journal of Product Innovation Management*, *37*(3), 212–227. DOI: 10.1111/jpim.12523

Verma, P., & Tan, S. (2024, September 18). A bottle of water per email: The hidden environmental costs of using AI chatbots. *The Washington Post*. https://www.washingtonpost.com/technology/2024/09/18/energy-ai-use-electricity-water-data-centers/

Viberg, O., Kizilcec, R., Wise, A., Jivet, I., & Nixon, N. (2024). Advancing equity and inclusion in educational practices with AI-powered educational decision support systems (AI-EDSS). *British Journal of Educational Technology*, *55*(5), 1974–1981. DOI: 10.1111/bjet.13507

Vidal, Q., Vincent-Lancrin, S., & Yun, H. (2023). Emerging governance of generative AI in education. In *OECD Digital Education Outlook 2023: Towards an Effective Digital Education Ecosystem*. https://www.oecd-ilibrary.org/sites/2a73a245-en/index. html?itemId=/content/component/2a73a245-en DOI: 10.1787/c74f03de-en

Villegas-Galaviz, C., & Martin, K. (2024). Moral distance, AI, and the ethics of care. *AI & Society*, *39*(4), 1695–1706. DOI: 10.1007/s00146-023-01642-z PMID: 37358944

Vygotsky, L. S. (1978). *Mind in society: The development of higher psychological processes*. Harvard University Press.

Vygotsky, L. S., & Cole, M. (1978). *Mind in society: Development of higher psychological processes*. Harvard university press.

Wach, E., & Ward, R. (2013). Learning about qualitative document analysis. *IDS Practice Paper in Brief*, 13, 1-11. https://hdl.handle.net/20.500.12413/2989

Wach, K., Duong, C. D., Ejdys, J., Kazlauskaitė, R., Korzynski, P., Mazurek, G., & Ziemba, E. (2023). The dark side of generative artificial intelligence: A critical analysis of controversies and risks of ChatGPT. *Entrepreneurial Business and Economics Review*, *11*(2), 7–30. DOI: 10.15678/EBER.2023.110201

Waititi, T. (Director). (2017). *Thor: Ragnarok*. Marvel Studios

Walter, Y. (2024). Embracing the future of Artificial Intelligence in the classroom: The relevance of AI literacy, prompt engineering, and critical thinking in modern education. *International Journal of Educational Technology in Higher Education*, *21*(1), 15.

Walther, C. C. (2024, November 12). Generative AI's impact on climate change: Benefits and costs. *Forbes*. https://www.forbes.com/sites/corneliawalther/2024/11/12/generative-ais-impact-on-climate-change-benefits-and-costs/

Walton, R. B., Ciarallo, F. W., & Champagne, L. E. (2024). A unified digital twin approach incorporating virtual, physical, and prescriptive analytical components to support adaptive real-time decision-making. *Computers & Industrial Engineering*, *193*, 110241. DOI: 10.1016/j.cie.2024.110241

Wang, F., King, R. B., Chai, C. S., & Zhou, Y. (2023). University students' intentions to learn artificial intelligence: The roles of supportive environments and expectancy–value beliefs. *International Journal of Educational Technology in Higher Education*, *20*(1). DOI: 10.1186/s41239-023-00417-2

Wang, P., Jing, Y., & Shen, S. (2025). A systematic literature review on the application of generative artificial intelligence (GAI) in teaching within higher education: Instructional contexts, process, and strategies. *The Internet and Higher Education*. Advance online publication. DOI: 10.1016/j.iheduc.2025.100996

Wang, Y. (2020). When artificial intelligence meets educational leaders' data-informed decision-making: A cautionary tale. *Studies in Educational Evaluation*, *66*. Advance online publication. DOI: 10.1016/j.stueduc.2020.100872

Wang, Y. (2021). Artificial intelligence in educational leadership: A symbiotic role of human-artificial intelligence decision-making. *Journal of Educational Administration*, *59*(3), 256–270. DOI: 10.1108/JEA-10-2020-0216

Wang, Z. (2024). Innovation in education management from the perspective of sustainable development. *Industrial Engineering and Innovation Management*, *7*(2), 139–148. DOI: 10.23977/ieim.2024.070219

Ward, A., Manoharan, S., & Ye, X. (2024, November). Exploring Academic Integrity in the Age of Generative AI. In *2024 21st International Conference on Information Technology Based Higher Education and Training (ITHET)* (pp. 1-5). IEEE. DOI: 10.1109/ITHET61869.2024.10837603

Watters, A. (2025, March 10). Agents versus Agency. *Second Breakfast.* https://2ndbreakfast.audreywatters.com/agents-versus-agency/

Watters, A. (2021/2023). *Teaching machines: The history of personalized learning*. MIT Press. DOI: 10.7551/mitpress/12262.001.0001

Weise, K., & Metz, C. (2023). When AI chatbots hallucinate. The New York Times, 4.

Wellner, G., & Levin, I. (2024). Ihde meets Papert: Combining postphenomenology and constructionism for a future agenda of philosophy of education in the era of digital technologies. *Learning, Media and Technology*, *49*(4), 656–669. DOI: 10.1080/17439884.2023.2251388

Whitbeck, C. (1996). Ethics as Design: Doing Justice to Moral Problems. *The Hastings Center Report*, *26*(3), 9–16. DOI: 10.2307/3527925 PMID: 8736668

Wigfield, A., & Eccles, J. S. (2000). Expectancy–value theory of achievement motivation. *Contemporary Educational Psychology*, *25*(1), 68–81.

Williamson, B. (2024). Code acts in education: AI in education is a public problem. *National education policy center blog*. https://nepc.colorado.edu/blog/ai-public

Williamson, B. (2023a). The Social life of AI in Education. *International Journal of Artificial Intelligence in Education*. Advance online publication. DOI: 10.1007/s40593-023-00342-5

Williamson, B., Eynon, R., Knox, J., & Davies, H. (2023b). Critical perspectives on AI in education: Political economy, discrimination, commercialization, governance and ethics. In *Handbook of artificial intelligence in education* (pp. 553–570). Edward Elgar Publishing., DOI: 10.4337/9781800375413.00037

Wilson, R. (2006). Policy analysis as policy advice. In R. Goodin, M. Moran, & M. Rein (Eds.), *The Oxford handbook of public policy* (pp. 152–168). Oxford University Press.

Wimmer, R. D., & Dominick, J. R. (2013). *Mass media research: An introduction* (10th ed.). Cengage Learning.

Witschas, A. (2023). Porn, Power, and Platforms: The (re-)production of hegemonic sexuality through Machine Learning systems. *Publications of the Institute of Cognitive Science, 2023*, 1.

Woolf, B. P., Lane, H. C., Chaudhri, V., & Kolodner, J. L. (2021). AI for educational technologies: Emerging research and opportunities. *International Journal of Artificial Intelligence in Education, 31*(1), 1–14. DOI: 10.1007/s40593-020-00227-6

Wordsworth, W. (1798). *The tables turned.* Poetry Foundation. https://www.poetryfoundation.org/poems/45557/the-tables-turned

World Economic Forum. (2025). *Future of Jobs Report 2025.* World Economic Forum. https://reports.weforum.org/docs/WEF_Future_of_Jobs_Report_2025.pdf

Xiao, J., & Bozkurt, A. (2025). Prophets of progress: How do leading global agencies naturalize enchanted determinism surrounding artificial intelligence for education? *Journal of Applied Learning and Teaching, 8*(1). Advance online publication. DOI: 10.37074/jalt.2025.8.1.19

Xiao, J., Bozkurt, A., Nichols, M., Pazurek, A., Stracke, C. M., Bai, J. Y., Farrow, R., Mulligan, D., Nerantzi, C., Sharma, R. C., Singh, L., Frumin, I., Swindell, A., Honeychurch, S., Bond, M., Dron, J., Moore, S., Leng, J., Slaghter van Tryon, P. J., & Themeli, C. (2025). Venturing into the unknown: Critical insights into grey areas and pioneering future directions in educational generative AI research. *TechTrends, 69*(3), 1–16. DOI: 10.1007/s11528-025-01060-6

Xu, X. (2025). AI optimization algorithms enhance higher education management and personalized teaching through empirical analysis. *Scientific Reports, 15*(1). Advance online publication. DOI: 10.1038/s41598-025-94481-5

Yang, T., Hsu, Y., & Wu, J. (2025). The effectiveness of ChatGPT in assisting high school students in programming learning: Evidence from a quasi-experimental research. *Interactive Learning Environments*, •••, 1–18. DOI: 10.1080/10494820.2025.2450659

Yar, M. A., Hamdan, M., Anshari, M., Fitriyani, N. L., & Syafrudin, M. (2024). Governing with intelligence: The impact of artificial intelligence on policy development. *Information (Basel), 15*(9), 556. DOI: 10.3390/info15090556

Yedatkar, A. S.Anju Santosh Yedatkar. (2024). Real-time data analytics in distributed systems. *International Journal of Scientific Research in Modern Science and Technology, 3*(6), 9–16. DOI: 10.59828/ijsrmst.v3i6.215

Yeo, M. A. (2023). Academic integrity in the age of artificial intelligence (AI) authoring apps. *TESOL Journal, 14*(3), e716. DOI: 10.1002/tesj.716

Yetişensoy, S., & Rapoport, D. (2023). Artificial intelligence literacy teaching in social studies education. *Journal of Pedagogical Research, 7*(2), 45–63. DOI: 10.33902/JPR.202320866

Yin, R. K. (2018). *Case study research and applications: Design and methods* (6th ed.). SAGE Publications.

Yin, R. K. (2018). *Case Study Research and Applications: Design and Methods* (6th ed.). Sage Publications.

Yin, W. (2022). Personalized hybrid education framework based on neuroevolution methodologies. *Computational Intelligence and Neuroscience*, *2022*, 1–16. Advance online publication. DOI: 10.1155/2022/6925668

Yükseköğretim Bilgi Yönetim Sistemi. (2025, January 19). *Türlerine göre birim sayıları raporu*. https://istatistik.yok.gov.tr/

Yusuf, A., Pervin, N., & Román-González, M. (2024). Generative AI and the future of higher education: A threat to academic integrity or reformation? Evidence from multicultural perspectives. *International Journal of Educational Technology in Higher Education*, *21*(1), 21. DOI: 10.1186/s41239-024-00453-6

Zawacki-Richter, O., Marín, V. I., Bond, M., & Gouverneur, F. (2019). Systematic review of research on artificial intelligence applications in higher education – Are the technologies ready for prime time? *International Journal of Educational Technology in Higher Education*, *16*(21), 1–20.

Zawacki-Richter, O., Marín, V., Bond, M., & Gouverneur, F. (2019). Systematic review of research on artificial intelligence applications in higher education – Where are the educators? *International Journal of Educational Technology in Higher Education*, *16*(1), 39. Advance online publication. DOI: 10.1186/s41239-019-0171-0

Zelkowski, J. (2024). To Praxis test or not? Mathematics content knowledge tests for teacher licensure and programmatic considerations on moving the preparation field forward. *Investigations in Mathematics Learning*, 1–20. https://doi.org/DOI: 10.1080/19477503.2024.2401728

Zewe, A. (2025, January 17). Explained: Generative AI's environmental impact. *MIT News*. https://news.mit.edu/2025/explained-generative-ai-environmental-impact-0117

Zhai, C., Wibowo, S., & Li, L. D. (2024). The effects of over-reliance on AI dialogue systems on students' cognitive abilities: A systematic review. *Smart Learning Environments*, *11*(1), 28. DOI: 10.1186/s40561-024-00316-7

Zhai, X., Chu, X., Chai, C., Jong, M., Istenič, A., Spector, M., Liu, J.-B., Yuan, J., & Li, Y. (2021). A review of artificial intelligence (AI) in education from 2010 to 2020. *Complexity*, *8812542*(1), 8812542. Advance online publication. DOI: 10.1155/2021/8812542

Zhang, R., Li, H., Meng, H., Zhan, J., Gan, H., & Lee, Y.-C. (2024). The Dark Side of AI Companionship: A Taxonomy of Harmful Algorithmic Behaviors in Human-AI Relationships. arXiv preprint arXiv:2410.20130.

Zhang, K., & Aslan, A. (2021). AI technologies for education: Recent research & future directions. *Computers and Education: Artificial Intelligence*, *2*, 100025. DOI: 10.1016/j.caeai.2021.100025

Zhang, X., Ding, Y., Huang, X., Li, W., Long, L., & Ding, S. (2024). Smart classrooms: How sensors and AI are shaping educational paradigms. *Sensors (Basel)*, *24*(17), 5487. Advance online publication. DOI: 10.3390/s24175487 PMID: 39275398

Zhao, X., Wang, L., & Li, Y. (2022). Developing AI literacy for primary and middle school teachers in China: Based on a structural equation modeling analysis. *Sustainability (Basel)*, *14*(21), 14549. Advance online publication. DOI: 10.3390/su142114549

Zheng, H., Xu, K., Zhang, M., Tan, H., & Li, H. (2024). Efficient resource allocation in cloud computing environments using AI-driven predictive analytics. *Applied and Computational Engineering*, *82*(1), 6–12. DOI: 10.54254/2755-2721/82/2024GLG0055

Zheng, L., Fan, Y., Gao, L., Huang, Z., Chen, B., & Long, M. (2024). Using AI-empowered assessments and personalized recommendations to promote online collaborative learning performance. *Journal of Research on Technology in Education*, •••, 1–27. DOI: 10.1080/15391523.2024.2304066

Zlotnikova, I., Hlomani, H., Mokgetse, T., & Bagai, K. (2025). Establishing ethical standards for GenAI in university education: A roadmap for academic integrity and fairness. *Journal of Information. Communication and Ethics in Society*, *23*(2), 188–216. DOI: 10.1108/JICES-07-2024-0104

Zuboff, S. (2019). *The Age of Surveillance Capitalism: The Fight for a Human Future at the New Frontier of Power*. Public Affairs.

About the Contributors

Aras Bozkurt is a researcher and faculty member at Anadolu University, Türkiye. With MA and PhD degrees in distance education, Dr. Bozkurt's work focuses on empirical studies in areas such as distance education, online learning, networked learning, and educational technology. He applies critical theories like connectivism, rhizomatic learning, and heutagogy to his research. Dr. Bozkurt is also interested in emerging research paradigms, including social network analysis, sentiment analysis, and data mining. Dr. Bozkurt's studies also cover the integration of artificial intelligence technologies into educational processes in the axis of human-machine interaction. His dedication to advancing the field is reflected in his editorial roles as the Editor-in-Chief of Open Praxis and Asian Journal of Distance Education, as well as his roles as an associate editor for prestigious journals like Higher Education Research and Development, Online Learning, eLearn Magazine, and Computer Applications in Engineering Education.

***

Sandra Abegglen, PhD, is a Researcher in the School of Architecture, Planning and Landscape at the University of Calgary. Her research focuses on online and hybrid education, collaborative pedagogies, creative teaching and learning practices, and fostering inclusivity in educational settings. Recognized for her innovative and impactful work, she has received numerous awards for her transdisciplinary and international collaborations, which bridge diverse disciplines and perspectives to enhance pedagogy and educational outcomes.

Hakan Altinpulluk received his bachelor's degree in Computer and Instructional Technology Education from the Faculty of Education at Anadolu University in 2009. In 2018, he completed his integrated PhD at Anadolu University's Institute of Social Sciences with his dissertation titled "Usability of Augmented Reality within the

Framework of Universal Design Principles in Open and Distance Learning." He began his academic career as a research assistant at Anadolu University's Open Education Faculty in 2014. In 2019, he was appointed as an Assistant Professor, and in 2021, he obtained the title of Associate Professor. Since 2023, he has been serving as a faculty member in the Department of Educational Sciences at Anadolu University's Faculty of Education. Altınpulluk's research focuses on open and distance learning, educational technology, and computer and instructional technology education. Throughout his academic career, he has published over 100 publications, including articles, book chapters, and conference papers. Between 2019 and 2024, he served as the Editor-in-Chief of the Journal of Open Education Applications and Research. Due to his contributions to educational technology, he has been honored with several awards, including the 2023 Anadolu University Academic Achievement Award, 2022 Article Performance Award, and 2021 Anadolu University Article Performance Award. His current research interests include augmented reality, virtual learning technologies, mobile communication technologies, and AI in distance education. Altınpulluk continues his academic endeavors in these fields.

Janine Arantes is a Senior Lecturer and Research Fellow at Victoria University, Australia. She co-leads the 'New Frontiers in Justice, Education, Policy, and Advocacy' discipline at ISILC and is internationally recognised for her work on AI governance, digital equity, and education policy. Her research explores the psychosocial risks and ethical implications of AI in education, with a focus on inclusion, human rights, and teacher agency. She currently leads foundational work for the AI Governance for Education (AIGE) Network, including research through the Smart Glasses Lab, the Digital Poverty Research Group and Teaching with Responsible AI Network (TRAIN).

Maha Bali is a professor of practice at the Center for Learning and Teaching at The American University in Cairo (AUC). She has a PhD in education from the University of Sheffield, United Kingdom. She co-founded virtually connecting, a grassroots movement that challenges academic gatekeeping at conferences. Also, Bali is a co-facilitator of Equity Unbound; an equity-focused, open, connected intercultural learning curriculum, which has also branched into academic community activities. Such activities are Continuity with Care, Socially Just Academia, a collaboration with OneHE: Community-building Resources and MYFest, an innovative three-month professional learning journey.

Hatice Bilgin received her BA in English Language Education from Boğaziçi University in 2005, followed by an MA in the same field from the same institution in

2010. She has been working as an instructor of English since 2005, gaining extensive experience in language education. She was awarded the Fulbright Foreign Language Assistant Scholarship, through which she taught Turkish at Portland State University in 2011-2012 academic year. Her research interests include the use of technology in education.

Merry Leigh Dameron is an Assistant Professor of Psychology and Human Services at Montreat College, where she began teaching in 2024. She holds a BA in Communications from Gardner-Webb University, an MA in School Counseling from Lenoir-Rhyne University, and a PhD in Counselor Education and Supervision from UNC Charlotte. Her areas of expertise include social justice in education, multicultural education and competency, and school counseling praxis. With more than a decade of professional and teaching experience, Dr. Dameron has served as a professional school counselor for Burke County Public Schools and held academic appointments as an Assistant Professor at Carson-Newman University and Western Carolina University. Outside of work, Dr. Dameron enjoys spending time with her husband, Jonathan, and their children, Zoe and Jack. Together, they love to travel, especially to places where they can hike and enjoy the beauty of nature.

Ioanna Georgia Eskiadi is a PhD candidate at the Aristotle University of Thessaloniki and a researcher at the Peace Journalism Laboratory within the Department of Journalism and Media, AUTH, where she contributes to important research projects. Her PhD thesis and writing work focus on innovation, new technologies, and their integration into news organizations. Throughout her academic career, she has been awarded fellowships from prestigious organizations such as the Portulans Institute and the Konrad Adenauer Stiftung, among others, in recognition of her research excellence. Ioanna holds a master's degree in risk communication and crisis journalism and a bachelor's degree in journalism and mass media, both from Aristotle University of Thessaloniki. She is proficient in English, Spanish, Italian, Arabic, and German. Through her work, she aims to provide solutions for news media organizations in the evolving media landscape, promoting innovation and sustainability in newsrooms. She has published her research on immersive journalism in scientific and academic journals, the adoption of emerging technologies by news media organizations, the role of AI in journalism, crisis communication, and audience acceptance of VR and AR in the media landscape.

Amy Flagler is the Director of Teacher Education and Chair of the Department of Education and Outdoor Recreation at Montreat College in Western North Carolina. Before arriving at Montreat College, she served as an educator in both public and private schools in Massachusetts, Virginia, Oregon, and Georgia. Dr.

Flagler completed her Ed.D. at Southern Wesleyan University in 2022 with research on how beginning teachers meet the needs of students with emotional and behavioral disorders in the general education classroom. She has co-authored several articles on the impact of disruptive technologies in the classroom and has presented at the North Carolina Independent Colleges and Universities (NCICU) Summer Faculty Institute and the Southern Wesleyan University Summer Residency Program for Doctoral Research. Dr. Flagler's research interests include improving teacher education to meet the challenges of today's diverse classrooms.

Gökhan Hınız is a researcher specializing in English language teaching (ELT), student engagement, and the integration of artificial intelligence in language education. His research focuses on technology-enhanced learning, AI-driven assessment, and professional development for educators. His recent studies include research on AI literacy in academic writing, the role of generative AI in ELT, customized online professional development programs for teachers and qualitative data analysis.

Sarah Honeychurch is Good Practice Adviser in Academic and Digital Development at the University of Glasgow. She has a BA and MA in Philosophy from the University of Southampton and a PhD in Education from the University of Glasgow. Sarah is editor for Research in Learning Technology and for the Journal of Social Media for Learning and a founder member of the Active Learning Network University of Glasgow Satellite Group. Her current research interests are participatory learning, lurkers, affinity networks, and bricolage.

Hakan Kilinc is currently working at Open Education Faculty, Anadolu University. He undertook undergraduate studies in the feld of Computer Education and Instructional Technologies (CEIT) between the years of 2009 and 2013 at Anadolu University. He received his master degree in the feld of Distance Education in 2016, May. In addition to this, he received his Ph.D. Degree in the feld of Distance Education in 2020, April. Hakan Kilinc continues to work in the feld of distance education technology, personalized learning environments, information and communication technologies, synchronous, asynchronous, and interactive communications, learner-generated content and online group discussions.

Apostolos Koutropoulos ("AK") is the Program Manager for the Applied Linguistics Online Program and a Lecturer for the Instructional Design Program at UMass Boston. He is also a lecturer for professional development programs at the Online Learning Consortium. AK holds a B.A. in Computer Science, an M.B.A. with a focus on Human Resources, an M.S. in Information Technology, an M.Ed. in Instructional Design, and an M.A. in Applied Linguistics from the University of

Massachusetts Boston. He also holds an EdD in Distance Education from Athabasca University. His research interests include: knowledge management, educational technology, social media, open education, and online learning. AK has published articles in the areas of technology in education, and has presented at professional conferences.

Chrysoula Lazou holds a BA in English Language and Literature from Aristotle University of Thessaloniki, Greece, an MEd in Distance Education, Athabasca University, Canada, and an MSc in Immersive Technologies, Training, and Game Design, International Hellenic University. Lazou is pursuing her PhD Degree in Immersive Technologies AR/VR/XR and teaches English and Instructional Design at the Democritus University of Thrace. Her academic interests focus on technology-enhanced learning, digital and media literacy, interdisciplinary studies, inclusive education, and project-based learning. Lazou is an IVLP Alumna, the coordinator of the CommuniTIES project for media literacy in Southeastern Europe and has received awards and distinctions for her work among which the UNESCO MIL Award 2022, the Gold Education Leaders Award for Innovation in Teaching, Governor General's Gold Award for Academic Excellence 2019/2020, and the Distinguished Alumni Award 2023, Canada.

Chrissi Nerantzi (PFHEA, NTF, CATE) is a Professor in Creative and Open Education in the School of Education and a Senior Lead of the Knowledge Equity Network at the University of Leeds in the United Kingdom. Her research interests are in creativity, open, boundary-crossing collaborative learning and imaginative and AI-enabled curriculum design. Chrissi is a GO-GN alumna, the founder of the international open #creativeHE community, the co-chair of the ICDE Open Education Network and has co-created many OER and initiated a range of further open professional development courses, networks and communities have been sustained over the years.

Nikos S. Panagiotou is Professor, School of Journalism and Mass Media Communication, Aristotle University. He has been a visiting Professor at APU University, Japan at Deutsche Welle. He has been awarded the following scholarships: Chevening Scholar of the Foreign and Commonwealth Office UK, RCAP Scholar from APU University Japan, Scholar to Beijing Foreign Studies University, Scholar of the State of Luxembourg. He has an extensive research work which has been funded from Google (DNI Initiative fund). He is the initiator and organizer of Thessaloniki International Media Summer Academy. He serves as the President of Digital Communication Network Global, Director of the Peace

Journalism Lab and oversees the International Center for the Safety of Journalists and Media Professionals.

Murat Polat is an associate professor in the Department of Educational Sciences at Niğde Ömer Halisdemir University, Türkiye. His research interests focus on educational sciences and educational administration/management. He has conducted various studies and research projects in these fields and resides in Niğde, Türkiye.

Sinfield, Sandra is an Associate Teaching Professor in the Centre for Teaching Enhancement at LondonMet and a co-founder of the Association for Learning Development in Higher Education (ALDinHE). Sandra is a co-producer of the learning development focused #Take5 blog that has national and international reach as part of ALDinHE - and that shares inspirational practice with LondonMet staff. She has co-authored Teaching, Learning and Study Skills: A Guide for Tutors and Essential Study Skills: The complete Guide to Success at University (5th Edition). Sandra is interested in creativity as liberatory and holistic practice in Higher Education; she has developed theatre and film in unusual places; and inhabited SecondLife as a learning space. Sandra is a University Teaching Fellow and was part of the #creativeHE collective that won the Collaborative Award for Teaching Excellence (CATE) by AdvanceHE 2022. Recently Sandra has co-edited the book Collaboration in Higher Education: A New Ecology of Practice, published by Bloomsbury (2023).

Lenandlar Singh is a Lecturer in the Department of Computer Science at the University of Guyana. He has approximately 20 years' experience teaching computer science and information systems. He has presented and published papers on topics in computer science, computer science education, learning technologies.. He is presently reading for his PhD at the University of Lancaster, England.

Özlem Soydan Oktay completed his undergraduate education at Anadolu University / Faculty of Economics and Administrative Sciences / Business Administration in 1993 and completed his first master's degree at Anadolu University / Institute of Social Sciences / Department of Business Administration in the field of Finance (with a thesis) in 1997. In 2021, the author completed his second master's degree in Distance Education (with thesis) at Anadolu University's Institute of Social Sciences, Distance Education Department, and continues his doctoral education in the field of Distance Education. Since 1994, she has been working in the Instructional Design and Scenario Department of the Anadolu University Video Production and Broadcasting Unit. SOYDAN-OKTAY, one of the authors of the book Interactive Scenario Design in Open and Distance Learning, has studied interactive scenarios, adaptive learning environments, learning analytics, immersive learning, immersive scenarios, immersive technologies, and third-age universities. Her research interests include learner-centered learning interactivities, psychological aspects of learning, learning performance, learning environments, heutagogy, inquiry-based learning, artificial intelligence, immersive learning, and immersive technologies. .

Bonnie Stewart is an educator and social media researcher fascinated by who we are when we're online. Associate Professor of Online Pedagogy and Workplace Learning at the University of Windsor, Bonnie explores the implications of digital infrastructures for institutions and society. Bonnie was an early MOOC researcher and ethnographer of Twitter as an academic environment, and currently investigates what it means to know, to learn, and to belong in a society shaped by our current information ecosystem.

Nurgün Varol is an independent researcher with a master's degree in educational sciences who continues her academic work in Türkiye. Her areas of interest include educational sciences, educational management, leadership, etc.

Tyler Watts is an Assistant Professor of Education at Mercer University. In his role, he teaches in the Tift College of Education and serves as program coordinator for the MS in Instructional Design and Technology. Dr. Watts earned his PhD in Education Sciences with a concentration in School Technology Leadership from the University of Kentucky. His research interests include instructional design, alternative assessment, online learning leadership, and teaching & learning centers. Dr. Watts is also an advocate for accessible and open practices in online education.

Index

G

H

I

L

P

Q

R

S

T

www.ingramcontent.com/pod-product-compliance
Lightning Source LLC
LaVergne TN
LVHW081544300926
849161LV00006B/1512